"*The Skinny on Success* is a funny, insightful and concise explanation as to why some people achieve ... this book is as good as it gets."

Jeffrey Kindler, CEO/Chmn, Pfizer

"Don't let the stick figures fool you ... Jim Randel will have you laughing and thinking at the same time. A very enjoyable read!"

Ken Blanchard, author
The One Minute Manager®

www.theskinnyon.com

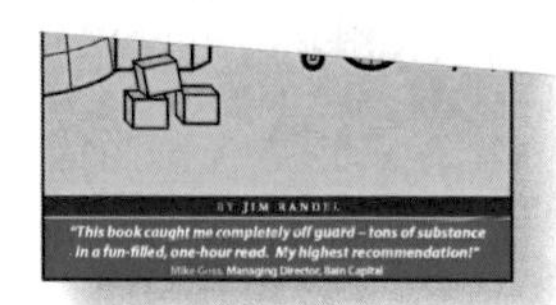

"This book caught me completely off guard – tons of substance. My highest recommendation!"

Mike Goss, Managing Director, Bain Capital

"This book takes about an hour to read and leaves you with a wealth of knowledge, sure to help you maximize your time, potential, and your network."

Tiffany Schlarman, bookpleasures.com

www.theskinnyon.com

"This book performs an extraordinary public service."

Richard Blumenthal, Attorney General State of Connecticut

"I've tracked Jimmy's incredible run of successful real estate investments for twenty years."

Jeff Dunne, Vice Chairman, CB Richard Ellis

"I love this book. It can literally save you a fortune!"

Gerri Detweiler, National Credit Card Expert

"I loved it. Substantive, fun and funny. I give it my highest recommendation."

Steve Pagliuca, Managing Partner The Boston Celtics

"A motivational quick read and a great little primer for a more detailed consideration of the topics covered."

Aaron White, VP, Touchstone Crystal

"I found myself nodding my head saying, 'that's so true'..."

Freshman, Sacred Heart University

The Skinny on Creativity

the skinny on™
creativity
thinking outside the box

Jim Randel

ISBN: 978-0-9844418-8-4
Ebook ISBN: 978-0-9844418-9-1
Library of Congress: 2010910705

Illustration/Design: Lindy Nass

For information address Rand Media Co, 265 Post Road West,
Westport, CT, 06880 or call (203) 226-8727.

The Skinny On™ books are available for special promotions and premiums.
For details contact: Donna Hardy, call (203) 226-8727 or visit our website:
www.theskinnyon.com

Printed in the United States of America

10 9 8 7 6 5 4 3 2
9 2 5 – 4 9 1 9

the skinny on™

Welcome to a new series of publications titled **The Skinny On™,** a progression of drawings, dialogue and text intended to convey information in a concise and entertaining fashion.

In our time-starved and information-overloaded culture, most of us have far too little time to read. As a result, our understanding of important subjects often tends to float on the surface – without the insights of writings from thinkers and teachers who have spent years studying these subjects.

Our series is intended to address this situation. Our team of readers and researchers has done a ton of homework preparing our books for you. We read everything we could find on the topic at hand and spoke with the experts. Then we mixed in our own experiences and distilled what we have learned into this "skinny" book for your benefit.

Our goal is to do the reading for you, identify what is important, distill the key points, and present them in a book that is both instructive and enjoyable to read.

Although minimalist in design, we do take our message very seriously. Please do not confuse format with content. The time you invest reading this book will be paid back to you many, many times over.

INTRODUCTION

Creativity ... WOW, what a big topic!

And such an important one, too, because no matter what you do, or where you are in your life, the ability to think creatively is crucial for your survival and your success. In short, the more you develop your skills at creative thinking, the better you will be able to master your environment – whatever it might be.

Creative thinkers are all around you. People who are juggling responsibilities and obligations. People who are finding ways to get a lot done with a minimum of resources. People who are using their talents to maximum effect. Creative thinking is the skill you need to overcome whatever stands between you and what you want to accomplish.

Creative thinkers will have an edge in the years ahead. Whereas once analytical thinking was paramount, today machines can perform analysis better than most humans. But machines can't imagine; machines cannot think creatively. And so, to compete and prosper you need to develop your ability to think creatively.

So, give us an hour of your time. That's about how long it will take for you to read this book. By the end of this book you will have a better understanding of the rules of creativity, and an enhanced facility for thinking "outside the box."

Jim Randel

• • • • • •

"The last few decades have belonged to a certain kind of person with a certain kind of mind – computer programmers who could crank code, lawyers who could craft contracts, MBA's who could crunch numbers. But the keys to the kingdom are changing. The future belongs to a very different kind of person with a very different kind of mind – creators and empathizers, pattern recognizers, and meaning makers. These people – artists, inventors, designers, storytellers, caregivers, consolers, big picture thinkers – will now reap society's richest rewards and share its greatest joys."

A Whole New Mind: Why Right-Brainers will Rule the Future
Daniel Pink (Riverhead, 2005)

"Think left and think right,
think low and think high.

Oh, the thinks you can think if
only you try!"

Oh, the Thinks you can Think!
Dr. Seuss (1975)

"Creativity: the ability to transcend traditional ideas, rules, patterns, relationships ... in favor of meaningful new ideas, forms, methods, interpretations."

www.dictionary.com

Hi. I'm Jim Randel.

In the next hour or so, I'm going to teach you everything I've learned about the subject of creativity.

And let me give you my most important finding right up front:

Creative thinking is a skill that you can develop – in other words, you can teach yourself to be more creative.

1

As part of our review, we are going to analyze some of the world's best known creators – people like Leonardo daVinci.

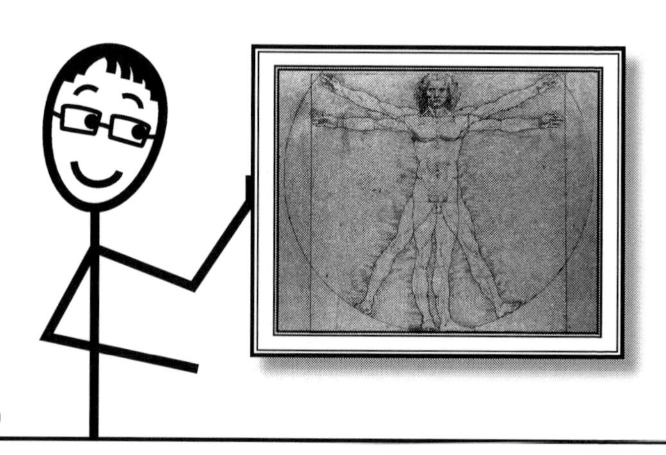

2

But, we are also going to speak about ordinary people.
People who utilize creative thinking to balance the competing demands and stresses of their lives – like parents for example.
3

Creative thinking is not just for inventors and artists.

"One woman, uneducated, poor, and a full-time housewife and mother … was a marvelous cook, mother, wife … She was in these areas original, novel, ingenious, unexpected, inventive … I learned from her and others like her that <u>a first-rate soup is more creative than a second-rate painting</u>."

Toward a Psychology of Being,
Abraham Maslow (Wiley, 1968)
(Emphasis added.)

4

Just before we get started, I'd like to answer a question that may be in your head.

"What's with the stick people? Why tackle such an important topic in a format that looks like something a second grader might do?"

There are several reasons.

One, I believe in simplicity – hence the stick people drawings. Less can be more. Studies have shown that people retain more information when a message is delivered in a concise, illustrated format than in just text alone.

Two, like it or not, your brain is changing. The Internet has caused all of us to process and retain information in new ways. When people use the Internet to learn, the experience is staccato – very quick, bottom-line focused, discrete bites of information. That is the exact format of this book.

Finally, clutter is the enemy of creativity.

Your mind is constantly being bombarded with stuff and noise. All this tumult hampers creative thinking. I don't want to add to the problem – I want to help you build your talents for creative thinking.

Every word and image in this book has been scrubbed for excess. I believe that if I can get your undivided attention for just an hour, I can jump start your creative impulses.

OK, in just a moment I'm going to start outlining for you 20 key points to understand about creative thinking.

But before we do, I would like you to try a little brain teaser.

As you can see, we have drawn a 9-dot square. The challenge is for you to connect all the dots by drawing just four straight lines **without your pen leaving the paper.**

Give up?

No worries. You see, the riddle is impossible unless you think **outside the box** – my first point about creative thinking.

1. TO IMPROVE YOUR CREATIVITY, FORCE YOURSELF TO THINK OUTSIDE THE BOX ... TO IGNORE ARBITRARY LIMITS.

SOLUTION

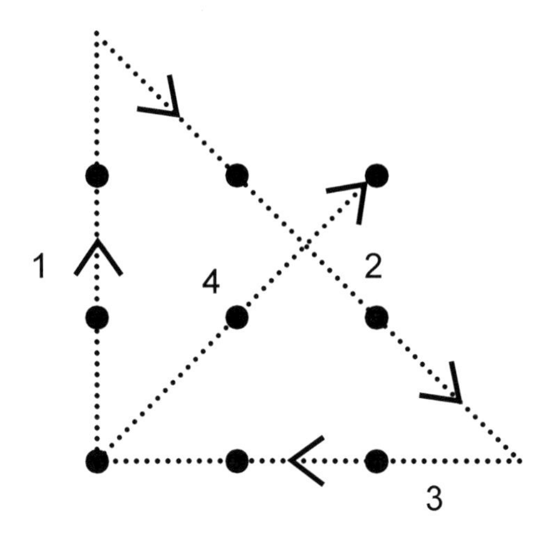

As you can see, the only way to solve our riddle is to draw your lines **outside the perimeter** of the square.

By looking at a challenge as if there are **no limits to your solution**, you sometimes see things in a different light and spur new and creative ideas.

History is replete with stories of great ideas that were the result of someone thinking outside the box.

One of my favorites is the story of Solomon.

Solomon was a biblical king. One day, two women came to him – clutching a little baby boy. Each claimed that the baby was hers, and that the other woman had stolen him.

They asked Solomon to hear their stories – and award the baby to the true mother.

But Solomon was not interested in the usual approach. He did not have the patience to listen to each woman's story. He decided to try something a little bit creative ... to think outside the box.

"Sorry, ladies, I don't have time for this. Give me the baby and I will cut him in half – seems like a fair compromise."

"NO, NO! Please, your Honor! Give her the baby."
And Solomon knew immediately who the real mother was.
15

By thinking outside the box, Solomon came to a very quick (and very accurate) resolution. Solomon "cut to the chase."

When you are confronted with a challenge, you should step back and think. Think about unconventional approaches. Think far outside the box; you can always pull yourself back in.

And that leads to the second of my points about creativity.

2. WHEN COMING UP WITH IDEAS, COME UP WITH LOTS OF IDEAS.

Most of our educational institutions teach us that there is **one** right answer. But that is not always the case.

When faced with a problem or opportunity, resist the impulse to come up with **the** right answer or approach. Instead, produce **lots** of ideas.

You can evaluate your ideas later – but first you need to have them!

"Nothing is more dangerous than an idea ... when it's the only one we have."

Emile Chartier, French philosopher

Author Roger von Oech writes about a creativity workshop he gave to a large computer company.

The president of the company was concerned with his employees' lack of innovation. Oech asked the assembled employees a lot of questions. But he told them what he wanted was not **the** right answer. What he was seeking was the **second** right answer!

In other words, Oech was pushing the attendees to ignore the first answer that came to mind, and to find an **alternative** right answer.

"One way to work around our assumptions is to ignore or 'forget' the initial right answers that come to mind when we're faced with a problem we've seen before ."

A Whack on the Side of the Head: How You Can Be More Creative, Roger Oech
(Hachette Book Group, 1983)

21

LEARN TO SUSPEND YOUR JUDGMENT

Some people judge their creative ideas **too quickly**.

By instinct, we all tend to practice what is called **convergent thinking**.

Convergent thinking is what helps us survive. It's the process by which we assess situations (some of which could be dangerous), and then make judgments as to how to deal with them.

22

DIVERGENT THINKING

The opposite of **convergent thinking** is **divergent thinking**.

Divergent thinking is when you let your mind flow – giving it a license to explore all the nooks and crannies of your imagination.

Creative thinking requires divergent thinking **before** convergent thinking.

In other words, before you start judging, let your mind go in all directions – wherever it feels like. Don't worry that your ideas seem nutty, silly or absurd. Your powers of convergent thinking will eventually throw out what is useless.

As creative thinkers we have to be careful not to reject ideas too quickly. We get a thought and then may think to ourself: "Oh, that will never work." And we never let the idea see the light of day.

One of the great stories in creativity lore is the invention of Post-It notes.

In 1965 the 3M Corporation was experimenting with different adhesives. It wanted to develop an ultra-powerful glue like the one I'm holding.

While trying to find a gooier glue, 3M had some “flops” – some glues that just weren’t that sticky.
One of the glues was so crummy that 3M let one of its employees have the formula.
That individual, Art Frye, did not know what to do with the substandard glue. Then one day a friend of his was complaining about having to scotch tape notes to himself all over his house.
25

The next thing you know, Art Frye invented Post-It notes.

In other words, what may, on first glance, appear to be silly, not useful, or “far out,” may actually have real sticking power.

26

EVERYONE IS A CRITIC

Because most people are convergent thinkers – and tend to shoot down new ideas (often just because they're new) – you should be wary about bouncing your ideas off other people.

At some point, you do want to solicit others' input. But if you do that too early in your creative process, you may be discouraged from pursuing what could be a terrific innovation or idea.

"Creative thinkers – authors, inventors and artists, for example – seldom talk about a work in progress."

The Art of Creative Thinking: How to Be Creative and Develop Great Ideas,
John Adair (KoganPage, 1990)

GO WITH YOUR GUT

Seeing around curves is hard. Most people cannot see change until it is well past them. If you gauge the value of your creative ideas by just what other people think, you may be disappointed. Sometimes you just need to trust your own instincts, your gut.

"In every work of genius we recognize our own rejected thoughts; they came back to us with a certain alienated majesty ... teach us to abide by our own spontaneous impressions with good-humored inflexibility when the whole cry of voices is on the other side. Else, tomorrow a stranger will say with masterly good sense precisely what we have thought and felt all the time, and we shall be forced to take with shame our own opinion from another."

Ralph Waldo Emerson

As Emerson suggests, there may be times when you have an idea you're unsure about and therefore don't pursue. Next thing you know, someone else has the same idea and runs with it.

"Hey," you say to yourself, "I had that idea months ago."

The point is not to reject your ideas too quickly. The key is to find a balance between imagination and practicality.

And that is not always easy because at times, **new = disruptive**.

3. CREATIVITY IS OFTEN DISRUPTIVE.

Sometimes creativity requires that you have a strong stomach.

99% of the world is comfortable with the status quo and resists new ideas. Creative geniuses throughout history have often been perceived as wacky – until their ideas were accepted or proven. Then, of course, everyone copied the creative's ideas.

"At every crossing on the road that leads to the future, each progressive spirit is opposed by a thousand men appointed to guard the past."

Maurice Maeterlinck,
Belgian Nobel Prize Winner

Many people are frightened by change. They see anything new as threatening.

Often creativity is an act of rebellion that requires a person to fight against the 1,000 men guarding the ways of the past.

Recognize this guy? Yes, Albert Einstein, of course – one of the most creative minds of the twentieth century.

I just finished reading a 550-page biography about him.

And you know what I learned?

I learned that Einstein was a rebel – he hated being told how to do things.

Einstein stuck his tongue out at accepted scientific "truths." He conceived new and different ideas, reduced his thoughts to equations, and at times dealt with tremendous skepticism.

"Einstein's life and work reflected the disruption of societal certainties and moral absolutes in the modernist atmosphere of the early twentieth century. Imaginative nonconformity was in the air: Picasso, Joyce, Freud, Stravinsky … and others were breaking conventional bonds."

Einstein: His Life and Universe, Walter Isaacson
(Simon & Schuster, 2008)

SOMETIMES CREATIVITY AND GENIUS TAKE TIME TO SURFACE.

Einstein was not a precocious child. In fact, he did not utter a word until he was well past the age of two. He was such a slow learner, that the family maid labeled him *"der Depperte"* – German for *"the dopey one."*

Einstein's inability (or reluctance) to speak reminds me of a joke.

There once was a little girl who, during the first five years of her life, never said a word.

Then one morning, to the surprise of her entire family, she spoke.

"This oatmeal is too hot."
41

"Oh my gosh, you can speak. But why did you wait until now to say something?"
"I had nothing important to say."
42

OK, not the funniest joke in the world but it makes a point.

Different people reach their strides at different times. Sometimes people, who by traditional measures don't appear destined for greatness, turn out to be world-beaters.

"Einstein's slow development was combined with a cheeky rebelliousness toward authority, which led one schoolmaster to send him packing and another to amuse history by declaring that <u>he would never amount to much</u>. These traits made Einstein the patron saint of distracted school kids everywhere."

Einstein: His Life and Universe
(Emphasis added.)

My wife wouldn't be happy with me eating watermelon in the living room. She thinks I can be a bit of a slob. But thinking about Einstein has inspired me. I need to be a little more rebellious.
45
UH-OH! Here she comes!
By pushing back against conventional thinking, you let loose your creative energies. You may come up with some really dumb ideas, but dumb is OK – so long as you reflect before you act.
46

I got nabbed. Now I need to be a little creative.

Why not play a little game with me? Pretend that you just got caught doing something not pleasing to your boss, your spouse, your parent, your teacher, or your friend. Come up with a few responses explaining your behavior.

Here is what I came up with when my wife confronted me:

"It's just water."

"I thought you said no 'felons' in the living room."

"I'm trying to be like Einstein."

"This is the pits."

No worries. My wife was very understanding. She just suggested that instead of playing golf with my buddies today, I spend my time cleaning the chair. Seems reasonable.
ONE HOUR LATER
Actually, I miss my buddies. I have trouble with solitude. This is all a set-up of course for my next point.

4. THE CREATIVE PROCESS WORKS BEST WHEN DISTRACTIONS ARE AT A MINIMUM.

Another enemy of creative thinking is distraction.

We live today in a 24/7, always-connected existence not necessarily conducive to the creative process.

I have read many books and articles about the mind. Here is the upshot of what I learned:

The mind can only process so much at once.

The majority of us are most creative when freed from distractions.

Inspiration and creativity are funny things. You never know exactly when good ideas are going to pop into your head. But if your head is filled with all sorts of mishmash, your cool ideas may never float to the surface.

That is why creative types tend to work in environments where they can control or eliminate distractions.

53

This is one of my favorite books on the subject of creativity. It is written by the American choreographer, Twyla Tharp. I'd like to tell you how Ms. Tharp boosts her creative juices.

54

"I know there are people who can assimilate a lot of incoming data from all angles ... They thrive on a multitude of stimuli, the more complicated the better. I'm not hard-wired that way. When I commit to a project, I don't expand my contact with the world; I try to cut it off. I want to place myself in a bubble of monomaniacal absorption where I'm fully invested in the task at hand.

I list the biggest distractions in my life and make a pact with myself to do without them for a week."

Here is what Ms. Tharp gives up in her effort to create a distraction-free environment:

1. Movies – one of her favorite forms of relaxation.
2. Multitasking – whatever she is doing, she does only that.
3. Numbers – she stops looking at clocks, bills, the bathroom scale.
4. Background music – she feels it "nibbles away at her awareness."

Although different people thrive in different routines, one way to jump start your creativity may be to build some solitude into your life.

When your mind is freed from the "noise," it is better able to roam, to imagine, and innovate.

"When I look back on my best work, it was inevitably created in what I call 'The Bubble.' I eliminated every distraction, sacrificed almost everything that gave me pleasure, placed myself in a single-minded isolation chamber, and structured my life so that everything was not only feeding the work but subordinate to it. It is not a particularly sociable way to operate. It's actively anti-social. On the other hand, it is pro-creative."

The Creative Habit, Twyla Tharp
(Simon & Schuster, 2003)

Although Ms. Tharp's routine sounds a bit extreme, she is nowhere near as monastic as one of American's best-known novelists, Philip Roth. Roth is the author of several great books including ***Portnoy's Complaint*** and ***American Pastoral***.

"I live alone, there's no one else to be responsible for or to spend time with. My schedule is absolutely my own. Usually, I write all day, but if I want to go back to the studio in the evening after dinner, I don't have to sit in the living room because someone else has been alone all day. I don't have to sit there and be entertaining or amusing."

Philip Roth
The New Yorker (May, 2000)

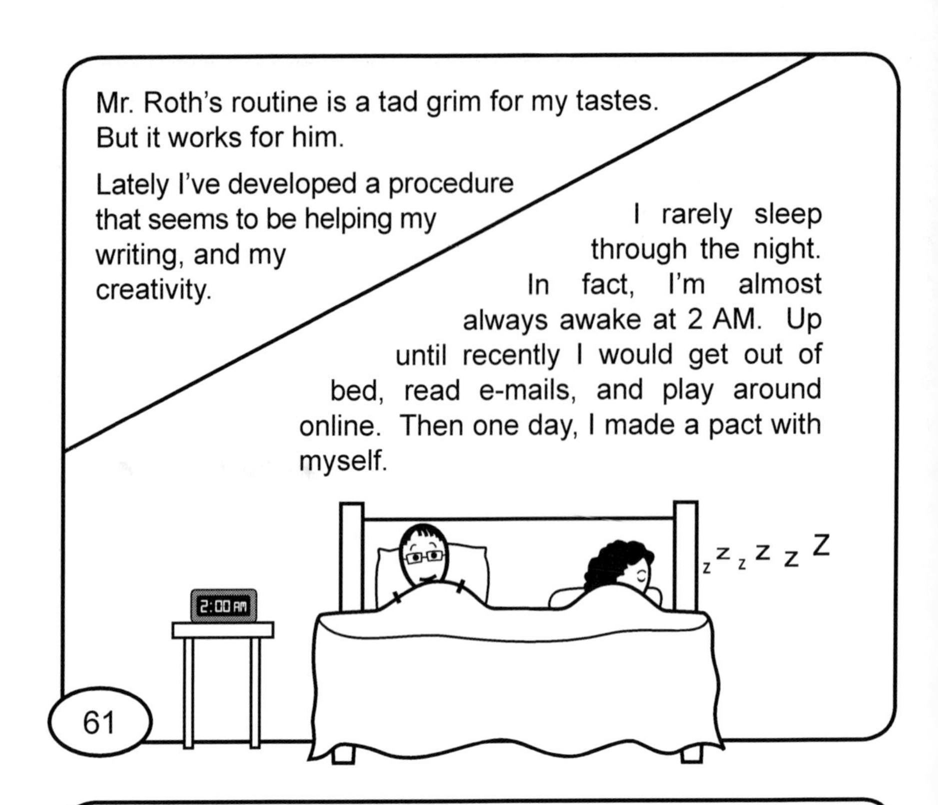
Mr. Roth's routine is a tad grim for my tastes.
But it works for him.
Lately I've developed a procedure that seems to be helping my writing, and my creativity.
I rarely sleep through the night. In fact, I'm almost always awake at 2 AM. Up until recently I would get out of bed, read e-mails, and play around online. Then one day, I made a pact with myself.
2:00 AM
z z z z z Z
61

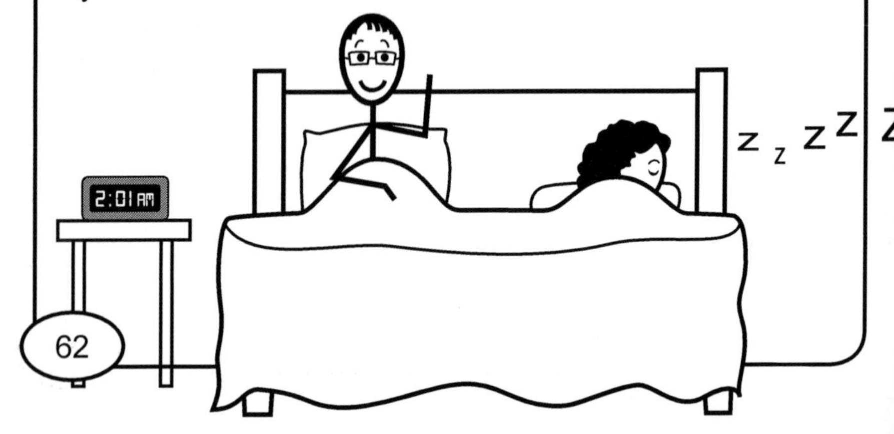
I decided that for at least 30 minutes I wouldn't leave my bed. Instead, I would stay put and reflect on projects I was working on. Obviously there were no distractions, and I found that in this quiet time, my mind would flow freely and ideas would follow.
If you want to promote your creativity, you need to give your mind room to breathe.
2:01 AM
z z z Z
62

"When I am completely myself, entirely alone or during the night when I cannot sleep, it is on these occasions that my ideas flow best and most abundantly."

Mozart

63

NOISE

There is a lot of noise in your head. But as teachers like Eckhart Tolle explain, you can control the tumult in your mind.

When you need to think, shut off the noise. Give your creative talents a chance to flourish.

64

It may not be a coincidence that some great creators had hearing problems.

Did you know that Beethoven lost his hearing when he was in his twenties?

And that Thomas Edison was partially deaf from birth?

"Edison claimed that the deafness was actually an advantage, freeing him from time-wasting small talk and giving him undisturbed time to 'think out my problems.' Late in life he would say that he was fortunate to have been spared 'all the foolish conversation and other meaningless sounds that normal people hear.'"

The Wizard of Menlo Park: How Thomas Edison Invented the Modern World,
Randall Stross (Crown Publishers, 2007)

In the digital age it's particularly hard to disconnect from all the tumult. A recent study indicates that about 1/3 of us are "hyper-connected" – totally engaged with all sorts of electronic devices. In this condition, it's hard to find the time to think … let alone to create.

• • • • • • •

"The best human creativity happens only when we have the time and mental space to take a new thought and follow it wherever it leads … Using screens as we do, constantly jumping around, we're ensuring that all of us have fewer ingenious moments and bring less associative creativity to whatever kind of work we do."

Hamlet's BlackBerry,
William Powers (HarperCollins, 2010)

67

Want to improve your creativity? Want to boost your innovative powers? Here's one tip: Disconnect for a period of time. Shut the world off. It will be there when you return.

Now on to my next suggestion – I need you to forget how old you are. I want you to behave like a child.

68

5. ONE WAY TO JUMP START YOUR CREATIVE JUICES IS TO BRING A PLAYFULNESS TO WHATEVER ENDEAVOR ABSORBS YOU.

An important factor in one's creativity is a willingness to discard accepted "truths."

A person who believes that everything is "open to review," is more inclined to look for new ideas – in other words, to think creatively.

And you know who has no regard for accepted "truths?" Yes ... children!

Children have no long history to fall back on. They are not set in their ways. They do not think in terms of practicality. They do not worry about consequences.

71

Remember the photo of Einstein sticking out his tongue? At the time of that photo, he was about 70 years old. But he had not lost his playfulness. In fact, it was that childlike approach to life that enhanced his creativity right up to the day he died.

OK, please indulge me for a moment. Think about something or someone that irritates you on a regular basis. Now stick out your tongue at that thing or person. Way out there! Make a loud noise, too!

How did that make you feel? Maybe just a little bit silly?

72

I hope so… because silly is part of playfulness and imagination.

Silly is liberating. It encourages irreverence … and unconventional thinking … and yes, creativity.

"He who laughs … lasts."

Anonymous

Hopefully you are enjoying our “skinny book.”

When I decided to start a publishing company, I did not want to do the “same old, same old.” I wanted to try something different.

Did I tap into my childhood when I started drawing stick people? Not deliberately, but once I disconnected from the “same old,” I opened my mind to new ways to communicate.

75

People who produce a lot of ideas may not be conscious of what they are doing, but at some point they act childlike. They let thoughts flow without worries about practicality, penalty or expense.

76

"The greatest invention in the world is the mind of a child."

Thomas Edison

77

Hey, I think I have a great idea for a way to light up a room!

Speaking of Thomas Edison, does this picture make any sense? Since Edison invented the light bulb, how could there be a light bulb going off over his head when he had the idea to invent the light bulb?

78

One of my favorite books on the subject of creativity is ***How to Get Ideas*** written by Jack Foster. Here is what he had to say about creativity:

"Let the child in you come out. Don't be afraid.

One of the ways to come up with new ideas is to be more like a child.

Loosen up. Run down the hall someday at work. Take everything out of your desk drawers and put it on the floor for a couple of days. Rearrange your furniture. Write notes with crayons.

Forget what was done before. Break the rules. Be illogical. Be silly. Be free.

Be a child."

One of Foster's ideas for inducing creativity is to rearrange the furniture in your bedroom or office. I decided to try it in our living room.

"I sure hope **you know who** doesn't stroll in right now."

6. ONE WAY TO BOOST YOUR CREATIVITY IS TO CHANGE YOUR SURROUNDINGS.

I like to do crossword puzzles. What I find most fascinating about doing crossword puzzles is what happens when I get stuck.

When I feel I am at a dead end with a difficult crossword puzzle, I put it down and do something else for an hour. Then I return to it, and quite often am able to complete words that had stumped me just an hour earlier.

But why?

No one knows how the brain produces ideas.

But what we do know is that ideas come to us at all times, and in all sorts of places.

83

Every minute of your day is dramatically different from all the others. Every minute of the day you are experiencing different stimuli. And your mind reacts to different stimuli in different ways.

84

Let's say you are working on a crossword puzzle (or challenge or problem). It's 10 AM and there are sounds outside your window. You have a certain energy level. You may be hungry or hot or both. You are thinking about a dispute you had with a friend. All those stimuli are causing your brain to work in a certain way.

OK, so let's say you stop thinking about your crossword puzzle, and you do something else for an hour.

85

It's now 11 AM, and you come back to the room. There are different sounds outside your window. Your energy level has changed, and you are no longer hungry or hot. You have forgotten about the disagreement with your friend, and are thinking instead about your plans for dinner.

You take another look at the crossword puzzle you couldn't finish, and all of a sudden you see answers to clues that had stumped you just one hour earlier.

86

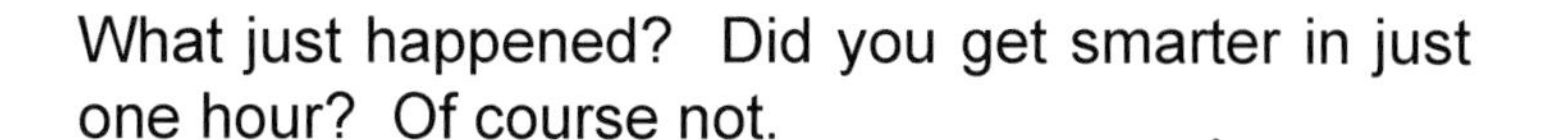

What just happened? Did you get smarter in just one hour? Of course not.

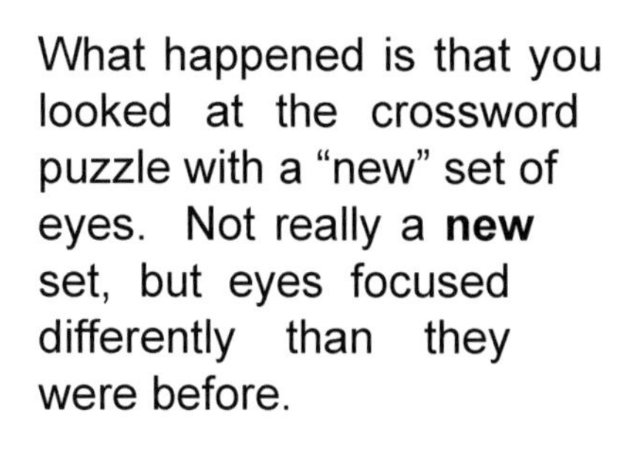

What happened is that you looked at the crossword puzzle with a "new" set of eyes. Not really a **new** set, but eyes focused differently than they were before.

87

The brain is an amazing organ.

There are 100 billion nerve cells (neurons) in the brain, and about 100 trillion different possible connections between nerve cells.

Even small changes in the stimuli reaching your brain, let alone skiing a triple black diamond, can cause major changes in your creativity.

88

"This morning you made a cup of tea or coffee and had your breakfast – the same as yesterday. But was it? You will never even brush your teeth in precisely the same way as yesterday. Every minute is unique."

The Art of Creative Thinking
(Emphasis Added)

89

Creativity experts tell you that when you are stuck – when you need a boost to your creative energy – you should stop whatever you are doing, and do something else. Walk your dog, put on some music, go for a swim.

The objective is to change the stimuli reaching your brain.

In this way, you may come back to your challenge with a completely "different" set of eyes.

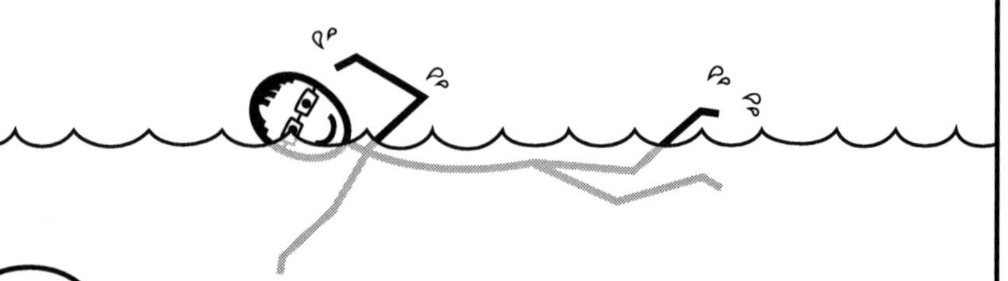

90

"Why didn't I think of that <u>before</u>?"

Anonymous

Wow, that swim felt great.

I'd now like to give you a clue to my next point about creativity.

It's actually an advertisement from the 1960's for National Library Week.

abcdefghijklmnopqrstuvwxyz

At your local library these have been arranged in ways that can can make you cry, giggle, love, hate, wonder, ponder, and understand. It's astonishing to see what these twenty-six little marks can do. In Shakespeare's hands they became Hamlet. Mark Twain wound them into Huckleberry Finn. James Joyce twisted them into Ulysses. Gibbon pounded them into The Decline and Fall of the Roman Empire. John Milton shaped them into Paradise Lost.

7. MOST OF THE TIME, CREATIVITY IS ABOUT REARRANGING, EXTENDING, OR COMBINING SOMETHING THAT ALREADY EXISTS – INTO SOMETHING NEW.

Occasionally someone discovers something new … as an example, the discovery of the planet Pluto in 1930. Well, actually Pluto was always out there, we just didn't know about it.

And that is pretty much the case with any creative endeavor … the words, the colors, the notes, the materials, the compounds are already out there. To be creative, you just have to combine them in a new way.

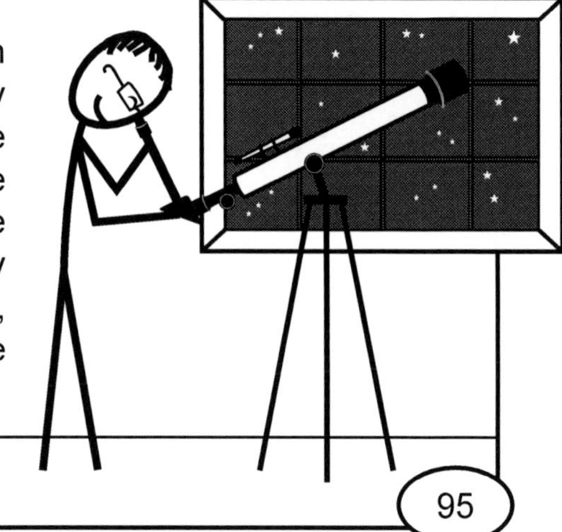

95

By the way, many people think Pluto was named after the adorable Disney character, the dog Pluto.

In fact, the planet was named after a Roman god of the underworld, and the Disney dog was named after the planet.

What?! I was named after a measly planet?

96

Henry Ford was once asked how he had accomplished so much, starting with nothing.

Here is what he responded:

"It's hardly correct to say that I started with nothing. Every man starts with all there is. Everything is here – the essence and substance of all there is."

97

When I sit down to write, I'm comforted by the fact that all the words I need to create a huge bestseller already exist. All I need to do is touch the keys on my laptop in the right sequence. That shouldn't be too hard.

98

Even in business, 90% of what appear to be new concepts are, in reality, variations or combinations of existing business ideas.

Google did not invent search engines. It was far from the first internet company to sell advertising. It was not even the first to tie its search capability to keywords.

Google's unique proposition – its creative input – was in developing an approach for ranking websites according to how often they were viewed or linked. Really just a tweaking of pre-existing business ideas.

Ditto for Facebook.

As you may know, facebooks – directories with student photos – were popular for many years before Facebook founder, Mark Zuckerberg, got the idea for putting photos and profiles online and facilitating communication between members.

Zuckerberg did not re-invent the wheel – he just did some tweaking.

"An idea is nothing more or less than a new combination of old elements."

A Technique for Producing Ideas,
James Webb Young (NTC Publishing, 1988)

101

"Discovery consists of seeing what everyone else has seen and thinking what nobody else has thought."

Anonymous

102

One way to see what everyone else has seen, and yet think what no one else has thought, is to **reframe the question** that everyone has been asking.

8. SOMETIMES CREATIVE IMPULSES WILL RESULT FROM REFRAMING THE PROBLEM OR QUESTION YOU ARE TRYING TO RESOLVE.

Einstein once said that if he had only one hour to save the world, he would first spend 55 minutes thinking about the problem.

105

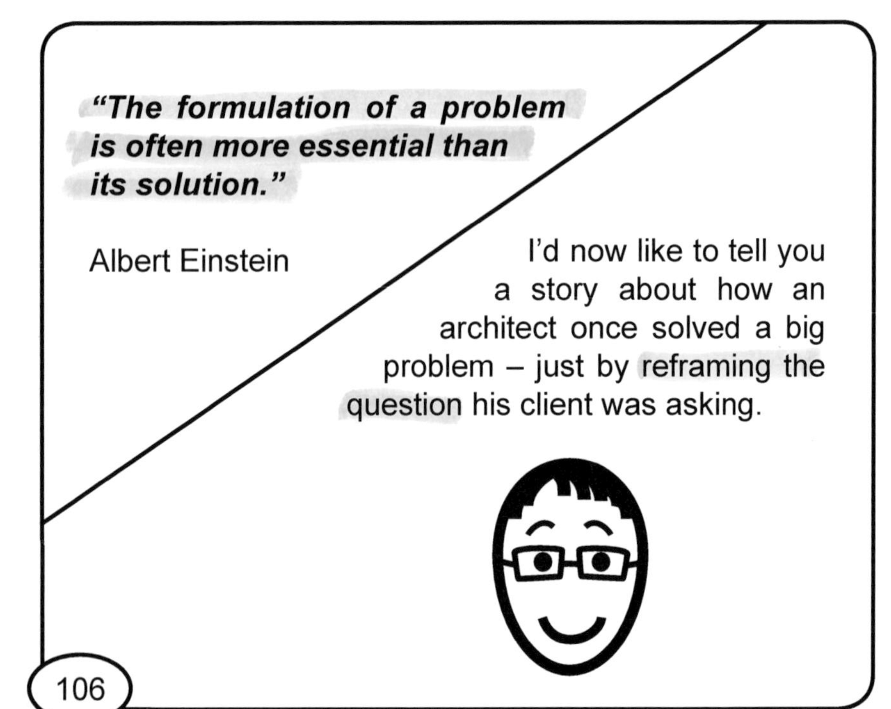

"The formulation of a problem is often more essential than its solution."

Albert Einstein

I'd now like to tell you a story about how an architect once solved a big problem – just by reframing the question his client was asking.

106

An office building owner once retained an architect to help solve the owner's problem.

The owner's office building was outdated, and its elevators were too old, small, and slow to service the number of people working in the building.

1
As a result, the people who worked in the building were always waiting for an elevator, and that made them unhappy.

The building owner asked the architect to improve the elevator system.

But given the physical structure of the building, the potential solutions were all very difficult and expensive.

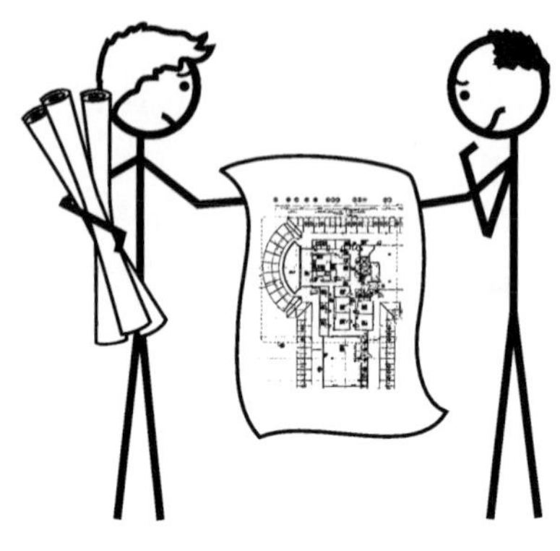

THEN ONE DAY THE ARCHITECT ASKED THE BUILDING OWNER A "SILLY" QUESTION.

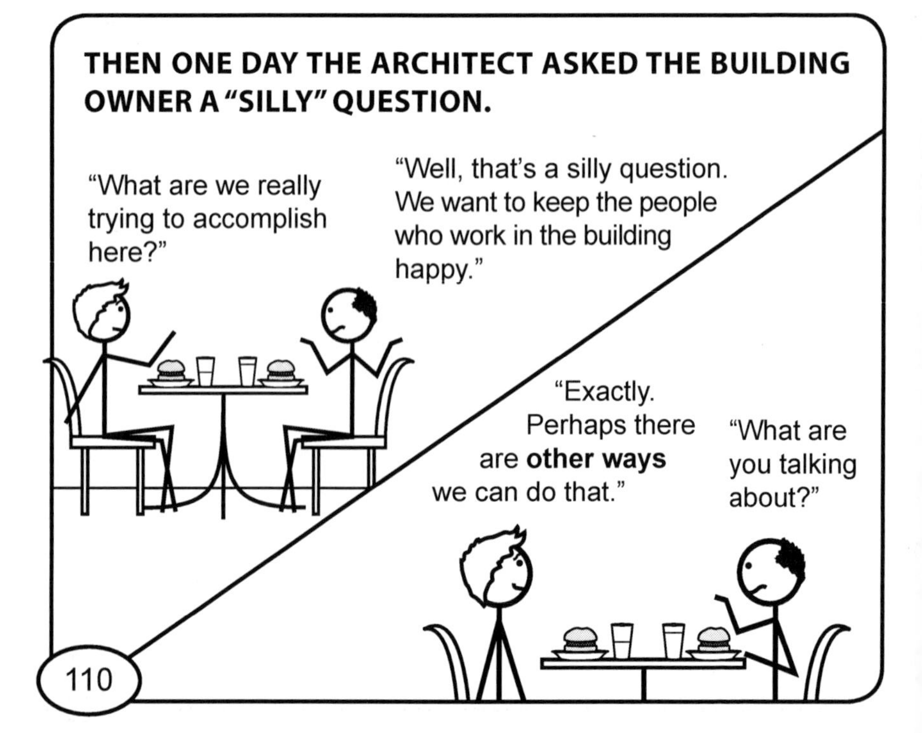

"What are we really trying to accomplish here?"
"Well, that's a silly question. We want to keep the people who work in the building happy."
"Exactly. Perhaps there are **other ways** we can do that."
"What are you talking about?"

And so the architect did something really easy and inexpensive.
He installed mirrors on all the walls in the building's lobby.
The mirrors were actually just a distraction. The elevators were still small and slow, but now the wait was a little less boring. While people waited for elevators, they fixed their neckties, touched up their make-up … or simply admired themselves.
111

In other words, the employees were not as unhappy waiting for an elevator – all because the architect reframed the question he and the building owner were asking.

By the way, have you ever noticed how many office buildings have mirrored walls?

112

There are many examples in history when innovators developed ideas simply by changing the question they asked themselves:

1. When Henry Ford stopped asking how to move his workers around the factory to where the work was, **and instead asked how to get the work to his employees**, he conceived the assembly line.
2. When Edward Jenner stopped asking why people get smallpox, and instead asked **why some people (milkmaids) did not get smallpox**, he discovered the vaccine for smallpox (exposure to relatively harmless cowpox).
3. When Leonardo daVinci stopped asking how to get people to bodies of fresh water, and instead pondered **how to bring water to people**, he designed the first modern plumbing system.

I'm going to take a break from writing right now.

I'm going to let my subconscious do some work for a while and let my ideas incubate.

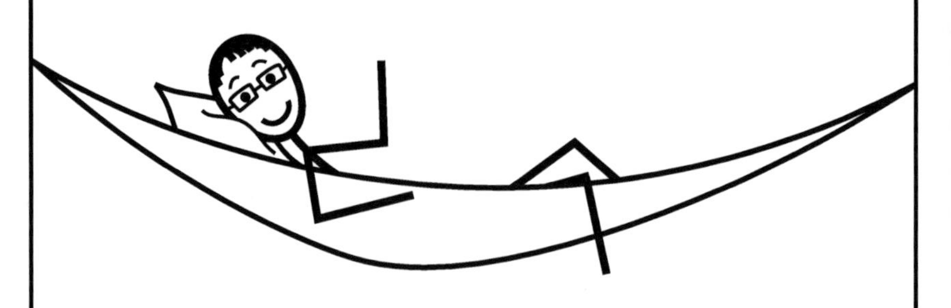

9. SOMETIMES YOUR SUBCONSCIOUS WILL DO YOUR CREATIVE WORK FOR YOU.

In many respects, the creative process is quite a mystery.

Ideas jump in and out of our heads seemingly at random. Psychologists call these "mind pops." Your job is just to pay attention so that you can snare the good ones.

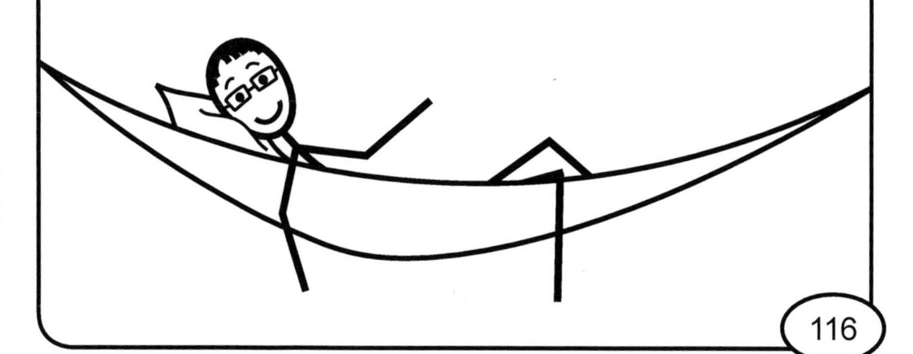

When engaged in a creative endeavor, you need to trust that your subconscious is working, even when you are not.

At any point in time you are aware of only a very small percentage of your brain's activities. Be assured there's a lot going on below the surface of your consciousness. Eventually this activity will bubble to the surface.

117

"In the creative state a man is taken out of himself. He lets it down as if it were a bucket into his subconscious, and draws up something which is normally beyond his reach. He mixes this thing with his normal experience, and out of the mixture he makes a work of art."

E. M. Forster

118

Did you ever have an intuition or premonition about something? Did an idea ever jump into your head from nowhere? Did you ever see the solution to a problem while thinking or doing something totally unrelated?

These are examples of your subconscious at work.

Researchers even believe that your mind is working when you are sleeping.

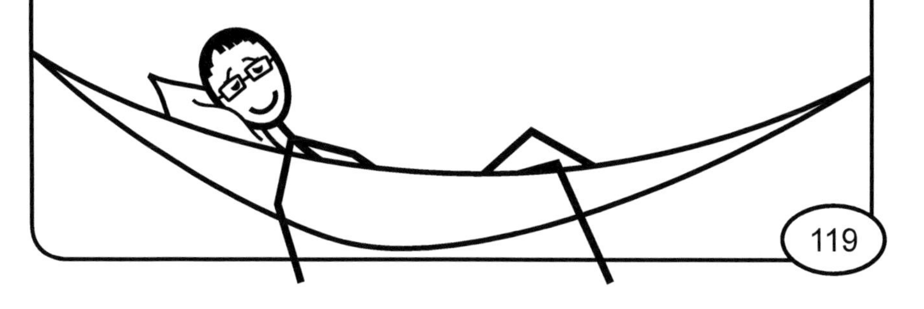

That is why some great inventors, Thomas Edison included, slept in their laboratories. They wanted to access their thoughts the minute they woke up.

One night I decided to try sleeping on my desk ... to see if I would wake up to some fresh ideas. Didn't work for me – I accidentally stapled two of my fingers together.

I'll be taking a little nap now.

Next time you are out of ideas, perhaps you should trust your subconscious and let your ideas marinate.

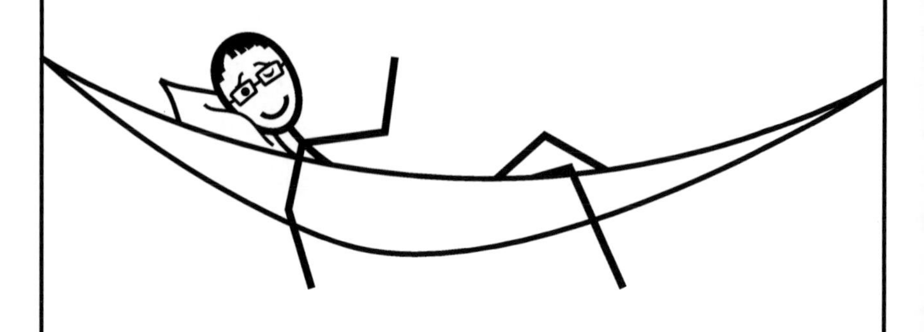

"Your subconscious mind never rests. When you quit thinking about the subject and decide to forget it, your subconscious mind doesn't quit working. The thoughts keep flashing freely in every direction through your subconscious.

They are colliding, combining and recombining millions of times. Typically, many combinations are of little or no value, but occasionally, a combination is made that is appreciated by your subconscious as a good combination and delivered up to the conscious mind as a 'mind-popping' idea."

Cracking Creativity,
Michael Michalko (Ten Speed Press, 2001)

As you can see, I'm up from my nap and jogging. Although I've never run more than one mile, I've decided to train for a marathon. I'm going for a personal best today. 1.2 miles. I realize that's a long way from 26 miles. But you have to start somewhere.

And that brings me to my next point.

10. TO BE CREATIVE, YOU HAVE TO START SOMEWHERE.

OK, not bad, 1.25 miles. I'm moving in a forward direction.
Most people never reach the potential of their own creativity because they never get off the metaphorical couch. Unless you give your creative talents a chance, you never know what you might accomplish.
125

Almost anything in your life can benefit from a new idea, a new approach, a new project, a new challenge. But first you need to start.

Many people feel their ideas will never go anywhere. So they never start. Other people fear failure, so they never let their creative thoughts run free.

These people defeat themselves before they ever get started.

Any idea that you pursue has a chance of failing; of making you look stupid; of embarrassing you. OK, those are the facts. Now move past them.

If you are going to let the possibility of embarrassment or failure stop you, then put this book down right now. I'm not going to sell you a bill of goods. Failure, embarrassment, humiliation, frustration – these are all part of the creativity game. You can't have one without the possibility of the other.

"To swear off making mistakes is easy. All you have to do is swear off having ideas."

Leo Burnett,
Advertising Executive

The good news is that once you start moving forward, inertia begins to work in your favor.

Once you start acting creatively, you build momentum. The act of planting your flag, of taking action, will ignite your creative fires.

I try to write everyday. Many times when I sit down to write, I don't feel particularly creative. But most days, just the act of starting to type brings forth ideas. Once you begin, it can be like flipping a creativity switch. The act of doing puts your mind in gear and boosts your creativity.

DON'T WAIT FOR INSPIRATION

"But what about inspiration?" you may ask.

"Shouldn't I wait to begin my creative journey until I know exactly what I want to say or do?"

Some people believe there is no point to taking off on a creative journey until they experience a sign – something that illuminates their path. That rarely happens. If you wait for inspiration, you may be waiting forever.

"If one had to wait for what people call 'inspiration,' one would never write a word."

Graham Greene

I love my new Nike running shoes. I mostly love their slogan: JUST DO IT.

Starting off on any new endeavor can be scary. **Creative thinking is not for sissies.**

"The first steps of a creative act are like groping in the dark: random and chaotic, feverish and fearful ... with no apparent end in sight."

Twyla Tharp

But nothing in life is riskier than just standing still.
"Even if you're on the right track, you'll get run over if you just sit there."
Will Rogers
133

I knew I could step on the curb before those bikers hit me. I saw them coming out of the corner of my eye.
And that is a lead into my next point about creative thinking.
134

11. ENHANCE YOUR CREATIVE TALENTS BY OPENING YOUR EYES A LITTLE WIDER.

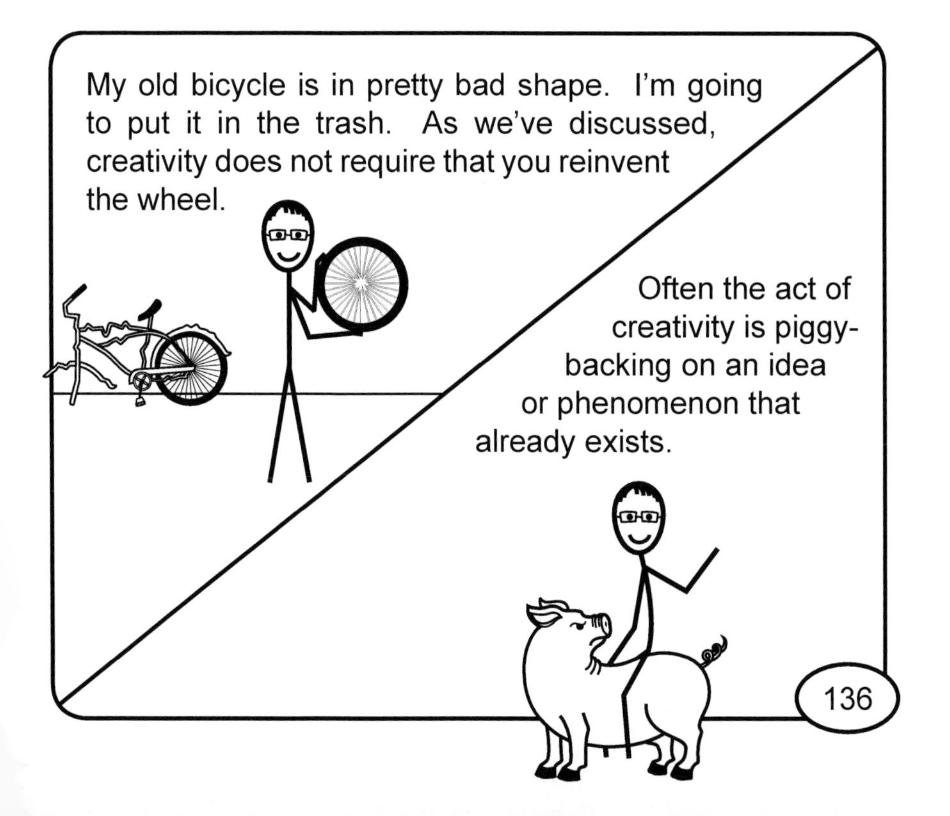

My old bicycle is in pretty bad shape. I'm going to put it in the trash. As we've discussed, creativity does not require that you reinvent the wheel.
Often the act of creativity is piggy-backing on an idea or phenomenon that already exists.
136

To build on something that already exists, however, you need to see and hear what is out there. You need to heighten your powers of observation ... let your curiosity go wild.

For example, did you ever really look at a flower? Hold it up to your face? Smell it? Take in the genius of nature?

"Stand still and watch the patterns, which by pure chance have been generated: stains on the wall, or ashes in the fireplace, or the clouds in the sky, or the gravel on the beach or other things. If you look at them carefully you might discover miraculous inventions."

Leonardo daVinci

Artists often see a shape or object or form and turn it into art. Picasso, for example, created artwork out of objects he found by the side of the road.

One day he saw a broken bicycle and used the twisted handlebars and seat to sculpt the head of a bull.

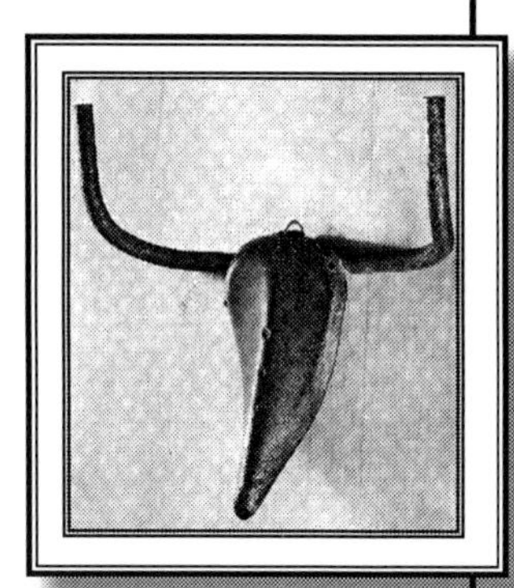

When you let your powers of observation run free, you open your mind to creative thinking.

ASSOCIATIVE THINKING

The ability to see one object or form, and relate it to a completely unrelated object or form is called associative thinking.

"Persons with low associative barriers may think to connect ideas or concepts that have very little basis in past experience or that cannot easily be traced logically."

Creativity in Science, Dean Simonton (Journey, 1980)

By opening up your senses, by developing your powers of observation, you enhance your associative abilities.

CULTIVATE YOUR CURIOSITY

Creative people are almost always curious people.

Curiosity may have "killed the cat," but as far as I know, most humans survive and prosper from their own curiosity. If you are interested in something, peel away the layers of what you see to be sure you understand everything about it. And, ask a lot of questions!

141

"Why, Daddy? ... But why? ... But why, Daddy? ... But why?"
Kids are great. They ask lots of questions. They want to know the answers to everything.
And so do creative people.

142

"Brilliant thinkers never stop asking questions, because they know that is the best way to gain deeper insights."

How to Be a Brilliant Thinker: Exercise Your Mind and Find Creative Solutions
Paul Sloane (KoganPage, 2010)

143

"We run this company on questions, not answers."

Eric Schmidt, CEO, Google

144

SERENDIPITY

As you open your senses to the sights and sounds around you, you also open yourself to serendipity – the occurrence of chance happenings.

Serendipity is the stumbling upon events, people, or things when you are not consciously looking for them.

Let me tell you one of my favorite stories about serendipity and creativity.

In 1945 a man named Percy Spencer was working with some radar equipment.

One day he noticed that the candy bar in his pocket was melting.

Percy could not understand what was happening, but figured something about the radar was cooking his candy bar.
What the Snickers bar is going on here?
So he placed some corn kernels next to the radar.
To his amazement, the kernels started popping like crazy.
POP!
POP!
POP!
POP!
147

Percy Spencer did not enter his lab that day thinking he was going to pop popcorn. Instead he planned to experiment with radio waves and radar systems. But, serendipity had a different plan for him ... and, yes, of course, Percy **built on this chance happening to invent the microwave!**

Everyday you are witness to thousands of little events. Are you watching for ideas? For oddities? For chance happenings? Is your mind wide open to possibilities?

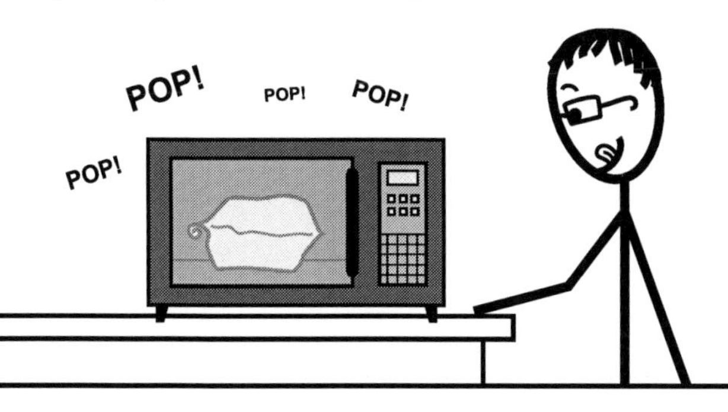

"In our everyday lives, we encounter odd moments when we see things beyond explanation. Our conditioned response is to ignore these moments or explain them away.

Yet these moments, for the innovator, are the future knocking on the door. How else will new knowledge appear to us, if not as strange, bizarre, or incomprehensible experiences?"

The Myths of Innovation,
Scott Berkun (O'Reilly, 2007)

149

Sometimes a serendipitous event can really jump start your creative juices.

150

TWO MEN ARE HIKING IN THE JUNGLE.
UNFORTUNATELY, THEY WALK RIGHT INTO A HUNGRY CHEETAH.
151

ONE MAN IMMEDIATELY TAKES OFF HIS BACK PACK AND STARTS PUTTING ON HIS RUNNING SHOES.
“Are you nuts!? Don’t you know a cheetah can run 70 miles per hour?”
“Of course I know that … but I only need to out-run you!”
152

That story always makes me laugh.

I doubt you're going to be bumping into cheetahs on a regular basis. But, by opening your mind to serendipitous events, you may inspire your creativity.

Take George deMestral for example. In 1941 he went for a hike in the woods and came back with burrs all over his pants. Wondering why they were so hard to remove, he looked at one under a microscope (widening his eyes so to speak). Next thing you know, he invents Velcro.

153

ZAPPOS AND SERENDIPITY

The founder of Zappos, Tony Hsieh, believes that random happenings and conversations can lead to great ideas. He even required his employees to funnel into their offices through one entrance – just in case a random encounter inspired some creative thinking.

"We made this decision when we moved into our building as part of our goal to ... increase the chances of serendipitous employee interactions."

Delivering Happiness, Tony Hsieh
(Business Plus, 2010)

154

12. IMPROVE YOUR CREATIVITY BY BREAKING EXISTING PATTERNS AND ASSUMPTIONS.

Like it or not, we all form **mental ruts** in our thinking. We tend to see and process and analyze what we observe today the same way we did yesterday, and the day before, and so on.

As a result, our creative joints get a little creaky.

Look at the two shapes I have put on my blackboard. Would you be surprised if I told you they were exactly the same size?

Most people will swear that the two shapes are not same size. But, they are exactly the same.

Because of the way they are positioned, most people cannot see that they are identical. This is an example of how the mind can become stiff – seeing and processing in set patterns.

157

To think creatively you need to break out of mental ruts. You need to spur your brain to new ways of thinking and analyzing.

Here are two suggestions:

A. Challenge Assumptions.
B. Disrupt Patterns and Reflexes.

158

A. Challenging Assumptions

In the 16th century, the scientist, Copernicus, challenged established scientific thinking when he proposed that the earth revolved around the sun – not the other way around. Until then, every astronomer was working off the wrong assumption – distorting all their findings and ideas.

You too have certain assumptions about how things work, what follows from what, and what methods work best.

To be as creative as possible, you need to test your assumptions.

If you want to maximize your creative energies, think long and hard about all of your assumptions.

"We've all had the experience of taking something for granted as the basis for opinion or action, and then subsequently finding that we had made an assumption – probably an unconscious one – that was unwarranted. Watch out for these preconceptions!

For we take on board all sorts of assumptions and preconceptions, often in the form of opinions or commonsense, which on examination turn out to be unproven or debatable. These are the main impediments to new ideas."

The Art of Creative Thinking
(Emphasis added.)

When you are thrashing with a problem or opportunity, try breaking it into smaller parts. Look at each premise or assumption you are making. Are you certain about each? Is there another way of thinking about each?

We all come to certain conclusions during our lives. And once we come to a conclusion or belief, we usually cling to it, always looking for examples to **support it**.

What we don't do, is search for examples that would **disprove it**.

LET'S SAY YOU BELIEVE ALL MOTORCYCLISTS DRIVE TOO QUICKLY.

ONE DAY YOU ARE DRIVING WITH YOUR FRIEND ON THE FREEWAY AND A MOTORCYCLIST FLIES BY YOU.

"See, I told you **all** motorcyclists speed."

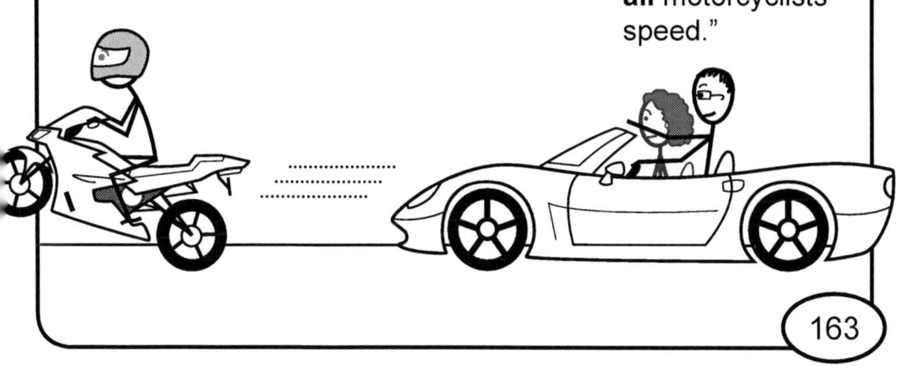

163

BUT YOUR FRIEND IS A LITTLE SMARTER THAN YOU ARE.

"Jim, witnessing an event that **confirms your assumption** is not the way to challenge your thinking. You must keep your eyes open and watch for facts that **disprove your rule**. There's one right over there."

164

In his great book, ***The Black Swan***, Nassim Taleb talks about assumptions.

He uses as his model the black swan. For years the world assumed there was no such thing as a black swan – until Australia was discovered where there were lots of black swans. Then everyone's assumptions changed.

Taleb maintains that it is dangerous and short-sighted to assume that **because we have never seen or experienced something, we will never see or experience it**. In creating, in problem solving, we must train ourselves to think about the possibility of "black swans."

166

167

"There are so many things we can do if we focus on anti-knowledge, or what we do not know."

The Black Swan,
Nassim Taleb

168

"If a man begins with certainties he shall end in doubts; but if he will be content to begin with doubts, he will end with certainties."

Sir Francis Bacon

B. Disrupting Patterns and Reflexes

The second way we can change how we think is to take conscious steps to alter our mind's patterns.

Let me try an experiment with you. Say the word "bloke" three times.

Now, tell me the word for the white of an egg.

Most of you probably said "yolk," which of course is the yellow of an egg. It is a natural reflex after repeating a rhyming word.

We are all subject to certain reflexes in how we think.

"When your attention is focused on a subject, a few patterns are highly activated in your brain and dominate your thinking. These patterns produce only predictable ideas, no matter how hard you try. In fact, the harder you try, the stronger the same patterns become.

If, however, you change your focus and think about something that is not related, different, unusual patterns are activated."

Cracking Creativity,
Michael Michalko

171

I recently read a book titled, ***Lateral Thinking***, by Edward deBono.

This book suggests that there are two kinds of thinking – **vertical** thinking which is logical and sequential (A to B, then B to C and so on).

And, there is **lateral** or sideways thinking which is not sequential. In fact, the point of lateral thinking is to disrupt your mental habits and provoke a new type or pattern of thinking.

172

Here are some of Mr. deBono's suggestions for spurring lateral thinking:

1. Take apart the pieces of a problem or opportunity and reflect on each. How can the components be reassembled in different ways?
2. Select a random word from the dictionary. Is there some way to connect this word to your creative endeavor?
3. Consider your challenge in a world of absurdities, e.g., water runs uphill. If such were the case, how might you attack your problem?
4. Focus on totally unrelated items – what can you learn from their similarities or differences?

The point of lateral thinking is to knock your mental patterns off their feet.

Lateral thinking is meant to be provocative – to jolt you out of your cognitive habits.

Many of the ideas you get from lateral thinking will be of no value to you. But, occasionally, the process of lateral thinking will lead to an epiphany ... a breakthrough in approach, analysis or understanding.

One of Mr. deBono's suggestions for inspiring lateral thinking is to reflect on unrelated objects, and consider how their differences or similarities apply to your challenge.

Before I wrote my first Skinny book, I tried several of deBono's ideas. In fact, one day I sat and stared at unrelated objects – including a feather and a bowling ball.

My hope was that this process would give me ideas for how to best communicate with you and other readers.

Here were some of my thoughts as I stared at a feather and bowling ball:

a) The feather and a bowling ball suggest weight – one light, one heavy.

b) The feather and a bowling ball suggest forward motion – one item moves gracefully while the other glides.

c) The colors of the feather and bowling bowl suggest states of mind – clean and pure against dark and foreboding.

After an hour or so I began to dwell on the contrast between the two objects.

What was most impactful on my brain was their dramatic differences – heavy and light, dark and white, hard and graceful.

And for whatever reason I thought about horror movies. I remembered two of my favorites, ***An American Werewolf in London*** and ***Psycho***. I won't spoil the suspense for you, but I will say that the most memorable scenes occur during periods of stark contrast ... someone happily strolling along, and then WHAM! A big, fat, horrible event occurs.

THE IMPACT CAUSED BY CONTRAST

And right then I decided that my Skinny books had to have a lot of contrast – silly little stick people juxtaposed next to a quote from Edison; goofy jokes preceding stories about Einstein; text against images and photos.

Having studied how people learn, I'm convinced that the contrast in this book will help you remember our points.

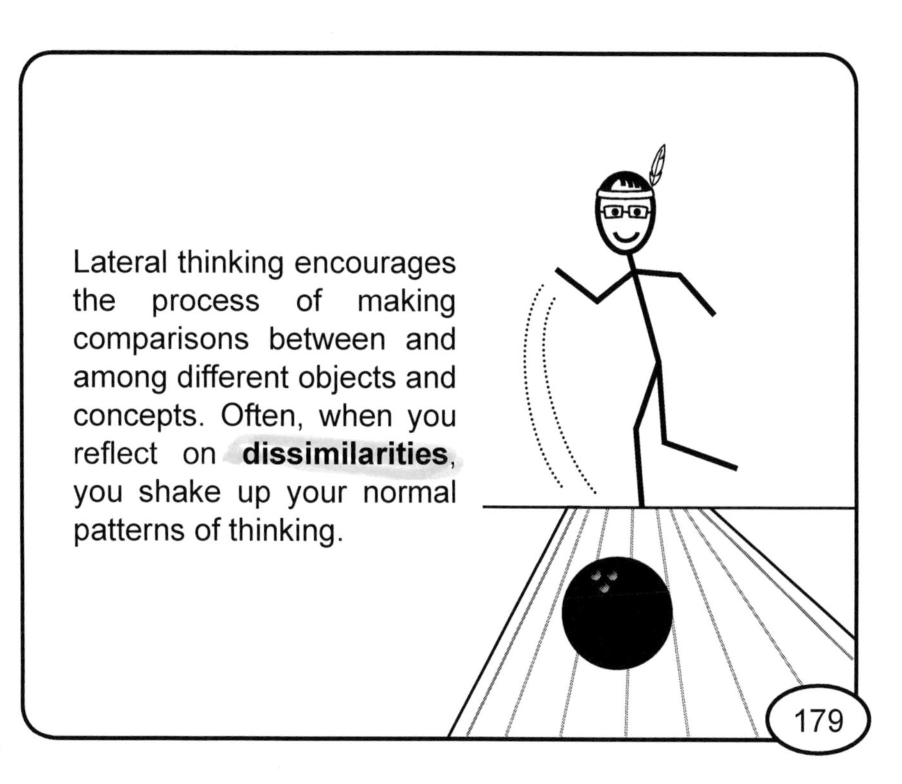
Lateral thinking encourages the process of making comparisons between and among different objects and concepts. Often, when you reflect on **dissimilarities**, you shake up your normal patterns of thinking.
179

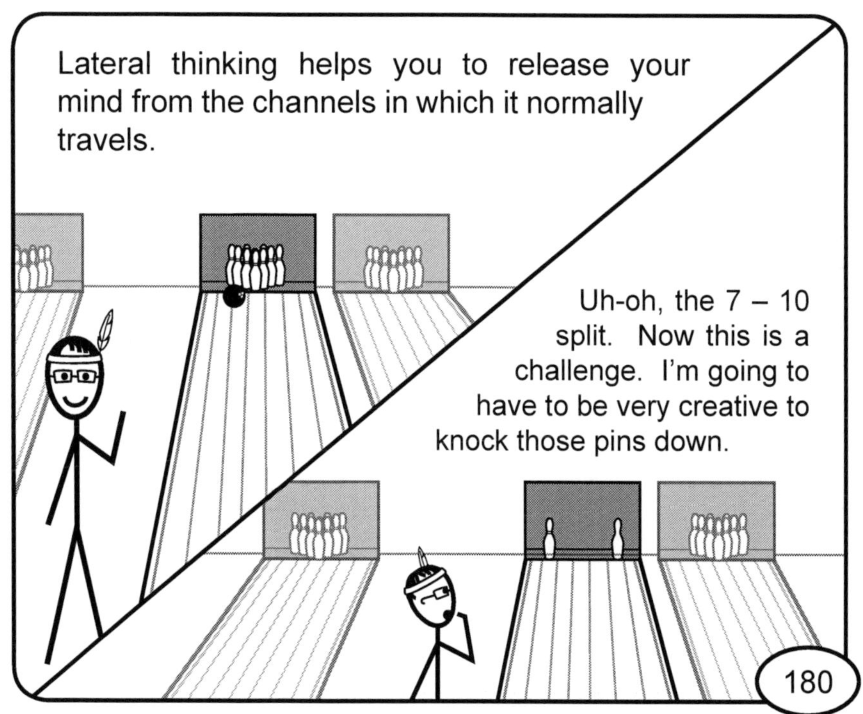
Lateral thinking helps you to release your mind from the channels in which it normally travels.
Uh-oh, the 7 – 10 split. Now this is a challenge. I'm going to have to be very creative to knock those pins down.
180

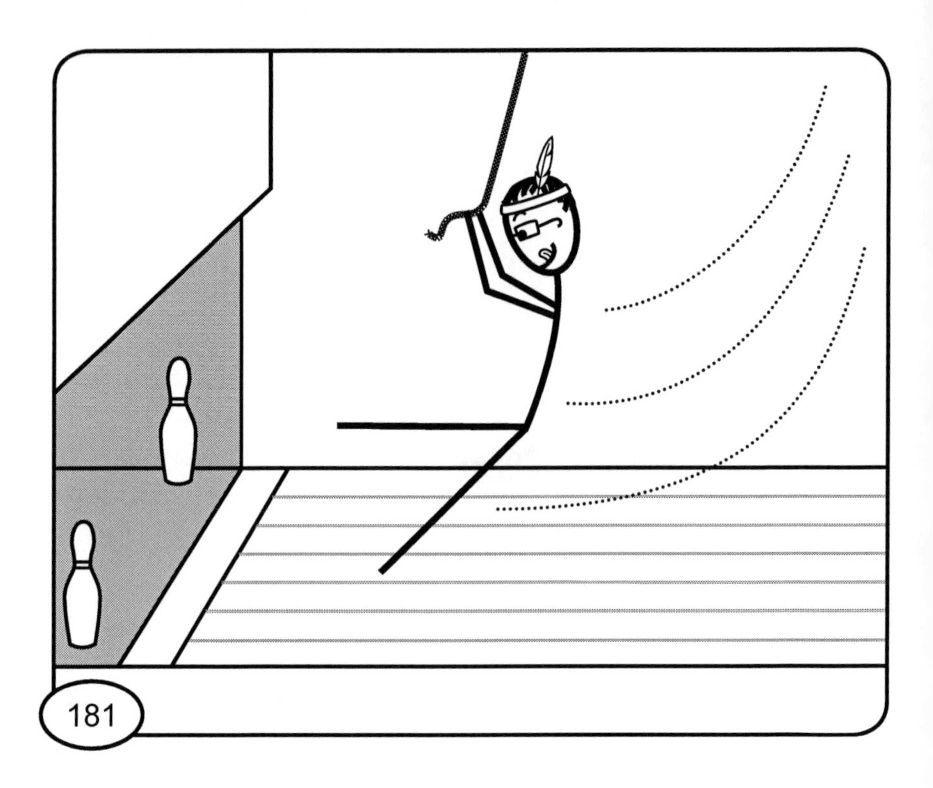

181

Just goofing. That's not allowed. Or, is it? I'm sure no one ever tried it before!!

Sometimes you have to think like a nut to disrupt patterns that have formed in your mind over many years.

Ouch, that hurt! Who knew bowling pins were so darn hard? Oh well, that's a good segue for my next rule of creativity.

182

13. CREATIVE THINKING MAY PRODUCE DISCOMFORT.

The creative process is not always a pretty one. It can be taxing. Humiliating. Anxiety-producing.

Over the years I have learned that I am most comfortable with certainty, order and familiarity. When I venture into strange ideas, places and experiences, I get anxious.

But this awareness has helped me. I realize that my instinct for safety is not always healthy, and certainly not conducive to maximum creativity.

I realize that to be more creative, I must be able to live with – if not embrace – some level of uncertainty and chaos.

"Some people by temperament find any sort of ambiguity uncomfortable and even stressful. They jump to certainties – any certainty just to escape from the unpleasant state of not knowing."

The Art of Creative Thinking

The creative process can be gut-wrenching at times.

The status quo can be so much easier.

But the status quo will eventually get stagnant.

187

"One does not discover new lands without consenting to lose sight of the shore for a very long time."

Andre Gide

188

I'm sure you've heard of the Rohrshach test ... where people are shown odd shapes and asked what they see in them.

A similar test was given to people who make their living in creative endeavors – writers, scientists, artists and innovators.

One group of cards had symmetrical shapes. The other group had asymmetrical shapes. The people in creative fields were asked to pick the cards they preferred, and almost all of them picked cards wtih asymmetrical shapes.

Other people (the control group) were much more likely to select the cards with ordered or symmetrical shapes.

189

"Creative people, as I see them, are distinguished by the fact that they can live with anxiety, even though a high price may be paid in terms of insecurity, sensitivity ... They do not run away from non-being, but by encountering and wrestling with it, force it to produce being ... they pursue the meaningless until they can force it to mean."

The Courage to Create,
Rollo May (Norton, 1975)

190

When you think creatively, there may be times when you are unsure of yourself... when you venture into stressful situations.

But, you must do your best to live with the discomfort. Find confidence in the fact that you are not alone ... almost everyone who leaves the safe ground of certainty experiences some level of angst.

There is even a line of thinking that the way to jolt your creative talents is to **deliberately inject** some stress into your life.

PUT YOURSELF IN A CORNER

As you can see, I have painted myself into a corner. I have done this purposefully.

I have done this because I believe our minds sometimes work best – **when they have to**.

It is said that creativity is your mind on tiptoes.

Don't worry about me. I will figure something out. In the meantime, I want to tell you about a friend of mine who ran an advertising agency.

193

Whenever his company started a new campaign, he kicked the project off with an idea fest. He wanted ideas – lots of them. So he told his creative team, "No lunch until you each have three ideas."

Of course, they all came up with the ideas – just before noon.

194

My friend was well aware that the mind sometimes needs to be inspired.

He knew that if he gave his team until dinner time to come up with ideas, then that is exactly how long it would take them to do so.

In other words, he created a time limit to help them ignite their creative fires.

WAS THE HEAD OF THE ADVERTISING AGENCY BEING UNREASONABLE FORCING PEOPLE TO HOLD OFF EATING UNTIL THEY CAME UP WITH IDEAS?

A man by the name of Alex Osborn would say "no."

Osborn is the author of a book titled ***Applied Imagination.*** He is the man credited with originating the concept of **brainstorming** (group creativity).

Osborn's research indicated that a group of four or five people, properly led, can come up with 50 – 100 new ideas in just one hour's time.

"Necessity is the mother of invention."

Plato

NECESSITY IS **THE MOTHER** OF INVENTION

When it comes to being creative, we humans **can rise** to the occasion. In other words when we are incited or cornered or inspired to achieve, we can be amazingly creative.

In a little while I'm going to list my candidates for the 10 most creative men of the last 500 years. But first, I'd like to speak to creative women.

Women have not had the same opportunities for achievement as have men – until perhaps the last 50 years. And so, my list of the 10 most creative women ever is much more current than my list of male creatives.

Mary Kay Ash – started Mary Kay Cosmetics
Jane Fonda – started the personal workout craze
Madonna – no explanation needed
Ayn Rand – author of ***Atlas Shrugged***
Anita Roddick – started The Body Shop
J.K. Rowling – invented Harry Potter
Martha Stewart – no explanation needed
Lillian Vernon – started the mail-order catalogue business
Dr. Ruth Westheimer – sex education and entertainment
Oprah Winfrey – no explanation needed

Each of these women forged new territory. Each was exceptionally creative.

I have researched the stories of each of them in trying to find a common thread. And my conclusion is that each, at some point in her life, was in a corner – needing to be creative to survive and succeed.

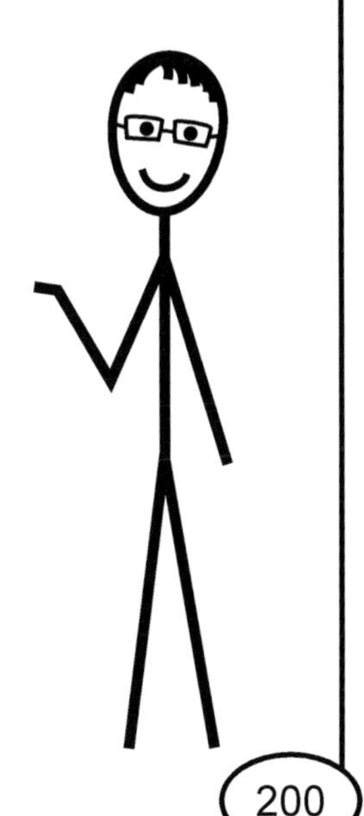

Look at my list again; look at the history of each woman:

Mary Kay Ash – single mother raising 3 children
Jane Fonda – mother committed suicide when Jane was 12
Madonna – mother died when Madonna was 5
Ayn Rand – fled Russian oppression
Anita Roddick – born in a bomb shelter during WWII
J.K. Rowling – single mom living on welfare
Martha Stewart – raised in Nutley, New Jersey
Lillian Vernon – fled Germany just before WWII
Dr. Ruth Westheimer – parents killed in Holocaust
Oprah Winfrey – raped as a teenager, gave birth to stillborn

My premise is that these ten super-achievers had a **need to succeed.**

And, as a result, they became very creative because **they had to.**

In other words, **necessity is the mother of invention.**

The upshot: You will never know how creative you can be unless and until you test yourself!!!

OK, so maybe my little room-painting illustration wasn't such a good one. I didn't factor in that I'd need to go to the bathroom before the paint dried.
PAINT
203

I now want to tell you about another powerful approach to boosting your creative juices.
PAINT
204

14. DRAW YOUR WAY TO CREATIVE IDEAS.

We skinny people existed well before written words did. We were drawn on caves in hieroglyphics 30,000 years ago. Writing, on the other hand, has only been around for 5,000 years.

Many people believe that drawings and illustrations are still the best way to communicate.

Certainly they are a great tool for creative thinking.

"Thinking in terms of pictures or diagrams is more than useful – it is essential for understanding and manipulating some issues.

We rely so heavily on the use of words to describe things that it is surprising how ineffective they can be for conveying information in some circumstances.

Try describing an unusually shaped object such as a corkscrew or coat hanger ...."

How to Be a Brilliant Thinker
Paul Sloane

207

DESCRIBING A CORKSCREW TO A MARTIAN

"You see there's this thing called a corkscrew. I don't have one handy right now but let me describe it for you. It's a little piece of metal that is twirly and then there's a piece of rubber or plastic on top and you screw it into a cork ..."

These Earthlings are worse off than we imagined.

208

"A picture is worth a thousand words."

Anonymous

Pictures and images can be very powerful. Many people believe that visuals are more impactful than words.

A few years ago, researchers showed volunteers 2,500 slides of photographs, one slide every 10 seconds. It took 7 hours to show all the slides. One hour later, the volunteers were shown another 2,500 slides – half of which were in the first batch (repeats).

The volunteers were then asked to indicate which of the second group of slides had been in the first group.

The results were surprising – the accuracy recognition was very high. On average about 90%.

The test was then sped up – showing slides every one second. Same result. A high level of accuracy in people's ability to recall what they had seen.

This test proved that our brains are well-equipped to remember pictures and images.

As the author of a scientific journal concluded: ***"the capacity of recognition memory for pictures is almost limitless."***

"The reason why, to quote the old adage 'a picture is worth a thousand words,' is that they make use of a massive range of cortical skills: color, form, line, dimension, texture, visual rhythm, and especially imagination – a word taken from the Latin imaginary, literally meaning 'to picture mentally.'

Images are therefore often more evocative than words, more precise and potent in triggering a wide range of associations, thereby enhancing creative thinking and memory."

The Mind Map Book,
Tony and Barry Buzan (Plume, 1997)

STRUCTURED DOODLING

A mind map is a drawing that causes a flow of ideas – what mind mappers call radiant thinking.

The point is to start with a central image or word and draw outward. Each new word or image will usually inspire another word or image, and at some point the totality of the drawing represents a framework for creation.

There is no exact form that needs to be followed to create a mind map. Just write or draw a central idea or image, and start doodling.

213

The 2008 book, ***The Back of the Napkin***, makes the argument that the best way to solve problems and create opportunities is to use diagrams and images.
How do you know which side is the back of the napkin?
"I'm afraid to ask what you're doing."
214

"We can use the simplicity and immediacy of pictures to discover and clarify our own ideas, and use those same pictures to clarify our ideas for other people, helping them discover something new for themselves along the way.

Visual thinking is an extraordinarily powerful way to solve problems, and though it may appear to be something new, the fact is that we already know how to do it.

We are born with an amazing vision system ...."

The Back of the Napkin: Solving Problems and Selling Ideas with Pictures, Dan Roam (Portfolio, 2008)

215

In the book, ***The Creative Entrepreneur***, author Lisa Beam suggests that people analyze their creativity with a visual diagram – what she calls a "mandala," Sanskrit for "magic circle."

Ms. Beam suggests that the best way to identify your creative strengths and opportunities is to draw a diagram which connects your answers to:

1. Where is your heart? What has great meaning to you?
2. What are your gifts? When does your work flow easily?
3. What is the economic value of what you do? How will it earn a profit?
4. What business tools and skills do you possess?

216

OUTLINE FOR AN ENTREPRENEUR'S MANDALA

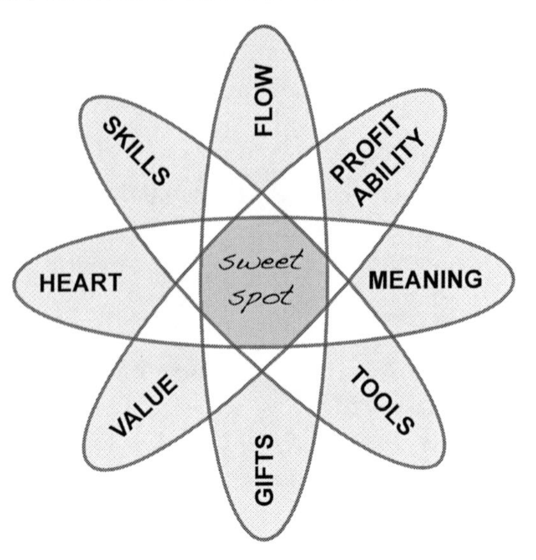

Ms. Jones suggests that the middle of the mandala is your **sweet spot** – that point where your talents, interests, and opportunities intersect.

Ms. Jones is a strong advocate for visual depictions.

"Visual journaling ... a powerful way to develop problem-solving abilities and gain insights in ways that linear, non-visual approaches to thinking and learning don't access. Visual journaling helps us go beyond what we know in our rational mind, so we can access other ways of knowing – the kind of knowing that results in truly original thinking, ideas, and creative breakthroughs."

Whether you try mind mapping, napkin drawing, or pictorial journaling, there is a lot to be gained by thinking visually.

Words are just substitutes for images and feelings.

When you draw or doodle, you engage parts of your brain you may not use on a daily basis.

Another way to access untapped areas of your braininess is to reach out to people who see the world differently than you do ... which brings us to our next point about creativity.

15. FIND CREATIVE IDEAS BY LOOKING FOR INSPIRATION FROM DIFFERENT FIELDS OR DISCIPLINES.

One of my favorite books is
The Wisdom of Crowds,
written by James Surowiecki.

I'd like to tell you a story from
the introduction to that book.
221

One day a scientist named Francis Galton attended
a state fair. At this fair, livestock were auctioned off.
And there were contests.

One of the contests
was to guess the
weight of a large
oxen.
222

People were asked to write their guesses on a piece of paper and put them in a jar. Some of the people in the crowd were knowledgeable about livestock. Others were just passer-bys with no particular expertise.

There were 787 guesses from people **in all walks** of life.

And here is what is fascinating: **when all the guesses were totaled and divided by 787, the average was <u>1,197 pounds</u> – within one pound of the oxen's actual weight of <u>1,198 pounds</u>!**

Was this just a weird coincidence?

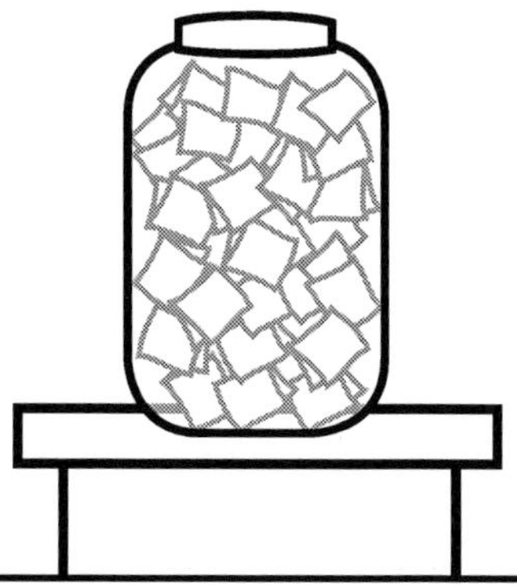

Surowiecki says, "NO." In fact, Surowiecki's book makes an excellent case for the proposition that the sum total of many different viewpoints will give you an answer that is far better than any one expert.

"If you put together a big enough and diverse enough group of people ... that group's decisions will, over time, be intellectually superior to the isolated individual, no matter how smart or well-informed he is."

The Wisdom of Crowds,
James Surowiecki (Doubleday, 2004)
(Emphasis added.)

Surowiecki's premise is that mixing people with lots of different perspectives and expertise will give you a collective wisdom that is surprisingly insightful.

This principle can work for you if you are stuck for ideas. Reach outside of your usual sources – solicit the views of people who see and experience the world differently than you do. The vision of those you engage can at times produce incredible ideas.

Such is the story of the printing press – one of the most important innovations of the last 500 years.

The printing press was invented by Johannes Gutenberg in 1440 when he enhanced his coin presses with elements he observed from a completely different field – winemaking.

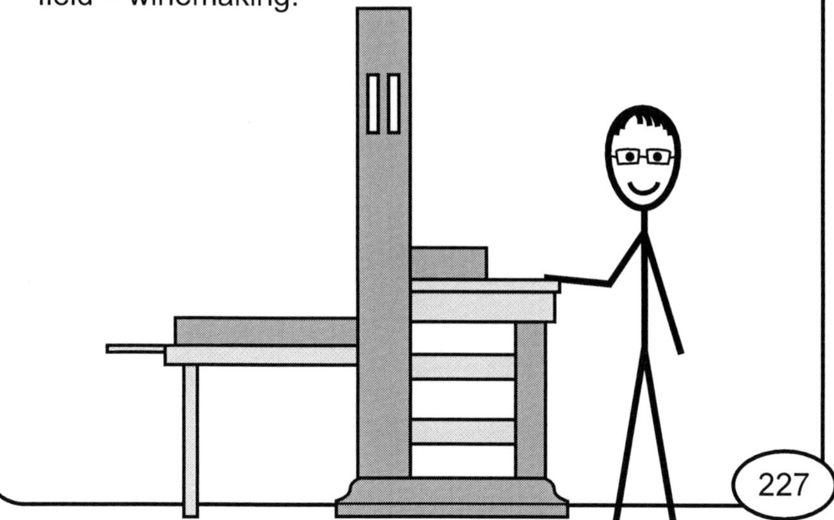

Gutenberg was a goldsmith, so he certainly knew a lot about minting coins.

And then, at some point in his life, he may have had a "eureka" moment while visiting a winemaker friend of his.

Taking inspiration from the wine press, and mixing it with his own expertise, Gutenberg invented the printing press – and opened up floodgates that led to the Renaissance.

Looking beyond your own turf can be inspirational.

Wherever you live and whatever you do, after a while you begin to experience the same people, places, and things.

That is why idea generation will often come from:

1. Travel.
2. Reading about subjects of which you know very little.
3. Asking people outside your field for help.
4. Studying innovations in areas other than yours.

229

Many of the most creative people have an eclectic group of friends. In other words, he or she engages with a diverse group of people – many with different interests and disciplines.

Reaching out to people with a wide range of backgrounds, educations, and viewpoints may help make you a more creative person.

230

16. WHENEVER AN IDEA HITS YOU, TRY TO CAPTURE IT AS SOON AS POSSIBLE.

I don't usually take my BlackBerry into the shower, but I had some great ideas while washing my hair and I wanted to get them down as soon as possible. I was worried that the minute I started shaving, I would forget them.

233

Doesn't it drive you crazy when you have a thought in your mind, something interrupts that thought, and then you can't recall what you had been thinking about?

That happens to everyone.

234

"'The horror of the moment,' the King went on, 'I shall never, NEVER forget!'

'You will, though,' the Queen said, 'If you don't make a memorandum of it.'"

Alice in Wonderland

235

At some point everyday, I'll stop whatever I'm doing for 10 minutes and make notes to myself.

It could be in my BlackBerry, or in a little notebook I carry, or on whatever scrap paper I can find at the time.

Then at the end of the day, I organize my notes into some kind of summary.

236

"Often an idea would occur to me which seemed to have force ... I never let one of those ideas escape me, but wrote it on a scrap of paper ... In that way I save my best thoughts on the subject, and, you know, such things often come in a kind of intuitive way more clearly than if one were to sit down and deliberately reason them out. To save the results of such mental action is true intellectual economy."

Abraham Lincoln

237

Some of the ideas I write down may look silly on rereading. But, that's OK because others may be helpful to a problem or opportunity I'm working on.

Still others may not be valuable in and of themselves but may lead me to another idea, or cause me to see a problem differently, or help me synthesize several ideas into a whole.

238

People who have studied creativity believe that it's very important to capture your observations and thoughts as and when they arise.

That's because the mind can only remember about seven chunks of information at one time. Once you start putting in additional information, older inputs fall out.

BUT, when you write or type something, you are telling your brain that it's important – and should be downloaded to your long-term memory.

Items stored in your long-term memory are there for retrieval – even if you don't know it. These items are embedded in your subconscious and, as we have learned, usually pop up when needed.

One of my personal heroes, Leonardo daVinci, was a diligent record keeper.

He carried notebooks with him wherever he went. A prodigious note taker, he died with thousands of pages of his ideas on paper – giving historians insight into the magnitude of his great genius.

Do you know which of the following daVinci created?

a) the Mona Lisa, or
b) renderings of the first flying machine, or
c) plans for the first submarine, or
d) the Last Supper, or
e) the predecessor to MapQuest.

The answer is ALL
of the above!!
And lots more!

Leonardo daVinci

At times, daVinci would take a break from his inventing, sculpting, and painting, and review his notes.

He felt that by reviewing his thoughts he would experience new insights and perspectives – which could lead to more inventions or creations.

Whatever daVinci did, I want to emulate. He was a creative factory – responsible for hundreds of significant inventions and works of art.

17. CREATIVITY IS NOT A SUBSTITUTE FOR TECHNICAL SKILL AND COMPETENCE.

I have an uncle Louie. He has never been able to hold a job for long. He fears that employment stifles his creative talents.

My uncle's hobby is photography. He believes that his photographs are special. He has never taken a course on photography. Or, read much about it. He just feels he is uniquely creative.

My uncle is sure that it's only a matter of time before his photographs are discovered, and he becomes rich and famous.

I hope it happens soon because he owes me money.

247

No matter how creative you may be, you need to hone your skills and work at your craft. Creativity, in and of itself, is not enough.

Creativity flows outward from intimate knowledge of a subject.

As perhaps you can tell, I'm a fan of great Renaissance artists like daVinci and Michelangelo. Both drew and painted the human body and, of course, Michelangelo's sculptures are amazing – including his breath-taking work, the David.

248

249

Michelangelo was fanatic about understanding the human body. He did not rely on his creativity. First, he had to have knowledge.

In Irving Stone's historical novel, ***The Agony and The Ecstasy***, Stone describes how Michelangelo risked death sneaking into crypts to autopsy fresh cadavers.

250

Here is an excerpt in which Michelangelo seeks help in finding cadavers:

"Michelangelo made it clear at once why he had come: 'Do you know if anyone is dissecting now?'

'Assuredly not! Don't you know the penalty for violating a corpse?'

'Banishment for life?'

'Death.'

After a silence, Michelangelo asked, 'And if one were willing to risk it? How could it be gone about?'"

The Agony and The Ecstasy
(Emphasis added.)

251

Whatever the forum for your own creative expressions, you too must learn all you can about your craft. Assist your creative genies by honing your talent and studying those who are great at what you do – thereby positioning yourself for inspiration.

252

CREATION FOR CREATION'S SAKE

I like to paint. I'm not very good at it. But painting relaxes me.

I have no pretensions of ever being able to sell a painting. I flex my creative muscles for no reason other than it brings me pleasure.

What do you think of my work? Pretty good, huh? Well, perhaps not. But, that's OK. I enjoy the creative process – even if no one else likes what I create.

Even with the greatest of talents, there is sometimes a disconnect between the energy invested and the recognition received.

"No painting ever sells for as much as it costs the painter to make."

Vincent Van Gogh

255

And while we are talking about energy, I want to speak to physicality.

I do not believe you can maximize your creative talents unless you pay attention to your health.

256

18. CREATIVITY IS AN EXPRESSION OF ENERGY.

The other day I was reading a book about daVinci and it says:

"What is your image of the body type of a genius? Did you grow up, as I did, with the stereotype of the skinny, 'four eyed,' brainiac nerd? It's amazing how many people associate high intelligence with physical ineptitude."

How to Think Like Leonardo daVinci,
Michael Gelb (Dell, 1998)

Being skinny myself, and of course four-eyed, I whipped off an angry e-mail to the author:

> ***"Dear Mr. Gelb. I happen to be a skinny, 'four-eyed' brainiac who resents your suggestion of physical ineptitude. I'm currently training for a marathon and have worked my way up to 1.5 miles … Any more questions?"***

I haven't heard back from him yet; I'm sure his apology is on the way.

YOUR CREATIVITY IS DIRECTLY RELATED TO YOUR ENERGY

The more energy you have, the more creative you will be.

And so I recommend that you take care of yourself. Eat well. Get enough sleep. Exercise daily.

Leonardo daVinci, for example, was known for his commitment to exercise and athleticism.

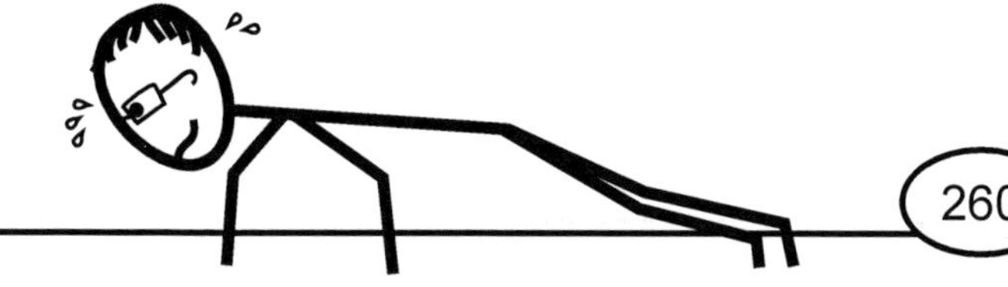

Do creative types take care of themselves?

Well, we don't know all the answers, but it's interesting to note that creatives do seem to be long-lived. Here's a list of some of the best-known male creatives of the last 500 years:

Leonardo daVinci – lived to age 68
Thomas Edison – lived to age 84
Albert Einstein – lived to age 76
Benjamin Franklin – lived to age 85
Sigmund Freud – lived to age 83
Galileo – lived to age 77
Michelangelo – lived to age 88
Sir Isaac Newton – lived to age 85
Pablo Picasso – lived to age 92
Mark Twain – lived to age 74

261

I can't prove that these men took care of themselves – thereby elongating their lives and maximizing their creative energies. They did, however, each live well beyond his life expectancy.

But I believe there is something more at work here.

I wonder if Einstein was a jogger.

262

THE PURSUIT OF THAT WHICH YOU ARE PASSIONATE ABOUT

There is nothing that energizes people more than pursuing something about which they feel strongly.

It is my proposition that engaging in what you are passionate about is, **in and of itself, life-sustaining**.

Perhaps that is the reason why the men on my list were so long-lived.

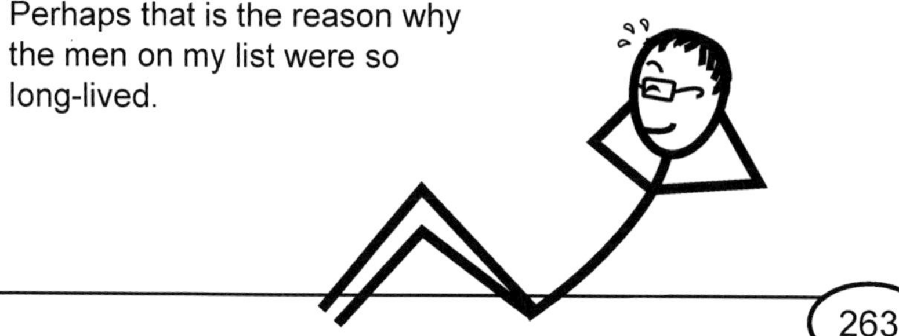

But there is one more reason you need to work on your energy level.

The fact is that if you try to create something new – something different from what people are used to – you are going to need a lot of energy to deal with the prospect of rejection.

We have discussed how creativity is disruptive. That scares some people. When scared, people push back. You need energy to stay the course in the pursuit of that which you believe in.

"Every great idea in history has the fat red stamp of rejection on its face. It's hard to see today because once ideas gain acceptance, we gloss over the hard paths they took to get there. If you scratch any innovation's surface, you'll find the scars: they've been roughed up and thrashed around – by both the masses and leading minds – before they make it into your life."

The Myths of Innovation
Scott Berklin

"You can write the entire history of science in the last 50 years in terms of papers rejected by <u>Science</u> or <u>Nature</u>."

Paul Lauterbur,
Nobel Prize Winner

"Don't worry about people stealing your idea. If it's original, you will have to ram it down their throats."

Howard Aiken, inventor

Perhaps I overdid the exercise thing today. I'm going to have to take a break pretty soon.

But first, I need to tell you about two more points.

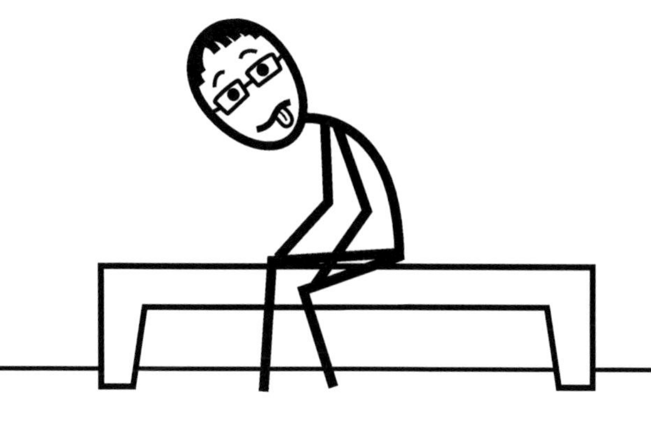

19. THE ACT OF CREATION CANNOT BE SCRIPTED.

"I don't know when inspiration will hit me. I just want to be working when it does."

Pablo Picasso

269

I've read perhaps 100 books and articles about creativity. Eventually, my brain started to overload; I wasn't getting much out of additional reading.

At some point you need to just let go and stop trying to create. You need to just go with the flow.

For better or worse, your mind is a whirling, swirling eddy of thoughts, ideas, worries, pleasures, images, and memories.

270

As we have discussed, there are ways to prepare yourself to think creatively and, ignite your creative impulses. But at some point you need to trust the process and stop trying. In other words, you need to be careful that you don't press.

Let me tell you a story.

TWO MEN WERE WALKING BY A RIVER, AND CAME UPON AN ENORMOUS WATERFALL. AT THE BOTTOM OF THE WATERFALL WAS A BODY.

"Oh no, someone has drowned!"

AND THEN, ALL OF SUDDEN, THE BODY STARTED MOVING TOWARD SHORE.
"Oh my gosh, the person is alive. How can that be?"
273

"You're alive! How could anyone survive that roaring surf and pounding water?"
"Easy … I just go up when the water goes up, and down when it goes down."
274

The point of this story is that sometimes in life you just need to let go.

Creativity is a wondrous process that no one truly understands. We can push the process a bit here and there, prod it forward, put ourselves in the right mindset for results, but eventually, we need to just go with the flow.

275

When Steve Jobs of Apple was asked, "How do you systemize innovation?"

He responded: ***"The system is that there is no system."***

In other words, there is no exact road map for the creative process. At some point, you just get on the road and start moving forward.

276

By the way, we can learn a lot from Steve Jobs. As you probably know, he is the founder of Apple and the creator of the Mac, the I-Phone, the I-Pod and now the I-Pad – all amazing and very successful innovations.

If you want to learn about how Steve Jobs creates, you might want to read **Inside Steve's Brain** by Leander Kahney.

277

Here's a mini-book report on ***Inside Steve's Brain*** that ties together some of the points we've been discussing.

1. Steve believes in viewing multiple versions of a new product before he settles on one – **he wants lots of ideas.**
2. Steve believes in **reaching across disciplines** in designing – the idea for the scroll wheel in the iPod came from a marketing guy, not a designer.
3. Steve believes in **lateral thinking** – provocative, off-the-wall creativity. He will sometimes ask, "What do we design if money were no object?"
4. Steve believes **everything already exists**. "We have always been shameless about stealing great ideas."
5. Steve believes **creativity flows from passion** – "You've got to have an idea that you're passionate about; otherwise you're not going to have the perseverance to stick it through."

278

I can't really surf. But since this book is my creation, I can create whatever world I want. And I have always wanted to try surfing.

Such is the lead-in to our last rule of creativity.

20. HOWEVER YOU BEST EXPRESS YOURSELF, CREATE THE WORLD YOU WANT.

Whatever you want out of life, it's not likely to just show up at your front door.

You have to use all your energies and talents to find and get it. And creativity – the development of ideas and pushing of edges – is most likely going to be a part of that quest.

281

I propose that every person should do something that taxes his or her creative talents. Design clothing, write a book, paint or compose, start an online business – anything that requires you to be at your most creative.

Why?

Because the world does not reward the "same old, same old." The world rewards risk takers and those who journey on "the road less traveled."

282

No worries, I'm OK ... Remember, I create the outcomes in my world.
You, too, can create the outcomes in your world.
283

THERE IS SOMETHING SPIRITUAL ABOUT CREATIVITY.

When you think about it, creativity is about extending your life. It is about leaving a part of you for future generations.

"Creativity is the yearning for immortality. We know that each of us must develop the courage to confront death. Yet we must also rebel and struggle against it. Creativity comes from the struggle – out of rebellion the creative act is born."

The Courage to Create,
Rollo May

Finally, the creative process can be amazingly joyful.

Lost in your imagination, pushing yourself into new territories, working at a challenge just beyond your reach … these can be times of real ecstasy!

As the great psychologist Victor Frankl said:

"What man needs is not a tensionless state but rather the striving and struggling for a worthwhile goal, a freely chosen task."

"Creativity involves the production of novelty. The process of discovery involved in creating something new appears to be one of the most enjoyable activities any human can be involved in."

Creativity: Flow and the Psychology of Discovery and Invention,
Mihaly Csikszentmihalyi (Harper, 1996)

287

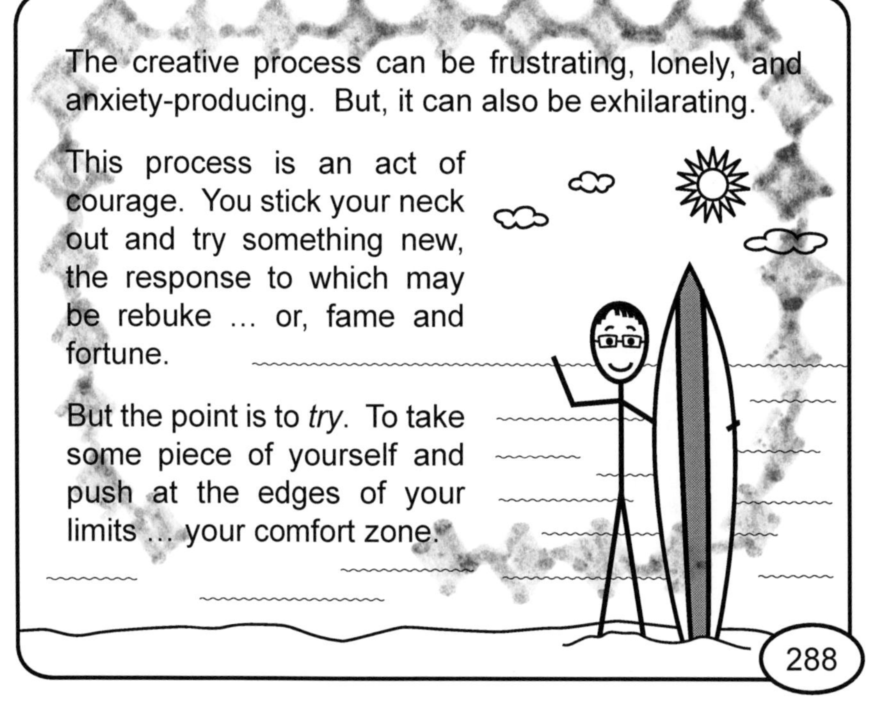

The creative process can be frustrating, lonely, and anxiety-producing. But, it can also be exhilarating.

This process is an act of courage. You stick your neck out and try something new, the response to which may be rebuke ... or, fame and fortune.

But the point is to *try*. To take some piece of yourself and push at the edges of your limits ... your comfort zone.

288

"It's not the critic who counts, nor the man who points out how the strong man stumbled, or where the doer of deeds could have done better. The credit belongs to the man who is actually in the arena, whose face is marred by dust and sweat and blood, who strives valiantly, who errs and comes short again and again, who knows the great enthusiasm, the great devotion, and spends himself in a worthy cause, who at best knows achievement and who at worst if he fails at least fails while daring greatly so that his place shall never be with those cold and timid souls who know neither victory nor defeat."

Teddy Roosevelt

289

"The reasonable man adapts himself to the world; the unreasonable one persists in trying to adapt the world to himself. Therefore, all progress depends on the unreasonable man."

George Bernard Shaw

290

A QUICK SUMMARY OF POINTS TO REMEMBER ABOUT CREATIVITY

#1: TRAIN YOURSELF TO THINK OUTSIDE THE BOX.

Don't restrict your thinking to someone else's limitations.

• • • •

#2: PRODUCE IDEAS – LOTS OF IDEAS.

Nobel Prize winner Linus Pauling said: *"The way to come up with great ideas is to come up with lots of ideas."*

#3: CREATIVITY IS OFTEN DISRUPTIVE.

Every so often stick your tongue out at convention.

• • • •

#4: THERE ARE TIMES WHEN YOU MUST KEEP DISTRACTIONS TO A MINIMUM.

Give your brain room to breathe. daVinci said: *"The painter must be solitary … For if you are alone you are completely yourself, but if you are accompanied by a single companion, you are half yourself."*

#5: BE PLAYFUL.

Never relinquish your inner child's belief in possibility.

• • • •

#6: IF YOU ARE STUCK, CHANGE YOUR ENVIRONMENT.

There are billions of cells firing in your brain at any one time. Changing the stimuli your brain experiences alters how these cells fire and the thoughts that emerge.

#7: OFTEN CREATIVITY IS JUST REARRANGING, EXTENDING, OR COMBINING WHAT ALREADY EXISTS.

You don't need to invent the wheel – just find new uses for it.

• • • •

#8: SOMETIMES THE SOLUTION COMES FROM REFRAMING THE QUESTION.

Remember what Einstein said – if he had only one hour to save the world, he would spend 55 minutes framing the problem.

#9: LET YOUR SUBCONSCIOUS WORK FOR YOU.

Go take a nap.

• • • •

#10: HALF THE BATTLE IS THE STARTING.

Don't wait for the muse to hit you. Muses are unreliable.

#11: OPEN YOUR EYES AND EARS.

The world around you is filled with tons of suggestions if you just let yourself experience them.

• • • •

#12: YOU NEED TO BREAK EXISTING PATTERNS AND REFLEXES.

By disrupting established reflexes, you sometimes see problems and opportunities in very different ways.

#13: CREATIVITY CAN BE UNCOMFORTABLE.

Most people feel safe with the status quo. Creative thinking sometimes takes you into uncharted waters.

• • • •

#14: DRAW YOUR WAY TO CREATIVE IDEAS.

Visuals – images, drawings, graphs, pie charts – are very powerful tools for jump starting your creativity.

#15: LOOK FOR INSPIRATION IN DIFFERENT FIELDS AND DISCIPLINES.

Soliciting ideas from people whose expertise is far afield from yours can be surprisingly helpful.

• • • •

#16: WRITE IDEAS DOWN AS SOON AS POSSIBLE.

Our short-term memories can only retain about seven thoughts before things start falling out.

#17: CREATIVITY IS NOT A SUBSTITUTE FOR COMPETENCE.

Hone your craft, learn all you can, position yourself for inspiration.

• • • •

#18: CREATIVITY REQUIRES ENERGY.

Take care of yourself. Engage in something you are passionate about.

#19: YOU CANNOT FORCE CREATIVITY.

The creative process is not mechanical. Sometimes you must just go with the flow.

• • • •

#20: GET IN THE GAME. EXERCISE YOUR CREATIVE MUSCLES.

There will be angst. There will be frustration. But there can also be incredible joy and satisfaction.

THE END

CONCLUSION

We here at **The Skinny On™** hope you enjoyed this book. We would love to hear your comments.

My personal e-mail is jrandel@theskinnyon.com.

Warm regards,

Jim Randel

BIBLIOGRAPHY

Here's a list of some of the books we read in preparing ***The Skinny on Creativity***:

A Technique for Producing Ideas, James Webb Young (NCT, 1994)

A Whack on the Side of the Head: How You Can be More Creative, Roger von Oech (Hachette, 1983)

A Whole New Mind, Daniel Pink (Riverhead, 2005)

Applied Imagination, Alex Osborne (Scribner, 1963)

Blue Ocean Strategy, W. Chan Kim and Renee Mauborgne (Harvard Press, 2005)

Business Beyond the Box: Applying Your Mind for Break-through Results, John O'Keefe (Brealey Publishing, 1998)

Cognitive Surplus: Creativity and Generosity in a Connected Age, Clay Shirky (Penguin, 2010)

Cracking Creativity: The Secrets of Creative Genius, Michael Michalko (Ten Speed Press, 2001)

Creativity: Flow and the Psychology of Discovery and Invention, Mihaly Csikszentmihalyi (HarperCollins, 1997)

Creativity Workout: 62 Exercises to Unlock Your Most Creative Ideas, Edward DeBono (Ulysses, 2008)

Delivering Happiness, Tony Hsieh (Business Plus, 2010)

Einstein: His Life and Universe, Walter Isaacson (Simon & Schuster, 2007)

Flow: The Classic Work on How to Achieve Happiness, Mihaly Czikszentmihalyi (Harper, 1992)

Hamlet's BlackBerry, (HarperCollins, 2010)

How to Be a Brilliant Thinker: Exercise Your Mind and Find Creative Solutions, Paul Sloane (KoganPage, 2010)

How to Get Ideas, Jack Foster (Berrett-Koehler, 2007)

How to Think Like Leonardo daVinci, Michael Gelb (Dell, 1998)

Ignore Everybody: And 39 Other Keys to Creativity, Hugh MacLeod (Portfolio, 2009)

Inside Steve's Brain, Leander Kahney (Penguin, 2008)

Lateral Thinking, Edward deBono (Harper and Row, 1973)

Leonardo daVinci, Sherwin Nuland (Penguin, 2005)

Leonardo daVinci: Flights of the Mind, Charles Nicholl (Viking, 2004)

Making Ideas Happen: Overcoming the Obstacles Between Vision and Reality, Scott Belsky (Portfolio, 2010)

Man's Search for Meaning, Victor Frankl (1946)

Oh, The Thinks You Can Think, Dr. Seuss (ICM, 1992)

Profiles of Genius: Thirteen Creative Men Who Changed the World, Gene Landrum (Prometheus, 1993)

Profiles of Female Genius: Thirteen Creative Women Who Changed the World, Gene Landrum (Prometheus, 1994)

Strategic Intuition: The Creative Spark in Human Achievement, William Duggan (Columbia Business, 2007)

The 12 Secrets of Highly Creative Women, Gail McMeekin (Conari, 2000)

The ***Agony and The Ecstasy,*** Irving Stone (Signet, 1961)

The Art of Creative Thinking: How to be Innovative and Develop Great Ideas, John Adair (KoganPage, 1990)

The Art of the Start, Guy Kawasaki (Portfolio, 2004)

The Back of the Napkin, Dan Roam (Penguin, 2008)

The Black Swan: The Impact of the Highly Improbable, Nassim Taleb (Random House, 2007)

The Circle of Innovation, Tom Peters (Knopf, 1997)

The Courage to Create, Rollo May (Norton, 1975)

The Creative Entrepreneur, Lisa Sonara Beam (Quarry, 2008)

The Creative Habit: Learn It and Use It for Life, Twyla Tharp (Simon & Schuster, 2006)

The Life of P.T. Barnum, P.T. Barnum (1855)

The Magic of Thinking Big, David Schwartz (Simon & Schuster, 1959)

The Mind Map Book: How to Use Radiant Thinking to Maximize Your Brain's Untapped Potential, Barry and Tony Buzan (Plume, 1996)

The Myths of Innovation, Scott Berkun (O'Reilly, 2007)

The Wisdom of Crowds, James Surowiecki (Doubleday, 2004)

The Wizard of Menlo Park: How Thomas Edison Invented the Modern World, Randall Stross (Crown, 2007)

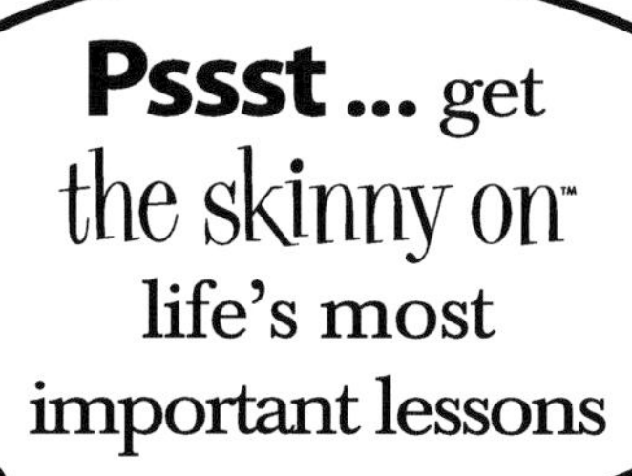

Pssst ... get
the skinny on™
life's most
important lessons

- Get 20% off your first purchase
- Receive exclusive offers, previews and discounts
- See excerpts from all **The Skinny On™** books
- Suggest topics for new books
- View and subscribe to **The Skinny On™** weekly webcomic
- Become a writer for **The Skinny On™**

www.TheSkinnyOn.com

Connect with us on:

GW00643472

Madness and Democracy

NEW FRENCH THOUGHT

SERIES EDITORS
Thomas Pavel and Mark Lilla

TITLES IN THE SERIES

Mark Lilla, ed., *New French Thought: Political Philosophy*

Gilles Lipovetsky, *The Empire of Fashion: Dressing Modern Democracy*

Pierre Manent, *An Intellectual History of Liberalism*

Jacques Bouveresse, *Wittgenstein Reads Freud: The Myth of the Unconscious*

Blandine Kriegel, *The State and the Rule of Law*

Alain Renault, *The Era of the Individual: A Contribution to a History of Subjectivity*

Marcel Gauchet, *The Disenchantment of the World: A Political History of Religion*

Pierre Manent, *The City of Man*

Marcel Gauchet and Gladys Swain, *Madness and Democracy: The Modern Psychiatric Universe*

Marcel Gauchet and Gladys Swain

Madness and Democracy

THE MODERN PSYCHIATRIC UNIVERSE

Translated by Catherine Porter

With a Foreword by Jerrold Seigel

NEW FRENCH THOUGHT

PRINCETON UNIVERSITY PRESS · PRINCETON, NEW JERSEY

Published by Princeton University Press, 41 William Street,
Princeton, New Jersey 08540
In the United Kingdom: Princeton University Press, Chichester, West Sussex

Translated from the French edition of Marcel Gauchet and Gladys Swain, *La Pratique de l'esprit humain* (Paris: © Editions Gallimard, 1980)

Library of Congress Cataloging-in-Publication Data

Gauchet, Marcel
[La pratique de l'esprit humain. English]
Madness and democracy : the modern psychiatric universe / Marcel Gauchet and Gladys Swain ; translated by Catherine Porter for Princeton University Press ; with a foreword by Jerrold Seigel.
p. cm. — (New French thought)
Includes bibliographical references and index.
ISBN 0-691-03372-2 (cl : alk. paper)
1. Psychiatric hospital care. 2. Power (Social sciences). 3. Mental illness—Social aspects. I. Swain, Gladys, 1945–1993. II. Gauchet, Marcel, 1938– . III. Title. IV. Series.
[DNLM: 1. Mental Disorders—therapy. 2. Hospitals, Psychiatric. 3. Power (Psychology) 4. Psychotherapy—methods. WM 400 G265p 1999a]
RC439.G2813 1999
362.2'—dc21
DNLM/DLC
for Library of Congress 98-45014

Published with the assistance of the French Ministry of Culture.

This book has been composed in Adobe Bauer Bodoni

The paper used in this publication meets the minimum requirements of ANSI/NISO Z39.48-1992 (R 1997) (*Permanence of Paper*)

http://pup.princeton.edu

Printed in the United States of America

10 9 8 7 6 5 4 3 2 1

Contents

Foreword

As its English title suggests, *Madness and Democracy* couples the history of insanity and psychiatry with the history of politics. On one level, what Marcel Gauchet and Gladys Swain give us is a story about the innovations in theory and treatment made by the French alienists Philippe Pinel and Jean-Etienne Esquirol in the years around 1800, about their utopian hopes for effecting radical and complete cures of mental illness, and about the institutions that developed as these hopes waned. But at another level, this history becomes the material for a meditation on modern democratic society, in particular on the relationship between individuals, power, and collective life that emerged in the era of the French Revolution. The book belongs to a genre that is little practiced in the United States, so that a word or two about its method at the start may help prepare readers for what they will find in it.

The history Gauchet and Swain write is also philosophy. Their way of combining the two disciplines belongs neither to the "analytical" philosophy of history practiced by Anglo-American thinkers who descend from Wittgenstein, nor to the "speculative" philosophy of history that we identify with such great nineteenth-century names as Hegel, Marx, Ranke, or Michelet. As historians our authors pay close attention to persons and movements, texts and contexts, but as philosophers they often meditate on these matters with a conceptual intensity to which historians—happily or not—seldom aspire. Nor do historians usually aim for as highly theorized an understanding of modernity, of how it contrasts with the forms of life that preceded it, and of what it has so far been and meant, as the one at work here.

One writer with whose method Gauchet and Swain share a good deal is the very one against whom their work is in many ways written, but whose powerful example and influence they acknowledge, Michel Foucault. The subject of insanity and its treatment is one of many topics that have been enlivened by Foucault's provocative dealings with them; it was he who first made clear how forcefully the understanding of mental illness bears on questions of modern individuality, freedom, and power.[1] Like Foucault, our authors make these crucial issues their intellectual quarry; their interpretations, however, their understanding of the history of psychiatry and their sense for the way its emergence helps to reveal the inner shape of modern life, are strongly at odds with his. One way to describe this difference, quickly and in a kind of shorthand, is to say that they draw some of the basic conceptual armature of their analysis not from Friedrich Nietzsche or the twentieth-century artistic avant-garde (two of Foucault's inspirations), but, like some other recent French scholars and theorists, from the problematic of modern democracy and liberty elaborated by Alexis de Tocqueville. This is not to say that Tocqueville was their point of departure, or that he is their only theoretical reference point, any more than Nietzsche or the avant-garde was for Foucault. But their general perspective owes much to Tocqueville's meditations on democracy. Like him, they simultaneously accept democratic society and worry deeply about its implications; they do not, in the manner of a Nietzsche, reject it as a disguise for the rule of the weak or search for ways to liberate the primordial, prerational human powers it is supposed to have denied and repressed.

For Gauchet and Swain, as for Foucault, what joins the history of insanity and its treatment to the history of politics and democracy is the question of human subjectivity: what does it mean that human beings regard themselves as the focal points and in some degree the determinants of their own experiences and actions? Such questions have long framed arguments about knowledge and agency. Immanuel Kant held that the very possibility of coherent experience, and of the scientific understanding that may arise from it, depends on some innate capacity of rational beings to give persistence and coherence to the ever-shifting flux of sense impressions that ties them to the world. And he identified the possibility of freedom, and hence of morality and of political liberty, with whatever power mindful creatures may possess to determine their own actions through the principles of reason itself. A century later Nietzsche would turn this vision on its head, arguing that the coherence and persistence Kant sought were protective barriers set up by weak creatures against the unceasing flux that was the world's deep, fearsome truth, and that actions mandated by transcendent principles of rationality did not liberate human subjects but enslaved them to a power outside themselves (no less constraining for bearing the name of reason), cutting them off from the energizing force of their own vital, creative wills.

Foucault's remarkable history of insanity, *Madness and Civilization* (originally published in 1961, at a time when Gauchet and Swain were still students), recast the beginnings of modern psychiatry in these Nietzschean terms, finding new and more insidious forms of oppression where Enlightenment reason and humanity saw emancipation. The long-celebrated image of Pinel freeing asylum inmates from their chains,[2] the practices he and his English contemporary William Tuke adopted in order to acknowledge the humanity of the insane and to institute a "moral treatment" that sought cures through mobilizing the reason that even humans afflicted with madness still possessed, these Foucault interrogated in order to reveal a different content behind them. The new doctors "substituted for the free terror of madness the stifling anguish of responsibility," instilling in the patient an organized sense of guilt that made him or her "an object of punishment always vulnerable to himself and to the Other; and from the acknowledgment of his status as object, from the awareness of his guilt, the madman was to return to his awareness of himself as a free and responsible subject, and consequently to reason."[3] Foucault would later generalize this view of the liberation offered to mad people so that it applied to modern individuals more generally, when he offered Jeremy Bentham's model prison, the Panopticon, as a blueprint for all the institutions and practices of disciplinary normalization that form modern individuals: wherever people assume the status of free subjects, they do so in contexts of confinement and domination that subject them to the powers infused through social and cultural life.

Although on one level Gauchet and Swain offer a different genealogy of the modern subject, on another their account renders the search for such origins beside the point. What distinguishes human beings from other earthly creatures is their ability to objectify their individual and social being, to become aware of the personal and collective dimensions of their existence in ways that give them some degree of independence from the world and from themselves, and thus some measure of power to alter the conditions of their lives. That human beings are, by their very nature, subjects in this sense has been denied often enough in human history (who but subjects could proffer such denials?), not just by modern figures in search of an intimate, mystical unity with cosmic being, such as Martin Heidegger, but by every human community that has claimed descent from gods or heroes, thereby delegitimizing any claim by ordinary people in the present to participate in determining the principles that organize their lives. Marcel Gauchet has analyzed the structures and strategies of such denials, and the consequences of their disempowerment, in his recently translated book, *The Disenchantment of the World*.[4]

But such human subjectivity is never pure or complete, never independent of the external conditions that shape and mold it, or the internal ones that often limit or weaken it. It is precisely in relation to these limitations of human subjectivity that Gauchet and Swain think modern theories of insanity acquire their greatest interest. What distinguishes modern understandings of madness and its therapies from earlier ones is the recognition that even in the maimed condition of mental breakdown, with all its loss of conscious control over thought and action, human beings retain their subjective integrity on some level. Their condition still belongs to them as the particular individuals they are; their insanity does not obliterate their personality and may even be a more emphatic translation of it. And they remain able to become aware of their state in some degree, to look upon it from a standpoint that is somehow both inside and outside of their malady. Certainly there are moments in human lives when, in Jacques Lacan's now-famous formula, "ça parle," when what speaks in human beings is the seething cauldron of desires and impulses that Freud named the Id; but should we think this so surprising? It is far more remarkable, Gauchet and Swain observe, that together with this thing-like being that speaks through us, there emerges a reflective self, an "I," whose firm rootedness in the human person is demonstrated by the acute pain with which it stands as witness to the forces that dissolve it. The phenomenon of mental illness shows that human subjectivity somehow persists in the midst of its own decomposition; it thus demands that we examine this mix of persistence and dissolution wherever and whenever human beings observe their own complicity in the suspension of their powers, reminding us of the many ways that autonomy and heteronomy may coexist as the terms of human existence.

The full and self-conscious awareness that mentally ill persons retain their powers as subjects, and that treatment should be premised on this recognition, only emerged in the 1890s, with Freud's psychoanalytic therapy, based as it was on a theory of the unconscious as a region of mental activity with its own kind of rationality. But Gauchet and Swain argue that this understanding was powerfully foreshadowed at the beginning of the nineteenth century. Implicit in the treatment Pinel began to provide from early in the 1790s, this new understanding became explicit in the thesis Esquirol defended and published in 1805, *Des passions considérées comme causes, symptômes, et moyens curatifs de l'aliénation mentale* (On the passions viewed as causes, symptoms, and means of cure for mental alienation). In this work Esquirol theorized the moral treatment he learned from his teacher Pinel, drawing from it implications Pinel himself seems never quite to have grasped. In the younger man's vision, hallucinations were not wholly irrational visitations, but the expressions of an "idée-mère," a parturient idea, and the apparently random sayings and actions of an insane person often revealed an inner coherence, a set of connections that led back to something that determined the whole shape of his or her personality. Madness was the form in which some individuals lived their particular existence.

Esquirol's approach set him apart from two groups of his contemporaries, one of which attributed insanity to some physical alteration, such as a lesion, that deprived the mind of the support it required in a healthy organism, while the other traced mental breakdown to some deliberate, perverse decision on the part of an individual, a voluntary alienation of his or her personality onto some fantasy image or desire: genius, royalty, or sainthood, for instance. For the first group only therapies that affected the body could have any chance of success, whereas the second demanded of people that they depart from their chosen state of weakness or corruption. This second approach implied a certain kind of "moral treatment," but here the phrase meant something like reform or correction, whereas for Esquirol it expressed the need to recognize the "remnant of reason" (as Hegel put it, in his appreciation of the French practice) that lodged within each instance of madness. The French doctors' aim was to liberate that rational kernel, so that the afflicted person recovered the normal ability to establish a reflective relationship between consciousness, the self, and the world.

The implication was that mentally ill people were not ones who had lost their reason but were rather dominated by a kind of hidden inner reason independent of their will, a sort of unconscious mind. To be sure, Esquirol was unable to formulate his understanding in this way, as Freud would do nearly a century later. Because he could not, he pursued his attempt to grasp madness as a complex whole, involving both the afflicted mind and the bodily existence over which it had gained control, by identifying the cause of madness with some disturbance rooted in "the passions," a region of the personality that communicated at once with intellectual and corporeal existence. In a way whose limits seem only too apparent now, Esquirol located the seat of the passions in the epigastrium. But Gauchet and Swain argue that we should not let the opacity of this theory, its false concreteness, blind us to the illumination it brought. If it was a myth, it was a rational myth, erected in the space where the linguistic and conceptual material at Esquirol's disposal (basically the psychology of the Stoics) reached its limits; within that space certain things could come to light. As a disorder of the passions, not the mind, madness was not the loss of reason, but the loss of the unity that normal selfhood may obtain, the unity that empowers the healthy personality to step back from itself and thus to achieve the distance from its own thoughts and feelings that allows for a measure of control over them. The insane were deprived of this ability to regulate their relations with themselves and the world, but not of the reflective faculty where the potential for it waited; as overwhelming as their loss of subjective wholeness was, it was not complete. Mental patients still retained their status as rational subjects at the core, and because they did, they were curable.

Such a perspective seemed to open up broad possibilities for successful treatment, and Pinel and Esquirol were each, at various moments, inspired with a powerful optimism about their therapeutic prospects. But their hopes were disappointed. Despite the advance in understanding that the moral treatment implied and promised, those who practiced it possessed very few instruments for making a difference in the lives of most patients. Their practical techniques involved less the kind of "talking cure" that Joseph Breuer and Freud would make famous than attempts to shock patients back to health by giving them some kind of moral or psychic "shake-up" (*secousse morale*), a dramatic encounter intended to make them see themselves from a different point of view. As the ineffectiveness of such interventions became evident, the early claims and expectations about rapid and near-universal cures were transformed first into theoretical explanations or excuses, and then into prospects for long internment, so that confinement itself came to replace the doctor's interaction with the patient as the basic instrument of psychiatric practice. As the number of asylums and inmates grew, the goal of cure declined toward mere socialization, the assimilation of patients to a more or less permanent population of the insane. Thus was the ground prepared for the disillusionment with collective treatment of the mentally ill that would grow so powerful in our century.

If Gauchet and Swain claim historical significance for Pinel and Esquirol, then, it is not by virtue of what the alienists achieved in their dealings with their patients; indeed, the pattern of enthusiasm and disappointment their efforts produced would reappear in good part with psychoanalytic therapy a century later. Rather, the significance of the moral treatment, and of the new understanding of reason and subjectivity it implied, lies at the point where the new psychiatry intersected with contemporary historical events and aspirations. The attempt to reform human institutions by an appeal to the universal power of reason, the utopian hopes to which this vision gives rise, and the collapse of such hopes, form a configuration we know all too well, above all in modern politics. By assigning responsibility over their personal and social being to people in the present, Enlightenment theory and Revolutionary practice made those same people the objects of their own reforming activity, setting up a possible equation between realizing the human potential of individuals or groups and subjecting them to rigid control by powers able to act in their name. Gauchet and Swain argue that it is precisely at the moment when human beings no longer agree to be ruled by powers outside themselves—such as gods or kings—that they become open to such interventions, since it is in this condition that society—or the particular individuals and institutions who represent it—assumes responsibility for realizing the humanity of all its members. "The individual who takes political possession of himself simultaneously opens himself up to an action by others that operates on the deepest regions of his being."

Such connections between psychiatry and politics were not only ideal or conceptual, they were also practical and concrete. Pinel became the director of the men's asylum at Bicêtre in 1793; and between 1797 and 1802 French officials undertook a series of initiatives to reform psychiatric treatment, first reopening the hospital at Charenton as a national treatment center, then appointing Pinel as director of the women's hospital at

Salpêtrière. By the last date Pinel's writings themselves had become a chief motivation for the reform efforts, but at the start inspiration came from other sources. The later eighteenth century saw a growing confidence that madness could be effectively treated, nurtured by the work and reputation of a series of lay practitioners, not trained medical men, notably (and in Paris) an ex-priest, François Simonnet de Coulmiers, and a former patient, Jean-Baptiste Pussin. They preceded Pinel in employing alternatives to the traditional physical therapies, replacing them with a commonsense approach based on air, light, movement, and humane interaction—in fact, most of the elements of what Pinel would call "moral treatment."[5] Reports of their success were widespread, and Pinel cited their work in his first writings on the new therapy, giving scientific approval and sponsorship to techniques that had developed outside the medical establishment. A good deal of his influence seems to have derived from his ability to generalize and theorize what had hitherto been ad hoc practices. Out of this synthesis of popular intuition and learned understanding there arose a remarkable spirit of confidence, evident both in the reopening of the hospital at Charenton, and at the time of Pinel's appointment to head the Salpêtrière in 1802. The aim had become to gather all the mentally ill together in a new kind of establishment, no longer referred to as a house of treatment but as a "house of cure." The optimism went as far as to envisage giving two-thirds or even nine-tenths of the afflicted back to society.

The new therapy thus seems to belong to the revolutionary universe where humanitarian projects to reform behavior, consciousness, language, and culture had flowered for nearly a decade. In Gauchet and Swain's Tocquevillian perspective, the reorganization of psychiatric treatment by revolutionary governments marked a new point in the secular expansion of state power that had characterized French history throughout the Old Regime and reached its culmination in the Revolution's attempts to give a central organization to the whole of national life, extending political authority deeply into society. In the basis of its claims, however, the Revolutionary state had become radically modern, replacing appeals to divine right or tradition with uncompromising adherence to the collective will of citizens. This changed vision of politics and social life gave the state a new, exalted, but dangerous dignity as the agent through which human beings became "the sole producers of their own history," the power to whom people looked for the realization of their humanity.

The new institutions for mental treatment thus had important features in common with other modern instances where expanded control over individual lives has been justified by the claim that virtuous rulers know how to activate the hitherto unrealized potential of the ruled. At this point in their analysis, Gauchet and Swain find Foucault's vocabulary quite apt and invoke it more or less explicitly. Although in democratic theory society appears as the source of legitimate political power, in modern institutions power becomes the determinant of social relations. As in the Benthamite Panopticon, the realization of humanity in individuals depends on their becoming subject to an agent of control, exterior to them and yet somehow suffused through the whole of social space, and claiming to animate them with the principles of their own nature. Hospitals, schools, factories, armies—all are sites where power transforms human objects according to some logic of individual nature or social needs, refashioning persons with a discipline that operates on body and mind alike, until they no longer feel the pressure that molds them as a constraint. No institution better defines and exemplifies this model than the asylum, where the institution organizes the whole life of its inmates in the name of humanity, and where the therapy applied to them must operate on, and liberate, the deepest, most hidden core of the self. Robert Owen, the British reformer whose treatise called *The Revolution in the Mind and Practice of the Human Race* provides the French title of the present book, *La Pratique de l'esprit humain*, imagined that physical and mental health could be restored to society as a whole by treating all people on the model of asylum inmates.

But a number of things distinguish Gauchet and Swain's understanding of these institutions, and the modern situation they represent, from other recent writers, including Foucault. The first is their view that the power that operates through these instances does not create or construct modern individuals as subjects but seeks instead to dissolve their separate existence in some collective whole. Foucault viewed modern political rule as breaking down collective forms of existence, with their possible solidarities, and operating through "the governance of individuality," a regime that is only made stronger when individuals seek to establish independence from it, unaware that their individuality "is not the vis-à-vis of power but one of its main effects." Gauchet and Swain regard the forms of control that turn modern liberty into its contrary as working in just the opposite direction, the goal being to "make the social reveal itself in its pure state through the absorption of individual identities." This "great dream, whose feverish pursuit has dominated, overwhelmed and exhausted our era," was pursued in asylums as Pinel and his successors sought first to insulate the hospitals from all exterior influences, and then to organize the community of inmates as a collective body, one that slept together and ate together, its members no longer inhabiting isolated cells intended to encourage reflection, but joined in a mode of life where everything safety and propriety allowed was done on a communal basis. Dissolved in this commonality, individuality could be made to flow into the molds intended to reshape it.

Such at least was the expectation, but here we come to a further contrast between *Madness and Democracy* and Foucault's writings. Where Foucault asks us to see asylum and Panopticon as models for a form of control that actually operates in the deep reaches of modern Western societies, and against which the potentially effective responses are not liberal restraints on power but some appeal to "subjugated knowledges" or a new aesthetics of the self, Gauchet and Swain remind us that projects of total control have repeatedly failed in the last two centuries. Some of them have been able to wreak havoc and violence on friends and enemies alike, to be sure, but all have fallen very far short of the kind of individual and social transformations for which their agendas have called. Far from being an instrument to bring the world under power's gaze, the panoptical eye has only peered into a void, since it is unable to recognize the subjects it seeks to oversee for what they are. In the human world, we never see less than when we try to see all. What has frustrated attempts to revolutionize individual and social existence has not been insufficient effort, but "the indomitable inventiveness" human persons bear within them. In workers' movements, in factories, in schools, in all the regions where the organizational ideal embodied in Pinel's asylum finds some sort of echo, planning has only worked when people have found ways to circumvent it, to take initiatives unforeseen by it. No institution better exemplifies this failure—or the limits of human self-creation—than the asylums whose numbers grew so rapidly during the nineteenth century, turning as they did from hoped-for "houses of cure" to holding-pens for those whose maladies remained beyond any effective intervention. Already in the 1890s critics were proposing to reverse the development that had so greatly added to the population of inmates during the past century, and simply release some of them into the outside world.

What relation should we see between such a return and the earlier history of the understanding and treatment of madness? Foucault presented that history as one organized around separation: the internment of the mad began, he argued, with the founding of the Paris Hôpital Général in 1656, an event he refers to as "the great confinement." Earlier, those considered to be fools or misfits were allowed to move about in society's midst, so that what defined the advent of modernity was the exclusion of those who belonged to the world of unreason from the world of the rational. The removal of persons was also the abstraction of one part of human nature from another, so that reason would not suffer contamination by what was considered to be outside its norms and bounds. These developments prepared the situation in which the mad would be "liberated" by Pinel, but only within an already established confinement. The twentieth-century campaigns to release inmates and allow them to participate in ordinary social life thus marked a reversal of this whole, long history, not just of insanity's confinement, but of reason's repression of human nature's other parts.

Gauchet and Swain argue for a radical reversal of this perspective. The medieval practices in which Foucault saw an opening to humanity at its margins were actually based on a more rigid sense of the mad as different, derived from ways of thinking that assigned particular forms of existence to separate places along the hierarchical chain of being ordained by God. Just as every degree of social life—clergy, nobles, peasants—had its distinct and permanent place on this chain, so did the mad have theirs. To encounter them in everyday life was to be present at the display of God's mysterious creative power, the same power revealed by the assignment of human beings to their particular place in the cosmos, or of life-forms and inorganic matter to their appropriate regions on the earth. Even more, the presence of the insane was an admonitory reminder of what human reason became whenever it stepped outside its limits, namely a kind of madness. Divine dependence made the order of society, like the order of the world, one that mere humans could not change, a limit that made clear why it was impossible to transform the mad into rational beings.

Against this schema, policies like the confinement decreed by the French government in 1656 exemplified a new sense of the human ability—even responsibility—to reshape social practices in accord with perceived human needs. In exercising this ability the absolutist government took the population as a whole for its object, acting in pursuit of a general social aim, even if to do so required treating different groups in different ways. The principle that all the realm's inhabitants were subject to state power implied a certain leveling-out of social distinctions, but under absolutism this leveling never went far enough to reject the old image of society as ordered by natural human differences. In accord with these limits, the state made the insane the object of its action, but no one regarded them as enough like others that they could be cured and returned to normal life. Only democracy would institute these more radical assertions, first the equal inclusion of all people in the body of citizens, based on their common right to share in the making of fundamental laws, and second the assumed rationality of all these citizens, even in the face of what appeared as a loss of reason in some of them. Absolutism and democracy represent two stages in an evolving logic of social inclusion, of which the moral treatment, with its hope for cures that would return large numbers of the insane to ordinary life, drew the implications with a kind of rigid optimism.

Such implications, however, were difficult to realize in practice. Within the asylum, old methods of keeping inmates isolated in separate cells or loges could be progressively replaced by common dormitories and refectories, but old fears that every insane person was potentially violent, and the sometimes crude or vicious behavior by guards and nurses such deeply rooted worries encouraged, were harder to eliminate, with results that were experienced and reported by so famous an inmate as Auguste Comte. The pessimism about cure that grew as the century progressed also worked to maintain the separation between the insane and others. Despite these limits, however, the treatment of inmates was animated by an Enlightened belief in their humanity and in the possibility of their reintegration. Even as long-term confinement came to be the norm, asylum inhabitants were expected to behave like other people, to wash and dress as others did, and to treat their fellows politely. Above all, asylums were to be places where people engaged in productive work, learning skills and habits that would prepare them to live on the outside. It is easy enough to deride such forms of behavior and living as petty, moralistic intrusions into the lives of disturbed people, as a narrow refusal to give validity to nonstandard forms of life, or as acts of obeisance to a bourgeois productivist ethic. Gauchet and Swain do not altogether reject these critiques, but they insist all the same that the direction given to the lives of inmates bespeaks a recognition of the humanity they shared with others, and thus an expectation that their destiny was to return to ordinary life. To call that life bourgeois highlights certain particular things about it, but being able to work productively, to act as others do, and to interact with them, are far from being exclusively bourgeois norms or conditions.

It was the irony of this logic of inclusion that it could only operate through segregation, thus giving a foothold to tendencies and beliefs that kept inmates in a world apart. Much the same happened with other attempts to integrate isolated groups in the years around 1800, notably the deaf; in our own time, we may add (and particularly in the United States), a similar dialectic of separation and inclusion is visible in the condition of various groups whose former status of inferiority or marginality is being challenged—women, homosexuals, people of color—leaving advocates for them divided between those who support universal inclusion and those who opt for difference and separation. Despite the countertendencies and resistances that develop toward it, the logic of modern social life operates with inclusion as its major premise. It is to this broader logic that the history of madness and psychiatry give testimony.

This way of recognizing both the threat and the promise born by asylums as institutions resembles the approach Gauchet and Swain take to other dimensions of their subject. One of the central arguments they share with Tocqueville, and with others who draw on him, is that democratic ideas are risky, even dangerous ideas, opening the way to new and more insidious forms of domination. But this is far from saying that liberal or democratic institutions are themselves merely forms of domination, as both Marxists and Nietzscheans in their different ways are wont to assert.

The totalitarian potential in democratic culture is the other side of the autonomy it institutes, since the society that recognizes no powers outside itself is the one that allows nothing to stand between its organized common force and the lives of its members. Collective autonomy and individual vulnerability to social power are two sides of a single configuration. But the threat to freedom this poses is only realized where the power that stands for the whole aims to reduce individuals to a mass, effacing their differences in the name of some kind of pure sociality. The failure to which this project succumbed in the history of asylums opened the way to a recognition of the need to found social practice (therapeutic in this case, but taking different forms in other instances) on a respect for individual differences.

Just for this reason the illumination the moral treatment brought must not be allowed to disappear behind the darker side of its history. Here we return to a point made earlier, that the modern conception of madness, even in the still inchoate form it assumed in the age of the French Revolution, points to a crucial turn in the understanding of the human subject.

Much influential commentary on this topic in the past half-century has presumed that subjectivity must be whole and integral or it cannot be, that the model for subjective existence must be the pure intellectual substance that is supposed to be revealed by the Cartesian cogito, or the primal and ever-unsullied self-positing power of the Fichtean absolute ego. In such a perspective, to recognize that human existence is shaped by external conditions, or dependent on bodily needs, or divided between a rational ego oriented toward the outside world and an unconscious attached to its own inner universe, is to deny that human beings are subjects. Such denials lose their force in the face of Esquirol's understanding that subjectivity survives even the descent into madness, that the subject is able to observe, painfully, the pressure that dissolves it, and that a core of coherence structures even the visions of those who lose control over themselves and the world. Against the modern Nietzscheans and Heideggerians whose hermeneutic of suspicion turns subjectivity into an effect of language, a defense against the flux of existence, or a reflex of humanity's loss of its primordial unity with the will or the cosmos, Gauchet and Swain insist that subjectivity must be reconceived as the capacity for self-awareness that survives even the kind of agonized suspension of wholeness that madness brings. It is never whole or complete, but it is no less what it is for that.

Such mixed and divided, but still effective, subjecthood is what democratic societies demand of their citizens, because the same historical act by which moderns reject control by outside powers makes them subject to interrogation and control by those who share the field of social autonomy with them. Such interventions found no place in the old universe, where social relations were inscribed in an order independent of human volition, and where individuals were subject to ruling powers whether they liked it or not. But where social relations are founded on the autonomous consent of those who engage in them, the inner condition of individuals comes to be a matter of much greater moment. The need to form individuals—to educate them, or to make them internalize certain ends—becomes much greater, and with it the notion that their inner being cannot be left out of public account. Where society can no longer assume that individuals owe it loyalty willy-nilly, each member of the group acquires an interest in what goes on in the interior of all the others.

Such an interest is not easily satisfied. It is not enough to hear what people may say about themselves, or even to assure their willingness to subscribe to a common faith. The knowledge required has to extend to whatever inner structures or forces may make people act in ways they or others cannot predict or control: it is knowledge like the knowledge that mind doctors seek about their patients. The modern individual, the democratic subject, is therefore not the independent figure portrayed in the Cartesian philosophy of consciousness. His or her social situation creates the presupposition of an inner being that is layered and complex, a home to hiding-places for things that associates claim the right to know; such subjects pay for their autonomy by an obligation to open themselves up to scrutiny by others. "The philosophy of the individual reduced to himself is in no way a triumphant philosophy of self-possession. On the contrary, it entails the painful discovery of a subject who is no longer master of himself, just as he is no longer free in relation to the other." This permanent crisis of consciousness is the other side of making the social bond depend on individual will and agency.

All this means that the Freudian vision of a subject divided between conscious and unconscious regions of psychic life is not opposed to the psychological assumptions that underlie liberal, bourgeois democracy but is the very view of human nature for which such a form of life calls. "Let us not be too sure that the discovery of the unconscious will come as a shock to the bourgeoisie. With the unconscious, the truth of the world in which it came into being has finally been found." Modern subjectivity is always challenged, always divided; to understand it, we must consider how it persists and survives under these conditions.

The lasting and positive significance of Pinel's and Esquirol's work arises from their role in bringing this problematic to light. Gauchet's and Swain's insistence on seeing them in this way, despite the darker developments in which they were implicated, constitutes an approach to ideas and their history that merits attention for its own sake. One very common practice in studying thought and culture nowadays is to assay ideas in terms of the interests they serve or the uses to which they may be put. Viewed in this optic, ways of thinking take on historical significance because they contribute to the hegemony one class or group is able to establish over others, or, in a narrower, more pragmatic perspective, because they become the instruments by which one or another profession or interest seeks to secure some terrain for itself against its rivals. Ideas about insanity and its treatment in the nineteenth century have been presented in both these ways, as elements in the rise of a hegemonic bourgeoisie, imposing its rationalist and productivist ethic everywhere, or as part of the attempt by physicians to claim that they, rather than lawyers, for instance, were the proper arbiters of guilt and innocence.[6]

That such ways of relating ideas to social life have much to teach us is beyond question. But the dominant place they have come to occupy in historical analysis and cultural criticism sometimes closes out equally important lessons. In his introduction to the posthumous collection of Gladys Swain's essays (she died in 1993), Marcel Gauchet specifically takes issue with arguments of this sort, as they appear in the work Foucault and some of his students did about the case of the nineteenth-century murderer and parricide Pierre Rivière. The insanity defense mounted on his behalf, despite the lucidity with which he recounted his deeds, may well have been inspired or colored by motives of professional rivalry and advancement. But to focus so intently on them hides the profound alteration in the understanding of crime, guilt, and responsibility that was under way in the early nineteenth century, and to which the debates between lawyers and alienists gave witness. In place of an old, religiously based vision that illuminated these questions in terms of the nature of evil, a way of thinking was emerging that centered on the categories of the normal and the pathological. But this distinction, *pace* Foucault, and despite the increased weight being put on it, was already problematic as soon as it could be recognized that the insane retained evident features of normality in the midst of their affliction. To argue that persons who knew perfectly well what they had done were not responsible for their actions created a scandal to many then, just as it continues to do now, and Gauchet insists that this whole way of thinking about agency and responsibility opened up a chasm of uncertainty from which we still seek to escape. Perhaps we must continue to explore it, as long as we recognize that what makes human beings human is their evident capacity to deviate from the norms set up to describe them, account for them, or discipline them. Here again we reach the still-mysterious boundary between our autonomy and our heteronomy.[7]

But this (if I read Gauchet and Swain rightly) is just the point: the history of thought may not always be the history of selfless devotion to truth; it may often be the history of self-interested or self-serving moves in a complex game of power. But it remains all the same the history of sometimes heroic attempts to make sense of things whose depths we cannot plumb. The limits of human knowledge are both temporal and lasting, partly imposed by the categories and ways of thinking, the stock of understanding, available at a given time, and partly by the overwhelming complexity of things, by the resistance the world, especially the human world, puts up against our attempts to grasp it fully. We in our present are as much confined by these limitations as were those whose projects we seek to understand and situate in some past, and Gauchet and Swain acknowledge this by allowing their book to take a form that reflects the always-incomplete process of seeking knowledge about the past, rather than one that represents authors as full masters of their subjects. Readers will find that this is a deeply meditative, ruminative book, organized along lines that follow out the implications and consequences of ideas and events in a multitude of directions, and whose style sometimes becomes complex and challenging. If the text is not always an easy read, however, the reason lies in the authors' passionate and deeply humanistic involvement with the people about whom they write, sharing with them a determination to grapple with human dilemmas at the limit of their solubility. This involvement is part of what makes them de-emphasize the alienists' service to their private or professional interests, in favor of a meditation on the more distant implications of their work. Such an approach recommends itself as a way to engage historical writing in a project of human self-understanding that lies forever before us, rather than as an appeal to the past to stand witness to a knowledge we think we already possess.

Because *Madness and Democracy* is such a book, I think it wholly appropriate to end this Foreword by raising a few questions about things in it that trouble me. Perhaps my skepticism about them is the predictable response of a historian and an American to a book that is deeply philosophical and French. In any case, it arises at points where the authors seem to pursue their Tocquevillian anxieties about democracy and its implications too rigidly, sometimes surpassing Tocqueville's own worries and doubts.[8] One instance has to do with what they make of Freud. The Viennese doctor is a large presence in this book, no less so for being only occasionally named. As the theorist who gave explicit form and powerful currency to ideas that Pinel and Esquirol left more or less in the realm of intuition, Freud is one of the most exemplary of moderns. By reading human beings "in the light of madness," he provided one of our age's most representative accounts of human nature. It is just this status as a paradigmatic modern that seems to determine Freud's appearance here (see the Introduction) as "a pure product of the totalitarian age," a thinker whose work, even more than Marx's, embodies "the perverse synthesis between enlightenment and subjection." These assertions are rooted in a stimulating idea about totalitarian thinking, that it operates by combining "a radical affirmation of historicity and a no less radical denial of history," and they point to elements of Freud's thinking that merit close scrutiny: the "ambiguous relation of crystallization and obliteration it institutes with the past," its ability to inspire its partisans with visions of a new age, its impermeability to disproof. In recent years Freud's reputation has undergone a barrage of attacks, some foolish, some powerful and effective; the clay feet beneath the idol are visible enough by now. But to assign him to the camp of totalitarian spirits because of his ambiguous relationship to history, or even because his "discourse functions as a mechanism for capturing and inhibiting thought," is to take flight on a philosophical balloon that has lost its historical moorings. Perhaps the figure of Lacan lurks somewhere behind these otherwise puzzling judgments. To describe Freud himself in such terms is to jumble together things that bear at best a superficial and abstract resemblance to each other.

A second, related matter is the argument (see Part Two, Chapter VII) about why the kind of knowledge modern psychiatry seeks became possible only under democratic conditions. The answer proposed is that earlier social forms neither required such knowledge nor represented the psychic interior as a separate realm to be explored. Psychic knowledge of a modern sort was not required in traditional communities because social existence was presumed to be prior to individuality, so that social bonds were not dependent on individual consent for their legitimation. And such knowledge was not to be looked for, because individuals were through-and-through those who occupied some naturally given place in the social order; thus there was no reason to look behind or beneath the direct indications they gave about themselves by way of speech and behavior, no cause to worry about a complex, hidden psychic reality. Democracy eliminated the assumptions that put these protective shields in place.

The argument is arresting, and it points to a larger modern anxiety about the masks individuals don and the deceptions they practice against others, a worry whose power to justify official techniques intended to pin persons to some unmistakable identity has recently been the subject of some original and stimulating reflections.[9] All the same, the account our authors give needs to be questioned in both its elements. Whatever claims medieval or early modern European societies and states made to legitimation based on divine right, cosmic patterning, or tradition, they were far from being tender or restrained in regard to the inner lives of individuals who seemed to pose some threat to order. In this regard the Reformation and Counter-Reformation mark a point when the intrusiveness of governments and religious teachers took a big step forward.[10] Not democracy but the space opened up for independent judgment and commitment by the breakdown of religious authority was what fueled these attempts at discipline, and the recourse to "spiritual exercises" intended to train the will in a kind of automatic obedience already suggests the kind of programming Gauchet and Swain attribute to democracy.

From the other side, the essentially negative cast our authors here give to psychic analysis, whether Pinelian or Freudian, makes it seem as if some will to know suffices by itself to produce understanding. But modern ideas about psychic coherence rest at least as much on the new sense of individuals as creators of meaning that developed out of eighteenth-century introspection, whether grounded in religion, humanitarian concern, or the beginnings of romanticism. Freud cited Friedrich Schiller as one source of his understanding that seemingly unconnected elements of dreams might be bound together by an inner logic, a point that should serve to recall how important literary analysis of thought and feeling was in creating the perspective from which it became possible to interpret psychic contents as meaningful wholes. The forms of self-discovery that literary sensibility encouraged often had painful consequences, as the example of Rousseau reminds us, and some of them resonate strongly with the picture of vulnerability and division Gauchet and Swain provide. But Esquirol's ability to understand hallucinations as connected to an "idée-mère," and subjective integrity as persisting in the face of powers that seemed to dissolve it, belongs as much to the modern appreciation of individuality as productive and meaningful as it does to the novel social need for knowledge about the threats that others bear inside themselves.[11]

A third instance of rigid adherence to a Tocquevillian schema appears where *Madness and Democracy* attributes so much efficacity to the state in bringing modern society into existence that individuals end up appearing more as products of state action than as agents of modern society's creation. What our authors say on this score (again mostly in Chapter VII of Part Two) seems hard to harmonize with the recognition they give elsewhere to the force of individuality, when they point to human inventiveness as the power that deprives the Panoptical eye of its reputed ability to infuse a transformative discipline through modern life. As clarified below, this way of thinking also yields a particular, and I think unsatisfying, account of how the therapeutic relationship relates to modern social life. Gauchet and Swain present the state, developing from absolutism toward democracy, as the source out of which modern social relations come to be. The very existence of the state created a challenge, at least implicitly, to the presumption that social relations between individuals were based on reciprocal obligations independent of human will, but only democracy made this challenge explicit, founding the social bond on the voluntary adherence of individuals to social power. In democracy, each individual possesses, in principle, a radical independence from every other, so that only state power can assure the establishment of bonds between them. Hence it is the state that both separates individuals and joins people together, becoming the exclusive agency through which modern social life is instituted.

Against this Tocquevillian perspective on modernity, there is much to be said for recalling one that comes from a philosopher whom Gauchet and Swain invoke at various points (he was an admirer of Pinel) but without developing his differences from Tocqueville, namely Hegel. Hegel's view of modern life also included a strain of suspicion about democracy, and it famously placed great weight on the state. But in Hegel's perspective modernity was a double-sided configuration, combining the "universal" freedom embodied in the state, the liberty that no individual can attain unless everyone's right to it is recognized, with the particular freedom given each individual to develop his (not yet her) capacities and satisfy his needs, even in ways that self-centeredly make others the means to private ends. What Hegel called the modern world's "prodigious strength and depth" came from this double-sided ability to recognize both the rational autonomy all individuals share and the complicated particularity that sets them at odds with one another. In this understanding of modern life, the universal principle of political right, guaranteed by state power, is indeed the ultimate (and in a sense even the original) guarantee of social cohesion, much as in Gauchet's and Swain's Tocquevillian view. But individuals, with all their partiality and egotism, are never simply the negation in principle of the social bond; their very propensity to use others for selfish ends sets in motion processes that establish limits to self-centeredness, giving birth to the principles of law and justice within the spontaneous relations of need that structure "civil society." The state becomes the guarantor of the social bond, but society prepares the joining; society has to work up the materials for such a guarantee inside its own sphere. From Hegel's point of view, one can—and I think should—make the same critique of Gauchet's and Swain's account of modernity that Hegel himself made of Rousseau's: that it provides an abstract, one-sided picture, devoid of the mediations between the social life of individuals and their political life that make it possible for social coherence to subsist without state despotism. The neo-Tocquevillian state appears as a kind of immediate emanation of the atomic individuals who contract to establish it, the one unity in a world of multiple particularities, so that the social bond must be the product of an outside power; here individuals make no contribution to social unity through the intermediary forms of interaction—at once competitive and cooperative—that develop in civil society.

Because Gauchet and Swain give so little play to this intermediate realm, they can only find the basis for the reciprocity of the doctor-patient relationship in a kind of anachronistic return to premodern principles of social interaction, still surviving in the midst of the democratic practices that dissolve them. In their view everything that defines modern life as modern works against the existence of a sphere "where the only thing at stake is the pure possibility of a relation among persons"; hence the doctor-patient relationship must draw on a spirit that is being driven out of modern life everywhere else. There is something right about such a view, to be sure: modern institutions and practices that validate utility and foster impersonality work powerfully against respect for the sheer humanity of others; and it may well be that relationships inspired by concern for such humanity need to be founded on principles or qualities to which modernity grants little or no specific recognition. But I doubt that premodern societies were really more likely to foster relationships based on pure personal interaction than modern ones are, and I suspect that what Gauchet and Swain see as pure reciprocity in Old Regime Europe was more often a mix concocted of indifference on the one hand and ideologically motivated justifications of hierarchical forms of domination, whether aristocratic or religious, on the other. If modern social forms can only recognize pure human reciprocity by going outside their own founding principles, then the same must be true of other societies as well, since no historical form can realize every potentiality human beings may eventually discover in themselves.

In sum, the neo-Tocquevillian view misses important elements of modernity if it equates modern social relations with the forms under which democratic political authority is established. To do so casts a veil over those features of modern life that make it potentially more, rather than less, humane than earlier social forms. Modern social relations are surely abstract in many ways, throwing us into contact with people whose anonymity we cannot fathom, and whose presence in our surroundings can be both puzzling and threatening. But just for this reason modern conditions require that human beings develop capacities for recognizing the humanity of others that traditional societies leave undeveloped or dormant. Modernity requires that we negotiate social interactions between people whose relations are not mandated by any set of established expectations, and that we activate capacities for perceiving the human qualities of those who differ from us, and for sympathy with them, that more stable and settled communities do not require. These are the positive modern preconditions for the kind of therapeutic relationship to which psychoanalysis in its best moments aspires, and for which the moral treatment of Pinel and Esquirol also provided an opening. To regard such interactions as made possible only by virtue of residues left over from a world we have lost is surely to miss something essential about what makes them modern.

These are, perhaps, not inconsiderable hesitations to offer in regard to a book that is here making its appearance in a new language, but even if they are valid, I think *Madness and Democracy* easily survives them. It is a work whose humanity and analytical power demand that we engage ourselves once again with the many important issues it raises: about rationality and madness, modernity and tradition, democracy and domination, subjectivity and its limits. If this Foreword encourages such engagement, it will have served its purpose.

Jerrold Seigel

Editors' Note

SINCE THE ORIGINAL French text is unusually long, the editors present an abridged American version of the book, with Marcel Gauchet's approval. Where entire sections have been omitted, they have been replaced by brief abstracts.

Madness and Democracy

Introduction

In a sense, an intellectual "accident" is at the origin of this book, which began as the preface to a new edition of J.E.D. Esquirol's *Des passions considérées comme causes, symptômes et moyens curatifs de l'aliénation mentale* (The passions viewed as causes, symptoms, and treatments of mental alienation, 1805). The text's disproportionate growth was surprising: the work first appeared limited and easily controlled but turned out during the writing process to be voracious, uncontrollable in its dimensions, prolific in demands, illuminations, and unexpected inspirations. Writers will attest that this is a perfectly ordinary experience of loss of control. But it is also an experience that an imperious tradition generally requires us to surmount: according to the rules we have learned, we ought to get a grip, eliminate our skidmarks, reshape the monster, restructure the project so that it looks more or less as though it had been initially intended to be what it has become. The point is to preserve the authoritative appearance of the author: he is on top of his subject, master of his thought, firmly maintaining power over the work. He is the only one who knows in advance where he is going and who has global mastery of what can be said; he follows the example of the authorities whose prominent positions put them in charge of evaluating the future for us and of organizing the emergence of what is new. These two "authorities" are equally derisory embodiments of an ancient illusion of power, an illusion inherent in the Western tradition according to which truth is always already given: it is unveiled by history, perhaps, but never produced *ex nihilo* as history unfolds—and thus it is integrally available to be possessed and dominated.

From its own special vantage point, our present work strives to shed some light on the ultimate and principal avatar of these embodiments of an illusion, and to denounce their disastrous consequences. For with the advent of democratic sovereignty, the inoffensive dream of theory has left the realm of books to be materialized in totalizing social projects, and to nourish the political aims of complete, exhaustive mastery of the collective destiny. The process has given rise to an unprecedent type of institution of which the insane asylum provides, in its exorbitant ambition and its constitutive failure, an illustration that is at once marginal and exemplary. The asylum episode offers an extreme example, but a highly significant one, of the massive impotence left over from two centuries under the sway of the idea of power. As we sought to bring to light the inexorable bankruptcy of the modern project of domination in all its forms, it seemed to us potentially valuable to show the consequences of this bankruptcy even in the organization of our own writing. If a new politics and a new ethics are to emerge from intellectual work—and the need for such a development is widely felt today—to counter the bureaucratic menace that threatens to stifle invention in the so-called "organization" of research and the planning to which it leads, and at the same time to counter the conformist disaster provoked by the egocrats of knowledge, this politics and this ethics ought to begin, among other things, by renouncing rhetorical postures that set up the phantasmagoria of ultimate power: the master-knower. Why not welcome instead the indetermination that traverses and constitutes all works of elucidation? Why disguise behind the artificially definitive logic of a program designed in advance and then masterfully completed, the real limits to our capacity to dominate the process through which something becomes and continues to become intelligible to us? A different relation between the "theoretician" and his enterprise is required. If we ourselves have not contributed effectively to the invention of the forms called for by this requirement, we should like to think that at least in our own way we have not entirely failed to recognize the requirement itself.

The position we have adopted entails a certain way of writing history, or rather of putting it in perspective. On the one hand, we reconstruct the history of the asylum as inscribed in the act of its birth; on the other hand, we analyze, in its various facets, the transformation of the idea of madness in relation to which psychiatry was instituted. We seek a way of rising toward the universal starting from the very heart of the particular, the accidental, the individual, instead of the classifications and crossings and progressive decantings whose overall truth we have been taught to expect to see emerging from its dubious manifestations of detail. This inversion of the standard perspective imposed itself on us in imperceptible stages; by adopting it, so far as we are able to judge, we have responded, here again, to a concern that permeates the spirit of the times in a diffuse, multiform, and insistent fashion.

The best way to get to the heart of this concern is via its key term, interpretation. For what is changing before our eyes is the entire order that presides over the operation of understanding. What is at stake, then, is understanding texts. The time-honored method of eliminating what is ancillary in favor of what is presumed essential in fact keeps us from grasping the complex movement of discourse, its subtle chinks, its discrete twists back on itself, the intimate struggles and sunderings in which the real work of thought is hidden. A major upheaval is under way. Still largely unnoticed, it has nevertheless already given rise to a few masterpieces; while these may not yet have the luster they deserve, they are destined in the long run to overturn the arrested vision of the historicist tradition in a radical way.

At the other end,in the closest possible proximity to the present and to the prose of the world, let us contemplate the new and promising reopening of historical sensibility to individual events. By events we do not mean pointless incidents or clamorous but empty gestures gleaned from the surface of human affairs, acts that turn attention away from the structures that really count and from the forces that displace the whole (and the critique of these forces, while remaining fecund, has become an overly facile foil). We have in mind the exemplary event, where in a tiny breach of works and days, a breach one might suppose to be without interest and without consequence for the long run, an entire universe has nevertheless been projected in miniature, a universe whose patient unfolding reveals without allowing any further distinction of levels the profound order of a society materialized, as it were, in the circumstantial meanderings of a local avatar, or emblematized in the fortuitous linking of a spectacular episode—a point of condensation of the temporal weft in which substance and accident, structure and symptom, are mutually and inextricably illuminated. It is useless, finally, to dwell at length on what has been acquired, indisputably, by psychoanalytic decoding. Anyone can put this to the test at any time: for the psyche, there is no meaning except embodied meaning, and only in the inexpressible singularity of a trace, a sound, a mark, are the most ordinary data of one's condition as subject concretized and lodged within one's very depths.

The abyss of the particular is the only way by which human beings can rejoin the common truth of their nature. Hieroglyphics of the personal past, the signifying profusion of the breaches provoked by events, the secret sinuosities of writing: these are scattered hearths of a vast reorganization of the relation between the universal and the singular that provides a foundation for the operation of knowing. This reorganization is well on its way, here and now, to transforming imperceptibly, on the obscure level of presuppositions, the bases, the tenor, and the horizon of all tasks of decoding and reconstitution of meaning. The intention obviously does not predetermine the result; the fact remains—and the relative peculiarity, even today, of the approach we have adopted justifies a clarification on this point—that our awareness of the ineluctable mutation in process has inspired and sustained our effort.

What has changed us humans into citizens of the modern world? This is essentially the question to which the present volume seeks to contribute some fragmentary answers. We moderns live according to an implicit representation of man that is in complete discontinuity with the representation revealed to us when we deal with earlier eras. In our everyday experience we rely on a feeling of who we are that has no real precedent, or so we perceive confusedly. The difference, we sense, is patent, enormous—and yet ungraspable. In what does it consist? What does it come from? Facing these questions, we are not entirely without reference points. We may lack clear ideas or developed certainties, but we do know in what places, in relation to what, and in what forms the new representation at issue has primarily been developed. Not within the activity officially recognized as "philosophy," not in the framework of a general anthropological reflection, but in another place entirely, a site initially remote from the academic scene: among practitioners dealing with mental illness, in connection with interpretation of its roots and its place in the subjective economy, and with ways of treating it. The representation of our intimate relation to ourselves shifted radically, at the dawn of the twentieth century, through the conduit of human insanity. Human beings read in the light of madness: the phrase sums up the tenor of the revolutionary operation at the origin of the strange concepts—best exemplified by the concept of the unconscious—that result from this shift. These concepts are charged with undeniable descriptive relevance, and they are symbolically powerful by virtue of the radical caesura they imply; yet they function at the same time as intellectual dead ends, attested by decades of sterile psychoanalytic orthodoxy.

Here, then, is the inevitable observation that triggers a renewed genealogical inquiry: if it is undeniable that the revolutionary idea of man that governs our lives has Freud's work as its principal source, it seems just as undeniable to us that that work not only fails to provide us with an adequate language for grasping and measuring the revolution, but also that it constitutes a formidable screen, one that hides at least as much as it reveals. A pure product of the totalitarian age (even more straightforwardly than Marx's revolutionary myth), the Freudian construct represents a maximally stupefying embodiment of the perverse synthesis between enlightenment and subjection that, as a project, permeates and dominates our century. It is a form of thought that provides food for thought only in order at the same time to prevent thinking (whatever the "personal intentions" of its author may be—and in this particular case those intentions are passably ambivalent).

Let us be clear: totalitarian thought is effective because it has the means to carry out its secret ambition, and it exerts its unfailing power to subject only because it is legitimately fascinating. It participates centrally in the totalitarian spirit through its ambiguous attitude toward history, through the way it reconciles a radical affirmation of historicity and a no less radical denial of history. It conveys a feeling of the absolute originality of the present; it insists on the equally absolute rupture that is to come or that is already in place and that must give rise *ex nihilo* to a society incommensurable with any society previously known to us. At the same time, however, it proclaims the end of history, an ultimate immobilization of the perspectives of human movement, the eradication of any temporal "beyond." A response to history, totalitarianism owes its incomparable imaginary power to the twin possibilities it offers individuals: on the one hand, they can conceive of themselves fully as historical actors (and even beyond this, as historical progenitors, destined phantasmagorically to create a world from nothing), and on the other hand, they can persist rigorously in a religious refusal of history, in the timeless drama of a world obeying an order fixed for all eternity.

All these ingredients are present at the heart of the Freudian revolution, whose power stems, similarly, from a twofold capacity: it allows its adherents to accept the rupture that has actually come about in the image of man and the sense of self, and it also constitutes the faithful as militants or agents of the new; at the same time it maintains its adherents in the illusion of a truth definitely acquired or formed. This truth is of course open to gradual improvement (as the imaginary "progress" of materialism, historical as well as dialectical, sadly proves); it is naturally a source of inexhaustible internal debates and a pretext for indefinite reformulations (but does anyone know a more disputatious and colossally graphomanic species than that of the theologically minded exegetes of a revelation that is nevertheless intangible?); in its ultimate content it is protected from any future subversion, however, and in the emptiness of its horizon it is destined to traverse the centuries, immutable.

The prodigious effect of deculturation that the Marxian work has exercised stems from the incomparable genius with which, in its day, it gathered together the elements of human history, making itself self-servingly self-sufficient to the point of seeming to condense all history in itself, and at the same time casting into oblivion the very movement that had nourished it and that might have made it possible to go further—to surpass Marxism. The Freudian work in turn owes its singular capacity for concealing the past to the multiple threads that Marxism has knotted together. External to all speculative tradition (whereas behind Marx there is Hegel), in no way referring to a real process supposed to have founded its discourse (whereas class struggle is rooted in reality, even if that reality just barely accedes to consciousness), directly constructed to appear as pure invention, without inscription, debt, or roots, and consequently without any conceivable "beyond," a perfect beginning that is at the same time an unsurpassable end point, Freud's work leaves even fewer escape routes from totalitarian adhesion than its Marxian homologue. For it is precisely through the ambiguous relation of crystallization and obliteration it institutes with the past that Freudian discourse functions effectively as a mechanism for capturing and inhibiting thought.

Woven of the denial of history that produced it even as it gathers up the results of history, orchestrated at the deepest level in such a way as to cut the reader off from his own origins at the same time as it brings them to light, the Freudian construction remains the prototype, one still unsurpassed today, of the unprecedented creation of modern times, a perverse mechanism for generating disciples and locking them into an irremediable repetition. As for the overwhelming success of the mechanism, there is no need to belabor the point: we all see it every day. The phenomenon does not violate the rule according to which political aims turn into their contrary, a rule that has tripped up the human intellectual or social enterprise from the beginning of the democratic age: once again, servitude will have come out of an emancipatory project; once again, the will to enlightenment will have found its outlet in an obscurantist abyss.

Thus if we are to reconstitute the meaning of the anthropological mutation that has imperceptibly separated us from our predecessors, we must free ourselves from the monopolistic and alienating language that denominates and symbolizes the new while skillfully concealing it from us. In other words, our task implies a need to go against the denial of history, a need to rediscover the thread of historical continuity. The only way to undo the totalitarian myth, to dismantle the intellectual screen, is to reintroduce that continuity as doctrine and practice into the process that made it possible and gave rise to it. A mature psychoanalysis requires us to give up the notion of a magical self-engenderment of the discipline, the obsessive infantile sexual theory of practitioners who have no illusions, it would seem, about anything. From this point of view, the enterprise initiated by Michel Foucault in his *History of Sexuality* strikes us as essentially just and necessary—whatever reservations we may have in other respects as to the details of the reconstruction he proposes. The subtraction of man from himself despite his reflective self-possession, a constitutive alienation, a subjective division, an enigmatic separation of the psyche from its living support: all that has been brought to light by the discoveries of psychoanalytic anthropology did not come out of nowhere, nor did it result from an absolute "revolution," self-aware and in full possession of its project.

Not that it is a matter of eradicating events. History does take the path of revolution, among others. If there was a French Revolution and a Russian Revolution, why should there not have been a Freudian "revolution"? And unquestionably there was one. Following the example of the French Revolution, indeed, it had something to do with the circumstantial conjunction of a series of factors, each one of which was necessary. Their explosive mutual enhancement contributed more than a little to the creation of one of those remarkable effects of beginning through which history seems to start up again from a new point of departure and become suddenly conscious of its design. Except that the full details, the motives, the real content, and the impact of the Freudian revolution are no clearer to us at present than the actual meaning of the French Revolution could have been to its actors or its immediate heirs. Moreover, these details have only just begun to be examined. To our knowledge, the only person who has genuinely accepted the challenge, indirectly with his *History of Madness* and more frontally with his *History of Sexuality*, is Michel Foucault. Anyone who takes up the question from now on is in his debt, if only because he conferred historical dignity on the subject.

The psychoanalytic revolution denies the obscurity that is constitutive of any historical rupture; in this respect it is characteristic of its times and participates fully in the logic of totalitarianism. For the characteristic feature of the totalitarian revolutions of our century is that they have been led by revolutionary parties modeling their action on the latest science of history. They claim to be fully aware of the necessity at work behind their enterprises, and they purport to know all there is to know about the new society that is to result from their efforts. Such claims betray an exorbitant ambition to total mastery of the meaning of one's action in history, an ambition that constitutes in fact a radical rejection of history, a denial of the gaps and excesses of meaning that any individual or collective enterprise entails by virtue of its immersion in becoming. In short, it constitutes a rejection of the *historical* unconscious, of that *other* unconscious because of which, when we are speaking of the *individual* unconscious, we are speaking inexhaustibly of something else, something other than what we think we are talking about.

Let us argue heretically that there is little more relation between what a psychoanalyst thinks he is doing today and what will appear a few short decades from now as the neglected truth of his practice than between the Jacobin discourse of 1793 and the actual political results of the French Revolution, or than between the program of the Bolshevik Party and the reality of the Soviet state from its inception. These commonplace observations are shocking only when they are juxtaposed with the strange regression of historical consciousness that in our century has allowed a double denial of the boundaries of human invention: the Freudian denial of its own past, and the Marxist denial of the future. More than ever, in this context, history turns out to be the weapon par excellence of political criticism. Emphasizing the importance of visible events together with the multiform, secular, and subterranean work to which they belong in every respect is the only way to break through the fiction of pure rupture and its empty fascination. It is the only way to reestablish minimal opportunities for a living reflection on the subject, which we should not hesitate to identify with the old-fashioned question, What can be said about human nature?

The approach to and the foundations of this problem have been completely renewed, of course, by the intellectual explosion for which, around 1900, the limited question of the therapeutic treatment of neuroses was the pretext and support; in connection with a particular type of pathological formation, this explosion simultaneously revealed the structural schism of the subject, its mode of establishment as subject in a personal process of development, its specific disinsertion in the laws of the species (the being for whom sexuality does not come naturally), and the principles of its possible transformation. But this is a problem that cannot in fact be treated or even confronted by the language of militant assertion, foundational incantation, and confused crystallization, a language in which a historical break that was scarcely conscious of itself was projected. It is a problem whose real renewal will begin to make itself felt in its full amplitude only when the episode of the Freudian subversion has been resituated in its direct genealogy, reconnected with its invisible antecedents, understood within the overall evolution of the society in which it was produced. It is with this program in mind, and with the intention of offering the beginning of a contribution to it, that the present work has taken shape.

Our sense is that the movement in question comes from far off, and that the undeniable, if uncircumscribable, anthropological rupture that structures our existence is the visible result of a great transformation that was initiated a century earlier and that remains rigorously inseparable from the great democratic revolutions of the late eighteenth century. If we are to grasp and comprehend the profoundly unprecedented aspect of our vision of man, we have to reflect on the light cast on the phenomenon of the personal by the unprecedented order of our democratic-individualist-statist-historicist-capitalist universe (all these adjectives actually designate different facets of the same thing). What we feel as an intimate dispossession, a separation from an invisible part of ourselves, is, paradoxically, only the refraction in internal space of the modern vocation to political autonomy. The becoming-other-for-ourselves that characterizes the reversal of our anthropological perspectives is the private face of the process that has, in the public sphere, done away with submission to the gods, with inclusion in the community, and with political dependence, and that has established individual sovereignty as the new foundation of the social edifice.

On the practical side, this new foundation has led to another paradox: human beings who have become socially independent and self-sufficient on the one hand are on the other hand human beings on whom a transforming grip can be exercised. The individual who takes political possession of himself simultaneously loses psychological power over himself and opens himself up to an action by others that operates on the deepest regions of his being. Outward emancipation turns back on itself to disclose inner servitude, and the dissolution of binding ties with others reveals an obligation to proceed by way of the other in order to act on oneself. The limited time period on which we have concentrated our attention is precisely the turning point when, in the aftermath of the French Revolution, the individual's successful reconquest of his "natural" rights and the wholesale reorganization of the relation of self to self and self to others that resulted from that reconquest bring about a new *"practice" of the human mind.*[1]

The enterprise, as it emerges in the early years of the nineteenth century, is in fact not absolutely without precedent or prefiguration. There is at least one very early precedent in whose lineage we need to situate it, namely, pedagogy—assuredly one of the inventions, here again, that most radically designate the originality of our culture. And it is all the more necessary to link pedagogy and psychiatry, despite the two centuries that separate them, as they mark two key moments of a single history, the history of the subject—which is another name, on another historical scene, for the individual. With pedagogy, the subject of reason was born; with the "moral treatment" advocated by the early-nineteenth-century alienists, the reflective subject entered into crisis; these two moments opened the way to what has become, for us, the constitution of the psychic subject, even though it has not yet really found its concept. The profound singularity of the modern Western approach to humankind, formational or transformational, is commensurate with the specificity of the representation of personal identity that developed during the same time period. From the outset, the freeing up of that indivisible kernel of consciousness and will, which had become a source of inexpressible particularity, has been accompanied by a continued effort to master the target thus exhibited. And it may be through its projection into the pedagogical order that we can best discern what the philosophical promotion of the subject of knowledge may have meant as a revolution in culture. In place of an apprenticeship that is based on the movement of a pupil toward the master, on the identificatory initiative, lateral participation, anonymous impregnation, and mimetic spontaneity, and that wholly neglects the operations through which the pupil gains access to what is to be transmitted to him, the organization of post-Revolutionary secondary education imposes a calculated inscription of the student in a progressive plan of study that is defined in terms of the child's presumed aptitudes, that is fundamentally selective in its aims, and that is wholly oriented toward the control of individual cognitive mechanisms and stages in the acquisition process.

This transformation of the educational process illuminates the passage from the old way of understanding what is human to the new one, and it highlights the autonomous principle of activity that is gradually being recognized at the heart of thinking individuality better than any philosophical treatise. Here, doubtless for the first time, in connection with the "discovery" that childhood was different from adulthood, the human mind became the object of a special practice that explicitly aimed to penetrate its mechanisms in order to direct its operation and content. Moreover, in the microcosm of the schoolroom, a number of precepts or methods were forged that we shall rediscover, carried to a higher power, in the microcosm of the asylum: from the imperative of isolation as a condition for exercising a determining influence on the individuality thus disengaged from its natural milieu, to the rule of programming existences as a means of shaping souls. There is, nevertheless, a significant difference: the fundamental limits that restricted the pedagogical ambition vanish as soon as the political triumph of individuality reveals the new face of modern subjectivity.

The pedagogical enterprise is centrally attached to the development of the cognitive faculties; that is, it is especially concerned with the impersonal, abstract part of the individual—in the last analysis, reason, that which is par excellence the same in every person. In the case of the madman, it is he and no other, the incomparable individual who is brought to light in his absolute subjective singularity by the aberration that cuts him off from his fellows, that the practitioner attempts to reach: it is the intimacy of the ego, the ultimate point of proximity where the self feels itself that the practitioner seeks not only to mobilize but to penetrate. Moreover, it is no accident that this change takes place just when the speculative disengagement of the category of the *ego* is reaching the extreme limit of its inventive curve, with German idealism. Thus, at the time when philosophy reaches its idealist peak, another history is beginning, haltingly, in a remote location. This new history is at once heir to the tradition of subjective identity and potentially subversive of the reflective being.

Furthermore, the pedagogical project puts insistent and explicit emphasis on the way in which a human being is to be taught, either by compulsion or persuasion, to take conscious control of himself and his behavior. The insane asylum, on the contrary, sidesteps and abolishes the postulate of autonomy that informs the work of education. The child is taught to conform, but his conformity is assumed—by Rousseau, for instance—to arise from himself alone, from his own inner movement. In insane asylums, the organization of the therapeutic machinery is destined to allow the alienist to exercise a perfectly concerted influence that is all the more integrally effective on the person of the insane individual in that it unfolds entirely without his knowledge. For this person is immersed in a world where everything is conceived so as to orient him without his awareness; he is traversed by a law that reconstitutes him through and through while he is reduced to enacting it. This exorbitant pretention to complete control and production of the individual was powerfully prepared, to be sure, by the empiricist and sensualist thought of the eighteenth century, but it could not be embodied as an actual institutional system except in terms of the unprecedented managerial relation between power and society (and between any power and any micro-society) that was inaugurated by the democratic revolution.

Here, then, are the two symmetrical aspects of the genesis of the approach to the human mind that we shall be examining further on: the establishment of machinery for taking control of human beings and engendering human qualities, and the invention of rules that make it possible to carve out a path within the individual to the point where he can escape from himself, and that allow the practitioner to act on the patient by playing on his divided state, simultaneously challenging the patient's resistance and winning his cooperation. A peculiar phenomenon of crystallization occurred over a period of a few years, at the very beginning of the nineteenth century, within the tiny psychiatric microcosm (which was made up of a few hundred people in Paris, five thousand at the most in all of France, as compared to at least one hundred thousand a century later: the increase constitutes part of the phenomenon). This process, which blended together recently emerged elements in an unexpected melting pot, gave madness the status of a critical anthropological indicator.

As it happened, the medical requirement of restoring order within a disturbed mind coincided directly with the project of power that had grown out of the emergence of the sovereignty of the people, and offered it a unique opportunity to develop in a perfected form, establishing the insane asylum as a political laboratory. The result was twofold. In the first place, the limits of man's power over man were very quickly brought to light. This discovery had significant consequences, since it imposed considerable sophistication on any undertaking that intended to transform human beings; indeed, it enjoined such an undertaking to start from an initial assumption of powerlessness. But, in addition, the aslyum produced a proximity and a likeness of the insane individual to other human beings that radically modified the earlier reading of his difference and that contributed decisively, on the infrastructural level, to an interpenetration of the normal and the pathological realms that has not yet ceased to upset our understanding of each. It turned out, furthermore, that, in the living enigma of an insane individual simultaneously foreign to himself and present to his own foreignness, the modern revolution of man's relation to himself found a vehicle through which it could be made perceptible. This encounter was inseparable from the concretization of new possibilities within the relation between practitioners and insane patients, and, by virtue of challenging the old norm of reciprocity, inseparable from the new possibilities in human relations that were opened up by the social atomization and dissolution of the old symbolic constraints. Thus a crucial part of our destiny was decided early on, coalescing within the marginal universe of madness.

Of the history that was inaugurated in that obscure site and that has been continually expanding since then, of this process of subversion that signals the transformation of the world within us, only a few essential consequences have seen the light of day thus far. To be sure, within ourselves, there is something unknown, something that, in the mirror of formations of personal alterity, has become incontrovertible to us. At most, we can make out signs of that unknown, and to a certain extent we can induce its effects, although only the most naive among psychoanalysts claim to know the full details of such effects. A proper speculative translation of the data set thus extracted and exhibited would already represent an overwhelming step in the direction of the reconquest and deeper understanding of that other identity whose virtuality inhabits us.

But the most determining effects of the contradiction within ourselves that was first conceived about 180 years ago at the heart of the eclipse of subjective power may still lie ahead of us. The aspects of madness that continue to escape us entail a renewal of the idea of the human being that is undoubtedly as important as the indisputable and elusive idea on the basis of which we are living now. What is there, in the structure of any subject, that resembles antagonistic suspension of the subject? If we were in a position to answer such a question, even in a very partial way, we would understand the contribution of insanity to our capacity to assimilate the real, to order and change it. What is the source of the subjective precariousness (within an indestructible subjectivity) that allows self-possession and communication with others to falter? Here we face nothing less than the question of the nature of human self-creation, the power of distancing ourselves from nature that has made us capable of acting on ourselves, the introduction of the reflective dimension owing to which there is not only subject, language, and society, but also the subject's power over himself, the invention of language within language, indeed the constitution of an artificial language on the basis of "natural" language, and finally people's power over the order of their society.

Madness unquestionably sheds a privileged light on what might be the capstone of the reversal in question: the integration of the point of view of the other within oneself. The capacity to perform this integration makes humans the only animals with a dimension of universality, for it allows them to conceive of themselves from a position outside of themselves, to look at themselves from elsewhere, as if they were other. Not only do they position themselves before the world in this way, but also in the world, in the same world as the others, for they are compelled to recognize themselves as relative specimens of humanity, as ones among others and equivalent to the others. Their experience takes on objectivity and impersonality: what I see, others see too; thus, what I see exists independently of me; what I experience, someone else could experience. This organization appears to be quite specifically the one that madness calls into question, on very different levels of psychic reality. On one level, I may be convinced that I am for some reason the only being of my species; this conviction may be viewed as the minimal feature of subjective pathology. On another level, I may find it impossible to situate myself in space or time. In between, I may be incapable of assessing the neutrality of the world (which ordinarily means nothing to me in particular, since it signifies simultaneously for everyone, but which suddenly sets about signifying everywhere for me alone), and I may be unable to believe in the relativity of my own existence amid all the others (which locks me into the certainty of being the only one, the best or the worst).

This point warrants two further observations. First, we should like to emphasize the pathogenic character of experience that drives the subject into a feeling of incommensurability. To say "that happens only to me" is a way of designating what is unbearable par excellence. (Let us recall that from time immemorial sorcery has had the function of conjuring up or conjuring away such experiences: that happens to me because someone else did what was required so it would happen to me; thus it could happen to anyone else. But the will of God has also had this function, allowing experiences that are unassimilable on the personal level to be resituated within the order of a universal ordeal.) Second, within the disorder of subjectivity that results from one's inability to take the other's viewpoint into account, we should like to clarify the mechanism of madness as classically embodied in delirium and hallucination. A mad thought is a thought that stems from the withdrawal of the internal reference points that give things simultaneous validity for myself and for others. Mad thoughts arise when it is impossible to consider what I believe from the virtual place from which another would consider it; these are thoughts that I therefore have no means to differentiate from myself, to put at a distance, and they are terrifying thoughts in that I know I am the only one who has them. A mad perception—a hallucination—is likewise a perception that cannot be shared, a perception woven out of its very lack of consistency for anyone else, a flash from the world that cannot be challenged, to the precise extent that it does not arise from this world in which I can always ask myself if the other has indeed perceived what I seem to have perceived.

These brief notations do not even constitute an attempt to name the problem. Rather, they seek to bring out, in contrast with the necessary inadequacy of their language, the foreseeable excess of the future over all currently available categories. And, since this work as a whole is a direct or indirect plea urging that the social process and the anthropological movement be taken into account simultaneously, let us add that the elucidation of the structure of exteriority that removes the subject from himself is surely not separable, in the last analysis, from the elucidation of the structure of alterity which provides society both with cohesion and with power to act upon itself. This alterity is wholly enigmatic in its profound necessity; it makes the community of human beings dependent on an agency at once produced by the community itself and detached from itself, an agency that defines a society and runs it as if from outside itself (and the alterity is imperious enough to have required, throughout almost its entire history, the sanction of a transcendent exteriority: the difference between the community and the State is only the intrahuman reflection of the difference between the community and the gods who make laws from an invisible vantage point).

This alterity is relative, and to a certain extent, as it were, illusory: it is natural that power should remain internal to society (even though the totalitarian enterprise is there to demonstrate to what extent the ultimate and constitutive ambition of the State is to move completely outside of society in order to gain a total grip on society. But it is also natural that one should not "truly" see oneself from the outside, which confers on the mechanism its essential precariousness. Still, if it is undeniable that one's continuous proximity to oneself cannot be abandoned, it is also true that one is at a distance from onself, at a partly imaginary yet efficacious distance, which needs to be accounted for. This distance is what assures us, on the practical level, of a quite verifiable operational capacity; on the theoretical level, it assures us of a capacity for objectivization, a capacity that is limited in a fundamental way but that is notably consistent within its limits. After all, the fact that the *id* speaks is not particularly astonishing. What is truly amazing is that where the *id* should never have done anything but speak, there could have emerged from that "mechanical" and self-productive flux an *I* that speaks—an *I* well enough anchored, as the experience of madness demonstrates with particular clarity, so that, when the *id* begins to speak in place of the *I*, there is frightful suffering of an *I* that is witness to the compulsion that is dissolving it.

The discovery of the unconscious has unquestionably marked a crucial turning point in the history of the idea of man. But the discovery of consciousness, which remains entirely ahead of us, and whose apparent obviousness conceals an abyss of difficulties, threatens to be no less upsetting—for it is clear that the bases for consciousness as we understand it are not especially "conscious" in the common descriptive sense of the term. This is why we began to search for the moment at which the unveiling of the subjective contradiction overturned the conditions of man's approach to man: we are interested in finding the historical fulcrum from which we can bring to light, taking the long view, the dimension of a possible future. In a world worn down with feverish immobilism, tottering with senile anguish, we should like to reconquer, to however small an extent, and without too many illusions, what we are losing, bit by bit, every day: the power of a future.

ABSTRACT I

The Moment of Origin

The opinions of Etienne Esquirol (1772–1840) on mental illness, as expressed in his important book *Des Passions considérées comme causes, symptômes et moyens curatifs de l'aliénation mentale* (On passions considered as causes, symptoms, and cures of mental alienation [Paris: Didot Jeune, 1805]), continued the work of his teacher, Philippe Pinel (1745–1826). Esquirol, like Pinel, believed that the origin of mental illness lies in the passions of the soul and was convinced that madness does not fully and irremediably affect the patient's reason. While Esquirol's later work, particularly his *Maladies mentales* (Mental maladies [Paris: Baillière, 1838]), mostly focused on the multiplicity of facts concerning mental illness and on the scientific techniques for gathering them, *Des Passions* sought to provide a speculative hypothesis on the nature of psychiatric disorders. *Des Passions* is, therefore, a crucial text for understanding the origin of modern French psychiatric theory.

PART ONE

Advent, Apotheosis, and Failure of the Asylum Establishment

ABSTRACT II

Esquirol's *Des Passions* capitalizes on the experience its author gained at La Salpêtrière, an insane asylum founded in 1802 by the French government. From its inception, La Salpêtrière aimed at isolating mentally ill patients from society in order to cure them. The idea of curing madness was not entirely new at that time: the asylum at Charenton had been pursuing this goal since 1797. From a humanitarian point of view, Charenton represented a considerable advance over the old Parisian institution of the Hôtel-Dieu, where the insane were imprisoned in gruesome conditions, with no effort made to heal them. Like La Salpêtrière later, Charenton fit well with the French Revolution's ideal of improving the lot of the blind, the deaf, and the mentally ill. Yet Charenton remained a basically archaic institution insofar as it sought to cure illness using exclusively nonmedical means.

CHAPTER I

La Salpêtrière, or The Double Birth of the Asylum

Establish a Hospice for the

Cure of the Insane

CHARENTON, or the experiment that went nowhere: that would be one way to sum up the meaning of the episode. Charenton bears witness to the prominent inscription of the problem on the agenda of the times. But it also attests to the difficulty of finding an adequate response to the problem from the start, finding a balance between the weight of the past and the seductions of false novelty. After the decision to set up a program for "full and complete treatment of insanity" at Charenton was made, it took five more years—five years of obstinate persistence in following the old model of the Hôtel-Dieu and of rapid disenchantment with the brand-new substitute—before the formula that was to succeed historically could be found and put into concrete practice. For what was established in 1802 at La Salpêtrière was beyond question an asylum in the modern sense. And in contrast to the archaic structures in which the attempt at Charenton was foundering during the same period, we can see what paths institutional modernity will take. The new structures entail the inauguration of an undivided, unchallenged medical authority, as has been widely recognized; but they also entail—and this has rarely been noted, though it is one of their essential features—a complete transformation of the therapeutic framework, based on a profound mutation of the representation of insanity in terms of its curability.

This mutation is widely translated as an awareness of a break and a feeling of discovery—the discovery that "the illness commonly known as insanity is not incurable." The break has been attributed to the effects of Philippe Pinel's *Traité de la Manie* (A treatise on insanity). At the literal level, this attribution is false, for Pinel was not the first to learn that the insane could be cured. And yet in that empirically inaccurate conviction there is a profound truth. For, in a special sense, Pinel was unquestionably the first to show, indirectly but in a radical way, that insanity is not incurable. He did so by revealing the need to view insanity in terms of what opens it up, what makes it accessible, in principle, to the therapeutic grasp, what keeps it, essentially, from being entirely closed in on itself—for such a self-enclosed state would make it inaccessible, would compel us to see insanity as "incurable," with some inexplicable exceptions. In this sense, the *Treatise on Insanity* is indeed the source book that its contemporary readers took it to be. The asylum project grew directly and immediately out of Pinel's idea. In chronological terms, moreover, it was in the wake of that book, a few months after its publication, that the bureaucratic roadblocks broke down and the field of practical experience opened up.

Even if they were in part accidental, the circumstances are highly significant. Events unfolded as if the institution of the asylum were an extension, a projection, a materialization, a transcription of Pinel's book, as if that text had been required to facilitate the simultaneous appearance of the possibility and the necessity of the new medico-hospital mechanism. It is clear, in any case, that we have no hope of understanding the special characteristics of the world of the asylum as it came into being in that period, the specific ambition around which it was constituted, or the real intention that inspired and permeated it, unless we go back to the thought process that is carried out in Pinel's work. In its historically unprecedented features, in its most singular aspects, the asylum arose from the conceptual revolution that made insanity accessible from the inside and restored the insane to the order of beings accessible through communication. This is its constitutive paradox: the asylum encloses an insanity whose secret pain is accessible to us; behind walls designating difference it sequesters an insane person who is just beginning to appear to us in his *sameness.* The uncertainties of this inherent rift have not yet been exhausted.

The reopening of Charenton in Year V of the French Revolution was purely a governmental initiative, conceived as part of a nationwide undertaking. The transformation of La Salpêtrière into a treatment facility in March 1802 was a measure that had essentially local impact; it was intended to deal with specifically Parisian problems, perhaps under pressure from the Ministry of Internal Affairs, but also under the impetus of preexisting reform plans developed by hospice administrators. Starting in 1797, the administration of the Hospices de Paris[1] was theoretically obliged to use the services of the Maison de Charenton, since the treatment of the insane had been prohibited in all other facilities of the capital by a decree of 27 Prairial, Year V. The Hospices de Paris were supposed to transfer their "indigents afflicted with insanity" to Charenton and pay their expenses until they were cured or sent back as incurable. In reality, service to the insane at the Hôtel-Dieu was never suspended despite the official prohibition, and the transfer of patients to Charenton at the expense of the Hospices de Paris must never have involved large numbers of people.

Things changed very little, then, for the vast majority of the insane, despite some inklings of modernization from above. For the most part, conditions remained stable for several years after the brief flurry of measures taken in Year V. Only at the beginning of 1801 did an overall reform project see the light of day. There was unquestionably a simple, fundamental reason for this development: after a period of faltering management, an administrative structure was established that had effective means for making decisions. Faced with the crisis situation created in Year VIII by the manifest deficiency of the five-member commission that had presided over the destinies of the Paris hospitals since Vendémiaire, Year V, Frochot, the new prefect of the Seine Department, decided to set up the administration of that enormous charitable apparatus (nineteen facilities, with a population of sixteen thousand indigents) on an entirely different basis.[2] At the head of that vast body, which had been spineless and more or less anarchic, he placed the Conseil général des Hospices, an authentic central decision-making organ endowed with visibly enhanced powers and equipped to develop a genuine hospital policy. Not only was the prefect newly appointed, but also the prefectoral administration itself; it had been instituted by the law of 28 Pluviôse, Year VIII (February 17, 1800). The reestablishment of public authority under the consulate, after years of fluctuation under the directoire, and the ongoing reconstruction of a stable administrative apparatus that was to culminate a little later in the strong Napoleonic state, clearly played a decisive role in the reorganization of the hospice.

Everything happened very quickly, since the Conseil général des Hospices, officially installed in its functions by Frochot (who was its ex officio president, moreover) on 5 Ventôse, Year IX (February 24, 1801)[3] was already addressing the problem of the insane on 19 Germinal (April 9) of the same year, just a few weeks into its work. Even before the creation of the Conseil général, Frochot had taken an interest in the question, or he may have been informed about a project originated by an unidentified third party.[4] Whatever the source of initiative, the subsequent chain of events suffices to prove that it grew out of a general awareness of the critical nature of the situation. Frochot and the members of the conseil were themselves strongly persuaded that there was an urgent problem requiring a rapid, specific, and comprehensive solution. Thus the anonymous recorder who mentioned "the establishment of a hospice devoted to the cure of Insanity" on 19 Germinal could ask for, and obtain, on behalf of insane patients, an exception to the policy the conseil had set for itself—"not to be concerned at this time with any partial improvement," but to devote itself first of all to the development of "general plans."[5]

The problem addressed was not, as it had been for Charenton, the isolated question of a "treatment house" (the implication being that for everyone else, that is, the incurables, general hospitals and poor houses would suffice). What was envisaged now was a general reform of the treatment of the insane in the hospitals of the capital, a reform that would consist in grouping them *all* in a *single* "hospice for the cure of the insane," formed by combining two huge adjacent houses, "the aforementioned convents of the Madeleine de Trénelle and the Filles de la Croix."[6] The prefect seems to have had his heart set for some time on those two buildings on the rue de Charonne in the Faubourg Saint-Antoine.[7] One was "entirely vacant" and the other "occupied only by a small detachment of the 64th half-brigade"; Frochet had already asked Clavareau, the hospice architect, to take a look at them. The Conseil général promptly took up the project on its own account and sent its own commission to the site, adding for the occasion not only the district mayor and Clavareau but also Mourgue, the general secretary of the Ministry of Internal Affairs, and Citizen Pinel. In their meeting of 24 Germinal, the commissioners acknowledged the truth of the facts contained in Clavareau's report and declared "that the two houses [were] perfectly suited for the establishment of a hospice for the cure of the insane."[8] And the conseil sent a report to the Minister of Internal Affairs the very same day, pointing out how advantageous it would be to "set up the hospice in two buildings which, owing to their contiguity, their construction, their courtyards, and their gardens, seem to have been built intentionally for this establishment that humanity has been demanding for so long in Paris."[9] The conseil thus urged him to release the funds needed to acquire the buildings, arguing that such an opportunity "might never come up again."

As it turned out, the minister let the opportunity slip by, and it was never repeated. The conseil took up the matter again on at least two occasions, on 24 Germinal, Year IX, and then on 28 Messidor of the same year.[10] Its efforts were fruitless: either the minister persisted in turning a deaf ear or he recoiled at the amount of money needed. For better or for worse, the conseil thus had to settle for transforming the existing widely criticized "asylums," "frightfully sad" places where "the stomach turns at the sight of the suffering of the unfortunate creatures who are condemned, for want of care, to perpetual confinement." And this is why Pinel, unable to put into practice the principles of the *Treatise on Insanity* in the vast establishment he had longed for, had to settle for modest reforms in the old workhouse for insane women at La Salpêtrière and give up all hope of the glory he would surely have won with the new facility. The "cure for

Insanity" had to remain a utopian dream. This limitation is conveyed quite clearly, in a way, by the myth attached to Pinel's name. According to the traditional view, Pinel merely liberated the insane *within* the unchanged framework of their confinement; he did not create a *different place* where the new course he had initiated could have been both implemented and symbolized. At least he cannot be faulted for failing to try.

Although it was short-lived, the project remains extremely interesting, in that it translates the critical mutation in perspectives on the treatment of insanity that came about after Charenton was opened. One small but meaningful change is visible at the outset: the project's very title emphasizes *results* rather than *means.* The term used in connection with Charenton was "*treatment* house"; now the text refers to a hospice "for the *cure* of the insane."

This shift, however slight, attests to a new confidence in the possibilities of therapy, and not just on the level of the successes one might legitimately expect, but also on the level of the aim one is entitled to set—as if from this point on, instead of having to resort to the uncontrollable vagaries of therapeutic trial and error, one felt that one had direct power over the inner pathways of healing and its outcome. But the fundamental change consists less in the goal therapeutic treatment now confidently sets for itself than in the tacit redefinition of the field to which that goal is to be applied, and specifically its extension to the asylum population as a whole. The plan outlined in 1801 no longer has anything to say about the distribution of patients and the two-pronged hospital organization that continued to prevail in the Charenton project without exception: on the one hand, there were potentially curable lunatics for whom treatment was worth attempting; on the other hand, there were incurables who simply had to be kept locked up. The essential novelty of the conseil's project, on the contrary, is based on the idea that the optimal solution would entail bringing all the insane together in a single establishment, those alleged to be receiving treatment at the Hôtel-Dieu along with those abandoned to their presumed incurability at Bicêtre, La Salpêtrière or the Petites-Maisons. The point is to apply the same regimen and treatment to all, giving everyone a real possibility, or rather a reasonable hope, of being cured. The important thing, in other words, is not specifically the intent to create a "hospice for the cure of Insanity" that, like Charenton, could have functioned alongside and in addition to already-existing institutions (regularly unloading its share of hopeless cases on those other institutions). What is important is the determination to replace facilities designed for confinement with a single hospice devoted to healing, with all the presuppositions that that substitution implies: the refusal to exclude any patient, a priori, from treatment, and thus the recognition of a necessary continuity within the medical enterprise. Instead of allocating a predetermined, fixed time for treatment, practitioners have to confront the undecidable individual chronologies of mental illness.

On this point, even though the little remaining evidence we gave of the conseil's activity is administratively elliptical, it is entirely unequivocal. The intention is to set up a mechanism that can be thoroughly medical in character. Bicêtre and La Salpêtrière are criticized precisely because "the arrangement of the facilities [there] has always worked against the means for healing," so that in these "asylums for unfortunate creatures, despite the great insights of Citizen Pinel, despite the experience and the continual care of Citizen Pussin, almost none of the unhappy patients has been restored to reason." "There are a few examples of this at Bicêtre alone," the recorder adds,[11] not as a result of Citizen Pinel's "great insights," we might add, however, but owing to "the experience and continual care" of Citizen Pussin, whereas the creation of "this establishment that humanity has been demanding for so long in Paris" would make it possible to "return to society nearly two thirds of those who up to now are condemned for want of care to perpetual confinement."[12] On the (mythical) basis of results allegedly obtained in England, elsewhere in the conseil's deliberations we find an even more spectacularly optimistic estimation of the prospects for cure: it would be possible to restore to reason "more than 9/10" of the insane, once the proper conditions had been met.[13] This can be translated as "virtually all," for the tiny remainder manifestly intervenes only to preserve a semblance of experimental plausibility for the claim. Of course one is bound to run into intractable cases from time to time. The fact remains that curability is the general rule; it is simply confirmed by the rare exceptions. In communications with the minister, the desire to convince encourages greater assertive prudence: the truly excessive figure of "more than 9/10" (a figure for internal use, arising from a discussion) gives way to the more reasonable one of "nearly 2/3." This probably suffices to explain the gap, which is after all a remarkable one, between estimates put forward by the same individuals just a few days apart.

Above and beyond their variations, whether these are purely formal or purely tactical, the estimates express a single conviction: that in virtually all cases, treatment of the insane can be undertaken with the greatest likelihood of success, notably including success with those currently deemed "incurable." There are incurable patients in the hospices only for want of care, or because of the "harmful effects" of ill-conceived care.[14] In any event, under the circumstances, the statistical estimates were necessarily indeterminate. They were not derived from experience, even though they may have invoked remote and mysterious precedents; they did not depend on any recorded result. They arose from belief; they embodied a presupposition; they were the projection of a postulate whose quite recent emergence was signaled by their striking and naive exaggeration. That postulate had much less bearing, in reality, on the actual outcome of the treatments undertaken than on the a priori possibility of implementing those treatments—or in any event the impossibility of ever hiding a priori behind the hasty verdicts of incurability to which the old medicine—and public opinion as well—willingly resorted. Every case of declared "insanity" gives forth some sign pointing toward a possible way out of insanity, assuming there is someone who can decipher its subtle dynamics. Such is the authentic event whose shock effect is transposed by these fantastic calculations into illusory but telling hopes of cure: not just a public production of an artificially optimistic *bottom line* that would have given rise to a short-lived euphoria, but a profound, global, and very precisely localizable mutation in the *approach* to insanity. This mutation has revealed insanity to be accessible in its intimate foundations, and thus eminently curable, though in an irreducibly special sense.

Concerning the project put forward by the Conseil général des Hospices, then, let us be clear about the dividing line between what is old and what is new. On the one hand, the project is inscribed in an already-lengthy series of similar projects. For a very long time, indeed, in the name of humanity, voices had been clamoring for the creation of a separate establishment for the insane in the capital, and steps had been taken in that direction. The wish and the attempt go back at least to the appearance of Tenon's well-known *Mémoires* on hospitals, published in 1786. From this standpoint, it is true that in 1801 the conseil is merely reiterating an old demand and reopening a dossier that had been exhumed and reburied several times (indeed, the Report of 24 Germinal, Year IX, to the Minister of Internal Affairs recalls these unsuccessful precedents). But the problem is entered on the short-term agenda at the beginning of 1801 not simply as a ritual return to old business by a newly installed administration. There is also manifest evidence of another cause, for the project put forward bears the striking imprint of an inspiration that is absent from its earlier homologues, an inspiration revealed by the fabulous hopes expressed by the unrealistic figures of our reporters. For in the meantime, Pinel has done his work: the quite recent shock of his undertaking is discernible behind the excessive accountings, as if minds had not yet had the time to get a grip on themselves.[15]

Pinel's ideas ultimately reveal a virtual hold over the insane patient, a hold that in theory operates in even the most intractable cases—a revelation promptly transmuted by the magic of arithmetic into a conviction that there is no insane person who cannot be cured. Pinel's work provides the conseil with the justification it needs to take charge of the dossier without delay: how could they not allow that "large class of unfortunates," currently neglected in the hospices, to benefit as soon as possible from a reform likely to reverse their condition? It is Pinel's ideas, finally, that covertly endow the conseil's project with the dimension of effectiveness that distinguishes it from its predecessors. For Pinel's ideas do not simply fail like the others. They succeed, to a certain extent, against all odds; they have consequences and effects. If they do not manage to wrest a special establishment for the insane from the vast confused body of the old Hôpital général, at least they manage to transform the universe of confinement from within, by irreversibly specifying the domain of insanity inside the hospital, along with an institutional practice that is presumed to answer the question they have raised.

However limited Pinel's undertaking may have remained, its effectiveness is nevertheless infinitely revealing. After Pinel it was simply no longer possible to leave things the way they had been. He did not succeed in creating the "hospice uniquely devoted to treating insanity" that he had hoped for. But a little more than a year after his *Treatise on Insanity* was published, he was nevertheless awarded the minimal means he needed to undertake research on "the general and particular measures to be taken for the regular treatment of the insane in a large hospice."[16]

An Effective Cure for Insanity:
From Belief to Experiment

The Conseil général des Hospices presented its enterprise quite openly to the political authorities by invoking the new direction taken by studies on mental illness. The report addressed to the "Citizen Minister" on 24 Germinal, Year IX, does not name Pinel, nor does it refer explicitly to his *Treatise*. But the reference is transparent nonetheless; what is more, at the top of the list of justifications for urgent reform, the report places the demonstration produced by the doctor of La Salpêtrière in his treatise. "The situation of the insane in the hospices of Paris," the preamble says, in effect, "has for a long time sought the attention of friends of humanity; that unfortunate and quite large class of unhappy creatures has not yet shared in the progress that the various sectors of the art of healing have made in recent years. *And especially the discoveries made recently as to their effective cure through moral treatment.*"[17]

There is no need to discuss the attribution of the aforementioned "discoveries" in the realm of an "effective cure for insanity," as an earlier (crossed-out) version of the text puts it. The very fact that the "discoveries" are evoked without further details suffices to indicate the character of public self-evidence that is attributed to them. The task that the Conseil général des Hospices sets forth and fleshes out as necessary is that of implementing the principles developed in the *Treatise on Insanity*. The goal is not merely the humanitarian one of reforming a troubling situation, but actually that of creating the conditions for the "effective" treatment whose methods have been revealed and defined by Pinel. Here we are intentionally borrowing and transferring the formulas used in the prospectus announcing the opening of Esquirol's facility. The parallelism of the presentation in the two cases is indeed striking: each begins with the book, with its power to demonstrate or the weight of its discoveries, and each goes on to express the urgent obligation to transpose into reality what has been discovered. In texts of such disparate inspiration as Esquirol's—the master's closest disciple making his pitch to the public—and that of an anonymous administrator struggling in some obscure bureau to wrest funds from the minister's budget, the presumed convergence of the paths of persuasion is unexpected enough to pose a problem.

There is truly a mystery involving the *Treatise on Insanity*: not only the mystery, as we have already seen, of the rapidity with which it found an institutional transcription, but also the mystery of the widespread conviction to which it gave rise, the mystery of its role as symbolic starting point, as source text. Given the repeated references, the recurrences of the argument, it is impossible to dismiss the book's transforming impact. There is no doubt about it: if Pinel was able to reform the treatment of the insane, his success came thanks to his *Treatise*. It was not so much the author in person who acquired the means to reorganize La Salpêtrière as it was his book. Through its power of conviction, Pinel's text won the resources for its own implementation and projected itself into the order of reality. Esquirol himself acknowledged this, after his fashion, when he wrote that of all the books published on this malady, not one "has had a more pronounced influence in France on those for whom it was written. *Since its publication . . . the fate of the insane has been infinitely improved.*"[18] He did not attribute the progress to Pinel's tireless personal efforts, but to the shock provoked by the publication of his work: an unaccustomed focus of praise, and a singular story whose driving force turned out to be the impact of a book.

To be sure, the data on which we have based our argument does not authorize us to be satisfied with the mere observation that the *Treatise on Insanity* had an impact in history. Our data require us to take an additional dimension into account: the fact that the *Treatise* owed its effectiveness to a particular illusion. What allowed it to trigger an actual break in the order of institutions was its own somewhat blind belief in the theoretical and general curability of mental illness. This obviously makes the relations between the source text and the effects actually achieved somewhat problematic. One hypothesis would be that Pinel's work created a pure mirage in public opinion, a mirage in the name of which an institutional apparatus was set up that finally had little to do, in its concrete reality, with the inconsistent phantasmagoria from which it emerged. Or we might go even further: perhaps our author came along at just the right moment to supply, providentially, the ideological cover for an operation whose deepest roots lay outside the social field, an operation that would have taken place in any case, under some other intellectual cloak. In this case, the link between the reality of the asylum and the *Treatise on Insanity* would be little more than accidental, for although the work might have served as a triggering cause, it could no way be deemed an essential source. One particular circumstance lends some credibility to the latter hypothesis: the rapid decline, at least in appearance, of the optimistic conviction that gave Pinel's book its generative power.

The great early confidence in the resources of moral treatment seems to have abated quickly; in fewer than ten years, it had fallen silent. Regularly invoked, indeed mechanically repeated during the five or six years that followed the appearance of the *Treatise*, the article of faith pronouncing the essential curability of insanity turned up very seldom later on, with a few scattered exceptions, and there too it disappeared quickly and rather mysteriously. After 1810, and for example in the critical literature produced in response to the second edition of the *Treatise* in 1809, there was virtually no further trace of it. Is this really so surprising? Is it not rather the infallible and banal sign of the inevitable decay of an unsupported conviction in contact with pitiless reality? Is it not quite simply that, regarding the "effective cure for insanity," people had to eat their words fairly quickly, and keep quiet? A normal instance of erosion, a fatal exhaustion of the illusion, the predictable annihilation of a dream lacking in consistency—these would finally reveal in its harsh nakedness the one solid and lasting result of the process: not the futile pretext-discourse, but the prison wall built behind the smoke screen of the therapeutic ambition.

On this point, two interpretations are possible. Either we consider the medical cover, adopted briefly by the asylum advocates, as a screen cynically adopted for an enterprise that was fully aware of its segregative ends, but also aware of their inadmissible character (the screen could thus be abandoned as soon as the project was well under way), or else we appeal to the cunning of Reason, which has once again concealed from the actors of history the true import of their actions and words. According to the old formula of guilty innocence, our naive alienists and their credulous partisans would have been agents, in good faith, of a confinement that had to suppress its name in order to be sure of winning out. But whether we lean in one of these directions or the other, the heart of the thesis remains the same. What is in each case taken as given is that the motives initially alleged have nothing in common with what was actually achieved. Whether we see the momentary confidence in the possibility of curing the insane as a dismal dream of misused intelligence or a subtle product of cunning, we will be left with little more than a deceptive alibi in the name of which and behind which a social mechanism was devised that had little to do, in its underlying logic, with the easy talk that presided over its advent.

In our judgment, neither one of these pictures is accurate. There were some illusions, to be sure, or at least some exaggerated assessments of the prospects for curing mental illness. But there was by no means total blindness on the topic; had there been, the utter foolishness of the position would have been quickly revealed or corrected by the rough law of experimentation. True, the figures did not measure up to initial expectations. But neither did they ever take on the appearance of bankruptcy or compel a confession of hopeless impotence. From 1805 to 1813, if we follow Pinel's summary reports, the proportion of cures was maintained, year in year out, at a rate of one for every two admissions. This is nothing like the nine-tenths projected by the Conseil des Hospices, but it is also a far cry from demonstrating the uselessness of therapy.[19] However the figures are interpreted, this crucial fact has to be kept in sight.

It is therefore not true that Pinel's asylum is no more than a simple lockup. Let us not get carried away with a statistical history of confinement, which in any event remains entirely to be written. Let us not extrapolate in time and space on the basis of this narrowly localized—but in every respect strategic—example. Let us limit ourselves to stressing the following fact: in the early phase of La Salpêtrière's operation as an asylum in the modern sense, for every two insane female patients who entered, one left, generally in less than a year. Thus we cannot legitimately impute the decline and gradual disappearance of the optimistic discourse of the early days to a categorical factual contradiction. That discourse could perfectly well have managed after all to come to terms with data that were in no way compromising—and it could have skillfully emphasized, for example, the contrast between the new conditions at La Salpêtrière and those that had prevailed until very recently (and indeed that continued to prevail outside of Paris), namely, hopeless, interminable confinement. What is astonishing in this matter, in fact, is the way the collective consciousness came to reject a conviction that had the best of reasons to persist. The scenario is not the ordinary one of an error finally becoming apparent. It is rather the much more complex and enigmatic scenario of an illusion that nevertheless contains a great deal of truth, and that without really encountering any contradiction nevertheless fades away, loses its interest, or ceases to appear meaningful.

The explanation presupposes a complete reversal, here, of the logic of appearances. Indeed, this is the first paradox we must confront if we truly wish to account for the strange destiny of the working representation that the psychiatric enterprise provided for itself at its inception. The excessive or illusory aspects of the initial confidence in the resources of the healing art are not what condemned the enterprise to silence or oblivion; on the contrary, what condemned it very early to silence was the profound truth that traversed it, the power it had to translate faithfully for contemporary minds the effectiveness of the Pinelian reform.

In a second paradox that sheds light on the first, this optimistic vision had the power of truth only owing to its illusory excessiveness. Had it been more moderate in its assertions, more calmly "realistic," it would not have fulfilled its function as truthful representation. To boast in advance that virtually all insane persons subjected to treatment would be cured was obviously to fly in the face of the most elementary experimental caution as well as ordinary common sense. The fact remains that it was only by embracing unreservedly the unrealistic prospect of total success that one could understand, at the time, the meaning of the transformation brought about by the *Treatise on Insanity* with a modicum of completeness and justice. For, on the one hand, Pinel's undertaking obviously involves thinking about insanity *in general.* How, then, could that dimension of universality be rendered pertinently unless one were to situate oneself on the horizon of *all* insanity? And, on the other hand, not only is it actually a matter of *curing*, but, in a certain sense, of nothing other than curing. This is why Pinel's contemporaries could legitimately think they had summed up the event in its totality when they called it the discovery of curability.

The break introduced by Pinel can indeed be formulated in wholly therapeutic terms. Furthermore, only in that language and from that standpoint could the break be clearly signified as such in its own time. On the therapeutic level, Pinel proceeds to a complete reversal of the previously accepted postulates, as they were given concrete expression, for example, in the context of treatment, in the form of an ordeal; the powerful influence of these postulates is evident from the Hôtel-Dieu to Charenton. The insane are incurable in theory, potentially curable in fact: this is a way of summarizing the implicit body of doctrine that lay behind the earlier procedures and that accounted for the fundamental hesitation between an a priori rejection of treatment as useless and a sense of the obligation to attempt some kind of treatment nevertheless. It does happen that insane individuals come out of their insanity, even though as a general rule there is no hope; the occasional exception only confirms the ordinarily disastrous dynamic of absence to oneself.

Pinel comes to precisely the opposite conclusion: curability in theory, potential incurability in fact. It is practically always possible to put a certain pressure on the mechanisms of insanity themselves. The patient may still sometimes turn out to be obstinately trapped in his disorder, despite the establishment of a therapeutic link; but the obstacle encountered in such cases does not invalidate the alienated subject's essential permeability to the therapist's grasp. This double postulation unquestionably sums up the overall significance of the Pinelian revolution in a concentrated way. What is not expressly formulated, in particular, is the central idea that provides this new regime of hope with its intelligible foundation, namely, the idea that there is no such thing as a complete eradication of subjectivity, even in what appear to be the most radical instances of insanity, and that, beneath the vacillation of his subjectivity, the patient always retains the possibility of protecting and defending himself against himself. For such is the real source of the a priori declaration that insanity is curable: a tacit thesis regarding its nature, its constitutive difference from total madness. No insane person is without some distance, however imperceptible, between himself and his illness. That distance allows him not only to defend himself against what is removing him from himself, but also to remain in proximity with others, despite the incommunicable nature of what he is confronting; furthermore, it allows him to remain open to the influence of others, or, more precisely, it allows others access to that inner aspect of himself that escapes his own control.

In this light, Pinel's reversal of the principles for treating insanity corresponds, on the one hand, to an anchoring of the therapeutic perspective in the intimate essence of insanity. On the other hand, it corresponds to a strict specification of the nature and modalities of the therapeutic activity. Therapy will take place as a form of human relationship and communication or it will not take place at all. There is no therapy that does not come about through the powers of discourse. Thus, to speak of the "discovery" of the hidden key to "effective cure" of mental illness through "moral treatment," in connection with the *Treatise on Insanity*, is not a bad way to express what happened. The fundamental aspect of the Pinelian break consists in achieving an opening onto insanity from within that reveals the principle of "effective" treatment. Such treatment apprehends insanity in its own element, at its very roots within the subject, in the very process in which the vacillation and the persistence of the subjective function are intertwined; this is why it can be called a fully "moral" treatment.

The nascent phenomenon of psychiatry found a relatively adequate expression in this discourse of therapeutic efficacy, in which it was immediately mirrored. It is neither a travesty nor a denaturing. On the contrary, the discourse offers a representation that is at once perfectly centered and comprehensive enough not to leave out anything important. In particular, the representation accurately situates the zone of maximum discontinuity, that of the postulates concerning what is possible and impossible in approaches to madness. This is not to say that the event played itself out in complete transparency for its actors, or that the rupture was instantly recognized and articulated in its full and definitive truth. For we can see at once what has remained irreducibly opaque and silent about the process: its intelligible core, namely, the transformation of the *conception* of insanity as such. The consequences of the overall mutation are articulated, one major consequence in particular: insanity is curable. But in the background, the underlying cause, the new idea according to which madness offers legitimacy to therapeutic optimism, remains unexpressed.

Owing to the very nature of insanity, which puts the human subject as such at stake, there is no way out without some form of intersubjective exchange. In other words, no matter how appropriate and faithful it may be, translating the Pinelian rupture in terms of curing produces a discourse that lacks the foundation it would need to sustain itself explicitly as a discourse of universal validity. Hence we find a quite awkward wavering between the imperative of targeting insanity as such and the absence of conceptual means that would make it possible to express insanity in its essence. When the curability of insanity is proclaimed, what is actually under discussion is insanity in general. But the terms are lacking, the terms that would guarantee authentic universality for the pronouncement while indicating, along with the *fact* of curability, the *reasons* why insanity is by nature curable.

The recourse to statistical generalization is thus an indispensable way of compensating for the deficiencies of the concept. For want of language adequate to the idea and in order to gain access nevertheless to insanity *in general*, people speak of a positively guaranteed cure of *all* insanity, or almost. This seems to us to be the compensatory mechanism that produced and necessitated the strange conviction of absolute empirical effectiveness: a need to embrace the entire field of insanity at least through numbers so as to procure an equivalent of what is felt to be lacking, some unutterable essence. Arithmetical maximalism is nothing else here but a substitute for conceptual universality. Thus the rigidity of the estimations of the number of patients cured is imposed by their secret symbolic function and their inherent inability to match the experiential data, even simply as modifiers. To adapt to the uncertainties of reality and to come to terms with the slippage suggested by the facts would have been to gain in verisimilitude at the expense of logic. To resign oneself to speaking of curing one patient out of two would have been to avoid the imperative of pinpointing the prospect for cure in mental illness as such, and thus to say nothing about the essence of the matter.

The therapeutic optimism of the early days was thus bound to vanish promptly and discreetly from the stage, as if through an inner renunciation of expression. It was impossible, in fact, for that optimism to accept a compromise with the fluctuations and mixed results of experience. But it was also impossible for it to be maintained in the face of even a relative contradiction by the facts. Silence was its only way out. Thus the confused but genuine self-consciousness of the psychiatric rupture returned to the shadows of the inexpressible. Nothing remained on the surface of history to signal the real tenor of the decisive moment that had been played out at the century's beginning regarding the understanding of insanity and its social destiny.

But the disappearance of this ambitious representation of its means and its task, in which a specialized medical approach to insanity was able to recognize itself and be recognized, however briefly, unmistakably refers us to a set of causes that are more diffuse and complex—because they have to do with the origin of that representation and with its very nature as representation—than the direct and immediate cause we began by identifying. It is a classic case of overdetermination: the manifest contradiction, under the circumstances, between the symbolic requirement (what there is to be represented) and the rules of verisimilitude (what can legitimately be represented) suffices to explain the disappearance of the belief in the resources of therapeutics; however, it does not therefore necessarily exhaust the significance of the belief. We are inclined to relate the loss of faith, or the depletion of the discourse, to a profound evolution inscribed logically in advance within the very premises on which the discipline is based—an evolution having to do with the way mental illness is viewed as well as with the implicit project of the institution constructed so as to correspond to it. It seems quite probable that the muting of the initial certainties also reflects an early shift of the alienists' attention toward new objects that were revealed or produced by the encounter between the principles that grew out of the Pinelian reversal and practical experience.

The Obstacle of Time

This is the case with what will later be labeled *chronicity*. We see this notion sketched out right away at the heart of the very earliest psychiatry. The idea takes root and takes on meaning quite precisely at the intersection, at the point of confrontation, between the paradigms presiding over the new therapeutic mechanism and what will rapidly be exposed as the irreducible obstacle of practice. On the one hand, we have the theoretical framework tacitly established by Pinel. Let us recall its terms: curability can always be postulated in theory; incurability always threatens to declare itself in fact. On the other hand, it is self-evident that when the actual results appear to entail fairly regular cures for a persistent mental illness that after a long ordeal appeared to be hopelessly incurable, the attendant uncertainty and surprise will provoke renewed reflection.

Weighing the figures for curability against those for incurability does not fundamentally contradict the newly won idea that the mentally ill patient is accessible in the intimacy of his suffering and thus essentially open to therapeutic intervention. However, attempting to keep the two in balance makes it necessary to consider mental illness from a previously neglected *supplementary* standpoint, and even to redefine it entirely, precisely in terms of the specific way in which it persists. The incurability revealed here actually has nothing in common with the incurability that once led to an a priori rejection of the possibility of treatment. The new incurability is not characterized by complete inaccessibility, by irremediable closure within the self, by the impossibility of any communication. On the contrary, the new sort of "incurable" patient may even appear eminently "curable" at the outset, in that he may be especially receptive to others and disturbed by his own illness. But nothing in his state really changes over the years, despite all the elements that justify the pursuit of moral treatment. The problem is not that unintegratable data pose a challenge to the postulates posited at the outset; it is that an exemplary figure appears *within* the field of observation marked off by these new reference points, the figure of a patient whose noteworthy distinguishing feature is that he integrates and reconciles within himself the extreme features of theoretical curability and pragmatic incurability.

One of Pinel's later texts offers interesting testimony to this crucial ambiguity and to the displacement of the medical attention that it implies. In 1816 Pinel was preparing a final summary of his observations concerning the patients of La Salpêtrière; in his preamble, he noted that recently, and especially since the publication of the new edition of his *Treatise on Insanity*, two objects in particular have held his attention: "1° the general progress of recently declared mania, which appears fully analogous to that of the acute illnesses; 2° the seriousness and the singular frequency of alienations marked by absolute incurability."[20] On the first point at least, Pinel's statement is clearly somewhat enigmatic on the surface. Without seeking to enter into an overly detailed decoding, let us recall that it is not by chance that the *Traité sur l'aliénation mentale* (Treatise on Mental Alienation, translated as *A Treatise on Insanity*) is also called *Traité de la Manie* (Treatise on Mania); Pinel uses the latter title again in the article we are quoting. For Pinel, "mania" is even more than the paradigmatic species of insanity that can shed light on all the others; it is truly the matrix species on which his own overall view of insanity is based. There is no mystery in his particular interest in cases of "recently declared" mania: these are cases in which the fewest contrary influences have been exercised, and consequently they are best able to reveal the inherent truth of the illness. The search for an analogy with "the acute illnesses" is directly related to the problem of curability.

We cannot deal in detail here with Pinel's neo-Hippocratism and his attachment to the doctrinal tradition of cautious "wait-and-see" medicine. Let us simply summarize his views by saying that, for him, the fundamental characteristic of acute illnesses is that they manifest a spontaneous dynamism inclining them toward a cure—they tend to pass, as he puts it, through "successive periods of graduated development, stationary state, decline, and convalescence."[21] The point Pinel has sought to verify through the systematic study of the "general progress of recently-declared mania" is whether mania is indeed invested, like acute illnesses, with a tendency that leads it naturally toward its own decline and extinction.[22] His research has been conclusive: mania is an essentially curable illness, a malady wholly open, in its fundamental dynamism, to a way out.

In other words, Pinel's primary concern, in the wake of the appearance of the second edition of his *Treatise* (though this publication was intended to show that his initial intuitions had been confirmed by experience), is with the actual validity of his theoretical model. What can be said about the true nature of mania, and, by way of mania, about insanity in general? The question is certainly not unrelated to the second object that has held his attention: "the seriousness and the singular frequency of alienations marked by absolute incurability." What if the curability that he had glimpsed and postulated at the outset were in the long run only an illusion? Between the lines, one can detect an uncertainty of this sort—and its defeat. In spite of everything, mental illness remains what it had been thought to be; a thorough study of its most exemplary form confirms this conclusion. But at the same time there is an unanticipated irreducible remainder that has to be taken into account—the "singular frequency" of mental illnesses that may well fall into the general framework but that still bring us up squarely against a paradox. These are cases in which insanity is invested, to be sure, as in all other cases, with an indication of its possible end, but in which it is also so irremediably suspended in time that indefinite duration seems to constitute its true fabric.

Such is the interrogative footing on the basis of which the idea of *chronicity* will gradually be constituted, throughout a multiform process marked by many hesitations and steps backward, a process charged with practical as well as theoretical implications. On the one hand, it is no longer particularly meaningful to speak of incurability, as soon as one acknowledges that throughout insanity's endless course, sometimes over an entire lifetime, some element of the intimate difference between the patient and his malady subsists. This difference means not only that in a profound sense the patient continues to belong to the category of reasonable beings, but also that he must continue to be maintained in a therapeutic context, since the end of his illness, while it cannot be predicted, can never be completely ruled out. On the other hand, it is also not very appropriate to keep using the term *curability* once the dimension of time has been introduced into the idea of madness, since time is the element in which insanity belongs to itself, as it were, the element in which it ultimately escapes our grasp.

Once again, we do not claim to be embracing the full complexity of the real historical process. On the contrary, we are attempting to abstract from it its intelligible framework. In brief, we are trying to accede to the kernel of reason behind the twofold phenomenon that dominated psychiatry in the last century, and that seems to us to constitute a single whole: the irrepressible rise of an all-encompassing category of chronicity, and the slow renunciation of the conceptual pair "curability/incurability." To be sure, what we are suggesting falls far short of accounting for the entire set of aspects that the idea of chronicity may have taken on, including, for example, the crucial notion of the recognition of a progressive and irreversible character in the productions of delirium as well as in the subject's advance into his alienation. But that very example allows us to illustrate briefly the way in which the central operation of synthesis occurred. For what we would have to show is that that notion of progressivity basically results directly from bringing together the categories of curability and incurability in such a way that they are both opposed and inextricably intertwined. Insanity is viewed as continually inclining toward its own "beyond," which on the horizon would be ultimate incurability; yet that horizon is blocked, deferred, postponed almost to the end, in a way that always offers the possibility of further progress toward curability.

These cursory remarks only hint at the major role played in the development of a new understanding of mental illness by the fusion, through reciprocal destitution, of the classical reference points that split insanity between hope and despair. The same fusion also governed the institutional debates over whether or not to create asylums for patients deemed incurable. From this perspective, the history of psychiatry merges in some sense with the history of the hard-won and crucial decision never to pronounce a patient incurable, and thus never to rule out communication and treatment. The history of psychiatry is the history of a slow infusion of curability into incurability, a process in which both terms faded away and owing to which from then on no insane person could be declared inaccessible.

In Pinel's case, the duration of the therapeutic experiment loses all common measure with that of the Hôtel-Dieu or Charenton: going well beyond the formerly prevailing limits of two months or six months, Pinel waits two years before pronouncing his verdict (Esquirol follows his example, moreover). After that time period, there is no more room for hope; Pinel emphasizes this repeatedly. There is no doubt about it: despite the intervening rupture, he continues to think within the old frameworks, which expand but do not shatter. And then, toward the very end of his work (he writes little after 1816), we see him discreetly establish the intellectual mechanism that will ultimately carry off the residue of tradition that has continued to hobble minds, the mechanism destined to take the novelty that had appeared at the beginning of the century as far as it can go. He manages to achieve this from the unique perspective of a certain pessimism in the face of the irreducible aspect of insanity. In the last analysis, at the core of the history of psychiatry, Pinel's pessimism may have been the instrument par excellence of the Cunning of Reason.

Treatment via Institutions

Doctrinal interests evolved quite early, then, in this very young specialized scientific field, and clinical attention shifted toward the persistent nature of mental illness. These developments were no doubt directly related to the retreat of the initial aggressive convictions. But we probably need to turn to a different evolution, one that developed more or less at the same time but even faster and more broadly, in our search for the determining factor that precipitated the dismissal of the initial therapeutic perspectives: we have in mind the evolution of the representations that presided over the practical approach to the insane in the context of the newly constituted asylums. Indeed, we should not forget that the proposition put forth in the first edition of the *Treatise on Insanity*—in whose wake we encounter the faith in the curability of insanity whose effects we have traced—is a pure statement of principle at the institutional level. In this statement Pinel understandably limits himself to positing the bases and determining the rules of a model establishment. He points out possibilities; he gives examples, he indicates paths to follow; in short, he defines the spirit of an institution that would be truly "devoted to curing the insane."

Now, what is remarkable is that the implementation—if not to "their full extent," then at least to a significant degree—of the principles developed in the *Treatise on Insanity* had a profound retroactive effect on those very principles, if it did not completely modify their tenor and orientation. Not only is the ideal of the institution redefined in the implementation process, but in addition and in particular, the goal of any possible treatment of insanity is radically inflected, as is, more banally and more generally, the very way the approach to the insane and the imperatives of their treatment are represented. "Following the observations that gave rise to my Treatise on Insanity, published in Year IX," Pinel writes in 1805, "there still remained to determine, through a vastly increased number of facts, what general and particular measures to take for the regular treatment of insane patients in hospices."[23] However, once the *remainder* in question was completed, it was not simply added to the original data recorded in the *Treatise*; instead, it required an overall recasting of the treatise, and a shift in its center of gravity. Here, *expansion* has become *revision.*

Pinel's systematic, universalizing development of a therapeutic method that was simultaneously official, consistent, and global was not limited to prolonging, exemplifying, and generalizing his initial approach to the treatment of madness; instead, this further development in a sense *closed off* the initial approach by extending it, or, more precisely, by incorporating it within and subjecting it to a different ambition, in that the new project extended to the institution of the asylum as a whole. The book's original aim was embodied institutionally, in a certain respect, only by being lost, by being transmuted and integrated into another project. For this reason, the establishment of the asylum is inseparable from a certain distortion of the idea behind it: if the impetus for the asylum came from the shock created by "discoveries as to the effective cure of insanity through moral treatment," it was only constituted as an institution by displacing the terms of the original invention to such an extent that they became largely unrecognizable.

Nothing better reflects this reworking of the initial idea than the way the organization of Pinel's *Treatise* changed from one edition to the next. Among all the wholesale restructurings and revisions of detail carried out in the body of the work prior to its republication in 1809, those dealing with the exposition of the principles of treatment stand out with particular clarity: first, because they take on a clear-cut form that makes them hard to miss; and second, because what is at stake in terms of their meaning is manifest from the start. To be sure, Pinel's move looks like nothing more than a basic rationalization of the book's argument. What had first been divided into two separate sections (widely separated in the 1800 edition)—section II, "The Moral Treatment of Insanity," and section V, "The Importance of an Enlightened System of Police for the Internal Management of Lunatic Asylums"—are simply combined and recast in a single section in the 1809 edition. The new section IV adopts the title of the earlier section V in a very slightly modified form ("The Importance of an Enlightened System of Police and Rules to Follow for the Internal Management of Lunatic Asylums"). Pinel seems to be trying to combat dispersion and seeking to give his exposition a more linear development; purely technical reasons such as these seem to account for the revisions, at least at first glance. But it does not take long to see that the logical reordering brings with it a major shift of meaning within the work. The text's formal reorganization is inseparable, here, from a critical, covert revolution in its content. For the import of Pinel's gesture can be measured in its capacity as a theoretical act: on this level, Pinel is now incorporating the problematics of moral treatment within the problematics of institutional operations, and, more decisively still, he is subordinating the therapeutic perspective to the perspective of institutional management.

In other words, what had been specified at the outset as the specialized realm of personal, "moral" relations with the patient, and as the no less specialized science of measures that would allow the various entrenchments of insanity to be overcome, is dissolved in this second phase within the general framework of institutional life and of an overall theory of the management of facilities for the insane. Not that the aim of moral treatment has been more or less discreetly abandoned, dismissed, or set aside; not at all. But from this point on it is meaningful only in terms of the operation of an entire establishment, only insofar as it is included in an overall therapeutic project of which the collective undertaking is recognized—at least implicitly—as the chief instrument. Pinel's text has not yet explicitly stated that the institution itself constitutes the most powerful means for healing.[24] But the intellectual framework he posits makes the formulation of the idea possible and necessary in advance, with the tacit transfer from the individual to the collective of the principle that is thought to be efficacious. For this is really what is at stake, finally, above and beyond the reorganization of the book's logical structure: a transfer of the mainspring of moral treatment from the realm of personal relationships to that of inscription and immersion within a communitarian order. With the benefit of hindsight, it is impossible not to see this crucial displacement as the act of thought that determined the destiny of psychiatric practice for over a century. This, then, is the nature of the fundamental revision of the therapeutic perspective which the experience of a "hospice especially devoted to curing the insane" very rapidly led Pinel to embody in his revised text. It might be called an extension of the goal of moral treatment to the dimensions of the collective individual; at all events it involved subsuming moral treatment within the overall task of administering and directing the establishment as a whole.

But as we can see, what is at stake far outstrips the vicissitudes of Pinel's reflection alone. What is refracted and played out at the same time in this modest reorganization of a book is nothing other than the intellectual event that presided over the emergence of the asylum model properly speaking: the fundamental conversion of alienist medicine to what is to be its specific and lasting ambition, and, we must add, the illusion par excellence of its aim, namely, the intent to have therapeutic action exercised entirely through the intermediary of the institution, and confidence in the possibility of doing so. To put it in less abstract terms, it is as though *treating insanity consisted first and foremost of governing a population of insane individuals*.[25] For it is one thing that doctors fought hard to create separate establishments for the insane; the way they invested the space they won, the way they believed in its resources, the way they reorganized, systematized, set up a disciplinary isolation that hospitalization by itself certainly did not require, are something else entirely. Once the specific nature of their establishments had been accepted, at least in principle, there was nothing a priori to keep the alienists from concentrating their prerogatives in a particular treatment sector, following the example of other hospital-based doctors. The fact is—and it is a crucial fact—that they set out in a different direction; they chose to take control of the institution as a whole, and to let nothing escape their sovereign authority. They declared their intention of defining a milieu that would work in every detail to further the therapeutic project.

We can understand very little about the nature of the asylum, despite what is suggested by the facile imagery that surrounds it, if we go no further than its walls. If we really want to understand what gave it its absolute originality in relation to all the other medical facilities, we have to return to the exorbitant project that presided over its definition and its organization. This project entailed the extension of medical power to all aspects of collective existence, in order to allow the institution to exercise total power over the souls of individual patients. The irreducible singularity of the asylum phenomenon was crystallized around that very precisely articulated aim, the same singularity that arose and imposed itself sometime between 1800 and 1809, with Pinel; we can reconstitute its gestation by studying the revisions of the *Traité médico-philosophique.* The specific project in terms of which the entire imposing apparatus of psychiatric assistance as we know it unfolded was determined quite precisely in that locus, between one version of Pinel's work and another. The therapeutic perspective was reinscribed at the heart of managerial authority: through that decisive operation the ideal of the institution was forged, the ideal that has guided and controlled the medical treatment of insanity for so long.

Thus something like a second birth of psychiatry is at stake in the redefinition of "internal management" and of medical authority that Pinel undertook under the impetus of his recent experience at La Salpêtrière. This second birth gave psychiatry its institutional form and the outline of its practice, after it had secured its intellectual foundation with what it called the discovery of the curability of the insane. Or, if it does not seem legitimate to speak of a second birth, it behooves us at least to speak of a two-stage birth, in which the second phase, in which the perspective opened up earlier, is transferred into practice, is also and inseparably the phase in which that perspective is not quite hidden from sight, perhaps, but covered over, buried, set aside within a new perspective that at once conceals and maintains it, keeps it, neutralizes it, and dissimulates it. For it is clear that the two moments of this complex gestation are not simply joined by addition. We do not find the breakthrough of an idea on the one hand and the moment of its concrete realization on the other, like two logical phases that need only to be added together to produce the complete process—even though in this case the realization is accompanied by a perceptible alteration of the idea. On the contrary, the operation presents itself under the auspices of the most straightforward continuity; the same moral treatment is merely displaced and raised, as it were, to the power of the collectivity.

With this sense of the continuity of the idea without regard to its change of level, we may well be getting down to the very root of the illusion that gripped alienist medicine when it originally identified itself with the institution in this way. The decoy par excellence that operated to ensnare psychiatry through the mirage of intrinsic efficiency in its apparatus for confinement was precisely the tacit conviction that, once translated from the individual pole to the collective pole, moral treatment remained essentially unchanged—as if, from one's hold over the subjectivity of one individual singular patient, one could move without the slightest discontinuity to a simultaneous hold over the souls of all; as if it were the same thing, or at least a gesture of the same order, to address oneself directly to an individual and to communicate indirectly with all through the intermediary of the institution; as if the latter constituted a necessary and transparent relay.

At the root of the upheaval through which psychiatry took recourse to the resources and presumed powers of the asylum, we find the intervention of this radically deceptive certainty that what had been initially discovered as moral treatment could be retained intact once it was transposed to the scale of an entire community. The blind spot, which under the circumstances served as a point of passage and a condition of possibility, was the complete distortion of the prospect of curing mental illness through moral means, a distortion implied by the change of register. The asylum apparatus was constructed on the basis of this primary misunderstanding, and consequently on the very principle of its failure: as soon as the illusion had time to declare itself, with the inexorable wearing down of the institutional aim, the impossibility of the asylum project came into view. The history revealed in these foundational years is a divided, contradictory one: on the one hand, there was a primordial opening to the truth of insanity, but almost at once, on the other hand—and it was all the more decisive in that it was destined to be materialized in an immense apparatus for treatment and confinement—there was an irreversible commitment to the pursuit of a chimera: the institution that cures.

Still, we must not be too quick to adopt the terminology of illusion and use it to relegate the long and arduous work of the asylums to the pure inconsistency of a phantasmagoria. For asylums did not exist for nothing; it is not as if on judgment day, at the conclusion of a long parenthesis, they left the problem in the state in which they found it. Invisibly but radically, they displaced the terms of the problem. If it is important to stress the profoundly illusory aspects of the goals of the asylum's advocates, it is just as important to pay attention to the transformation of insanity that actually occurred by means of and under cover of that chimerical vision. The asylum no doubt failed to cure the insane in the sense in which its inventors intended. But by virtue of its very project, by virtue of the means it adopted, by virtue of the methods it had to use in order to conform to its own goal, and—this cannot be stressed too strongly—*entirely without its agents' knowledge*, it completely changed the face and status of insanity, by functioning, as we shall see, as a gigantic apparatus for socialization, as a machine for reducing the insane person's highly resistant alterity.

The authentic task of the asylum was, then, throughout its history, to contribute to its own disappearance or at least to the methodical, though unconscious, demonstration of its own uselessness. It was constituted around a blindness that predestined it to failure, in terms of its explicit ambition. But on the other hand it was destined to work tirelessly, though unwittingly, toward its own demise. As much the trajectory of an illusion as the hidden progress of an essential revelation, the history of the asylum has thus been oriented toward effacement from the beginning. Except that—here is an ultimate reservation provoked by recent debates about its usefulness—perhaps something else still remains to be brought to light in the history of the asylum. Perhaps there is a final component that would contribute, on the contrary, to maintaining it in spite of everything, and even to making its disappearance impossible. For a long time now the asylum has appeared irremediably condemned, and yet it survives and resists, as if at some level beneath its obvious defects, it were taking root in a reason for being that is more powerful than surface intentions and visible determinations. Might it not be the case that a profound connection has developed between insanity and institutions, one that we remain powerless to dismantle? It may well be the case that the birth of the asylum coincided with the search for an institution that would remedy the disorganization of the subjective being; in any event, after the project of a therapeutic collectivity has come undone, the question remains, unsurpassable, and continues to challenge us.

Treating insanity remains fundamentally a matter of seeking to organize the world around psychosis in such a way as to repair its deep rift. This is *also* what was at stake in the beginning when the project of moral treatment was extended to an entire population: the extension of imperatives of "neutrality"—let us have the courage to use this word—to the human and material environment of the insane, imperatives called for by the singular nature of insanity, and initially used on the level of the individual. Whatever we may think of it, this generalizing move remains for us a vital problem and an insurmountable necessity.

CHAPTER II

The Politics of the Asylum

Changing Man, Producing Man

If we try to reconstruct the way the crucial conversion came about, it appears as though the insane asylum began to dominate medical thinking with its own logic, that is to say, its own phantasmatic construction, almost from the start. For it is clear that the pattern of authority within which psychiatric practice was integrated is a borrowed model, endowed with an abstract general validity. While this pattern found an exemplary embodiment in the insane asylum, it could not have been invented there. Doctors did not use the asylum to create a unique, unprecedented structure. They took their cue from a recently developed ideal of institutional order, an ideal that was explicitly prevalent in one entire sector of activity but that actually traversed the full extent of the social field in a diffuse way, for it was derived from the very essence of the society that had grown out of the democratic revolution. In short, doctors espoused, or, more precisely, allowed themselves to be subjugated by, the paradigmatic project of *an organization of collective space that could change man.*

The project was inseparable, in its emergence, from the immense rupture that is at the origin of modern societies and to which the French Revolution lent the exceptional strength of its language. As we know, the explicit restoration of the principle of sovereignty to the people was the central feature of that event. But another well-known phenomenon needs to be emphasized here as well: the way in which society's full recovery of the right to define itself and the power to organize itself, a right and a power until then ascribed to divine will as manifested in the person of the king, was translated into concrete reality. If the rejection of the transcendent roots of power instituted a perfect harmony, on the theoretical level, between the motivations of society and the will of its officials, in practice what emerged was the state's unlimited right to act and its unlimited pragmatic power over society. Taking a Tocquevillean interpretation to the extreme, then, one might plausibly view the revolutionary moment as the decisive incident in a lengthy process of growth and assertion on the part of the state. In stripping the supernatural world of its status as true source of legitimacy and authority, the revolution might be seen as simply removing the final obstacle separating the process from complete fulfillment. The revolutionary developments that put the principles of collective organization at humanity's disposal and acknowledged human beings as the sole producers of their own history also allowed the state to come fully into its own by appropriating society's newly liberated power over itself.

In a supreme paradox and an enigmatic reversal of the democratic experience, wherever society was proclaimed and instituted as its own master it also experienced the ordeal of an unprecedented dispossession. In theory and in practice, it is society that produces power. And yet, beyond constitutions and rules, or through them, as never before in history, it is power that concretely and symbolically produces society. Here is the key point in the development of the political model whose roots we are seeking: by virtue of the democratic revolution, a standpoint of power from which society as a whole appears to be managed, organized, and constituted, is imported within the social field itself—a standpoint of absolute power, as it were, provided that the term *absolute* is not understood to mean "arbitrary capriciousness," absolute power in Tocqueville's sense: "an immense, protective power," "thoughtful of detail, orderly, provident, and gentle," embracing "the whole of social life" so as to cover it "with a network of petty, complicated rules that are both minute and uniform."[1] Not power that seeks above all to impose its own particular will, but power that aims to know society inside out in order to be able to control it concretely, even in its limits and its depths—as if, to bring society into being, it were necessary to give shape to public power. Power takes on the ultimate task of perfecting the constitution of society as such by recombining its most discrete elements. Its goal becomes twofold in a remarkable way, and the extraordinary—and necessary—division between masters and subjects comes into play. On the one hand, power requires the establishment of a place from which nothing can escape, from which everything can be known, controlled, supervised, and verified at all times. And, on the other hand, owing to the pure externality of that vantage point, power is accompanied by the will to produce a society that coincides perfectly with the sacred principles that have been instilled from the outside.

Here we have reached the political source of the dominant schema of modern societies, the level of *organization.* On the one hand, there are people who define—in the name of *knowledge,* it is important to note, not in the name of their own desire—the right way to proceed, to behave, to act; and, on the other hand, there are people who are asked only to merge with the order thus determined. To the extent that that order has been established precisely in view of its correspondence with the immediate possibilities of individuals and the collectivity, it requires neither reflection nor feeling but rather a virtually mindless adherence. We find this division everywhere in our own society, from pedagogy to the scientific organization of work; it subtends everyday bureaucratic rationality just as it traverses the most grandiose of revolutionary dreams. Across the breadth of the social it endlessly refracts the exorbitant good will of secularized power. This new power is exclusively attached to the production of a good society and destined by that very token to put itself in society's place, to know society via substitution, in order ultimately to restore society to itself while sparing it the need for thought.

The ideal of absolute separation between learned elaboration and mindless execution is the truly specific property of the modern mechanisms of power. At one extreme, this ideal will be translated into the implacable and aberrant rigor of industrial work, which is organized in terms of a radical separation between polar opposites: the overall conception, which has both to grasp the entire process and to break it down as finely as possible, and the execution of detail, in which each agent is not only deprived of any overall understanding of the chain of gestures in which he is inserted, but is also *thought by the other*, right down to the smallest shifts of body position. But at the other extreme, the ideal will become the dream of a society so in harmony with its own mode of organization and the intimate necessity of its laws that it functions without representation, in the limpid tranquillity of a natural progression.

Such a society seemingly has nothing in common with slave labor. Yet the perspectives are analogous and the thought patterns, if we look closely enough, are in a profound way the same. For what is it that makes it possible even to formulate such a project of conciliation, if not the existence of a power structure that presents itself as capable of bringing the project to fruition on the one hand, and that entertains the project as its own secret ambition and, as it were, its obligatory illusion, on the other hand? The will to make society and social organization coincide is expressed, consciously or unconsciously, from the standpoint of power. Behind the idea of a society that coincides perfectly with its own rules and its own way of being, an omnipresent and omniscient state is presumed to intervene. The state not only produces a society in complete harmony with truth, but it also puts itself in society's place so as to conceptualize it in its truth. The state is entrusted with all thinking about those aspects of society that society embodies and deploys without thought. The experience of various nations in this century is sufficiently fraught, as we know, to verify the hypothesis and to reveal the absolute political constraint that parallels and conditions the noble and recent goal of a society without difference.

Between the factory and the contemporary totalitarian state, the gap is immense in all respects, to be sure, and nothing would be more absurd than to seek to merge in a single category phenomena that have so little in common in scope and register. But the very difference between these phenomena allows us to see the extraordinary fact that *the articulation of power* remains fundamentally identical at both poles. Pure agents viewed as destined to the blessed opacity of nonreflection are split off from leaders defined by the sovereign knowledge that they are presumed to possess. Those who know oversee those who do not, shaping their existence and claiming, literally, to constitute them. On the one hand, we find mute conformity with a rule or with the specifications of a plan whose very tenor it is best not to know; on the other hand, we find a methodical replacement of those who obey by those who know, and the artificial, exhaustive, and meticulous recreation of their world.

To be thought by others, to think in the place of others: here we have the ultimate, perfected form of the bond of power in modern societies, a bond that is in essence, properly speaking, totalitarian. We have deliberately chosen to focus on it in a place where its exercise implies coldblooded compulsion or overt violence—thus in a place where the bond of power is on display, along with its means and its ends, in unequivocal nudity. But under more neutral and sometimes more attractive faces, this bond has been diffused throughout the social fabric; it has dismantled the traditional figures of hierarchy and given rise to new institutional arrangements.

Turning to what may be the most original undertaking in this vast enterprise of reinvention and imposition, we find that Michel Foucault has admirably restored to us an obscure but decisive chapter involving the genesis of the *disciplines* and of what could be called programming of the body. The development of the gestures of military life (both marching and exercise) that Foucault traces is striking, almost allegorical in its scope. His book illuminates with particular clarity the transition marking the entry of the various powers into modern forms for the management of human concerns. In describing the way military marching is controlled, Foucault points to the transition from the injunction to respect a collective rhythm, as defined by a drumbeat, to the detailed redefinition of a soldier's step in which "the act is broken down into its elements; the position of the body, limbs, articulations is defined; to each movement are assigned a direction, an [amplitude], a duration; their order of succession is prescribed."[2]

In short, Foucault describes the shift from an external understanding of authority, in which the proper form of the act is obtained by submission to the rule imposed, to an expropriative, substitutive understanding that is productive of order, in which authority ensures in advance the proper execution of the act by programming it in all its details; "it controls its development and its stages from the inside" (ibid.), exhaustively reconstituting the intimate connections into which the gestures are made to flow. A shift from an imperative that it behooves you to respect to a plan that traverses you, a plan that governs even the smallest components of your movements in your stead, a plan that you are asked merely to implement. To be sure, this controlling aim has the body as its target, and the dispossession implied appears all the more singular in its exorbitance, since it is depriving you of the most intimate and most basic self-mastery. But the model adopted is not so very different, even if it is not anchored in such spectacular anatomical materiality, when the pedagogic relation that presides over language learning, for example, becomes a relation between a programmer of exercises based on the science of unconscious linguistic structures and a pupil who is presumed to be invested with the laws of discourse without even being aware of them—a relation functioning solely through the intervention of precisely regulated and wholly programmed discourse. Here the dispossession of the executing agent may be imperceptible, gentle, and protective, but it remains strictly the same from the structural standpoint. Similarly, the ambition of the conceiving agent remains formally analogous, even though it is aimed only at a child's development rather than at the inhuman cohesion of military troops. In both enterprises the objective is to make oneself master of the entire process through which the other (soldier or schoolchild) must pass. That process is to be reconstructed on the other's terms and in his order in such a way that the other, ideally, can merge so completely with the program governing his actions that he will be unaware of the overall constraint.

In the final analysis, the two enterprises take their inspiration from a single schema of power. The one stems from a violent and pioneering effort to make authority penetrate into the deepest, most primitive levels of the social fabric, the other from the humanist, if not "revolutionary," desire to put an end to the techniques of coercion in the educational process; they are separated by nearly two centuries. And yet, despite divergences and distinctions, the aim that subtends both enterprises is identical in form and structure. This aim was just beginning to emerge when the process for fabricating footsoldiers that Foucault analyzed was being put in place. Since then, it has been broadened and generalized, and also sublimated and softened; today its subtle omnipresence makes it virtually unlocalizable. When it comes to identify itself with *organization* as an activity and an end in itself, or, to use Max Weber's terminology, when it reaches the point of espousing the rationalizing ethos of bureaucracy, that aim is consubstantial with the nature of power in modern societies.

The specific functioning of this mechanism is characterized, as we have already seen, by expropriation, substitution for the other, determination to make the other coincide wholly with the program to which he is assigned. More abstractly, the mechanism might be defined as a combination of three elements: a certain *localization* of power, a specific type of operation, and a precise notion of the intended effects. In the first place, then, the agent of power must be in a position that enables him to know everything; no aspect of the sector of humanity or sociability he controls may be allowed to escape him. Within the historical framework he chose to examine, Foucault highlighted this first principle as an imperative of visibility that was implemented, signified, and embodied in exemplary fashion in the great architectural dream of panoptic machines.

We shall not embark upon a discussion here of the more symbolic than utilitarian character that those too-perfect surveillance mechanisms seem to us to have acquired; let us simply note that those mechanisms seem to have had the particular function of translating, in a concrete and thus telling way, a thought whose abstract extension to the new field opening up to power was in other respects highly unclear. This new field was "optically" free, as it were, from inspection and control. Now, somewhere between metaphorical experimentation and allegorical embodiment, a self-definition of power couched in topological terms sought to establish itself through the invention of the panopticon. The defining feature of the panopticon is an eye from which nothing is hidden owing simply to the place it occupies: the panopticon articulates a place, a space, and a task that constitute the inexhaustible matrix of the modern bond of authority. Its gaze is all the more infallibly efficacious in that it is itself removed from the vision of those it envelops—and because in fact it is not supposed to be inscribed on the same level as the objects of its gaze. It institutes a topological disjunction between active and passive, viewer and visible, that constitutes modern society's version of the old dissymmetry between Masters and Subjects, between directors and executants.

In the guise of architectural figuration, what is at stake is the shaping of a fundamental social schema destined one day to control hierarchical relations and the mode of exercise of authority as a whole. On the one hand, then, there is a requirement of readability—the need to conceptualize action and organization in such a way as to make them globally graspable from a presumed outside; there is also a postulate of integral exposition and universal accessibility—the possibility of an exhaustive command of information in a given sector. On the other hand, that requirement and that postulate are necessary because the possibility exists that one may remove oneself from the common space of social action so as to reach a global vision of that space from an entirely different place (a postulate of the spatial "transcendence" of power), and because by the same token the agency that maintains itself elsewhere, apart, has a unique legitimacy based on knowledge: power has its own right to know, which determines the scope of its mandate. On the one hand, in other words, there is a strictly defined type of submission, and on the other, a no less specific project of domination. The bond of subordination may not have been created yesterday; nevertheless, its visage is not timeless. It takes on a very particular form in societies that, like our own, come to see themselves as free from what had been from the outset the external source of all legitimacy and sovereignty, namely, the power of the gods.

For the modern distinction among functions and roles based on power has new characteristics that stem directly from the emancipatory choice through which human autonomy was affirmed and recognized. Nothing remains in society—customs, rules, traditions, received forms—whose unintelligible necessity would refer back to the creator's unfathomable wisdom or to mysterious decrees of providence. Nothing remains, then, that is exempt from investigation; nothing remains in human space that is not deemed available, a priori, to the grasp of intelligence and open to full explanation. The social-human universe is in theory readable. But in the same way, there is no longer anything superior to the power that can endow it with legitimacy and meaning through delegation or reflection; thus nothing can confine this power to a limited role as intermediary for an omniscience and an omnipotence reigning independently elsewhere. Consequently, nothing remains to keep power from appearing as the ultimate agency of right, reason, and truth in the social order, as the general source of intelligibility of the human world. Thus we have the fatal conjunction, in sum, between the opening of a field of knowledge whose extension and depth are unprecedented, and the emergence of an intellectual agent invested with incomparable legitimacy holding a unique position of monopoly. At one extreme, there is the all-encompassing state; at the other extreme, there are minor authorities scattered over the full extent of the social realm; these gradually come to reproduce, in miniature, the schema that pairs good authority from which nothing must be dissimulated with human beings educated to believe that everything concerning themselves can be known and to expect that the other, the state, with global information at its command, will take them in hand.

Even so, the knowledge involved, which becomes as it were the very element and the inherent stake of the power relation, is inseparable from a certain form of *action*, for the state has responsibility for literally *making* society *exist*. In reality, the recognition that society explains everything in terms of society itself cannot be separated from the awareness that it *produces* itself, that it changes owing to a set of purely internal causes and forces, that it never ceases to create itself, that it bears within itself the full power to *make itself*. Ours is the first society to be inaugurated without reference to an external foundation. By that very token, it is the first to assume its own historicity explicitly. This historicity takes the form, to be sure, of an immense legacy from the past that must be inventoried and managed, but it also takes the form of a vertiginous appeal to the future. Tomorrow will be another day, something else again, necessarily; the shape it will take is entirely up to us.

Our society is the first to take on the task of looking inward in order to reshape itself completely, the first to require itself to reexamine itself through and through in order to fabricate itself, in view of an absolutely other form that it knows it possesses and to which it has the primordial imperative of giving birth. One can appreciate the renewal of the prospects for social action provoked by such a compelling consciousness of change, with its immediate corollary, the obligatory reckoning with the dimension of the future. Nothing in the legacy, nothing we have received or been given, can legitimately be deemed untouchable. On the contrary, everything has to be viewed with an eye to revision, reform, or replacement. Conversely, there is nothing in the social-human order that cannot be knowingly produced, or even wholly fabricated. What was unconscious work for our predecessors has to become for us—we who know ourselves to be authors and who think we are in charge of tomorrow—the fruit of a deliberate project, an explicit intention. Here no doubt lies the most remarkable feature of the representation of power inherent in our will to history: the artificialism, the underlying vision of a world whose components are all created by art and calculation—the tacit postulation, in other words, that it is possible to recreate any sort of human milieu or segment of sociability, both in a radical way, by going back to the most elementary levels, and in an exhaustive way, by using science to rediscover an authentic organic coherence. This is what will henceforth indicate to power its practical horizon and give full meaning to its vantage point of knowledge. Its elective function will be precisely to constitute the social realm that requires the production of a future, that is to say, first and foremost, to organize it.

The inaugural task of modern power is to put an end to the anarchy of things that merely exist. One cannot be content simply to register the mindless incoherence of what is already here. One must be able to give an account of what is: hence the need for an inflexible and patient enterprise of inventory, definition, and rule-making, an undertaking destined to ensure compatibilities, communications, and consistencies at all points. The institutional detail has to be woven into the uniform fabric of the general will. In short, the social must be constructed as an organizable entity, that is, a chain of elements, mechanisms, and relations, all perfectly known and thus transformable and reproducible at will. Such is the gigantic adaptation of society to its duty of historicity, to its own capacity to change itself, which the agent par excellence of social transformation—the State—has been ceaselessly promoting over the past two centuries. Henceforth acting in the name of the need for the human community to constitute itself, this State has found no obstacles to its subtle, capillary penetration of society.

Even so, what is at stake here is in a sense only a preliminary and minimal organizing task in view of organization itself, aiming above all—and this is by no means self-evident—to guarantee itself an effective and direct hold on society. This initial rationalizing endeavor does not have its end in itself. It is meaningfully carried out only when it is supported by a limitless phantasmagoric ambition. The ambition may be open or hidden, enacted or suppressed; in any event, it is always there, underlying the attempt at rationalizing as the signifying schema that alone justifies the effort. This time we are dealing not merely with the project of making the social something potentially masterable, but also with the concurrent, globalizing decision to *bring it fully into being*, without reservation or remainder, through an operation that would possess full knowledge of the workings of the collective machinery and that would generate those workings concretely. In reality, this phantasm of generative omniscience has met various fates, from the totalitarian states to the micro-embodiments dispersed throughout a social fabric that is in other respects more slack or more resistant. The fact remains that, whether it is silent or triumphant, explicitly advocated or obscurely active, the phantasm haunts our societies, reflecting back to them the dream image of their power.

Self-construction: in the abstract, here is the true and unsurpassable dimension of a society thrown outside of itself, as it were, and into a posture of self-directed omnipotence by the revelation of its dynamism and the prospect of its future, except that in the actual process of production the terms are reversed, and what is involved is *being constructed*. It is as if the agency of power were appropriating and reserving for itself the sort of social reflectivity that is aroused by historical consciousness, in order to constitute from without an order based entirely on thought, an order that is to that very extent opaque, at least ideally, to the executants who are to be integrated in it. The symbolic power of society to construct itself is the power of the state, along with the various scattered relays of institutional authority, to construct society. In other words, the state is empowered to posit itself as the *self* of society, as the agency that concentrates the clear self-consciousness of the community within itself; it takes on the community's capacity to refabricate itself on a rational basis, and in its benevolent monopoly it spares the community from having to think itself.

On the side of power, there is omniscience and radical productive power; on the other side, there is the happy, mindless coincidence between pure agents and a framework and a plan in which they can be fully incorporated. Here is the very situation we noted earlier as the modern form par excellence of the division between directors and executants: a situation properly designated as the *ideal of organization*, in the strong and full sense of the word, if we bear in mind the inextricable intertwining of its two aspects. On the one hand, it entails a belief in the possibility of constituting from without, and in a purely rational, artificial way, a system of places, roles, and relationships among the individuals who make up the society; on the other hand, and correlatively, it entails a belief in the possibility of putting everyone so precisely in his or her place, of assigning each individual such a specific and clearcut function, that there is no need for individuals to understand the whole in which they are included; it will be "natural" for them simply to act out, in complete ignorance, their assigned parts in the program.

On the one hand, then, we confront the most resolute artificialism. But on the other hand—and this is a particularly important point—we encounter the apparently contradictory aim of complete correspondence, of perfect, spontaneous, nonreflective, "natural" adjustment on the part of the individuals in question to the norm, plan, or program that is imposed entirely from without. The point is clearly crucial, and it becomes intelligible only in relation to the essential transformations of the idea of law that are implied by the revolutionary reappropriation of sovereignty and the restoration to society of its own founding principle. We shall have to be content with tracing the broad outlines of this upheaval very briefly. Still, we cannot overemphasize the fact that the upheaval is central to the spectacular mutations that the representation of humankind has undergone over the last two centuries; indeed, it may well constitute one of the most powerful driving forces behind those changes.

Within the framework of a transcendent conception of the foundations of society, law lies inherently *outside* individuals in some sense (even though they encounter it within themselves); it is different in its essence from what human movement conveys on its own, so that the obedience that law requires is also an intellectual act of submission to a will superior to one's own. However we interpret the bond that subjects creatures to their creator, an irreducible alterity will always remain, an alterity that defines our relation to the fundamental injunctions designed to guide our existence as an encounter with exteriority, a straightforward, unmediated collision with the outside. Whereas as soon as it is postulated, to the contrary, that law is the expression of the social will alone, and that it has absolutely no meaning except insofar as it formulates what one takes to be good and right for society, law can be conceptualized under the sign of coincidence.

Modern law, then, is expected to provide the basis for immediate harmony between the deep-seated desires of society and the nature of things. And if such harmony were taken to the extreme, we would no longer be aware of the law's existence. We find fault with our laws precisely to the extent that they violate the spontaneous consent of subjects, that they take on a form of external opposition that makes them artificially constraining, that they demand a forced—and therefore pernicious—obedience. We criticize laws in the conviction that, if such artificial constraints still exist today, and if there exists a more profound difference or separation between the law and the collectivity in action, the reason is that society is divided, traversed by a conflict that pits the oppressed against the oppressors. In a future society truly in harmony with itself, however, there can be no such distance between its actual tendencies and its rules. Such a society must eliminate the violence of imperatives, generally speaking, in favor of a harmonious coincidence between collective activity and the principles destined to guide it. To be sure, law is always the expression of what must be, but no longer in the sense in which there would be an inherent, unbridgeable gap being human beings and their duties—on the contrary, instead, in the sense in which what must be *will be.* The prescriptiveness of law proceeds from the movement of minds and things; it simply assigns to that movement the forms it is to take. According to the modern view, law takes on body and necessity only through its possible and virtual *identity* with the behaviors it is supposed to govern. And as we can see quite clearly today, this is how law comes to be degraded into norms. Rather than allying itself with what is imposed from the outside, with what requires an awareness of obligation and a will to obey, it tends to adopt what happens to be enacted by the majority, what is indicated through collective practice, as the rule to which it conforms unquestioningly, of its own accord. On the one hand, there is an understanding that the intimate harmony between the collective will and the social being is what makes law; and on the other hand, it is understood that humans are made to live spontaneously according to the rule of law, that they do not need to impose such a rule on themselves by force and reflection, that on the contrary they are destined to respect it, from the outset and unconsciously, since respect for law is in the final analysis what constitutes them as subjects.

This idea is incontestably the most revolutionary idea of our time, not only because it has overturned our anthropological conceptions, but also because it depends in every respect on the process unleashed by the political revolution out of which our democratic societies have grown. It leads to one of that revolution's most significant results: the idea that the foundation of law is also the condition of possibility of human subjects, that, in the animal-that-is-the-human-being, law is the pivot around which a subject is constituted, the conduit through which the subject comes into being; the idea, consequently, that humans relate to law through inherent conformity with what defines their being at the deepest level, not by adhering to it, plying themselves to it, or obeying it, but by slipping themselves into it unthinkingly, by postulating it unconsciously; the idea, correlatively, that every unmistakable transgression stems from a primary failure of the process of constitution of the subject, from an inherently defective integration into the dimension of law.

This idea has not come to prominence, of course, in such elaborate academic language. Nevertheless, without passing directly through discourse, it has prospered in what could be called the social perception. Reigning by delegation, it is even increasingly omnipresent in collective consciousness, in the form of an elementary conviction that sums up its practical consequences: in essence, all crimes are pathological. Behind this cursory article of faith that is nevertheless unsurpassable in some sense for the spirit of the times, as is demonstrated by the constant use its detractors make of it, an immense revolution has completely upset the relation of individuals to law. Law has been brought back from the irreducible difference in which it demanded conscious choice to the most immediate of proximities—the proximity of the very thing of which you are unaware and that institutes you.

This transfer of the place of law toward the unconscious inner space of the subject has an additional consequence, one that may be less striking but that is of the utmost importance in the context that interests us. It does not involve the interpretation of pathologies but rather the orientation of therapies. How can one cure what is denounced as illness? The premises governing the diagnosis indicate a suggested treatment response. The whole problem clearly lies in the development of strategies that will allow the law to permeate the individual and that will restructure his personality without his knowledge, without his awareness. These strategies will have to focus on the dimension that was deficient at the outset, the dimension that is to be restored as if by osmosis.

This redefinition of the legal principle within society, and the crucial transformation of the role and the prospects of power that it necessarily implies, have a direct political impact. Power was classically charged with preserving the laws, making sure they were observed, pursuing infractions, and imposing sanctions: it was the power of interdiction, overt constraint, and punishment. Power construed in this way tends to bring out the striking externality of law and to highlight its character of coercive injunction. But as soon as the ideal of law becomes the ideal of coincidence between acts and rules, its function changes completely. It now has to strive to predict behavior and adapt norms. Through an extraordinary effort to anticipate the conduct of its subjects, it has to develop normative frameworks into which individuals can fit, frameworks that their acts can espouse without violence and even without conscious decision. The problem is no longer one of imposing rules, of making it known that imperatives exist. The problem is one of anticipating the spontaneous movement of individuals and containing it. It is no longer a matter of securing obedience, of obtaining explicit submission, but of producing conforming behavior as if from within.[3]

Authority in operation will thus take on the character of programming, by and large. There can be no viable commandment without prior reflection about what good execution can and must be, or without a detailed determination of its paths and means; the agent will merely have to provide effects and substance for an act already fully composed in the abstract. There can be no good government on any scale without an exact and constructive science of behavior, capable of penetrating the hidden laws of government and producing an inventory of its mainsprings so as to reconstitute its best possible forms from within. And the best possible forms are those that are most regular, most economical, easiest to deploy; consequently, they are the forms that, once adopted, require the least explicit intervention of will, owing to their coincidence with the primordial constraints of action. For the programming ambition is guided by a double ideal: to use artifice to create something more natural than nature, and to do so in order to reduce proportionately the need for conscious participation on the part of the executants.

This strange science proposes obstinately and methodically to produce ignorance in the beings it studies. We have limited our purview to transformations in the status of law, that is, the explicit and codified body of fundamental prescriptions framing the collective practice in a given society. But the meaning of the evolution we are describing clearly lies in the tendency to dissolve the specificity of the imposition of law within the undifferentiated whole constituted by the rational organization of authority and regulation-driven management. There is no further need, in fact, for a violently manifest agency of difference charged in its absolute preeminence with reminding people of the existence of an order and a will that surpass them, and of imperatives that in some sense overwhelm them. The state gradually loses its sacred aura and begins to appear as just one element among others, in a vast branching network of agencies that define norms and develop the framework of action for social agents. It is a crucial element, to be sure, by virtue of its coordinating function, but it has no special dignity. Hence the idea, to a large extent legitimate, that in such a system power consists in a *relation*, and that truth is not to be sought in the direction of a special foyer that would monopolize the exercise of power in society, but rather in the direction of the multitude of relations through which it passes concretely—and in which it reveals itself to be substantially the same everywhere. This occurs because, in our society, power takes on the consistency of a uniform and global *management of the other*, and because it comes in fact to be embodied electively in a type of operation in which, if one seeks to define its essence, *who* commands and *who* obeys, and the very nature of what is to be executed, matter less than *how* the process works—the mode of the relation, as it were. Nor can one legitimately credit any specific agency of society with a monopoly on such operations, for all types of authority tend to merge; they appear to operate on the same level, flowing together into a single structure.

What the state develops is no different in theory, at the level of the model, from what any holder of a modicum of power generates in his limited sphere. However, if we place too much faith in the undeniable functional uniformization of power, we lose sight of the overall social project that obscurely produces it and in relation to which it takes on meaning. That project, for its part, can be explained only in relation to the new power with which the state finds itself invested in a society that claims to define itself, and in relation to the quite specific power to produce a perfected, integrally organized society that coincides fully with its own norms and operational rules—a society that will be defined by the project itself.

At the root of the atomization of powers into a multiplicity of local foyers of production and organization of the other, there is an unprecedented phantasmagoria of social Oneness from which each of these microenterprises draws its principle and its aim. The dispersed and multiform effort to know the other in his stead, to elaborate his gestures and his thoughts, to adjust him to the proper shape, exists only against the background of a great dream of ultimate unification. The state provides not only an image of this unification, but also the means for its patient enactment on an everyday basis—if it does not end up adhering to the dream as if that dream were the ultimate meaning of its own mission, and decreeing its terrifying realization. The model for this power has taken on the consistency of a relation, and it has a birthplace in history: the place in which the relationship between state and society takes precisely the form of a *relation* between ideally disconnected terms. The state separates itself from society in order to embody its productive externality with respect to itself and its full power to construct itself. We have moved from the natural superiority of the prince to a difference in the location of the governing agencies, a difference that simultaneously defines their task and assigns them a goal. The aim is to exploit that potential for difference to the utmost, to take separation to the extreme, in order to acquire more and more power to know and to produce society from the outside. Thus it will finally be possible to institute a society in ultimate conformity with itself—that is, to bring about the division between an omniscient regulatory agency and pure agents who have been restored once and for all, in the clarity of immediacy, to the ultimate simplicity of an existence that follows the rules so closely that it no longer needs to be aware of itself.

On the horizon of every particular effort to achieve strict coincidence between individuals and the program that embraces and moves them, we find a concealed will to accomplish itself completely through the end of history. For beneath the surface features of the society that has finally been reconstructed according to the truth of its natural laws or restored to its unique essential necessity, and thereby delivered from the need for representation, so that it has only to produce itself as action, there is an ultimate goal: the advent of the good society toward which the future is understood to tend. This is the prospect that gives fundamental meaning to the action of power in our societies. Power seeks the definitive correspondence of human beings with what is viewed as the ultimate law of their organization; power is what invisibly provokes and nourishes the phantasmagoria of such correspondence. Power pursues this correspondence tirelessly, whatever it may claim, and even when it denies or fails to recognize that it is doing so, it is destined to progress in that direction alone, to decode itself in that mirror alone, to understand itself in that idea alone. The meticulousness and subtlety of the smallest agency of power, of the finest mechanism of subjection, cannot be understood apart from the excessiveness of power in search of its absolute, and in pursuit of the most total of projects. And this latter power is well localized; it is not at all discreet: we know it as the state.

We have been endeavoring to retrace the abstract genesis of the *institutional form* that prevails in our society, that is, the genesis of the way in which the exercise of authority is articulated in society. We have strongly emphasized the extent to which form is inseparable here from *content*, and the extent to which the originality of the prevailing mechanisms of power lies precisely in their capacity to imply a representation of the good society, or even in the fact that on the humblest level they unfold concretely only in relation to a specific, though implicit, idea of the ultimate ends of the human adventure. But there is one particular point in this overall conceptualization of power that we must highlight in terms of our own special focus. The project of *changing humanity* may seem to be a trivial one today, at least in its expression; yet it is actually quite an extraordinary endeavor. It constitutes a direct consequence, an obligatory corollary, an exemplary figure in any case, of society's enterprise of self-production. It would take another hefty volume to reconstitute the formation of such an idea; we shall limit ourselves here to noting its obvious links with the appearance of a clear historical consciousness.

Man becomes. He is not confined to a single, fixed, timeless form; on the contrary, in every respect—his seemingly most spontaneous dispositions, his affective reactions, his most thoughtful inclinations, his customs, the overall orientation of his thoughts—he changes, and profoundly, according to the situation and the epoch. This means that he himself is in some sense a product. It also means that it must be possible, to some extent, to produce man deliberately, now that we have access to the idea of this undertaking that the human race has pursued unwittingly for so long. Within this overall interpretive framework, we can identify the intermediary role that notions such as milieu may have played, and we can recognize the multiple influences that have helped form a representation of man as the result of a process of constitution and fabrication. Finally, from a properly philosophical viewpoint, we know what role is played in the formation of this genetic, artificialist vision of humanity by the empiricist rejection of innate ideas, by the empiricist image of the intellect as a blank slate, and by the theory according to which things of the spirit are acquired exclusively via the senses and on the sole basis of impressions produced by the external world.

The boldest visionaries of concerted production of the human soul borrow their language from this notion that the individual is primordially rooted in the universe of his sensations, that his ideas and his inner leanings depend in a radical way on what he is able to perceive. Bentham writes, for example, that "education is simply the result of all the circumstances to which a child is exposed." Consequently, to concern oneself seriously with a man's education ought to mean "watching over all his actions, placing him in a position where one can influence him as one likes, by choosing the objects that surround him and the ideas that he is to develop." Thus the educator will not settle for inculcating a few bits of knowledge and some vague principles. He will create and shape a personality from start to finish; he will also determine the gamut of feelings to which the individual will ultimately be susceptible, as well as the successive thoughts that may occur to him. And in a general way, to the extent that the educator ends up "becoming master of everything that can happen to a certain number of men, controlling everything that surrounds them, in such a way as to bring about in them the impression that one wants to produce, to assure oneself of their actions, their relationships, all the circumstances of their lives, so that nothing can escape nor counter the desired effect," one would be in possession of "a very energetic and useful instrument," Bentham writes.[4]

The instrument in question is nothing less than an instrument for fabricating human minds. The extremist nature of the project brings it into sharp relief, but it is nevertheless not unrelated to what the theoreticians of the time expected from the expressive powers of public architecture, for instance. It is no coincidence that this project is inscribed in the revolutionary context, where political leaders are preoccupied, significantly, with the problem of using the controlled play of symbols, ceremonies, and institutions to produce a new species of individuals thoroughly imbued with their civic duties and with their essential membership in the nation. Let us recall, for example, the astonishing debate, in 1793, over the establishment of the republican calendar. What is at stake, indeed, for the proponents of "reforming the vulgar era," if not, above all, ensuring control of the very foundations of the public mind by shaping its organization and contours? "We can conceive of something only through images," Fabre d'Eglantine declares before the Convention, in a report on the new calendar. "In the most abstract analysis, in the most metaphysical combination, our understanding apprehends only through images, our memory leans and relies only on images." Thus priests, "whose universal and definitive goal is and always will be to subjugate the human species and enchain it under their control," have skillfully instituted the various religious ceremonies in such a way as to imprint dogma on souls through striking scenes," and "longstanding familiarity with the Gregorian calendar has filled the memory of the people with a considerable number of images that it has long revered and that are still today the source of its religious errors." Reform must thus consist in thoroughly transforming "the people's understanding," basing it definitively on "the realities of reason" and "the truth of nature," and it must no longer allow anything to penetrate "that does not convey a significant character of public utility." For "visions of ignorance" and "priestly prestige," it must substitute images that are in harmony both with the requirements of free thought and with the imperatives of society—images drawn for the most part, as we know, from "agriculture and the rural economy."[5]

Various other proposals for designating the months had been suggested before Fabre d'Eglantine's won the day. But for our purposes it matters little whether the principle finally adopted involved "consecrating the agricultural system through the calendar" or "reminding citizens every day of the revolution that made them free and reviving their civic feelings through an eloquent nomenclature," as had been suggested. What interests us is the singular power that the leaders attribute to themselves in all cases, the power to forge the thinking and feelings of an entire people according to a well-thought-out, methodical, and comprehensive plan. The moral individuality of citizens is viewed as a perfectly malleable matter that can be disposed of at will with the help of an adequate and literally demiurgic strategy. *"Seize man's imagination and govern it"*: Fabre d'Eglantine deserves to figure prominently among the prophets of the new age if only by virtue of the brilliant formula with which he summed up the enterprise. For in that short phrase he expressed a major axiom of the modern politics, and he gave conscious expression to a dimension of social possibility that was as unprecedented as it was to become essential. All authorities have the power and the duty to seize souls and reform their contents, to put the organization of human souls on an entirely new footing. The governance of men henceforth goes hand in hand with a concern, whether urgent or remote, for the production of man. This point needs to be stressed: it is a matter of *producing* personalities and not simply, trivially, of manipulating minds, as a hasty interpretation might allow us to suppose. It is not a banal matter of skillfully exercising influence or using artifice to capture the goodwill of creatures whose profound intangibility as constituted individualities would by the same token be acknowledged. It is a matter of moving into the sphere of explicit, intentional, and self-governing social action a process that has up to that point been left to improvisation, anarchy, and obscurity: the process of forming human beings in their intimate singularity, in their most immediately compelling subjective structure.

Societies have never ceased to fabricate, unwittingly, the total personalities of their members. Now they are not only to become aware of this critical task but they are to take conscious responsibility for it. Perhaps no one has put it better than another great precursor, an illustrious and celebrated one who clearly has his place among the founders of our present world, Robert Owen. "From the earliest ages it has been the practice of the world to act on the supposition that each individual man forms his own character": here is the fundamentally erroneous principle on which all systems instituted up to this point have been based. And we need to pay attention: "This is not a slight mistake, which involves only trivial consequences; it is a fundamental error of the highest possible magnitude; it enters into all our proceedings regarding man from his infancy; and it will be found to be the true and sole origin of evil." Consequently, it is only by adopting the inverse principle, which has been amply proved by the facts, attested by every honest examination, that a happy and just society can be established. We must start with the observation that the human being "never did, nor is it possible that he ever can, form his own character." "Without a single exception," this person receives it "always formed for him." It is formed for the person from without. Essentially, says Owen, it is a person's predecessors who "give him, or may give him, his ideas and habits, which are the powers that govern and direct his conduct."[6] The power of this formative operation is inherently limitless, he assures us: "*Any* habits and sentiments may be given to mankind."[7] In other words, the solution to the social problem has to begin with an explicit integration of this immense creative resource, which has been misunderstood and held in contempt up to now, into the register of public authority. No peace or happiness among people can come about without a rational and responsible reckoning with the limitless power to constitute their humanity. It is easy to see in profile, between the lines of the Utopia, the luminous and grandiose image of the *New Man*, the contemplation of whose advent was to be the distinguished privilege and, as it were, the ultimate truth of our time.

As we all know now, there was no New Man, in the end, in the terrifying test tubes of the revolutionary chemistry—but we have not yet completed the difficult task of learning this. Could it be that the power to change humanity does not exist after all? If that were the case, we would have to reconsider the very bases that have permitted us to think for the past two centuries. Let us be clear: it is not a matter of the preeminence of some ideas over others; what is at issue is the whole stock of principles governing the entire set of discourses we use, those that claim to subvert the established order as well as those that endeavor to defend it. At issue, to put it briefly and bluntly, is the common theoretical root of both the conservative idea and the revolutionary inspiration. Who today does not believe, more or less, in the power to produce personalities? Who does not subscribe to it and nourish it? Who has an alternative frame of reference? And yet a revision of that very belief is mercilessly required by the massive, extreme, irreversible, and this time no doubt truly ultimate, political experience of our time. We are going to have to revise the very belief that not only nourishes thought but shapes institutions and gives form to social life at all levels.

We have reached the moment—all indications point to this conclusion—when the epoch of that belief, which was inaugurated, as we have seen, with Bentham, Fabre, and Owen, is coming to a close. From one exemplary revolution to another, from an age of invention and promise to the instant of realization that marks a glaring failure, the historical parenthesis is closing. Two centuries of confidence in the power of human beings over the order of their world—and the only outcome has been the unleashing of state violence along with the most incontrovertible powerlessness to transform souls. This observation points with limpid simplicity to the tenor of our future questioning: *What can we do?* At the same time, it allows access to new interpretations of the past. An impossible endeavor lasting two centuries was minted in a multitude of particular experiments, all equally determined to conquer the power to change humankind and simultaneously to produce a perfected society, all equally permeated by periodic failure and yet tirelessly recommenced—until, finally, in an experiment so all-encompassing and so radical that it no longer leaves any way out, we have discovered that failure was inevitable, that it was ineluctably inscribed in the institution's guiding principles and its ideal. Must we not get our bearings, now, from that unsurpassable horizon of failure within which the effort to produce society and to seize minds has continually been generated? Must we not be sensitive first and foremost to the dimension of impossibility, wherever it is a question of reforming personalities or transforming subjects, whenever we are dealing with the powers of institutions or the integral organization of collective space?

The Social Imaginary and the Therapeutic Aim: Conditions for an Encounter

The phenomenon of the insane asylum can best be understood historically, it seems to us, in the light of the perspective we have just outlined. Whether we are looking at its origin, the project in terms of which it was organized, or the dismal end in which its earliest ambitions finally collapsed, the insane asylum is intelligible only as a moment or fragment of the immense and futile attempt to embody, by way of good government, our power to create ourselves and to act on others. How are we to understand the alienists' early and almost exclusive faith in the resources and powers of the institution as such, unless we relate it to the emerging general confidence, at the dawn of the democratic age, in the full power of the spirit of a well-conceived collectivity over individual minds? And how, at the other extreme, are we to grasp the profound meaning of the failure of the so-called "instrument of cure," unless we resituate it within the framework of the overall, constitutive failure of the political effort to take charge of others' souls—an effort which, in a thousand different guises, has permeated and shaped our society ever since it began to relate to itself from the exclusive perspective of its self-constitution?

What was played out at the beginning of the nineteenth century in the narrow domain of the insane asylum was even something exemplary, something experimental, in that it translated the new requirements for the exercise of authority and invented forms designed to give the institution total control, through its implementation alone, over the personalities of its inhabitants. There are two simple and powerful reasons for this. Both stem directly from medicine's penetration into the world of confinement or, more precisely, from medicine's appropriation of the space formerly reserved for the seclusion of madness. For such is the overall paradox of this genesis: the medicalization of the asylum is what tended to make the asylum an eminently political space. So long as the insane are simply removed from circulation when their state is judged critical or dangerous, they are just prisoners among others, posing the same problem of confinement as do any others. But as soon as they cease to be ordinary prisoners, as soon as they become something like patients who need perpetual care and on whom it is appropriate to act in view of a cure, an extraordinary problem of power arises in the framework of therapy, a problem that produces the absolute specificity of the category to which the insane individual belongs. For, unlike ordinary patients, insane people are not afflicted in their vital force, in a way that would still leave them their autonomy as individuals; rather, they are afflicted in their very humanity, in their capacity to sustain themselves as subjects.

What is affected in the insane is precisely their capacity for autonomy. Thus the heart of any therapeutic enterprise necessarily consists in taking total charge of their existence. There is no other path, if the goal is to achieve effective proximity to madness and an authentic reckoning with madness in its originality. As an author from the 1850s put it very well, medicine is "put in charge" of the insane individual "body and soul."

> Medicine is not only to take care of the patient, but also of the man, of the moral, civil and political person of whom it is in a way the tutor. Medicine has the responsibility, while the effects of treatment are pending, to control the patient's relations with his family and with society. It disposes of the patient in all respects, for his own good. It provides appropriate dosages of air, light, space, food, freedom of movement, and communications with other men. What power! But also what a duty, what a responsibility! Moreover, since this sovereign right over the madman has to be exercised by some authority, what is more reasonable than to invest it in science.[8]

It would be hard to formulate more eloquently the exorbitant dimensions of the problem of authority that comes to light when "the sovereign right over the madman," instead of being exercised principally in the form of more or less definitive sentences of exclusion which trivialize their victim once again, becomes the condition, the very principle, the everyday fabric of medical practice.

The first, immediate, massive effect of the entrance of the therapeutic idea into establishments previously reserved for the mere detention of the insane was the revelation and implementation of a perspective of power, a perspective that is of course striking owing to its scope but even more astonishing in its tenor, since there is nothing less at stake than complete management of someone else's life. This is the first reason, in our view, why the insane asylum at its inception naturally became a sort of laboratory for power, a place where the organizational ideal that grew out of the revolutionary invention could be put into concrete experimental practice.

In a providential encounter, the alienists' newly discovered obligation to envisage an integral assumption of responsibility coincided with society's latent and diffuse but compelling dream of a truly authoritative state capable of permeating and constituting the other. And the encounter was all the more productive in that it was rendered possible and necessary by a second factor, one involving the *goal* it was appropriate to set for the insane patient rather than the *means* to be used. In fact, insane people are, par excellence, or at least in a more meaningful way than anyone else, *people to be changed.* This is in any event how the subjects appear at the point of the Pinelean breakthrough. Such people, at once specifically afflicted in their humanity and preserved as human beings, demand to be restablished in the plenitude of their personal means, solely through the appeal to what persists within them of ineradicable humanity. Insane patients will thus typically serve as figures embodying the gap between others and themselves, a gap that a just collective order will have taken on the task of abolishing. Here, too, there is an encounter between the most advanced forms of the social project and the particular stakes of alienist practice. To strive to restore insane people to reason, in any case, following the new line of moral treatment that operates by way of personal relations and the element of speech, is to enter into the symbolic framework of a transformative enterprise destined to reestablish people in their essential humanity, or to restore that humanity to them—an enterprise whose aim is moreover inseparable from a specific type of power and from an extremely precise logic of organizations. Hence the inevitable mobilization, with respect to the asylum, of a general model of an institution apt to "seize souls and govern them" and, what is more, capable of recreating the socio-human dimension. Hence, too, the almost unique opportunity offered by the asylum: it will serve as an exemplary, exhaustive embodiment of the abstract, embryonic project of creating a social mechanism that can condense and make masterable the power to forge individualities and to take charge of their most intimate mainsprings.

This is the spirit in which we need to understand the very early conversion that led Pinel to institute moral treatment within the management of establishments devoted to the insane, and to rely on the resources of a well-understood "distribution" and on constant, comprehensive order. Maintaining his original commitment to the idea that regular communication with the insane patient is the therapist's first priority, he soon encounters the inevitable twofold problem: how to organize the collectivity, and how to act on individuals. Now, this is the very problem that the new social order sees itself as centrally destined to solve. Hence the enthusiasm for a solution that has already been found always in its entirety. Hence the nearly immediate crystallization, within the hospital, of the ideal of power that emerged under the influence of the democratic rupture; hence the takeover of alienist medicine by an all-institutional aim, even by an entirely (albeit unwittingly) political representation of its own task. This is how the asylum became one of the places of pioneering clarification in which a nascent world was able to make readable for itself the imperatives that had been guiding it obscurely and the perfect form to which it aspired. The asylum became one of the first places, if not the very first, where one could see a concrete and transparent affirmation of the dual ambition of a power that seeks both to understand the other in its stead and to ensure that it has the means to transform the other.

This political exemplarity, however indirect and symbolic it remained, did not escape the most perspicacious among its contemporaries. Owen, for example, a precursor of scientific socialism, recommended that the model presiding over state action be adopted in the asylum.

> The time is coming when it will be discovered that the quickest way to bring an end to the countless physical, mental and moral illnesses provoked by the irrational laws that men have invented and introduced during their slow progression from unreason to reason, will be to govern themselves or to treat society in the same way that the most advanced doctors govern and treat their patients in the best-organized insane asylums: there, indeed, patience, goodness, and total tolerance of each paroxysm of the various illnesses constitute the line of conduct of all those who are responsible for the unfortunate souls, the latter having become what they are in consequence of the insanity and injustice of a perfectly irrational social system.[9]

In political terms, it is true that one might see in these lines only a banal apology for the most traditional philanthropic paternalism. While such a reading would be accurate on the literal level, from a historical viewpoint it would totally miss the point: the text signifies in striking fashion the transformations of power that Owen's proposition—that one should greet the paroxysms and deviations of illness with "patience, goodness, and tolerance"—may have implied at the time.[10]

For power that depends on a principle of *acceptance* in place of the ordinary principle of *repression* is power that no longer derives from the classical image of a guarantor of the law, concerned with preventing, with precluding at the outset, any hint of disobedience or transgression among individuals, through a permanent display of force. It is power that, conversely, is more interested in reforming motives than in proscribing behaviors, power that knows how useless it is to offer direct opposition to deviations that are never in the last analysis truly deliberate, but on the contrary are always essentially unwitting ("man [is not] master of his affections," as Owen writes elsewhere). As a result, this power does not attempt to annihilate deviance at the root; it allows externalizations, but it anticipates and circumscribes deviant behavior and brings the deviant back gently, by that very token, to the rational truth of the rule. The patient is not consciously aware of that truth, and he does not need to recognize it; nevertheless, the truth embraces and constitutes him. The task of power is to disengage that truth from any impediment, to let it operate in its natural pertinence. The power in question is a psychological power. It does not expect individuals to comply explicitly and consciously with the law that it posits; on the contrary, strengthened by its science of motivations, it posits laws that are in conformity with the deepest human inclination, in such a way that individuals can slip into them without thinking about them. This comes about in the ultimate perspective of people's full reconciliation with themselves, in which, since behavior would no longer be anything but the enactment of a rational exigency, and an enactment inherently adequate to itself, there would no longer be any "physical, mental or moral illnesses."

Thus the criterion of free externalization that Owen used to characterize the politics of the insane asylum is infinitely less anodyne and banal than it first appears to a retrospective gaze. In its way, it goes straight to the heart of the radical reinvention of the forms of authority that were familiar in the last century and for which the asylum supplied an at once marginal and privileged theatre. For the liberal laissez-faire approach is indissociable from what, on the other hand, constitutes the most specific and the most virulent ambition of the new power—its will to take charge of minds, to control the circle in which they develop and rebuild its foundations. Behind the principle according to which one must, without exception, "allow all deviant acts that compromise neither the individual's safety nor that of the other patients,"[11] we find the implicit idea that there is no other way to circumvent individuals wholly, in order to penetrate their most secret motivations and to act on them effectively. This is the very idea of control and transformation that gave the insane asylum its exemplary character in the realm of control of human beings.

What is being advocated here is the free manifestation of concrete effervescence: aberration at the level of acts. But later on, when it is a matter of giving free rein to the wholly peaceful disruption provoked when private images and senseless language emerge from a subject's inner depths, political stakes of the same order—that is, of the same symbolic nature—resurface. Today, once again, in a still confused but already obsessive way, we sense or suspect that an exemplarily advanced and premonitory form of the mechanism of authority is being manifested via medical embodiments of "total tolerance" with respect to the aberrant singularity that waits only to express itself in each subject. And we are unlikely to be mistaken. For the injunction that underlies psychoanalysis—the injunction to "let oneself go," to tell all, to "let it all hang out," entails a pioneering expansion of the scope of power, and also an unprecedented refinement of the procedures for penetrating human beings. It is as if the lesson of panoptic blindness had been pursued to its logical end: decidedly, the procedure does not teach one to see very well. Even if one observes everything, one still learns nothing. Let us listen, then. Let us abandon our initial and logical suspicion of speech. For common sense suggests that letting the other talk and trusting what is said may only be a way of ensuring that one will be deceived; only by looking for oneself can one legitimately guarantee the objectivity of information about the other, all the more so in that the individual unwittingly reveals himself in his behavior. But this commonsense view is a gross error, as we have had to learn. The eye espies only the void, and it is only in discourse that others offer up their captive truths. They may seek to deceive; they may simply lie: this matters little, since their calculation reveals them, since their lies exhibit what they do not know to be the most truthful aspect of themselves. Let us not try to find out whether they are telling the truth. Let us be content to register what cannot deceive: the subjective truth that comes across in their speech without their knowledge.

A displacement from *seeing* to *hearing*: this is doubtless what best characterizes the changes of destination in the quest for psychological efficacy. But while the goal may be adapted and transformed, the structure through which the other is displayed and replaced remains unchanged. What is uniformly at stake is getting the others to reveal themselves wholly, so that one can know in their place what they, from their place, cannot know: their own truth. If people give free rein to the disorder of their acts, it is in an attempt to get back to what can be discovered there: some grasp of the others' difficulty in adapting to the rule, and, consequently, some inkling of a way to help them do so in a lasting fashion. If one frees up the disturbed, painful expression of the dreams and signs that haunt the subject's private world, it is with the intention of rediscovering the secret of the strange discord that opposes us to ourselves, and the means, consequently, for a harmonious reconciliation with the laws of our condition.

The psychoanalytic emancipation of discourse reveals a power that is more and more forceful as it becomes more and more benevolent, more and more tolerant, the power of *listening*. It opens up a world with more and more room for self-expression and subjective affirmation, less and less room for the autonomous and contingent decisions of the individual. The power of prediction that belonged to the insane asylum in its day has been rediscovered. But there is a notable difference: its sign is reversed, and the figures of the future will be deciphered from this point on with more anguish than pain. We hardly expect, now, that good government will set up the New Jerusalem, to borrow Owen's terminology, or that it will finally restore to human beings the ultimate harmony with themselves to which history destines them. And we know, on the contrary, that we have everything to fear from the indefatigable expansion of the powers that want only what is good. Hence the current awakening of a critical consciousness that is still very unsure of its motives and its target, and that can be mindless in its categories, but that has deep roots, with respect to the "liberations" of all sorts promised us by contemporary ideology—and especially with respect to the freedom of expression promised by psychoanalysis. Hence, too, no doubt, in this phase of crystallization of anxieties in the face of the inexorable rise in power of the agency of production of the social, the strange retrospective contemporaneity that the specter of the asylum has taken on, or regained, during the past two decades, under the sign, this time, of unanimous denunciation and anathema, if not conjuration or exorcism. For, at some obscure level, the asylum has remained an institutional model, even if it was never merely that. At a time when everyone is concerned with getting to the roots of the specifically modern forms of domination, the asylum is spontaneously rediscovered as a primary, elementary, symbolically perfect incarnation of what has since its inception never stopped growing, unfolding, and refining itself, to the point where it now envelops us in an embrace that is as agreeable as it is fatal.

Taking Charge of Minds: The Economy of Power

The asylum came into being under the sign of a luminous and direct expression of institutional principles derived from the literally revolutionary revelation of our power over the human mind. Governed by the principle of centrality first of all, the asylum is organized around an opening at the middle point from which everything is equally and immediately readable; thus decisions can be made on the basis of pertinent information. As Claude-Nicolas Ledoux wrote early on, "one of the principal devices connecting governments to relevant activity on a continual basis is the overall arrangement of a plan that gathers all its constitutive parts around a center." And like a visionary poet he offers an image to convey the infallible optical authority thus conferred on the being "placed at the center of the radii": "Nothing escapes surveillance; it has a hundred eyes open while a hundred others sleep, and its ardent pupils tirelessly illuminate the restless night."[12]

Pinel takes a similar line: "One of the capital points of any well-ordered hospice is having a general center of authority that decides with no appeal."[13] And the position the formula occupies in his book is telling: in the second edition of the *Treatise*, it opens the chapter entitled "General Precepts to Follow in Moral Treatment," which has been moved to the heart of the fourth section, "The Importance of an Enlightened System of Police and General Precepts for the Internal Management of Lunatic Asylums." More than a strategic position, it is a highly emblematic one: the *general center of authority* is what connects management of the collective to therapeutic treatment of souls. Hence the particular importance of this imperative of centrality: its critical role in the edifice of alienist medicine is repeatedly affirmed. The principle of centrality establishes the relations according to which a transparent organization can unfold: "A methodical distribution of the insane of the hospice among various departments makes it possible to grasp immediately the respective measures to be taken for their feeding, their hygiene, their moral and physical regimen."[14] Even more importantly, the principle of centrality allows the prospect of moral treatment to expand spontaneously to the entire institution, which is thus transmuted from a collection of people that is ordered but fixed in its rigid classificatory abstraction into a globally coherent, unified, fusional mechanism materially animated by an idea, traversed by a will, and consistently intelligent in its action. Owing to the clear subordination of collective existence as a whole to a source of authority that is visible, instantly perceptible from all points, *one* person (the doctor) can simultaneously and continually communicate with *all* (the patients). Pinel puts this very well in a passing remark about the basic conditions required for the treatment of maniacs: "A unique center of authority," he says, "must always be present to their imagination in order for them to learn to control themselves and master their impetuous enthusiasm."[15] The conviction that emerges pointedly from such a proposition is unequivocal: a specific ordering of power in space, or rather a specific way of structuring space in terms of and in relation to the place of power, in itself keeps the governing principles constantly present in the patients' minds. Within the special framework of the asylum, such an arrangement or structuring allows the doctor to have uninterrupted control over the minds of all the patients at once. In other words, the distinguishing feature of good organization, and the secret of the incomparable efficiency it generates, is that it absorbs the ungovernable multiplicity of individualities in the unity of a mass that is at once perfectly homogeneous and perfectly penetrable, perfectly governable from within.

This effect of "social condensation" is induced by the institutional topology whose discovery was the chief challenge to alienist medicine. It precipitated a redefinition of the prospects of moral treatment and gave rise to the later developments of the asylum project. For once the gravitational equilibrium of the collective field around a central point of cohesion had been found, the entire enterprise took on clarity and a firm direction, beginning with the therapeutic task. Within such a framework, moral treatment has to consist first and fundamentally in making oneself one with the soul of a population that is itself made to live in unison, so as to maintain that population in an imperturbably regular order of thought.[16] On the one hand, then, the doctor has to be certain that he has access to, and can control, both the intimate details of the cases and their overall distribution. Hence the familiar obsession with classifying patients: in the last analysis, the process is intended less to circumscribe and segregate patients according to the intrinsic interest of their particular symptoms than to render human beings instantly available as a collectivity that can be traversed and mobilized in its totality. In other words, the process is designed to produce a population that can be integrated into an overall, controlled process. In addition, it is designed to incorporate individual patients into the collective project, to integrate them within the network of community constraints, to a greater and greater degree. The aim is to produce an increasingly docile, compact mass—increasing "communism," as certain alienists will not hesitate to say.

The originality and the socially avant-garde character of the asylum lie precisely in its ability to develop such a "collectivist" model. In comparison, in other institutions of the same order, such as schools or prisons, it is also a matter of directly imposing constraints on individuals or inculcating them with information in view of transforming them, using models that are relatively archaic from the standpoint of the economy of power. The insane asylum, for its part, organizes the existence of its wards not only in the name of an all-encompassing tutelage but also and especially in the name of full integration into the operation of a community. Thus it can offer an image of society in miniature—a society that is, moreover, if we may be permitted the expression, exemplarily social.

Still, if the principle of centrality is to be fully developed and fully effective, it presupposes the intervention of a second principle that will ensure its control of the space in which it operates: a principle of *circumscription*, which rigorously delimits an inner world that can be constituted and controlled at every point in its insularity.[17] From this principle stems the celebrated isolation that is so strongly promoted by the alienists and that is easy to identify as an indispensable condition for an institution that means to act on minds and reconstruct personalities. To begin with, how can one control without exception all the influences that are to be exercised on an alienated mind, in order to restore that mind to itself, except by making a radical break with its ordinary environment and the habits in which it has been entrenched? On this point, our authors are unanimous. One insists that "the insane must be separated from the objects that have excited their alienation or that maintain and aggravate it."[18] To isolate the insane, says another, is to procure the inestimable advantage of "removing from the disordered mind the support it finds in a multitude of ever-renewed impressions, associations of ideas, emotions, and memories."[19] Never again will the break be as clean or the separation as spectacular. As one of our authors writes, in a curious burst of imagination: "I would like these hospices to be built in sacred forests, in steep and solitary places, amid great upheavals, like the Grand-Chartreuse. . . . It will often be useful for the latest arrival to be brought down by machines, for him to traverse ever new and ever more astonishing places before he reaches his destination; the ministers of these places should wear special costumes"! And elsewhere, as if that debauchery of means did not suffice: "Phantasmagoria and the other resources of physics, music, water, lightning, thunder, etc., would be used by turns."[20] If there is an imperative need for special establishments, the same Fodéré declares, it is in order "to offer to the senses of the insane objects entirely different from those to which they were accustomed, new faces, other furnishings, other sites, other manners, a total change, finally, in all the objects that surround them."[21]

Given such a dramatic caesura in vital continuity and its external reference points, a break that puts the entire set of forces, correspondences, and influences apt to orient mental flow into the doctor's hands, it becomes possible to envisage an indirect but methodical and all-encompassing strategy for reconstructing psychic individuality on the basis of impressions received and the general effects of a calculated environment.[22] Indeed there is nothing in this closed universe that cannot be related to the goal pursued, nothing that cannot be skillfully utilized or deliberately orchestrated in terms of the goal. Whether it is a matter, to use Peisse's telling formula, of the amount of air, the amount of light, space, food, freedom of movement, or communication with other people, everything must be deliberately conceived so as to contribute to the restoration of the patient to harmony with himself through harmony with the surrounding world.[23] Thus the literature of the period highlights the special, artificial, studied character of the asylum milieu, often emphasizing it in a strangely abstract way. "To isolate the insane is to substitute *establishments set up in a quite special way* for ordinary localities . . ."[24]

But isolation, understood simultaneously as rupture and as closure, is not only the imperative condition of existence for an instrument capable of circumventing and enveloping the insane patient from the outside. It is also the condition through which a direct, intimate, and total hold over the mind of the individual can be ensured. "In the special establishments, isolation is complete: the patients soon know that they are under the authority, and even at the discretion, of the director."[25] "Isolation," someone else says, is a way "to impress vividly on the insane the conviction that they are subject to a superior force destined to control them."[26] And indeed, can one conceive of a society whose citizens could boast of competing laws and lay claim to different but equally legitimate authorities? A single law, a single purveyor of force, a single agency in which popular sovereignty is concentrated: these are obviously the first principles of political sociability—the very principles by virtue of which the asylum accedes silently, but profoundly, to political existence. What does this mean, finally, in the realm of the imaginary, and of course without any possibility that it can be explicitly acknowledged, if not *separation* from global society and *entrance* into another society similar to the first one, since that first one too is centered on an ultimate, exclusive, and incontestable power, which the insane must simply be made to see as such? Thus the closure of the institution on itself and its own system of norms tends to confer upon the doctor a power that is truly political in nature, just as it tends to transform the patients into political subjects—they are members of a society in the fullest sense of the term.

At bottom, the goal of isolation is to transfer to the heart of the asylum the ultimate power that a society has over its members. This means of course the power to control their behavior openly through the exercise of political authority, but also the power to shape their personalities, to mold their minds, invisibly but despotically, and to govern their souls without their knowledge; this is the only power on which it truly makes sense to rely, when reforming deviant subjectivities is at issue. The only difference is that the formative power of society is usually exercised in a largely unconscious and also anarchic mode, whereas in the restricted and fully concerted framework of the asylum, the active potentialities of the social bond can be mobilized in an intentional and precisely focused way. To inaugurate a society that has the power, through its very order and its working principles, to prevent people from being mad: such is the utopia to which isolation has removed the world of the asylum.

The utopian vision is by no means dead. Indeed, it undoubtedly has a promising future, for it is inherent in the great dream of power that torments modern societies. To be sure, it is impossible to continue to believe in the possibility of making the properly social process of producing personalities transparent and controllable, within a small, segregated experimental republic at the heart of the larger one, a republic that has become a society in its own right by virtue of its very insularity. The point has been won. But these are only the effects of a metamorphosis in the way a society lives out its dream in practical terms, effects that scarcely affect the tenor of the dream itself. There remains, in our society, the certainty that an intelligent and just collective order will have enough reconciling power over souls to abolish madness.[27]

But the political form of the institution appears most clearly in two related principles that define the rule of asylum life: the principle of *mobilization* and the principle of the individual's *absorption* within the collectivity. Here, there is no longer any medical equivocation, and hardly even anything that remains implicit. The logic of the model appears naked, as it were. How can one act more surely on minds than by organizing their daily existence in a way that continually solicits them, ceaselessly offers them objects to keep them busy, so as to circumscribe, anticipate, and saturate the circle within which they are to evolve? And how can one establish the unanimous harmony of the good rule more effectively than by making the communitarian law the very fabric of a general operation into which each person is absorbed? On this terrain, it is no longer solely a matter of the particular application of a model drawing its legitimacy from the mutations of global society, and descending from on high, as it were, into the multiple depths of society, but stems from an actual encounter between a possible response to madness and a dreamed-of solution to the enigma of history. What is the problem posed by the insane, indeed, if not that of their confinement within the uncoercible solitude of a belief that belongs to them alone? Practitioners must therefore work to draw them out of the constricting self-centeredness of their dreams and restore them to the bosom of the community of minds by seizing their attention, mobilizing their faculties, and making them participate fully in the collective intellectual process. Viewed in another light, the issue can be formulated as follows: the insane are people removed from the common rules of conduct and judgment by their own inner deficiency; thus they must be made to live according to the collective rule until their life is one with it, if they are to recover their senses as if through impregnation, and if they are to reopen themselves at the same time to the possibility of existence for others.[28]

Now, how would one define the successful society, a society restored to its true essence at the end of history and the ultimate resolution of the antagonisms that have been at work among men from time immemorial (or at least such is the phantasm that arises with, and is nourished by, bourgeois society and its manifest conflicts, for bourgeois society is the first society to make the mirage of surpassing itself a consubstantial element of its own reality)? The successful society is first of all, unquestionably, a society that knows it is a society, that is to say a society whose members—who are as remote from ignorant servitude as they are from the obtuse individualism of the Dark Ages—are fully imbued with the feeling that they are part of a collectivity and share in their community's global outlook: a society, one might say, where the participatory openness of each member toward the whole works to abolish all difference between individual consciousness and collective consciousness.

Next, the successful society is no less certainly a society that rejects any separate law imposed from the outside on beings who would be spontaneously inclined to behave differently. It is a society that reconciles complete freedom and total conformity with the higher demands of the collectivity, which are in fact spontaneously enacted by individuals. Bourgeois society clearly has not limited itself to summoning up this phantasmagoria of revolutionary deliverance as its necessary underside. If bourgeois society did not invent the historical agent that is quite concretely capable of undertaking to bring that phantasmagoria into being, it has certainly provided the agent—namely, the state—with means adequate to the task. If it is not inherently the state's project, if is has not been awakened, set in motion, and maintained by the state, the dream of a society restored to coincidence with itself intersects and nourishes the practical ambitions of the state in a fundamental way, as these ambitions derive from society's declared determination to produce itself.

The conjunction of the state and this dream, at any rate, was inevitable; the idea of inaugurating an undivided, classless society was destined on the one hand to turn into an unprecedented domination of society by the state, and on the other hand to come to terms with the sophisticated forms of exercise of authority whose organic link with the expansion of the state we have also seen. While the state has been the effective agent in building the representation of a society aware of itself and in harmony with itself, it does not much matter for our purposes whether the state has also been the major source—if only indirectly, through the shadow it has cast—of that representation. We need only observe the objective collusion between the unconscious workings of power and the explicitness of a revolutionary aim—an aim that is, moreover, unaware of its means. What interests us for the moment is the hidden but effective presence at the heart of every schema of authority—the schema that prevails not only in the framework of the state but also in any cell of the collective tissue: the production of a twofold image of a perfected social entity, that is to say, a society that is nourished by the unanimous and constant participation of agents but that no longer differentiates between actual actions and the laws of action. An effort to secure an opening toward collectivity and the congruence of thoughts, an effort to promote a collective functioning that would absorb individuals within the rule: here are the reference points according to which, obscurely to be sure, most often unwittingly, but inexorably and infallibly, powers have been continuously guided starting with the moment when, within society, the gaping question of its own invention was raised.

We have already shown how the asylum turned out to be an ideal place for the crystallization of the most advanced forms of authority. Here we can see how it came to be the site of an intersection between therapeutic perspectives and the authority that secretly aims to constitute the social bond. The institutional arrangements that appeared to be conducive to restoring insane patients to reason—incorporation into the general activity of minds, integration into the enactment and application of a common law—are the very arrangements that power conscious of its ultimate goals or aware of its dreams would be determined to adopt and stabilize.

The character of totalitarian anticipation that was acquired by many aspects of the asylum has to be understood in relation to the foregoing conjunction. This is not a retrospective projection on our part. It is an authentic prefiguration that becomes clear once it has been related to the quite singular conditions that permitted and produced it. The very imperative that madness be taken into account so that a way out of madness might be found constituted something like an appeal to the mobilizing and integrative force that was destined to a prosperous future. Still, it would probably not be false to say that, on the contrary, the presence of a fixed phantasmatic figure of the social at the heart of the practice of authority is what allowed those particular responses to madness to be conceived and embodied.

A medico-political knot of this sort is almost bound to be a hopeless tangle. In any event, there is no doubt that the discourse of the alienists on this point always occupies a dual register, so that, even where medical concerns alone are at issue, the tacit quest for good institutional order in general breaks through. Let us consider the following sample, for instance:

> An Establishment for the insane must be governed by regulations, to which all must submit. This will serve as a response to all objections, and aid in surmounting all repugnance, at the same time that it furnishes motives to obedience, less unpleasant, than the will or caprice of a principal. There is, in a house of this kind, a movement, an activity, a vortex, into which by degrees, all enter. The most infatuated and jealous lypemaniac finds himself, almost without knowing it, forced to live out of himself; carried along by the general movement, by the example, and by the impressions, often strange, which are perpetually striking his senses. The maniac himself, attracted by the harmony, order and regularity of the house, defends himself better against his impulses, and abandons himself less to his eccentric actions.[29]

Everything is there. Of course it is simply a matter of bringing the "lypemaniac" out of the stubborn solitude of his belief and his defiant distance from others, or of containing the exuberance and the aberrant behaviors of all sorts of maniacs. But, in an exemplary sense, it is also a matter of an institutional system capable of drawing each patient out of his own self-absorption, away from the exclusive pursuit of his own private chimeras, and getting him to live "outside himself" in thoroughgoing harmony with the collectivity, in communion with the "general movement." It is a matter of an institutional system capable, too, of getting individuals to think consistently of themselves from the place of the other, from the viewpoint of the impersonal, anonymous other constituted by the collectivity as a whole, so that, taken to the extreme, there is no more need for external control over subjective deviations from the "harmony, order, and rule" of society—since, on the one hand, all individuals control themselves adequately from within, and since, on the other hand, the deviations inherent in individual personalities tend to disappear gradually on their own as each individual is imbued with the requirements of the collective persona. But it is a matter, too, of an institution structured in such a way as to understand and define in advance all cases, all situations, all behaviors—all the "answers to objections."

Nothing is to be overtly imposed; no one is to be subjected to a leader's "will" or "whim." The organization anticipates and codifies the everyday fabric of activities and tasks, down to the most intimate details, so that there is no choice but to blend in. One does not *submit* to it; one *enters* it without feeling any constraint. No doubt the organization strictly determines the form of your impressions, the tenor of your feelings, and even the order of your thoughts, but it does so without your being aware of it for a second, "carried away" as you are by a law in action that does not call for assent or even comprehension. Thus the "lypemaniac" is "*forced* to live outside himself," but "*unwittingly*," without futile scoldings or superfluous coercion.[30] What is presented to us in this way, in its utter completeness, far surpasses the asylum: we are encountering the abstract ideal of an institutional form that contains, owing to the anticipatory intelligence that drives it, the solution to the problem of making a community coincide with itself through its law. And from this standpoint it would doubtless be hard to find more extreme formulations than those the alienists produced to characterize immersion in a collective that is indissociable from the rules that govern its operation. Thus Morel explains that the cell system, while it may have "great advantages" in penitentiary establishments, is to be absolutely proscribed in the context of asylums, where on the contrary "everything must tend toward the fusion of individuals under the aegis of a gentle but firm discipline."[31] The comparison between prison and asylum is highly instructive, to the extent that it sheds light on the origins of the divergent destinies of two institutions that were nevertheless both designed to change people by bringing them back within the law, and which were for this reason moreover regularly juxtaposed by good souls infatuated with philanthropy.

Morel announces a division between the old and the new, between the tenacious old idea of the power of human beings, guilty sinners, to reform themselves from within, and the emerging representation of society's power to transform its members. On the one hand, then, we have the congenital archaism of a system in which correction is expected to come from the patients' reflective return to their inner worlds, and from the forced examination of conscience that isolation in a cell is supposed to produce—except that, in the case of prisons, overt transgressions are at issue, transgressions that correspond to an accepted definition of illegal behavior and to the prevailing moral image of ill intent, so that the pressure of traditional ideas is logically decisive. On the other hand, we have the involuntary gradualism of a collectivist experiment aiming to guarantee constitutive rather than regulatory control over souls through the dissolution of intellectual singularities at the heart of a mass that is intimately and unconsciously one with the law that comprehends and directs it. However, while in the case of the asylum we are still dealing with transgression, it presents itself here as transparently involuntary, just as it obscurely implies a representation of the law that is incommensurable with the classic representation: rather than an external law that you respect, there is a law that constructs you as a subject from within and without your knowledge. The lack of such a law is precisely what alienates the subject. Thus curing madness requires the enactment of a power that thinks in the place of its subjects and of a law the collectivity is destined to embody actively.

From the very moment when madness is discovered to be intrinsically curable, it foreshadows the future representation of people and the future growth of social power. For, if we look closely, we discover a radical and unrestrained ambition, as is the case, for example, when someone speaks of the "fusion of individuals under the aegis of a gentle but firm discipline." It is no longer even a question of "transforming the human brain into an exact mirror of the external order," something Auguste Comte could advocate as the goal of politics at the time; such a transformation continues to presuppose personal limits and the self-enclosure of the individual. What is at stake is contained, to be sure, within narrow boundaries and marginalized by its point of application, but positively articulated nevertheless: it is the great dream whose feverish pursuit has dominated, overwhelmed, and exhausted our era: the dream of making the social reveal itself in a pure state through the absorption of individual identities, the dream of opening individuals onto others to the point where the derisory frontiers that isolate them in their particularities are abolished, of opening them up to the point where they lose themselves and at the same time realize themselves in their truth as social beings in the living unity of a mass without discord or difference. Here is the immense chimera of modern power, a chimera for which the asylum project, emerging by chance from the tortured paths of history and in the obscure times of gestation, indeed constituted a minuscule but privileged point of crystallization. The process was not necessarily an unconscious one. In 1848 one could read—in the *Annales médico-psychologiques*, the central organ of the profession, in a text written by Bouchet, one of Esquirol's closest disciples—concerning the organization of asylums in view of moral treatment: "Social individuality must disappear and blend into the common life. . . . The very principles of communism are the ones applied to the governance of the insane. Most of the time, illness is only the consequence of individualism taken to extremes. Its remedy thus is to be found in the contrary disposition."[32]

CHAPTER III

Impossible Power

Totalitarianism as an Illusion

NEED WE DWELL on the inexorable, obligatory, constitutive failure of the phantasmagoric totalitarian mechanism? Perhaps so; for some of our contemporaries have a peculiar tendency to be credulous. They are inclined to take a project literally, no matter how excessive, and put it on display like a scarecrow; they remain untroubled by any hints of the inherent lack of realism that makes the project impotent or inapplicable. They act as if the project could work; as if, for example, the "eye of power" that is positioned at the core of the panoptic machine, infinitely open and theoretically infallible in its exhaustive force, although lacking a gaze, could finally notice anything but the void; as if—even supposing the impossible, supposing that the eye could see everything—even the fact that nothing remained unknown about a human being, the fact that that person's environment could be completely controlled, offered any measure of control over the individual's personality, any power to direct its development. So far as we know, even where it has been brought to the pinnacle of panoptic perfection, prison has never put large numbers of people back on the right path.

Is that last observation an insignificant banality, merely "empirical," as it would be labeled scornfully today by the bizarre "epistemologists" who profess quite seriously to respectful audiences that science has nothing to do with facts? Or is it an important sign of the fact that the most elaborate of surveillance mechanisms, in principle irresistible, still leaves its unhappy victims entirely free to pursue and perfect their most disastrous inclinations? If the latter is the case, how can one fail to take into account the avowed ineffectiveness of the mechanism, its definitive impotence, when one symbolically houses the unbroken servitude that is supposed to threaten us within the sovereign field of vision that power claims for itself? Indeed, power wants to see us. But what does it see? What does it understand, in what it sees? And in particular, what forces, what means for moving us without knowledge does power actually derive from its continual, obsidional, interminable investigation?

The panoptic installation works well enough as a symbol: let us grant that it offers a fairly adequate figure for the ambitions of universal readability and integral accessibility which have been induced in the authorities on a massive scale by the restitution of society's omnipotence over itself. But let us also agree not to see it as anything but the symbol of a project, luminously expressing the excessiveness of an aim, but having nothing at all to say about its practical opportunities or its potential for success. And it would hardly be enough to describe these latter as mediocre, or weak; nonexistent would surely be a better term. Thus, before terrifying ourselves with the specter of implacable mechanisms brought forth by the authorities, let us avoid being duped; let us not espouse the fiction that subtends and animates these authorities and holds captive the supposed masters of the mechanism. Let us avoid entering into the illusion that leads the most ingenious of the government's architects astray and undermines their most subtle fortresses in advance—an illusion that certainly does not prevent the arrangements from being constraining, but that unerringly disarms the essential pretention of power that inhabits and justifies them.

In the last analysis, no power is more blind than power that believes it can see—which does not keep surveillance from being intolerable, even when it is futile. No power has a less effective hold over souls than power that claims to possess and transform them—which certainly does not prevent the sterile ambition of reformers from being unacceptable to those who are its victims. If one lesson is beginning to emerge fairly solidly from the two centuries of history that have unfolded under the sign of the Revolution, it is indeed the lesson of the actual impotence of the collective body over itself—incomprehensible, but inescapable, given the violent evidence. It is the lesson of human beings' ultimate lack of power over the order of their societies.

The time for revision is at hand. But its flow is from here on inexorable. However repulsive and fraught with implications the task may be, little by little we are going to have to register and assimilate, then to act and think in terms of, the gigantic failure constituted in its very principle and under its countless forms by the productive-organizing-programming action of society on itself. At this turning point, whose scope is as yet inconceivable, other paths will have to be invented; human beings will have to devise a new way of managing the full and rightful sovereignty that they have over their world. At this turning point, too, new illusions will doubtless emerge regarding what is desirable and what is possible—but perhaps, just perhaps, this time human beings will discover the right way to get around the limits on which the old enterprise foundered and to surmount the indecipherable obstacle that the social realm admittedly constitutes for itself.

The fact remains—and this is the only certainty to date—that *the imaginary of mastery* that has dominated the management of our societies up to now is over and done with, the imaginary that assigned that management its global aim just as it determined in detail its empirical paths and its material forms.

The enterprise we are considering has led to failure everywhere. The failure to control the other, to conceive him in his stead and to constitute him integrally was flagrant at the outset, yet it has long been invisible; after tirelessly recommenced attempts it has become more and more striking but it remains curiously unthinkable. The failure of surveillance mechanisms is of course exemplary, though they continue to be regarded quite oddly as redoubtable by those who hold them in the greatest contempt, whereas they are only unbearably derisory. But let us move directly to the most overwhelming, the most obvious failure, *the failure of the state*, a massive, bloody, critical failure; and yet this one too is misread with singular consistency by the very critics who doggedly denounce its effects. How can anyone fail to note the striking ambiguity that mars the recent "discoveries" of the totalitarian phenomenon by very good minds whose new vigilance and brilliant asperity does not keep them—and this observation is somewhat troubling—from remaining mired in the totalitarian illusion?

One can only approve the indictment that finally designates plainly—though never virulently enough—the concentration camps and the reign of everyday terror that results ineluctably from the project of producing a society by and only by the state. Similarly, one can only reject the aberrant thesis in which the short-lived lucidity of our new ideologues immediately founders, the thesis that tends to depict the state, with its aspiration to omniscience and omnipotence, as the long-awaited temporal embodiment of a fatal "Master" that has reached us from the depths of time and that is destined, we are told, to bend reality, history, and human beings to its Law—a Master against whom our only remaining weapons are moral refusal or hopeless rebellion. For if there is one certainty to be drawn from the totalitarian experience, out of the unleashing of violence that it implies, it is indeed the blinding certainty of the formal bankruptcy and the inglorious collapse of the so-called Master. Yes, the state claims a monopoly on knowledge and decision-making. Yes, the state purports to make society transparent and thus malleable at will. But can anyone fail to see the result even for a second? Can anyone be unaware for the briefest instant of the incommensurable disorder, the generalized dissimulation, the vertiginous anarchy, the abyss of chaotic obscurity into which those lofty ambitions have fallen? The figure of the "Master" is decidedly a pitiful one: something between the shady operator with no scruples and the illiterate lush, a figure all the more despotic and vindictive for being lamentable, dull-witted, and stumbling.

The state that posits itself as all-knowing and all-powerful in truth knows virtually nothing about the society it dominates, and it can do very little—except try desperately to take back what its own actions repeatedly allow to escape, or else blindly avenge itself on a world that eludes its grasp, and ward off its own impotence with ferocious or delirious exorcisms. Much more than a deliberate and constitutive project, much more than the ultimately technical necessity of imposing its will through coercion, it is the deficiency of its hold over the social body and its ultimate inconsistency that condemn the state to violence, that lock it into violence as its requisite element, whether it is a matter of passing off obvious absurdities as realities or of acquiring on its own behalf, for want of an accessible understanding of things, the concrete thickness, the solid anchoring, the unavoidable weight of death. The less it masters, the more the state persecutes and murders, arbitrarily; from beginning to end it succeeds only in offering a bloody and definitive demonstration of the fact that mastery is essentially *impossible.*

Within the human order there is no Master capable of separating itself from others enough to know them truly, to control them integrally, and to dispose of them freely: this is the irrefutable observation imposed by the totalitarian disaster, an unprecedented experience of the limits of the political. Of course there are leaders who are capable, even sometimes to a very considerable extent, of dominating, governing, and controlling; but if we look closely, we discover that they succeed only provided that they recognize and accept that they are anything but true Masters, that a great deal escapes them, and that they cannot achieve everything. Totalitarian power, unaware of that condition, transgresses it and is thus blinded, both to itself, to its own possibilities, and to the collectivity that it is supposed to be governing. The ultimate paradox of power is that renunciation of mastery alone can allow it really to be exercised—by which we mean exercised in reality, starting from approximately verifiable data and in view of a measurable result. Under these conditions, to evoke the mythic figure of a featureless "Master" with regard to totalitarian states is nothing more or less than to extend, or even to help accredit, the very myth of power in which the totalitarian enterprise and its sinister depravations are rooted. It is to continue to nourish, through repulsive fascination, scarcely less alienated than yesterday's enthusiastic advocacy, the bloody mirage of something whose enemy one intends to be.

The observation needs to be extended, moreover, to an entire literature which, in the crush of this belated (and very relative) antitotalitarian awakening, is now "rediscovering" the state, finding in it the universal explanation of all our troubles, and accusing it of all crimes in a way that contributes, without their authors' knowledge, to the fundamental myth that has been and that remains at the root of the irresistable growth of the state. Imprecations against a supremely evil spell do not unmask it, under the circumstances: they conceal, they entice, they reinforce the common illusion that also nourishes—for the process works both ways—both the appeal to the state emanating from below and the bureaucratic expansion dreamed of on high. To make the state an infallible monster that can know us at will, that can possess us and sport with us at its pleasure, that can manipulate us without our even being aware of it, is to reinforce the obscure belief that legitimizes the state's action and allows it to prosper—the belief according to which there exists a point in human space from which the collective universe is entirely intelligible, completely masterable, and even freely manipulable. There is no need to emphasize the extent to which that belief is the cornerstone of a society that sees itself precisely as having the full right to act on itself and that finds itself consequently looking for means to put into practice its theoretical domination of the problem of its own organization. But the question is allegedly resolved even before it is raised. The means supposedly exist; they lie in the state, which is instantly projected into the imagined place from which the social landscape proves entirely decipherable and entirely reconstructible; by the same token, the state is endowed with untouchable legitimacy as the instrument par excellence of society's potential; the state is the revolutionary arm that will allow society to become what it must be.

The state itself—rather than the people in power at the moment—is in an impregnable position of strength, since it is tacitly understood that whatever happens must happen by way of the state. The more one demands transformations in society, the more one appeals, consciously or unconsciously, to the state—again, not to its current representatives, but to the abstract power that the state materializes and that it derives from the position in which it is believed to be installed and that its agents of course think they themselves occupy. Its most ardent detractors reproachfully credit the state with that very position of virtual omniscience and proximate omnipotence, a position whose radically illusory character ought on the contrary to be unmasked by an authentic critical effort—for that is the only angle of attack capable of guaranteeing to critics any destructive impact. In order to make the state's expansionism illegitimate in its very foundations, it is necessary to bring to light the nonexistence or at least the theoretical impossibility of occupying such a place of exhaustive vision and global mastery, and to shed harsh light, in the process, on the ultimate inconsistency of enterprises undertaken in the name of the so-called specific power conferred by the separation of state power from society.

Inquisitorial inventories that seek to penetrate and embrace everything are useless. They inevitably allow what is essential to escape them in the end, despite the weighty apparatus they generate and nourish, despite the plethora of information they stock up. The living enigma of social creation invisibly eludes the most meticulous of surveys. Such attempts mark the regular, inexorable degradation of the efforts of power to orient collective activity and to model rational organization. The efforts undoubtedly lead to profound and sometimes massive transformations, but never those that were expected or targeted; instead, the transformations produced always increase incoherence just where it was supposed to be alleviated, and they secrete irrationality in step with their rationalizations. These transformations arise from aberrant forecasting and inherently faulty programming; even when they succeed in imposing constraints, their effects are sterilizing, and they may be annihilating; at all events they are fated to see the truly new emerge elsewhere. No one with his eyes open can fail to see the incommensurable waste that the mad ambition of a society, as concentrated in the state, carries along and heaves up, the ambition to take control of everything and to institute itself as what it is not, what it cannot be: master of the general will, capable of knowing what moves it and where it is going, truly aware of what it can do, conscious of what in truth it ought to be. The waste in question is extraordinarily generative, moreover, and even eminently inventive in a number of respects, so much so that it may well constitute the principal mode of production of historicity in our universe. And this waste tends to feed on itself, by virtue of a commonplace circular process: the more disorder and irrationality spread and come to the surface, the stronger the will to control them becomes—the will to reduce them, to absorb them definitively back into the framework of a social organization in full possession of itself—and the more the opportunities for failure increase, as a result, the more the uncontrollable aberrations of the bureaucratic machine proliferate. As if our society were incapable of conceiving itself, even if only to despair of itself, except in the prospect of an ultimate reconquest of itself and except insofar as it is destined to the interminable construction of the gigantic administrative apparatus that promises it that one day it will know itself down to the most intimate detail and will master itself in all its parts.

No doubt the most conclusive testimony to this belief is the exasperated feeling of impossibility that permeates the derisory denunciations of a state that has become the whipping boy of French suburban universities. But the movement is already irresistible, the movement that will substitute the critique of impotence for the impotence of criticism. Although it is still unimaginable in its forms, its outcome, and its incidents, there is nothing obscure about the rupture to come, at least in its principle. It will require that we stop hoping that the state will get a new grip on itself, a prospect necessarily destined to radical failure. It will require that we begin to understand the unmasterable inventivity that the social encompasses. It will require that we stop thinking of ourselves in the horizon of a definitive reassertion of self-control. It will require that we start accepting the abyss always gaping just ahead.

Let us not be misled as to the breadth of the reversal in the offing. The state organ in its spectacular hypertrophy is not the only thing that is in question. The reversal has to affect the entire set of institutions and mechanisms at all levels of social life that relay and materialize the project of power of which the aim of state control constitutes only the extreme figure. The principle of power, entailing the will to expropriate others, the claim to possess them intimately, to rethink them through and through and to produce them, is the same wherever it unfolds, as we have seen, wherever there is a division in society, on any basis at all, between directors and executants. The same face of the impossible is uncovered everywhere, the same failure is repeated—and the same transformation becomes imperative. There is no such thing as an assured hold over the other, no such thing as a truly efficient organization of the other's world and behavior. Every success in a particular sector is counterbalanced at once by an adjacent failure. Troops may be made to carry out maneuvers with almost total mechanical perfection, but that does not guarantee success on the battlefield, to say the least. No planning or programming succeeds in completely stifling the initiative of agents in a predetermined framework within which they are presumed to be no more than cogs.

The most intrinsically enlightening and also the most crucial example of this, owing to its centrality—however symbolic—in a social formation that believes it is determined by economics, lies in the organization of industrial work and the political struggle of which that organization is the stake from the start. In the case of industrial work, ambition is at its paroxysm of clarity, and the constraints involved are brutal enough, moreover, to deny individuals the convenience of abstention, which is so widely practiced elsewhere. They cannot remove themselves from the order in which the least of their gestures is intended to be confined.

Under such conditions, the lesson cannot help but be convincing, and indeed definitive: to be reminded of this, we need only return to Cornelius Castoriadis's luminous and particularly effective demonstration.[1] On the one hand, despite all the science mobilized in order to construct an individual and collective program of work corresponding so closely to the natural law of bodies that the worker's only role would be to implement it concretely, with remarkable regularity the process turns out to be accomplished along pathways other than those anticipated; in addition, despite surveillance and policing of the material framework, implementation always escapes control in some respects. On the other hand, far from constituting an impediment—let alone a major obstacle—to the smooth operation of the production process, the constant resistance to which the system invites its workers, even as it claims to understand them in advance and define them in their stead, proves in reality to supply the very condition of possibility of that operation. For the supposedly rational plans into which agents are to be inserted are generally—and, owing to their very mode of development, constitutively—so defective that without the operations of refusal, deviation, and recomposition carried out by the executants in a shifting and informal fashion, the work process would end up, if not in paralysis, at least in a state of intermittent disarray. Indeed, if the reifying will at work in the so-called scientific organization of industrial activity were to achieve its ends and succeed in constituting individual workers as pure executants deprived of all understanding of their tasks, the system would collapse owing to the interplay between its lacks and its inconsistencies.

Here we have an irremediable contradiction: a theoretically perfect mechanism, based on the complete exclusion of initiative on the part of its agents, in reality succeeds in working more or less satisfactorily only thanks to initiatives taken in spite of it and against it. It is not just the dehumanizing and annihilating logic of "piecework" that gives rise to refusal and revolt. It is also the impossible objective it is trying to reach and the aberrations it engenders, aberrations that do not simply invite struggle on the part of the executants but require it, make it literally necessary. And not only does the "master" of the mechanism—the one who is supposed to know the others in their stead and to be the sole possessor of an overall vision of the process—not know with any certainty what is happening, not only is he incapable of preventing operations from going their own way rather than his, but it is only through the systematic opposition and methodical disobedience he encounters that he obtains something rather than nothing. In other words, the conflict between directors who direct much less than they think they do and executants who cannot help but do much more than execute is what ensures minimal cohesion, in such a framework, cohesion without which the system either would grind to a halt or would break down into anarchy.

Conflict is a factor of integration as well as of subversion. To put it in still other terms, the system lives on its own failure. And to the extent that the organizational model, the programming vision of authority—entailing a "rational" breakdown of tasks so a precisely determined sector of activity can be assigned to each person, for only the agency at the pinnacle of the hierarchy has the overall logic in hand—tends constantly to spread and become generalized, it is not absurd to maintain that the contradiction inherent in the aim of defining the activity of the other in his place constitutes the fundamental form of social antagonism today, and also that it is properly speaking the impossibility it confronts that supplies the axis around which it can function. It is inconceivable that one could really substitute oneself for another person to the point of penetrating into his body and producing his gestures; it is unreasonable to hope that the other can be subsumed within a program-rule through activity alone, without consciousness: yet our society not only fails to acknowledge this, in its dominant dynamics, but it organizes itself in large part in terms of a radical refusal to acknowledge it. Still, in the last analysis, from the inexorable failure to which society's central aim is thus destined, from its deepest disorder, it nevertheless derives something like a vital principle of cohesion.

The Failure of the Insane Asylum

Although the asylum project was very much less elaborate than the extensive modern developments of the organizational schema that have arisen from the revolutionary reinvention of power, that project and the fiasco to which it led need nevertheless to be deciphered as a particularly significant and even in many respects premonitory episode in the murky drama of power that has continued to play itself out at the heart of our universe. In the insane asylum, the model of order found a perfect place to unfold: the failure of the asylum project turned out to be commensurate with the rigorous clarity of the principles applied. It is an exemplary, limpid failure that prefigures, peacefully and in miniature, the immense disasters our century has known. It is impossible to control with a single gaze, impossible to master a population, however appropriately supervised and distributed, as if it were one person. It is impossible to transform individual souls at will, impossible even to act effectively on personalities by means of a suitable environment. It is impossible to mobilize minds in a lasting way, impossible to absorb them in the movement of an implemented rule to such an extent that individuality dissolves. All of these limits, over which the great political dream of our time has come violently to grief, were encountered earlier by the psychiatric experiment within its institutional microcosm. It is true that that early encounter had no consequences—and here naturally is the crux of the difference—except for the painful and slow degeneration occasioned by imprisonment; its consequences were admittedly on a very small scale in comparison with the bloody ills of the world. But the encounter was nonetheless not necessarily without profound political implications, indirect and diffuse ones no doubt, but of considerable impact.

Starting at the end of the nineteenth century—useful reference points are found in discussions about the "open door policy," and, in France, the positions taken by the principal advocate of "the method of freedom in the hospitalization of the insane," Marandon de Montyel[2]—the cause is irrevocably won: the body of convictions that had nourished the asylum effort from the beginning is no longer available to well-meaning minds. The walls still stand, but nothing vital remains of the conceptions and perspectives that initially justified them. The transformation now required, says Marandon de Montyel, is the equivalent of a "condemnation of everything that has been undertaken on behalf of the insane since Pinel's day. The magnificent establishments that we have built for them and the special hygiene to which we have subjected them may be said to have contributed in large measure to the increase in the number of incurable cases."[3]

It would be hard to mark the end of an era more clearly: the moment when the initial intentions turn into their opposite has become manifest, irrefutable. Separating the insane from the rest of the world does not further their treatment but on the contrary only tends to keep them confined in their disorder. Criticism has focused on the isolation of patients. But via isolation, which is the most perceptible and spectacular aspect of the system as well as its indispensable keystone, it rejects the entire mechanism of mastery as illusory and harmful. It is useless, as a general rule, and most often therapeutically dangerous as well, to cut the insane off entirely from the milieu they come from (a practice long deemed essential), because, in the first place, the wholesale availability of the patient to the doctor that is supposed to result from this isolation is from beginning to end a deception, and it has devastating consequences.

The institutional transparency or at least readability that was assumed to be produced by the appropriate classification of patients is thus a myth, and a pernicious one. For what is theoretically knowable is not yet knowledge. Only in the abstract can one offer up an ordered collection of human beings to a sovereign gaze capable simultaneously of descending into particularities and embracing their universal totality. God, perhaps, might profit from the doctor's effort to organize the space of illness and make it materially intelligible. The only thing we know for certain is that the doctor himself, the practitioner, will benefit little from it, if at all: the order *in itself* that he struggles to promote becomes all the more foreign to him as it becomes more perfect. The more impeccable it is, the more it is order *for some other* who is imagined to take in the whole at a glance—an other who is never oneself, the one in fact responsible for seeing and hearing. One result in practice, as incisive writers emphasize painfully, is that patients are neglected or even simply forgotten, in a process engendered and maintained by the machine designed to comprehend them. The alienist is at the heart of a mechanism conceived to make all cases immediately accessible to him in theory. But this is a false miracle of organization and a *trompe-l'oeil* trap: as the critics who have no use for isolation will point out, the alienist actually knows very little about what is going on, and even his limited knowledge is superficial; he is materially incapable of devoting more than a few minutes per year to each of his inmates. He reigns over a vast confinement ward where order masks indifference and neglect, and where what finally prevails is incarceration without attention or hope.

For what else is there to say about the so-called grip on the collective soul that would be authorized by the same intelligent distribution of individuals and species? If there were a first prize for illusions, this one would surely win. It is possible to imagine that a rigorous classificatory mechanism might permit a certain narrowly objectivist type of acts of knowledge. But it is impossible to see how such a mechanism could unleash a potential for the simultaneous communication of one with all, owing to which moral treatment could be applied in one fell swoop to the community of the insane as a whole. Here we have the mythic figure par excellence that has absorbed and blinded the medicine of alienation: the figure of the *mass*, an at once self-assured and elusive image of a collective being that lacks shape or form but that gives the impression of tangibility owing to its density. The image produced by the absorption of separate existences is that of a being without subjective consistency that nevertheless authorizes nearly individual and bodily commerce for anyone able to mobilize it and get it to coagulate. This eminently political figure is completely unsuited to the field of asylum practice, but it was put to a truly essential use there, in that from the outset it raised the aim of treatment to the global level of the institution, and in the end it crudely revealed its nature as an untouchable and perilous mirage.

We have to face facts: it is simply not possible to take hold of human beings en masse. No matter how one goes about it, the distinctness of individuals turns out to be unsurpassable. Whatever one does, subjective singularity remains unalterable; it resists dissolution within the collective entity to such an extent that the effort to deny it makes it stand out more sharply. Any effort tending to destroy the elementary bonds of coexistence in order to replace them with an undifferentiated, undistanciated mass succeeds on the contrary only in privatizing and further isolating individuals. In short, every alleged instance of fusion of beings must be radically challenged, along with every fusional figure gravitating around the central one: fusion with the law, fusion with the benevolent inspirations of authority, fusion with the harmony and order of the environment.

No law is experienced in reality as more external and more visibly constraining than the law that allegedly corresponds intimately to the spontaneous movement of subjects rejoining the anonymous enthusiasm of their community and effacing themselves in it. No power is more distant, more foreign, than power that believes it is plunging its roots into the population it controls, becoming one with that population, allowing it to live in harmony with its deepest truth, and communicating to this truth the general impulse to which it aspires. No organization is perceived as more artificial than the one conceived so that individuals can enter into it in such a natural way that they end up being entirely permeated by it and oblivious of it. The same illusion is involved on all these points: the illusion of a coincidence of the subjective with something that lies outside itself (other subjectivities, forms of sociability, the order of things and of the world), a coincidence that provides a way of literally entering into the subject and that makes it possible to act on the subject from within.

In a sense, the asylum experiment tested the irreducible character of a personal alterity that is never surmounted except through phantasmagorias. It is impossible to get a grip on human minds by drawing them in some way outside of themselves so that they will lose themselves in a collective movement that is for its part tightly controlled. Despite the disciplinary regimentation, the asylum was never anything but a place of intimate solitude, where each individual, sheltered by the daily repetition of collective gestures, faced the mechanical emptiness of a life with no horizon and had virtually no way out but persistence in his or her all-consuming chimeras.

However evil we must judge it to have been, however critical we must be toward its intolerable and futile, prisonlike oppressiveness, we must not forget that the asylum effort was first and fundamentally *the experience of an impotence* that was unaware of itself. That experience was in large measure the source of the uncontrollable aberrations into which it strayed: sometimes useless constraints, sometimes wretched oblivion if not terrifying abandonment. Our means for acting on the soul of others are weak, and perhaps even in the last analyis nonexistent; at all events, those that people thought they could attribute, in the wake of the revolutionary experience, to social influence are absolutely derisory. Here is the real bottom line of the experiment that played itself out over nearly a century in the space of madness and the confines of the machinery for reforging minds.

The experiment has remained unpublicized, and though premonitory, it has obviously prevented very little, which is not to say that it has remained without sequel or consequences; but quite to the contrary; silently, even secretly, the lesson has been registered. Confusedly, obscurely, the failure has been taken into account, reflected upon—to what point we do not know, but sufficiently, that much is certain, to bring about a radical change of direction, if not a complete reversal in political orientation. How can we fail to observe, indeed, that it is at the very moment when the institution intended to reform personalities reveals its patent impotence that a therapeutic technique arises, taking as its starting point the rejection in principle of the exercise of any direct effort to transform the patient's personality? Can one believe for an instant that the two events are unconnected? On the contrary, it is precisely because of that long effort to produce humans and to reconstruct the subject—and in a direct relation to the impossibility encountered in that effort—that the founding reversal of Freud became possible. The point of Freud's reversal was not to try to take control of souls, not to try to master from start to finish the process through which subjects get hold of themselves, de-alienate themselves, reconstitute themselves at a distance from their problems, but instead to accept from the outset, on the contrary, that one does not have immediate power over whatever it is that allows an individual to change; one does not really know its paths; one has to allow a transformation to occur without having access to its ultimate motive force.

There is a profound ambiguity in the psychoanalytic relation. On the one hand, psychoanalysis participates fully in the great projects of gaining power over ourselves that traverse the epoch. It stems from the avatars of our furious will to give ourselves the means to act on ourselves and, in the end, to *make ourselves.* But on the other hand, its approach is based on a tacit awareness of the limits of such an enterprise. Its approach originates in an acknowledgment that there is something impossible in the aim of penetrating others and influencing them in depth. And it is on this basis that it stems from the asylum experience, which in a sense it had to play out in reverse. Yes, subjects can to a certain extent change themselves and/or be changed. But solely on condition that one clearly recognizes, posits, and assumes, first, the impossibility of directing and controlling the process of one's own transformation oneself (one has to work through the other); and, second, the impossibility for others to lead as they please, and to channel with full awareness from the outside the transformation on which they are collaborating (others have transforming power only to the extent that they abstain from exercising power directly and from claiming mastery of the effects that they induce). There is no mechanism capable of procuring mastery over souls and their transformations. The terms have to be reversed: the transforming efficacy of the mechanism presupposes not only that it is based explicitly on the unmasterable, but also that it is deployed concretely in such a way as to make all positions of mastery untenable.

We know what was, historically, the theoretical and practical occasion that allowed or required such a reversal: the problem of hysteria, construed precisely as the problem of power over the soul of another, with its mirages, its traps, and its limits. For the hysteric is potentially the patient who is maximally open to action by the doctor, the most spectacularly influenceable, the most strangely susceptible to the hypnotic will of the other. Yet beneath his or her surface availability, dependency, and submissiveness, the hysteric is the most intractable being there is, the most irreducibly manipulative, the most resistant to the other's grasp even in the state of automaton-like abandonment in which the patient acts only on the master's orders. In short, it is the hysteric who gives a living face to the irremediable contradiction that power over the mind is destined to encounter. One may well manage to control others entirely, in appearance, even to the point of supplying their thoughts and dictating their movements, but one nevertheless always ends up acknowledging that in the last analysis others have escaped completely and irremediably, or even that one has actually been led unwittingly by them. Hence the radical renunciation and inversion in principle to which the hysteric invites us: if there is any possibility of going to the depths of the soul of another human being and mobilizing it, this can only happen without a manifest seizure of visible control, without illusions of mastery. Thus there is never a question of denying the strategically determining character of the episode of hysteria. That episode enabled the shift to occur; it functioned as an obligatory relay for invention. At the same time it is impossible not to take into account, in the background, something much less immediately visible, but just as decisive, if not even more profoundly causal: the avowed failure of the alienist system and of its aim to control the destiny of souls via the institution of the insane asylum.

The challenge that took the form of the hysteric's evasion brought forth a direct, explicit response. But it also raised a question, tacitly: what are the full consequences of the impossibility of getting an effective grip on subjects, as one had thought one could do by means of a collective organization? In this light, we can identify three moments in the development of the idea of a properly psychological cure for alienation. The first moment could be called Pinelean: it involves the discovery of an ineradicable "remnant of reason" in the insane, the discovery of the continual opposition in which they always dwell, somewhere in the vicinity of their deviation; this opposition is precisely what allows the practitioner to enter into a relation of intimacy with the patient's disorder. This first moment offers an opening between acceptance and reservation, between a refusal to counter the discourse of the insane and an effort to remain at a benevolent distance; it allows the discovery of a therapeutic space in the element of communication.

From this point on, quite rapidly, as we have seen, the principle of treatment thus brought to light is transferred and projected within the space of the institution. This is the second moment, the asylum moment: perhaps we need to call it psychiatry's political moment, the moment when it is invested and taken over by a pioneering institutional model that came straight out of the revolutionary upheavals of the social world. The logic of this collectivist implementation of the alienist project is completely transparent. We have to begin by noting that the institutional approach to treatment conforms perfectly with the fundamental requirements of moral treatment, as they had recently been formulated: do not counter the delirious convictions of the insane patient, do not pander to them either. Within the asylum framework, one must not exhort patients to think differently; one must not make statements intended to show patients the error of their ways. One must say nothing that is apt to upset them in their delirious faith; but one must say nothing, either, that is apt to support or encourage their beliefs. These restrictions are not in contradiction, then, with the conditions that have to preside over a moral cure. And the institution seems to offer in addition, as a crucial supplement, infallible means to mobilize the subjective element that has remained intact in the insane. It offers the possibility of drawing all the patients out of the solitude of their aberrations and getting them to live in unison in the impersonal and normal order of a common thought; thus it allows them to distance themselves to some extent from their madness, whether to forget it or to conquer it. The only problem is that the institution's alleged power to take hold of minds and blend them together arises from a pure mirage: in reality, there is no way to seize subjects from within so as to bring them outside themselves into the controllable field of a coherent and fusional community. Hence the Freudian reversal, once the bankruptcy of the institution that treats patients en masse has become incontrovertible.

In the first place, Freud takes the irreducibility of the individual into account, without making any concessions at all to the illusory figures of the absorption of separate existences within some collective entity. Second, and especially, the Freudian reversal establishes as a principle that it is impossible to maintain oneself in a place from which one might penetrate others, play subtly on their inner mainsprings, and seize them in their very depths. If we want to see the chasm in operation, the chasm that disconnects them from their aberrant element, that obliges them to question it, that supplies them with the power to rid themselves of it, there is only one way to proceed (and this is the third moment): we have to make them experience an absence—the irremediable, unfathomable absence of someone who could pierce them through and through, control their emotional reactions and their inner movements, and dictate their behavior from the outside.

We can see now that in this third moment, the cure of the soul leaves the political terrain onto which the asylum had brought it. It has decidedly left behind the time when its role was to supply an exemplary embodiment of the social ideal of power. Henceforth the converse is true, in many respects. The cure of the soul serves as an anti-mode; it offers the subtly polemical image of a gap and a renunciation with respect to the will to power that continues to nourish the phantasmagoria of society getting a radical new grip on itself. But we have to wonder whether this power of nonpower, which today constitutes the heart of psychiatric practice, may not also be weighed down by a secret political exemplarity. Is it not here that we must seek the cause of the diffuse but insistent feeling that there is a politics of psychoanalysis, the exact tenor of which escapes us but which we know to be of crucial import? This feeling is translated, in a way, by the persistent association of the names Marx and Freud. In Freud, the radical consequences drawn from an illusion of power that continues moreover to govern the social project are particularly premonitory. The cure of the soul had the opportunity to undertake a premonitory experiment, via the asylum: it experimented both with supreme power as it is dreamed of in the mirror of revolutions, and with the outcome of enterprises that propose to produce humans. The experiment may be said to have done no good whatsoever, if one means that it was not even *seen,* and that in its total insignificance it did not prevent the reutilization and diffusion of the same model, the pursuit of the same effort, this time on the scale of planetary apocalypse. Nevertheless, now that contemporary societies are numbly experiencing the undoing of the illusion and the discovery of the incomprehensible, the experiment signals very locally and very modestly, by its sequels and its developments, the path toward the agonizing revision that they will have to undertake: no claiming of power, if one is seeking to liberate the possible; no aiming at mastery, if one is seeking authentically to act.

CHAPTER IV

A Socializing Machine

Madness Transformed

HOWEVER ACCURATE our evaluation of the failure inherent in the asylum project itself may be, we must not allow it to blind us to the critical operation that was actually carried out in that context, or to keep us from examining its unintentional success. Although a certain number of insane patients were surely cured in asylums, the asylum itself could hardly have been "the instrument for curing" that its advocates expected. Even so, it was not without an instrumental function. In other words, from a historical point of view, its role was not limited to the purely segregative function of sequestering individuals who were unacceptable or problematic in terms of the requirements and norms of their society. Objectively, and at the most elementary level, the asylum indeed served to exclude. However, it would be quite mistaken to depict it as a mere social parenthesis, an inert apparatus for confinement, simply a walled compound adequate to contain its inmates and therefore destined, the day it disappeared, to leave the problem of insanity intact.

Asylums may not have treated the insane, but they *changed insanity*. The insane asylum may well have been the most powerful instrument of transformation that has ever come into play in the course of the history of madness. Far from serving simply to keep the insane at a safe remove, the asylum modified basic assumptions about their condition and status, to such an extent that it actively demonstrated its own futility and even its harmfulness. Although it failed to produce the anticipated therapeutic results, either in terms of mobilizing minds or absorbing individuals into the community, in the long run disciplinary and collectivist mechanisms that were implemented in the asylum context had the indirect but decisive effect of making evident, or at least perceptible, the fact that the insane were fit to live among other people, and that they continued to participate in the multiple networks of the social bond. These mechanisms brought to light the dangerous absurdity of a confinement that definitively breaks the social ties of individuals whose capacity for human relationships has been affected but who are nevertheless still indissolubly inscribed, in some sense, within the order of human communication.

The isolation imposed by the asylum is paradoxical. The asylum separated the insane from the rest of the world, but it also drew them out of the primitive abyss of their solitude. It cut them off from society, but it brought them out of their self-containment, from their confinement within their own bounds, from their inaccessible otherness; it brought them back to the open, multidimensional space of coexistence. No doubt the asylum restored their reason only to a limited degree, if it did not thrust them more deeply into their unreasoning pain. But through a slow accumulation of signs of identity and proximity, which corresponds chronologically with its own breakdown as a system, it symbolically restored the insane to society, by revealing incontestably and tangibly their nonseparation from ordinary human beings. No doubt the asylum left its inmates subjectively alone, if not in a state of intimate abandonment; thus it left them with the perilous freedom to fill the terrible moral emptiness of their lives as best they could. But at the same time, though it failed to seize hold of souls, the asylum at least succeeded in integrating individuals into a collective organization. It revealed the insane as human beings whose tragic singularity nevertheless does not cut them off from dealings with others and from social authority.

Two factors in the practice of isolation were closely connected, in the early stage of the asylum, then became progressively dissociated. In the first place, there was confinement itself, a forced removal from one's original milieu and a withdrawal from the gaze of the world. In this respect, the asylum was not innovative; at most, it systematized an ancient practice by elevating it to the status of a therapeutic requirement. A second circle of seclusion was no less crucial, though it was less spectacular—and for good reason—within confinement itself: the mutual isolation of the inmates. All patients were assigned to the rigid boundaries of their own cellular islands. In the early days, the two strategies were mutually interdependent. The insane removed from society also had to be set apart in their essential solitude. At least this was the ideal, when circumstances allowed—when lack of space, for instance, did not make it necessary to cram patients in. In cases of overcrowding, moreover, chains were frequently used in an attempt to ward off the perils of promiscuity. In another, rarer case, at hospitals like the Hôtel-Dieu in Paris, the insane undergoing treatment were admitted into a separate but common room. The custom at the time was to tie them down to their beds. But in principle as well as in practice, the form of confinement most commonly adopted and generally deemed adequate was the isolation of patients in their "boxes" [*loges*], to use the term in fashion at the time. Until the 1800s, new establishments devoted to madness were always built in terms of that imperative: one inmate, one cell, one unit of space (whether that space was conceived as an old-style box or a more modern bedroom, a monk's cell or a prisoner's, a shed or a dungeon).[1] In the early nineteenth century, haphazard housing for the insane was still devised in buildings that lent themselves badly to the desired individualization of confinement. Thus the recourse to the frightful wooden cages or the unspeakable huts described for example by Fodéré,[2] always in the obstinate effort to separate individuals whatever the cost, and to reduce insane patients to their own resources: the classic institutional paradigm of exclusion.

The utilitarian reasons for this compelling ideal of solitude—preventing violence, the general economy of surveillance—are not hard to grasp. But there are other quite particular reasons of a symbolic order: the institutional form corresponds point for point with the presumed nature of the illness. If one thinks that there is no better way, no more humane way, so to speak, to behave toward the insane than to remove them absolutely from the company of others and leave them alone, the reason is that one assumes madness to be in itself a complete withdrawal into the circle of the self and an absence from the world, a cutting off of the self in the empty autism of dreams or a convulsive forgetting of the self in the blindness of mad rage. Physical confinement simply accepts and confirms the insane person's own state of inner confinement, the imprisonment within the dark space of his or her chimera. The solitude of the box is exactly commensurate with "moral isolation," the "sort of civil death" that is striking and moving in the insane, as a quite enlightened writer could still put it in 1816.[3] The same Moreau—who happened to be Pinel's friend, colleague, and eulogist—writes that complete separation from others is "what makes the spectacle of madness less laughable than pathetic. . . . These patients, deprived of their social life, deprived of their usual communication, reduced to an animal state or involved in their supposed relations with supernatural beings, are in situations that powerfully grip the heart and provoke a lengthy, painful emotional reaction." Under these conditions, the only way a doctor can gain access to the intimate tenor of the problem is by accompanying the madman, as it were, in his "intellectual isolation" and "the interruption of his moral existence," as Moreau puts it. Thus the celebrated Père Poution de Manosque, one of the best-known of the entrepreneurs in the treatment of madness who began to proliferate outside the field of medicine at the end of the eighteenth century, reveals how the strict isolation of his patients was for him not the principle behind an apparatus for confinement but the basis for treatment. "They all live separately," he stresses; "they eat separately; they take walks at their own special times."[4]

The goal of separation continued to be widespread well into the nineteenth century. In 1866 at Evreux, a visitor could still find 32 cells for 40 inmates in the section of the hospital reserved for the insane. At Pontorson in 1833, the proportion was even more overwhelming: 78 boxes for 80 patients.[5] Moreover, at the time these arrangements were perfectly in keeping with the official vision of what an establishment of that sort could and should be, as we can see from the circular of September 14, 1833 sent by the ministry in charge (Commerce and Public Works, curiously enough) to the departmental administrations. Inquiring about the needs and the currently available means for accommodation, in the context of the investigations that would lead to the law of 1838, the civil servants of the Bureau for the Insane continued to make the box the basic accounting unit that allowed them to assess the capacity of the "special establishments" ("Are there special establishments for the insane in the department? How many boxes?").[6]

Committing patients to confinement always implies asserting and officially recognizing the subjective self-containment of the insane themselves. And remarkably, Pinel's reforms changed practically nothing, in the early stage, either in reality or in the conceptual framework. On the contrary, the need to prioritize improvement of the deplorable material conditions that prevailed at Bicêtre and La Salpêtrière led reformers to insist from the outset on the benefits of separating the patients, in contrast to the earlier overcrowding and promiscuity. Thus when the Conseil général des Hospices asked the Minister of Internal Affairs in 1801 to release funds that would allow the acquisition of the "former convents," Madeleine de la Trainelle and Filles de la Croix, the writers did not fail to highlight, among the advantages of those two houses, the fact that one of them, the convent of the Madeleine, "consists of 4 very large buildings that contain many offices and rooms ready for use," so that "one can receive insane women, whose numbers are greater, in them." "Almost without expense," they concluded, "that house will be able to hold more than 400 women *in separate rooms.*" Similarly, the house that had belonged to the Filles de la Croix could easily be set up so as to accommodate "300 insane men *in separate rooms* in the healthiest and most secure manner."[7] Here is a happy meeting between monastic architecture and the imperatives of welfare.

The subject was apparently dear to the heart of the administrators of the Conseil des Hospices, for two years later, deploring the failure of the requests addressed to the Minister, one of them, Camus, returned to the matter to insist that fatal limitations had resulted. "The Conseil," he observed, "has succeeded in reforming the earlier state of affairs [the treatment of madness, especially in the Hôtel-Dieu], but very imperfectly, very incompletely, and in a way that is not at all comparable with the successes that would have been achieved if we had been able to gather the insane of each sex together in a separate house, *with a cell (not a box) for each one*;

extensive gardens, areas of shade, water . . ."[8] Doctors themselves were slow to change their thinking on this point. E. Georget, for example, declared in 1823: "In general, single-bed cells are preferable in almost all cases; patients can leave them during the day and meet together; at night, they do not need each other."[9] The model of the complete solitude of the box has been abandoned, to be sure, and communal existence has been recognized as the normal mode of daily life. But the powerful underlying idea remains: the conviction that, left to themselves, removed from surveillance and from interactions with rational people, immersed anew in the element of their dreams at night, insane people are incapable of sustaining ordinary social life.

This situation is after all not so astonishing. For while psychiatry breaks radically with the old representations of the insane patient's "moral isolation," in its nascent stage it nonetheless maintains a narrowly restricted view of the patient as an isolated individual. The insane patient is open to communication and capable of exchange, but only within the limits of his singular, assymmetrical, and privileged relation with a skilled practitioner. Psychiatry may well have gotten its start by breaking with fallacious images of self-contained unreason and irremediable alterity on the part of the insane, and by revealing the contrary possibility of an intimate living relation with a deficient but viable subject. Still, it continued to view that subject only in isolation, only as grasped in his essential separation by a doctor or a specialist in moral treatment, such as Pussin. For that very reason, however revolutionary it may have been in other respects, Pinelean psychiatry did not have the intrinsic vocation of subverting or even disturbing the traditional order of confinement. It infinitely humanized confinement, moving patients from boxes to cells. But it retained the principle of confinement as its foundation. Psychiatry integrated itself within the symbolic space of confinement as organized by a basic principle of separation. It revealed the opening maintained by insane patients toward others—but within the exclusive framework of one-to-one therapeutic relations. On the one hand, it restored the patients' potentialities as subjects; on the other hand, it left them completely cut off from the possibility of casual relations with ordinary people, or even their companions in misfortune.

Strictly speaking, of course, the division is untenable, and the distribution necessarily unstable. Patients' elementary capacity for sociability, revealed in the therapeutic relation, will necessarily exceed its initial framework and spill over into their overall social environments. The distribution will unquestionably be eradicated in the long run, for once the power of the subject has been recognized and liberated within the narrow field of moral treatment, it can only expand, progressing toward self-realization in the form of the ability to stand on one's own as a person among others.

Still, it took time for that process of recovery to be completed and for the insane patient to progress from abstract participation in the order of sane, communicating beings—a premise of psychological treatment from the start—to concrete participation in the universe of social beings, evident in the ability to coexist immediately and autonomously with others.

This inaugural defeat of the insane individual's alterity was crucial, and it contained the potential for everything that followed. Breaking through the obscure confines of insanity, the pioneers of alienist medicine managed to penetrate the estranged victim's soul, where they found the ineradicable vestige of reason that could restore sanity. But what followed was equally essential: the lengthy work of erosion, eliminating the prejudice that the insane had to be isolated from society, locked away in their difference, condemned to inhuman solitude. Just as crucial as overcoming this barricade was patiently reintegrating the insane patient back into the living community of humans, isolated perhaps by illness, but never totally released from involvement with society. For this function the asylum deserves credit. It was the intermediate stage supplying the space and the conditions for resocialization, which gradually diminished the pragmatic alterity of the insane. This outcome was not necessarily intentional, of course: in the last analysis the asylum may have contributed as much through what it lacked, through what it failed to control, as it did through its explicit project (though that project itself was no small undertaking). One thing remains certain, despite all the clichés and prejudices: the critical shift took place in the asylum.

Sleeping

From the asylum's earliest years, as soon as doctors had acquired the right to oversee the organization of the facility and the treatment administered, we see the beginning of a move away from the cellular framework and its presuppositions and toward a system based, on the contrary, on the patients' latent social skills. The step was measured and cautious, but also highly significant in view of later developments. Pinel was still dealing exclusively with convalescent females—just under a quarter of the inhabitants of the treatment section of La Salpêtrière, if we are to believe an 1805 estimate.[10] But for these women, from the outset, it had been formally established that there would be no more boxes. The hospice administration was persuaded to allow a dormitory as one of the first improvements indispensable for a regular treatment program. "People are admitted there," Pinel says, "to learn to moderate their behavior, to calm their agitation, if any, to learn to live in communication with their fellows and to develop the taste for work that is the only safeguard for a solid and lasting cure."[11] A "common workshop" was located next to the dormitory, for sewing; there, the convalescents "gather to pass almost all day in company, encouraged by the slight progress they make every day, which in the end gives the most active ones a certain resource when they leave the hospice, as they will resume the habit of working when they return home."[12]

If we avoid naive claims about the insidious intention to inculcate the "bourgeois" work ethic, or moralizing platitudes about complicity with triumphant industrialism, we can pay attention to the context and find something of much more historical significance, a fundamental mutation of sensibilities: insane individuals are beginning to be reintegrated within the social framework. As Pinel comments tellingly, "One cannot describe often enough how salutary to the return of reason are the periodic gatherings of several people where they can converse freely about the interests of their families, whom they left behind several months earlier, and whom they hope to see soon, after a necessary absence, however long. Their days thus go by quickly, spent in communicating to each other their troubles and fears."[13] And even during the period when Pinel was presiding over La Salpêtrière, the mechanisms of the institution were still perceptibly evolving, for the measures first adopted exclusively for female convalescents were expanded to include other categories of patients. In 1816 the proportions were virtually equivalent: 349 boxes on one side against 321 dormitory beds on the other. The same report also specifies that "another dormitory that has just been finished can hold nearly one hundred melancholic patients."[14] It also mentions construction projects undertaken at Bicêtre after the 1806 reform and the inauguration of treatment, in particular a suitable building "divided into six rooms, each capable of containing 28 widely-spaced beds, 168 beds in all."[15]

We do not want to exaggerate the exemplary impact of this movement. Most of the establishments that opened at the beginning of the century continued to be organized according to the traditional model ("every insane patient has his cell"; "sixty other patients, each in a separate cell"). Treatises, prospectuses, travelers' accounts all endlessly repeat the same long-established and stubbornly prevalent cliché of solitary confinement. The fact remains that, even though the experiment was relatively isolated, the shift toward a collective structure at Bicêtre and La Salpêtrière already attests to a decisive shift in the pragmatic categories of alienist medicine. An increasingly pronounced inflection soon becomes an open break and ends up completely transforming the tenor and form of isolation. Patients are still cut off from the rest of society, but within the circumscribed universe, the closed world, of the hospital there is an opening toward others, an immersion in the collective dimension: not just the freedom to wander about within the walls—that freedom had already been advocated by eighteenth-century philanthrophists, and it is in no way incompatible but actually coheres with the representation of the insane person as inherently unsociable, so absorbed in his own thoughts that he cannot pay attention to others, so oblivious to others that he moves among them as if they did not exist (thus taking no risks and encountering no problems). What the more and more collective style of the asylum organization posits is a presence to others that has been maintained in the insane person to a sufficient extent that relations of coexistence among individuals can come about spontaneously. The mass dimension acquires a strategic character here: when a hundred people suffering from melancholia are put together in a dormitory, no matter what surveillance precautions are taken, the authorities know that the human relations that will develop within such a gathering must escape them. Thus the inevitability of these relations is acknowledged at the outset, and patients are allowed to pursue them according to their own dynamics, free from any hindrance or external intervention.

Unaware of Pinel's premises, Parchappe goes no further than Esquirol in his effort to discover the origins of "the predominance of dormitories as compared to the usual lodgings." To him that predominance is "still not very pronounced," moreover, in the model plan proposed in 1818, and rightly so. To judge from Esquirol's well-known 1818 paper on the "establishments devoted to the insane in France," or "Maison d'aliénés," an article that appeared the same year in the *Dictionnaire des Sciences Médicales*, it is obvious that his reasoning is still largely confined to the archaic framework of cellular isolation. We may take this as a telling sign of the extent to which practice is ahead of consciousness, given what we already know about the context of La Salpêtrière where Esquirol is working. The alienist promotes concrete arrangements for which he lacks the theoretical keys; his historical thinking does not measure up to his actions. Parchappe sees the Desportes project (presented in 1821, published in 1824) as containing the first clear acknowledgment in principle of the predominance of dormitories, a predominance, he notes, that "is more and more pronounced in the projects successively proposed and realized."[16] In 1853, then, an informed visitor no longer hesitated about the direction the history of the asylum was taking: the developments of recent decades continue to emphasize and increasingly validate an approach to the use of space that was still uncertain in 1820.

We have very interesting evidence of this definitive crystallization of the idea, after the half-century mark had passed, in the "scientific excursions into insane asylums" described by a certain Berthier, a little-known alienist but an attentive and representative investigator.[17] What makes his tour of France so telling is that he has very firm views of his own. His is a resolutely modern mind; he does not hesitate to pronounce stern judgments on what seem to him to be barbaric remnants of another age, or to shower praise on supporters of successful innovations. His central criterion, the basic dividing line, is the cell, first as a principle of construction, and second as a disciplinary instrument or means of containment. He judges everything first and foremost in terms of these two points; he vigorously deplores the persistence of institutions that are still made up almost entirely of boxes, and he condemns the excessive use of isolation in cells as a cheap way of securing peace and quiet.

Berthier's viewpoint is clear: he favors minimizing individual confinement. His general observations and his fundamental, pressing imperative allow us to see a clear dividing line between the two eras of the asylum. On one side, there are the facilities built or remodeled at the beginning of the century according to an essentially cellular model, and others still governed primarily by the ideal of individual enclosures even though they are organized around dormitories.[18] On the other side, there are the "good" establishments, most often of recent construction, designed to be as collective as possible in all respects. The slow but inexorable evolution toward the second model signals a major transformation in the status of madness. The gradual disappearance of boxes corresponds to the fate of the insane, who, imperceptibly but surely, become less and less "other." Less and less presumed prisoners of their own psychic solitude, they gradually regain their status as participants in a world in which one never really leaves others behind or stops needing them.

Eating

We have stressed the issue of how patients were housed, first because of its explicit importance for practitioners themselves, and also because of its inscription at the most immediately visible level. In a tangible and lasting way, the dormitory issue determined the overall structure of asylum buildings. Its influence was not limited to residential units, moreover; indirectly, it also affected the way patients were grouped. Taken to the extreme, the box eliminates the problem of grouping patients by categories; it makes it possible to put any patient next to any other. What makes the issue of boxes as opposed to dormitories an acute, obsessive problem is the organization of space according to a generalized principle of coexistence.

At the same time, other institutional changes, while they may be less important and more difficult to grasp on a broad scale, tend in the same direction and are just as clearly significant. The slow, laborious conquest of the dining hall is a central and privileged example. Pinel mentions the problem only once, in passing, in connection with the prevailing practices in Esquirol's establishment. But insofar as one can form a precise idea of daily life at La Salpêtrière from the few pages Pinel devotes to "the preparation and distribution of food," it seems certain that his silence corresponds to the renewal—without controversy or pangs of conscience—of the old practice of distributing food individually: to each his box, to each his portion. It is perfectly natural that Esquirol's wealthy wards should be concerned with forms, in keeping with the original dignity of their condition. But for the broader hospital population, of humble origins, there is no concern. And yet a great deal of caution is required, even given the genteel tradition the private facility is obligated to recreate: "Dinner is at four o'clock; the convalescents, the calm patients, and those who are only intermittently agitated are accepted at M. Esquirol's table; the others, unless they are dangerous, dine in a common room, each one at an individual table and attended by his own servant; the remainder, few in number, eat in their rooms."[19] The precautions taken are eloquent: while it is viewed as desirable to integrate the insane into a common space, it is also judged very difficult. In the best case, patients are invited to eat at the doctor's table, which is elevated to ensure effective surveillance. At the other extreme, there is the classic meal taken in the solitude of the cell. Between the two, we find the astute compromise of a tête-à-tête with a servant—the patient is still isolated, but surrounded by others nevertheless. Under no circumstances, however, are the insane left on their own.

In the face of such deeply rooted mistrust, which we find even among the most enlightened figures and in the most favorable material situations, in the face of this quite tenacious feeling that the insane must be cut off from others, it should not surprise us that change was so long in coming. In 1818 the same Esquirol observes that there are still "very few establishments where the insane are served together. In some, there is a common table for the convalescents and for a few calm, privileged patients. In Pyrna, Doctor Bietlnis has required all the patients to eat together, except for the most violent. In Avignon, in Charenton, in Bordeaux, there are rooms for this purpose."[20] Here Esquirol paints a dark picture of the countless disadvantages that arise from the widely practiced system of "distributing food at fixed, regular hours for all the inhabitants," typically once a day. "What torments, what laments, what cries, what furious displays" because the distributions are made uniformly, without concern for individual needs, "because having their daily bread at their disposal, the patients destroy it" and then suffer from hunger, because for fear of supplying them with a weapon, the management "does not entrust the agitated patients with dishes," so that "they often have neither vegetables nor soup and are almost limited to black bread."[21] Furthermore, when dishes are used to serve food to the insane, they "are in frightful condition" (or nonexistent); "the imbeciles, after receiving their food in their hands or in containers made of wood, pewter, or tin, wander around in the stairways, corridors, and courtyards devouring their food in a most disgusting manner." At La Salpêtrière, Esquirol explains, they have had to act against the most flagrant abuses, and he lists various steps taken to ward off the complaints and recriminations that arise from hunger and thirst. But he makes no mention of measures to establish dining halls, even though such measures have been declared "useful everywhere," because they "get the insane accustomed to resuming social habits."[22]

The same text allows us to identify, at roughly twenty years distance, the period in which common meals in asylums became a widespread practice. Esquirol corrected himself when he reworked his 1818 article for inclusion in *Des Maladies mentales*: "The insane used to eat in their cells," he wrote in place of the passages cited above; "today, almost everywhere, the insane gather in dining halls and sit at common tables." He noted a significant detail: "There are houses where [the inmates] are entrusted with knives. In England they are given thin knives with a round point and a blade that is sharp only in the middle, two or three inches wide."[23]

Around 1838, then, the principle of taking meals in common must have been almost universally accepted. Still, we must be cautious here: it may well be that Esquirol was exaggerating somewhat, out of optimism. This is the feeling one has, at any rate, when one compares his account to that of an approximate contemporary, a certain Leuret, a doctor at Bicêtre, which was still a relatively advanced and privileged facility at the time. Leuret confirmed the existence of a movement in favor of the new form of collectivization of daily life, but he also emphasized its recent, local character: "In several hospitals, especially during the last several years, the need has been felt to bring the patients together for their meals: this is a way to get them to eat neatly, to encourage those who, out of uncooperativeness or forgetfulness, might be otherwise be deprived of food; finally, it is one more resource for establishing social relations among them and distracting them." And in this connection he reports that Ferrus, at Bicêtre, had already succeeded in getting "several hundred incurable insane patients together at the same table: they were—and still are —served individual portions, which they eat more or less properly."

Here is an important limitation. The patients are gathered together, but they are served; each receives a portion that has been prepared ahead of time. They are still viewed as incapable of behaving like fully social beings who could divide up the food and share among themselves. The tacit postulate is that they can be asked to tolerate each other at most, not to model their behavior on that of others or even to take the others' existence into account. Leuret had sought to break with this limitation "a few months before"—let us recall that he was writing in 1840, two years after the publication of Esquirol's treatise—when "the Conseil général des Hôpitaux ordered that a dining hall be set up for insane patients undergoing treatment," and that as the person "responsible for the service at Bicêtre," he was to take charge of "designating and classifying the patients who would be admitted to the table." Esquirol's factual indications arouse a certain skepticism about his brisk generalizations. Perhaps there were indeed dining halls "almost everywhere"; however, in Paris, around 1840 and in one of the country's greatest hospitals, headed by the most prestigious masters of the special science, the insane patients undergoing treatment—recent arrivals, among whom a lingering paroxystic state was suspected—continued to take their meals in private, presumably in the isolation of their cells. But when the administration officially decided to end this state of affairs, Leuret for his part was not prepared to settle for a mere extension of the Ferrus system; he was determined to reestablish the ordinary and complete forms of mealtime sociability. Here is how he describes the execution of the reform for which he was responsible:

> I chose eighty patients, and I divided them into groups of ten. In each group, I took a leader whose job it was to get the tablemates together, bring them to the table, and make sure that they all took off their hats and washed their hands when they came in. The leader was to preside over the table and make sure that at the end of the meal everyone put his spoon, fork, and knife back on his plate; for I am not afraid to give them knives, on condition of course that they never take them away, and I take precautions so I will know right away who is not respecting this duty. From the very first day, everything proceeded in an orderly fashion, and from that point on letting the inmates eat in the dining hall has been a favor to grant them, a favor that works to the benefit of their cure. I have allowed no nurses to sit at the inmates' table; nor have I allowed the portions to be cut in advance, because I was determined that everything should be done without visible authority, and I wanted to remove as much as possible everything that recalled the hospital. Every table head has to know the names of his tablemates; he must make sure each one is properly served, and must treat them as if he had invited them to dine in his home.[24]

Leuret's description makes the whole process clear: the paternalistic calculation, the hierarchical strategy, the abundant precautions. And of course, for those of us who imagine that we can look down on such language as terribly dated, there is a great temptation to focus exclusively on what strikes us immediately as hypocritical authoritarianism and moralizing weakness. Here, too, there is much we may be tempted to criticize: the infantilizing inculcation of good manners (take off your hat, wash your hands); the skillful selection of low-level leaders who serve as intermediaries for enforcing the rules; the appearance of freedom achieved through concealed but rigorous surveillance. We may be inclined to see these as dirty tricks taken straight out of the "Master's" inexhaustible bag. But to do so would be an unfortunate historical misreading, for such an interpretation completely fails to take into account the inscription of the experiment in an ongoing process and its very real significance as rupture.

The rigorous accumulation of precautions and the groping meticulousness of the staging both help signal the historical break. We should also not forget that each of these detailed measures was a novelty at the time. It was not self-evident, at the time, that the insane should be left to themselves—"I have allowed no nurses to sit at the inmates' table"—as if they were in a position to constitute themselves, through their own actions, as a community, however fleeting. It was "because I was determined that everything should be done without visible authority," Leuret says, that "[I did not] allow the portions to be cut in advance." But whatever Leuret may be saying in other respects about visible or invisible authority, what we have to see here—and it represents a considerable step forward—is the form of collective management that Leuret reintroduces in an elementary but still significant fashion. With the patients' participation in the minimal universe of exchange, the dimension of subject-group is symbolically restored. Is it an insignificant detail that the table head is required to know the names of his companions? Not at all, if we recall that in the 1800s, to enter an institution for the insane still often meant losing one's name, because the family honor was at stake, of course, but also because being mad meant that one existed only for oneself, that one no longer had to know others or to situate oneself in relation to them.

Leuret is explicitly attempting to create a world where you care about knowing who you are, where you have to know who the others are; he is combatting a time-honored and still overbearing tradition that reads madness as loss of self. We may well be shocked today by the petty concern for maintaining control over knives and forks. But it is important to understand what plates, spoons, forks, and knives meant to the insane, at a time when many establishments still followed the old custom of distributing food in disgusting bowls made of an unbreakable material (wood, pewter, or tin, according to Esquirol), if they did not put the food directly into the inmate's hands, for fear of some violent gesture (Esquirol again). Similarly, for us the trivial point of making sure the patients washed their hands before meals is no longer anything but the mindless imposition of so-called "good" manners. But seen in its own context, the preoccupation with "cleanliness" takes on a completely different meaning: it indicates a concern for *humanity* that counters a persistent representation of *animality*. It marks a break with the deeply rooted idea that elementary forces, which surface owing to the patient's absence from self, condemn the insane in every case to bestial voracity and uncleanliness. That same idea continued to make it acceptable, in these early decades of the nineteenth century, to distribute food directly into the patients' hands and to let them wander about in the courtyards "devouring their food in the most disgusting manner." If Leuret for his part wants the Bicêtre patients to wash their hands before eating, this may well reflect the narrow-minded authoritarianism of a custodian of bourgeois morality. But there is a more important consideration: Leuret is also acting as an agent—although of course he cannot be aware that he is playing this role—of the diffuse, multiform, almost imperceptible but inexorable process in which the radical otherness of the insane is being slowly dismantled. As we know, the image of bestial lack of consciousness has been attached to the insane for centuries. If Leuret wants his patients to wash their hands, it is in part because he refuses to keep on seeing them as beings set apart by the automatic indifferentiation of instinct. It is because he recognizes them as individuals who are not only immediately and fully aware of their surroundings, but who remain potentially capable of taking others into account, of acting for others.

Leuret's enterprise can thus be viewed as a global, systematic, painstaking endeavor to reconstitute the dimension of sociability in a nodal point of daily life. The challenge for us is to find the meaning and logic of the enterprise behind what may strike us, at a distance, as a rigid insistence on orderliness in a project of authoritarian reeducation. After the fact, once the phenomenon has been achieved and constituted as self-evident, it is easy enough to be stirred up, in the very name of that self-evidence, by the appearance of regimentation and paternalistic cautiousness. Why the useless apparatus of mobilization and support for people who are indeed perfectly capable of taking their meals peacefully together and of working things out quite well among themselves? However, one small detail has been forgotten amidst these good sentiments, and it changes everything: it is that the most elementary integration of the insane among their neighbors and companions had to be *produced*, in both meanings of the term—and it had to be constituted from start to finish, down to the humblest details, in a struggle against the millenial weight of custom and images and against the silent violence of power. Such integration had to be manifested in action; its very possibility had to be demonstrated, in order to counter the persistent reticences of a public opinion under the sway of ancient phantasms.

Working

Dormitories and dining halls are strategic places: beyond their functional importance, they sum up a way of being and even symbolize a condition. The vast mutation of the status of madness, of which the nineteenth century was the theatre and alienist medicine was the principal agent, is perhaps nowhere better reflected and attested than in the patient reform of the internal arrangements of the insane asylum and its inhabitants' way of life. But if we are genuinely seeking to arrive at a thorough evaluation of the work of socialization that was accomplished within confinement, we need to enumerate a whole set of additional initiatives and measures; we shall have to identify their sources of convergence and trace their evolution. At issue here is everything with which the doctors strove to fill the perilous emptiness of daily life, to "ward off the effects of idleness and boredom."

Idleness had been identified fairly early as the great danger of the asylum, and it was increasingly felt to be its inherent vice, as efforts were made to draw the insane patients out of themselves and as their need for the external world was recognized. In the beginning, there was no problem of this sort, for the insane were perceived precisely as so involved with themselves that there was no hope of distracting them for a regulated activity that would restore them even for a moment to the truth of the outside world. Forgotten in the depths of their boxes, or, more humanely, given the freedom of the courtyard, the mad were thought to be occupied with themselves and themselves alone, either singlemindedly pursuing their chimeras or releasing the surfeit of energy that possessed and agitated them. Thus the new concern for the way the insane spent their time takes on immediate importance: questioning their absence to the world meant putting an end to their intrinsic idleness. Work then became the first way to signify their continued participation in a universe of which the center stood outside themselves.

Pinel's formula is well-known: "Mechanical employment [is] essential to the successful management of lunatic hospitals."[25] He is quite firm on this point:

> Very few lunatics, even in their most furious state, ought to be without some active occupation. The scene which is presented in our national establishments by the insane of all descriptions and character, expending their effervescent excitement in antics and motions of various kinds, without utility or object, or plunged in profound melancholy, inertia and stupor, is equally affecting, picturesque, and pitiable. Such unrestrained indulgence of the natural propensities to indolence, to unproductive activity, or to depressing meditations, must in a high degree contribute to aggravate the existing evil. Laborious employment, on the other hand, is not a little calculated to divert the thoughts of lunatics from their usual morbid channel, to fix their attention upon more pleasing objects, and by exercise to strengthen the functions of the understanding. Where this method is adopted, little difficulty is experienced in the maintenance of order, and in the conduct and distribution of lunatics, even independent of many minute and often ineffective regulations, which at other places are deemed indispensibly necessary.[26]

Pinel goes on to invoke the example (apparently a mythical one, moreover) of the "asylum" in Saragossa.

Now, while on paper the point may seem to have been definitively won, while the critique of the "afflicting" effects of inactivity seems to have been established once and for all at the outset and thus seems to be available for interminable repetitions, in reality things are not so clearcut. First, because despite the generality of his theoretical claim, in practice Pinel adopts a restricted approach: if we look closely, we find that he is actually concerned with providing occupation for convalescents alone. In this connection, we may recall the description of the sewing workshop in La Salpêtrière cited above; at Bicêtre, Pinel reports, "I made . . . every exertion in my power to obtain from the government an adjacent piece of ground, the cultivation of which might employ the convalescent maniacs and conduce to the reestablishment of their health"; however, the "disturbances which agitated the country" after the Revolution prevented this project from being carried out. For considerable distance remains between having an idea and seeing it carried out, seeing it tangibly—and even then never fully—embodied among the self-evident aspects of the world. It is one thing to posit as an axiom that "few lunatics, even in their most furious state, ought to be without some active occupation."[27] It is something else again to encounter the patient, to perceive him immediately as a human being capable of working. On this point as elsewhere, perceptions lag behind ideas. Practitioners may know perfectly well that the insane are not as completely walled off within themselves as had been supposed; they may very well view them as accessible. Still, they continue to see insane patients as incapable of adapting spontaneously to the unpredictable contours of reality or of submitting to the demands of a long-term enterprise.

It is always possible, of course, to use force to turn patients away from their demented convictions and their senseless "gaps." In this regard Pinel evokes the example of a farmer from northern Scotland who was "famous" for his treatment of insanity:

> The great secret of his practice consisted in giving full employment to the remaining faculties of the lunatic. With that view, he compelled all his patients to work on his farm. He varied their occupations, divided their labour, and assigned to each, the post which he was best qualified to fill. Some were employed as beasts of draught or burden, and others as servants of various orders and provinces. . . . Disobedience and revolt, whenever they appeared in any of its operations, were instantly and severely punished.[28]

But once violence is ruled out, along with its theoretical correlate, the impossibility of conquering the insane person's subjective autarky except by brute force, and once the hope of a cure is shifted onto the patient's own movement toward the outside world, it remains obstinately understood that such movement is to be expected only as the illness declines, only "when, amidst the languors of an inactive life," convalescent patients may be offered "a stimulus to their natural propensity to motion and exercise."[29] As for the other patients, there is not much point in seeking to remove them from their overly intense preoccupations or their convulsive wanderings, even if one knows that an attempt to do so is perfectly conceivable.

The Contradictory Nature of Isolation

During the progressive reintegration of the insane into the realm of everyday practices, recognition of their ability to undertake regular activity was continually extended and broadened until it completely transformed the approach to the problem. At first a medical prescription that broke with the tacit presuppositions of confinement, work gradually came to be viewed as an elementary need to be satisfied, apart from any medical considerations.[30] Moreover, confinement proved to pose an increasingly insurmountable obstacle to satisfaction of that need. How could ever more numerous patients be provided with occupations, given the necessarily limited resources of a closed space? Little by little, this question becomes the acute, insistent, insoluble question of asylum managers.

Shifting away from the idea of an inherent idleness that was initially attributed to the insane, practitioners began to conceive of an artificial idleness, secreted and maintained by the structures of confinement, which could only incite to madness, further sequestering individuals within their illness. Here we encounter the polemical theme of "confirmeries," institutions seemingly designed to fabricate incurables. In 1840 Leuret is already formulating the problem in almost these terms. He warns pointedly against the "disadvantages" and even the "dangers" that may result from isolating a certain type of patient.

> Owing to his illness, the monomaniac is quite disposed to live isolated from the world, to entertain himself with his ideas alone; the friction he experiences in society obliges him to live outside himself; self-esteem and the fear of appearing ridiculous may keep him in good habits; the contact with reasonable persons supports him; his habitual occupations, if he is still capable of pursuing them, offer a happy diversion from his delirium; as soon as he is deprived of all these advantages and sequestered, as soon as he has no company other than that of the warders or of other unfortunates who, like himself, are insane, he falls into a state of moral impoverishment that is more or less advanced but usually very pronounced and very prompt; and unless multiple efforts are made both by himself and by the doctors, he runs the risk of falling into dementia.[31]

To be sure, Leuret's reservation applies to only one category of patients, and these probably would not even have been confined thirty or forty years earlier.[32] However, this does not prevent Leuret from saying that isolation is "often useful" and may even be in typical cases "almost always necessary." The fact remains that Leuret's reservation makes it possible to measure the distance covered since the period of absolute faith in the asylum, as exposed in the early 1800s. Pinel had been able to see that idleness kept insane patients in their state of "effervescence" and "delirious exaltation"—although it did not lead to any aggravation of their condition. At the same time, he was untroubled by doubt on at least two fundamental points. He was convinced that the hospital framework was the only context in which one could remedy the patients' "spirited outbursts" and make "mechanical work" available to individuals whose illness would keep them from it anywhere else. He also believed that a well-conceived establishment could provide all the resources to this end.

Leuret differs with Pinel on both points. For him it is no longer self-evident, in the first place, that an asylum is absolutely necessary to reconnect the insane person with the external world. To a perhaps limited but still signficant extent, the representation of the insane as estranged from the world has receded, and patients are beginning to be seen as human beings who still have an essential need to "live outside of themselves," despite their tendency to turn exclusively inward toward their delirium-induced preoccupations. And it is less obvious still, in the second place, that an asylum ever makes it possible to offer an adequate, let alone advantageous, substitute for "the duties and habits of society." The suspicion we see developing in Leuret is that, whatever doctors do to fill up their wards' existence, they will never succeed in providing the consistency of a life filled with all the spontaneous solicitations of an ordinary environment. Confinement itself proves to be an obstacle to the creation of a milieu sufficiently endowed with its own dynamic to absorb individuals and thus sufficiently dense in necessary relations with others to re-create within a self-contained system the authentic tenor of the social bond.

Here we are observing the beginning of the great reversal through which the asylum effort finally became capable of self-criticism. Constituted, transformed, traversed through and through by the aim of socialization, the asylum was destined to appear in the final analysis, and as a function of its very success, as the ultimate and principal obstacle to the complete realization of its own project. To the extent that it managed to produce and unveil in the person of the insane man or woman not only a being capable of adapting to the external forms of organized manual labor, but a being with an indestructible need to associate himself with the affairs of the world, the asylum inevitably reached the point of bumping up against its own necessary insufficiency as an artifical microcosm, against the "moral poverty" inherent in its self-enclosure, against its ineluctably desocializing effects. This is the movement that one can trace in Leuret, in a still incomplete way, but in unambiguous terms. The representation of the intimate potential of insane individuals has already been sufficiently broadened—in the eyes of a privileged witness, to be sure—to impose a clear though embryonic awareness of the deficits of activity and sociability that isolation implies.

In Leuret's case, the two inspirations intersect and remain in balance. The primary task consists of returning the insane to ordinary rituals—we define the insane here as individuals who have succumbed to the exclusive solitude of their singularity—the dual dimension of coexistence with others and integration within the common order of things (the dining hall is an example of this effort). In addition, we see the beginning of an effort, doomed at the outset, to compensate for the congenital social deficiencies that characterize any closed gathering of individuals of the sort the asylum produces. How can an asylum ever equal the pressing multiplicity, the complex thickness of the outside world?

It is manifestly in this spirit that Leuret poses the problem of work. He notes that "the distractions available to patients in a clinic or a hospice are very few in number," and that their effects are necessarily "quite secondary." Only work offers a valid remedy against the void, and the ideal is work "organized absolutely as it is in a factory." Leuret reports he has seen such an arrangement in Germany, in the Halle hospice directed by Damerow.[33] But a large farm might also serve the purpose, although it offers few outlets in winter. Similar declarations appear throughout the second half of the century like a leitmotiv in literature about the asylum. These declarations have been interpreted by others, moreover, as marking a concerted will to reinculcate the work ethic in individuals tempted to evade it, or as marking a rational project for readaptation to productive tasks—the language may vary, but the overall idea remains the same. That interpretation has some general validity: the therapeutic ambition goes hand in hand with the project of restoring individuals—of "adapting" them as best one can—to society as it is. It is hard to see how it could be otherwise. However, this inoffensive bit of conventional wisdom hides what is essential. To begin with, it hides the historical inscription of enthusiasm for manual labor in the asylum context; as if from time immemorial the insane, themselves without history and malleable at will, had waited for someone to come up with the project of putting them to work—whereas in reality, a long preliminary transformation and a properly productive operation were needed in order to bring the insane patient into a regulated network of occupations; as if doctors had only imported the norms of a society under the sway of the demons of productivity from outside the asylum in order to impose them within—whereas what was asked of them first of all was to respond to a problem internal to the institution, the problem posed quite precisely by the contradiction between the sustained potential for activity in insane patients, which situates them in some way among the ranks of beings in the outside world, and the limits within which confinement restricts them; as if, finally, the grandiose prospects of transforming asylums into agricultural or industrial niches had led in the slightest degree to systematic, lasting, and satisfactory realizations even from the point of view of their supporters. Such, assuredly, is not the case. In general, the project of putting the asylum population to work remained for the most part a pious wish, tirelessly reiterated but no less constantly disparaged.

Bicêtre is a good example. In Leuret's time, the doctor did not have a factory, but he had access to a farm, granted to Ferrus by the hospice administration. Thus it was possible, at least during the summer months, to employ most of the able-bodied insane. ("As for the small number of those who, while able to work, are nevertheless neither strong enough nor astute enough to be sent outside," Leuret adds, "they are kept busy making door mats or hats.") The farm was an exceptional resource for the capital city, and it soon came under scrutiny. A few years later, indeed, the lands were used for the construction of the Sainte-Anne asylum, and that spelled the end, if not of work at Bicêtre, then at least of its principal resource.

This example, in no way exceptional, brings to light one of the chief obstacles with which the alienists had to contend: the crowded conditions in the asylums. The continual admission of patients congested the facilities, diminished the level of supervision, and created a constant demand for new construction; thus available space was often whittled away.[34] No doubt there are local successes here and there—in one place a remarkable system of workshops, in another a vast farm absorbing all the available labor force in a beehive atmosphere. But these were also often precarious—highlighted by the specialized literature at one moment, but quickly undermined by circumstances, routine, or demographic changes. There was certainly a vast array of studies and experiments: one example is the movement to set up asylums as agricultural colonies in the 1860s.

A precise, meticulous, in-depth history of all those undertakings has yet to be written. It would probably reveal a situation more complex than the one we can see here; there would probably be a number of exceptions, partial adjustments, or limited successes. Still, such a history could not greatly modify the overall impression that, in general, and despite the obsessive efforts of its managers, the asylum did not keep its inhabitants occupied. By and large, attempts to put the mentally ill to work met with large-scale failure. Thus it makes no sense to judge the enterprise on the basis of declarations of intent. Each one may have been more radical than the last, but all were almost equally devoid of effects and consequences. It is precisely this gap between the ambitions declared and the results actually obtained that needs to be questioned. It brings us back to the root of the problem, that is, the insoluble contradiction of an institution that more or less consciously pursues the goal of reestablishing the insane within the order of objective existence, that is, the existence that is required by the outside world yet tends to relegate them by its very principle to an aimless life. This is what fundamentally gives rise to the desire to make the insane work. But here, too, does that desire not come to grief, at an even deeper level than the level of material obstacles? For if the insane were actually put to work, would that not further aggravate the contradiction instead of resolving it? Work is not everything, in fact; a human being can demonstrate aptitude for a perfectly ordinary activity on a daily basis and still be condemned to the "moral poverty" of a closed community. Perhaps it is here that the emptiness of the asylum world, even when partially filled, stands out most sharply. Making the world inside the asylum virtually the equivalent of the world outside may be the surest way, in the end, to reveal the harmfulness of the walls that separate the two. Perhaps it is in this murky zone that we must seek the ultimate reasons for the alienists' impotence in the face of this gigantic and unreformable apparatus. Their outlook is reminiscent of the disturbing demoralization of soldiers fighting for a cause they suspect is lost.

Insertion into a Community

Leuret set out to run an impossible race against the "moral impoverishment" that inevitably results from the self-contained nature of the asylum. His commitment distinguished him as visionary, beyond the critical turning point where the asylum, almost as soon as it was systematized, quietly became a problem in its very principle.[35] Nevertheless, he belongs to the early stages of psychiatry's evolution, as primarily and insistently determined to reconstitute ex nihilo the communitarian dimension of the insane population. He occasionally followed authoritarian paths, even "somewhat military" ones, as he himself acknowledges. Here again, we inevitably find his means disturbing today, for we have inherited a representation of the "madman" that has been shaped and transmitted by that very authority, and not at all given as self-evident from the outset. Thus, concerning the barracks-style training imposed on patients "who are able to walk and who cannot or will not work," we are told: "Whenever time permits, [they] are brought together in the courtyard of the hospice and made to exercise by marching like soldiers at drill. Imitation is such a powerful lever, even over the laziest and most stubborn of men, that I have seen several among these latter who, having first refused to do anything at all, nevertheless consented to march. This is the beginning of methodical, regular, and reasonable action, and this action leads to others."[36]

It is easy to anticipate the indignation of today's fine minds before the odiousness of such activity and the sterile absurdity of such a remedy for idleness. For we should recall, even before we examine the political arguments, that finding a remedy for idleness, figuring out against all odds how to avoid leaving the patients unoccupied, is always the primary concern. But perhaps this is precisely where we shall find the answer to the retrospective reproach of regimentation. Work is a vivid affirmation that for all practical purposes every insane person can be included in a collective activity; in each one, it is possible to arouse, at least in an elementary, instinctive ("imitative") fashion, an awareness of the need to relate his gestures to those of others, an awareness of the material, bodily sensation of moving in concert with others.

Despite what we may be inclined to believe, such points have not always been taken as self-evident. Let us recall the then quite recent images still attached to the "liberation" of the insane, the liberation advocated by Tenon, the one initiated by Pussin: what was actually at stake was bringing the insane out of the dungeon (or their chains) and allowing them freedom of movement in the courtyard—both the "furious" ones, as Tenon would say, "in a continual, vain mobility, flailing about to no purpose," and the "imbeciles," "sadly immersed in inertia and stupor." "An afflicting sight," Pinel observes, and one that the iconography of the asylum continues to preserve until very late in the century; we can all call to mind swarming scenes where a cacophony of gestures and attitudes bursts forth, a tragic or comic juxtaposition of solitudes, depending on the artist, scenes in which no one even sees anyone else, in which no one exists any longer except for himself. Leuret's enterprise has to be evaluated in contrast to these backward visions of the insane person's uncontrollable, indomitable reduction to particularity. Disciplinary, primitive, mechanical: all these terms no doubt apply to Leuret's project. But it was also transformative: in its own rudimentary and modest way, it helped produce the new system of self-evident verities in the name of which some of us can now pass lofty judgment.

Moreover, the recourse to military drills constitutes only the most extreme and, as it were, the most desperate measure of a set of provisions that look less incongruous. For us, this extreme measure has become impossible to defend; as a result, it opens up the depth of a historical field, the remote reaches of a mutation. Alongside marching in step there was also, more acceptably, a school for the insane, which had the dual advantage of "instructing and distracting" the wards at Bicêtre, who were almost all products "of the poor and unfortunately ignorant class." Above and beyond the actual classroom instruction dispensed by a teacher, the school supplied the framework for meetings devoted to collective reading, recitation, play rehearsals, and singing, always with the omnipresent intention of bringing the insane patient back into the presence of others. At the most elementary level, the patients may have had to take turns reading aloud and thus pay at least some attention to what the others were saying. Or, via play productions, they may have become aware of the need to modify their discourse by virtue of the fact that it was addressed to others, to an entire eager public, and that they might need to adapt their speech according to audience reactions. Or, finally, when it was a matter of "singing together harmoniously," they may have been asked to adjust their voices to the others and to work toward blending into the collective sound.

A single, common preoccupation lies behind all the exercises in their diversity: the point is of course to distract the patients, to use studious activity to fill the long winter evenings during which the patients, sent to bed at sundown, had previously been left to themselves.[37] Leuret explicitly justifies his actions in these terms, pointing to the therapeutic effects traditionally expected from diversions. But there is also something else, something at once silent and self-evident, something left rigorously unexpressed and impossible to miss: an exclusive, systematic preoccupation with rebuilding at its root a bond of mutual belonging among individuals, a concern for bringing insane patients back to the point of self-determination in even the humblest matters, which relates to the fact that they dwell among others. This concern on the part of practitioners operates simultaneously against the inner inclination that tends to isolate the patients concretely, and against the inherited representation that sequesters them in their dementia and excludes them from the social dimension.

Commerce with others first of all: although it was not openly acknowledged, this was actually the behavioral goal that guided the alienist from start to finish. To take just one illustrative detail, Leuret reports that "since a rudimentary library has been made available to the teacher in charge of the school, the educated patients can spend time reading in the evenings and during breaks from manual labor." However, he hastens to add that "this is only a distraction on which I do not count very much; I am much more inclined to advise the educated patients to help the teacher, by giving lessons to the uneducated themselves; in that way master and pupil work together toward curing each other."[38] The most intelligent distraction is useless if it continues to leave patients trapped in the curse of their solitude. The only distraction that really counts is one that leads them to manifest themselves positively as human beings capable of even more than respect for rule-governed forms of coexistence, one that allows them to show their capacity for exchange and authentic reciprocity, and not just within a privileged relation with a representative of rational individuals, but with fellow human beings, those from whom they are a priori the most remote, since they have all been brought together by a common indifference to outside truth and public opinion.

Leuret pursues this set of provisions, as it happens, within a therapeutic perspective. The point is of little importance: elsewhere, measures inspired by similar concerns are advocated by people who do not have much faith in moral treatment and who embellish their work with different justifications. The theoretical options and the systems for action that they are intended to justify do not have primacy here. The explanations come after the fact; they provide a cloak of rationality for requirements of a different order. Under the circumstances, these are not so much medical requirements as social requirements that have in fact remained obscure and unformulated throughout the history of the asylum; continually active, these requirements have been invoked under a wide variety of names, but they have never been recognized in and for themselves. What is astonishing, actually, is that the internal transformation of the asylum in order to transform madness itself took place in a largely independent fashion, with its own rhythms, halts, and critical phases, but without many inflections dictated by doctrinal reversals and without many substantive disagreements attributable to antagonism between individuals or schools of thought. What is remarkable is that, in this area, practitioners with differing views ended up adopting the same practices. Innovators who for the most part rejected the legacy they had inherited nevertheless continued along the lines of their precedessors in this respect. The prevailing opposition occurred between conservative inertia and reforming dynamism rather than between contradictory visions of mental pathology.

Below the level of any official justifications, the insane asylum was the site and the stake of a specific process—a slow one, obscure even for its actors, not consciously mastered by them, but one in which the true historical function of the asylum has to be recognized. It entailed a shrinking of the social principle of difference that had from time immemorial identified the essence of madness as separation from the rest of humanity (however that separation may have been implemented institutionally). We have offered a few glimpses of that entirely material operation. Its history, which remains to be written, would have to take into account the nebula of modest initiatives, humble measures, and minor reforms through which the most sensitive aspects of change often passed; it would focus on the subtle evolutions of daily life, and it would neglect none of the registers on which the social bond is simultaneously formed and signified.[39] The buried truth of the psychiatric phenomenon remains to be exhumed.

To reinscribe the insane patient among the others is to gain control over him or her: what the alienists were pursuing through the socialization of their institutionalized patients was basically a mechanism for gaining a comprehensive, enduring hold over their minds. And this is no doubt in large measure why they remained silent about the task of meticulous reconstruction of the forms of coexistence, even when they devoted all their efforts to that end. For the project of instituting interaction among the patients is not apparent to them as such; they literally do not see it, so fully is it incorporated in and subordinated to a perfectly clear, explicit, and central aim, that of taking hold of souls and governing them (to borrow Fabre's superb formula once again). A lunatic locked away half the day in her box and wandering freely about the rest of the time is someone who fundamentally escapes me, as therapist, aside from the few, brief moments that may be devoted to dealing with her in private. When she is kept busy with the entire body of her fellows, when she is associated with some matter that mobilizes the whole group at once, even if it is only a simple meal taken in common, when she is integrated into a collective task, I will not only have the means to hold her virtually at my disposal, like the others, but also the possibility, if not of communicating directly with each individual, at least of being implicitly and simultaneously present in the mind of each by way of the organization I am running. Beyond any doubt, the effort to open up the asylum space onto itself, to collectivize it, to activate it, as it were, requires control, mobilization, and mastery of the patient population. Dormitory, dining hall, workshop, school, chorus: these are all melting pots to mold individuals into a mass that can be dealt with globally and governed in principle at will, to the extent that one finds oneself the demigod with power over that artificial being. If the insane asylum succeeded at bringing its isolated wards into contact with one another, if it made a profound effort to re-create a space of mutual belonging among its inhabitants, its goal was to establish and perfect itself as a machine for capturing and governing minds. The asylum was a machine built on faith in an illusion, and it never provided effective tools for any sort of moral government of the phantasmatic collective entity it envisioned. But as a machine, on the other hand, it confirmed the actualizing power of illusion once again, for it totally remodeled the social image of madness.

A Counter-Society

The logic of an institution that seeks to exert mass control over individuals does not suffice, however, to account for the internal transformations of the asylum. At least one other factor was crucial in the increasing affirmation of the collective dimension in the asylum: the implicit or concealed identification of the institution as a society—a society in miniature, of course, but a complete and self-sufficient society all the same. Alongside the asylum-as-instrument, conceived as a doctor's mechanism, and set up to manipulate patients as much as possible, there was a more covert model, but finally perhaps an even more influential one, that of the asylum-as-social-island. According to this model, the asylum functioned as a closed system, ideally something like a small autarkic republic: Pinel speaks of its "little government."

From the choice of site to architectural preferences, from management decisions to trends in medical practice itself, this image of a community that has to find a space of plenitude or of properly social density in its own self-enclosure weighs continually on the fate of the psychiatric institution. Asylums are built in remote locations, insofar as possible, in an economic isolation that is particularly propitious for the institution and so that implementation of specific new principles of governance can proceed unimpeded. They are built to resemble, as far as possible, not so much a single, highly specialized building (one that would thus refer by default to the rest of society) as a fairly large and diverse set of buildings, in order to create the impression of a self-sufficient locality. "Asylums built on ground level," Esquirol argues, "made up of several isolated buildings distributed over a larger surface area, *resemble a village* whose streets, squares, and walkways offer the patients more varied and extensive spaces for the exercise that is so necessary in their state."[40] Finally, they will be set up to meet most of their own needs and come as close as possible to the perfection of a closed circuit.

All these perspectives culminated around the 1860s with projects for creating asylums that were real agricultural colonies. These projects may well have been largely inspired, as we have suggested, to address the primary and obvious deficiencies of the system, but they nevertheless served as a logical conclusion to the utopian logic that had governed the model since its beginning.[41] The headlong rush toward an ideal future has always been seductive: if one encounters difficulties, the reason is that one has stopped along the way, because one has not really been given the material, spatial, and symbolic means to establish a community that would form an organic whole on its own to such an extent that its members could find in it the plenitude of social existence.

The image of an island, serving here as a vanishing point toward which projects tend indefinitely, is characteristic of its day. It does not inform the asylum project alone: the figure permeates the entire social field. It stems from a specific moment in the collective imaginary that could be called the moment of utopia as practice: the moment of belief in the possibility of constituting a different social microcosm ex nihilo, in the vacant space left outside of society. This microcosm would be at once entirely specific (answering only to its own rules) and fully social. We should note that this belief is no longer viable: it has been swept away or defeated by the movement of history, and its eradication separates us irremediably from the great utopian thrust of the nineteenth century. None of us today can believe we are removed from the social space, or capable of exiting from it, of leaving it behind. We now know that difference, novelty, and social alterity can be experienced only within society, on its margins perhaps, but oriented toward society and in continuity with it. Over and beyond its directly political effects, perhaps this reversal helps explain the crisis of a whole series of institutions whose conception depended significantly on that schema of insularity and extraterritoriality—the insane asylum is in the first rank, but it has plenty of company. It is too late to set up a perfect microcosm outside the walls. On the contrary, the time has come to assert belonging, to manifest openings to the outside, even to the point of total transparence; it is time to demonstrate that one never ceases to be inside of society, at its very heart.

However obvious the imaginary schema that nourished the social project of the period may have been, dependence on it still does not suffice to explain everything. We also have to take into account the special destiny that led the insane asylum to posit itself as a virtually self-sufficient social unit. It was as though the alienists had had to resign themselves to a tacit compromise. On the one hand, insane patients could be brought back among others and helped to form a community; on the other hand, this could take place only among the insane themselves, in a separate space where each could be brought out of his solitude while remaining in physical isolation—as if, once the separation of madness had been implemented, it could never again be *completely* abolished; as if, once the confinement of the insane person within himself had been overcome, there should subsist irremediably around him, in spite of everything, something like an aura, something evoking the difference of madness, as if one could restore the patient to the company of her fellow beings, then, only within the bounds of a different society, one irreducibly distinct from society in general. The weight of inherited representations, the particularly powerful resistance of figures of otherness, can never be dismantled all at once, and they lead to compromises in each of their fall-back positions; here is surely the primary reason for the essential ambiguity that suspended the psychiatric enterprise between the restoration of the insane person to a collective sameness and a reaffirmation as other.

This is hardly astonishing if we are acquainted with the almost geological slowness of this sort of transformation, and especially given what is at stake: the immense historical operation through which the time-honored forms of the outsider have been systematically questioned in Western culture over the past two centuries (though the movement has much older roots): representations embodying the divisions of the human species and the categories of the outsider as a whole, including savages and the proletariat, women and—naturally—the insane. How could doctors have had the power to wipe out in a single blow the power of one of the richest and most profound symbolic images of foreignness, of difference, of which we are capable with respect to ourselves? They subverted it on one crucial point; they proved it false, patiently and concretely; but they were able to do so only within a framework that ratified and reproduced at another point the ultimate social form of difference that they were dismantling. If the insane are just as capable as we are of behaving like social beings, we still cannot conceive of them doing so except apart from us, in a society outside of our own.

A parallel comes to mind here, one that makes it possible to evaluate the structural necessity of passing through this phase. We can compare approaches to the insane with the prospects and limits Itard assigned to the education of the deaf (the segregative tenor of Itard's approach was to be quite sharply criticized later on[42]). The comparison may appear surprising today. In context, however, it seems to us an obvious one. The education of the deaf, the education of the blind, the moral treatment of the insane: all these enterprises are inseparable in their origins, since they were motivated fundamentally by a common inspiration; each movement arose from the same decisive mutation of sensibility.[43] At bottom, in each case, one finds an invisible but efficacious shared revolutionary postulate: no "moral isolation" is irremediable; no withdrawal into the self away from interaction with one's fellows is so definitive that it cannot be undone, reversed, or overcome. There is always a possibility of establishing a bond of communication despite the barrier of the senses or the soul that cuts the individual off from the rest of humanity. Afterward, the practical paths to be followed diverge according to the difficulties specific to each case. But the various approaches draw on this common foundation, on a shared refusal to compromise with alterity, a shared goal of penetrating it, a shared project of reintroducing into human exchange beings who up to then had been excluded from it. And no one contributed more actively to this enterprise, in his field, than Itard. It is hard to challenge his position as one of those who did the most to prove, as he put it, "that the deaf are no less perfectible than others, and that, brought together, aided and developed by their mutual commerce, they truly form a society that is progressing toward perfection." The fact remains that even as he expressed his ideal vision of the ultimate perfection of his enterprise, with all the freedom of an acknowledged utopia, he was still unable to imagine anything but a separate society for these beings whose inherently sociable character he struggled to demonstrate all his life.

> If I dared to utter here one of those cheerful projects that the imagination produces when, rising above all obstacles, it wanders off in pursuit of an ideal improvement, I would propose to bring together in a single place all the deaf people in France and even in Europe. There, under the absolute authority of a governor, and under the direction of some teachers chosen from among the most educated of the group, they would form a colony organized like a soci-

> ety. If I am not mistaken, in very little time we would see the emergence of people remarkable through their genius and their original talents, and the observation of their progress, the particular direction of their industry, of their minds, the nature of their relations with us, and especially of their relations with their children, some hearing and others deaf, would be the most admirable spectacle that could be offered to the meditation of a philosopher.[44]

Far from appearing as opposites, then, under the circumstances, socialization and segregation function as complementary and necessarily associated terms. The original collective power of the deaf, will be liberated as soon as their access to communication has been assured; this will be all the more evident in that care will have been taken to group them together, apart from others, and, if possible, in the solitude of a virgin land where they can establish a truly different community. The obligatory price for retrieving each individual from his solitude is collective isolation. Restitution to the social dimension comes by way of separation from global society. To be sure, in the case of the deaf, the special issue of language no doubt plays a significant role in strengthening the segregative option. It seems perfectly appropriate and justifiable to bring them together in a separate place, since they use a special language that is known by very few in the speaking and hearing community. Itard's project was surely influenced by that singular determinism, if only in its trenchancy. But the sort of obligatory translation between integration and exclusion that he advocated derived nevertheless from a much more general necessity—which might well be nothing other than the necessity of a very specific moment in the global process of dissolution of human alterity. Perhaps something like an intermediate step was required in order to restore individuals excluded from communication to the society of beings for whom others exist, a step in which the aim of reinsertion in the sphere of reciprocity could be reconciled with a separation that is still deemed socially insurmountable. Perhaps Itard was expressing the exact truth of this transitory phase, which constitutes an inevitable passage destined to be overcome, a phase in which one could not yet imagine ever reintegrating to society as a whole human beings who were, however, demonstrably not outside of human exchange.

As far as we know, no alienist pronounced himself quite so clearly about the life prospects of his patients. This is not hard to understand. The condition of the deaf is a state whose permanence invites us to think in terms of a definitive status. Madness stems, on the contrary, from an existential accident; it remains transitory in essence, even when it lasts. It gestures toward a way out; even if the exit from madness is uncertain or suspended, its very possibility, except in special cases, precludes thinking in terms of an irrevocably fixed destiny (even though one of the great temptations of psychiatry was precisely to represent the madman as a creature of a separate sort). Thus conditions modeled on the ones Itard proposed could never have been established in an insane asylum. The institution destined to harbor madness can in principle only be a place of passage, organized less to manage the existence of individuals than to restore them to the outside world.

Despite the limits imposed by this principle of circulation, the model Itard advocated, the model of the "colony" constituted as a small, specialized, closed, marginalized society, nevertheless left a profound mark on the actions of the supporters and leaders of the asylum movement. Although it never fully prevailed, the model continued to offer a counterweight to a strictly therapeutic orientation, in that considerations having to do with the life of the institution regularly took precedence over the imperatives of therapy and the release of the patients. Owing to this autarkic temptation, the asylum constantly oscillated between being a place for treatment oriented primarily toward the outside world, and a place for living from which one rarely returned, and where the first priority was to organize a framework suited to a way of life that was fixed once and for all. And it seems unquestionable that the effort to institute a collective functioning within the walls was governed to a large extent by a similar aim of creating something like a parallel world that would allow people who had been irremediably excluded from the common destiny to rediscover, at least among themselves, an opening toward their fellow beings.

This aim is suggested by certain details in Pinel's account of the reforms undertaken at La Salpêtrière in 1802, particularly the way he managed, with Pussin's help, to overcome the opposition of the staff. "At first they objected strongly," he reports, "they protested against the innovations and the injustice, and it is easy to imagine the resistance and the surreptitious plotting of more than forty serving girls, deprived of their so-called rights to treat the insane patients with extreme harshness, and henceforth reduced to passive obedience. They carry on in various ways, sending complaints and demands my way."[45] But what is interesting is the remedy finally applied to this stubborn challenge. Owing to his own skill and authority, Pussin managed to hold out, so that "most of the serving girls sought to retire and were successfully replaced little by little by convalescents known for their intelligence and their zeal, and inclined to adopt the paths of gentleness presented to them as an inviolable law."[46] The way to guarantee a kinder, more tolerant staff was thus to keep cured insane women on hand to look after the patients in treatment. The measure is revealing in more than one respect. It indicates, first, the still crushing weight of a destiny: it was difficult, and in many cases impossible, for patients to return to society once the threshold of madness had been crossed, despite the various transformations that had already occurred. Given this uncertain exclusion, little could be done except to try to provide the "unfortunate women" with work on site, mediocre work perhaps, but still preferable to the unpleasant existence that awaited them on the outside.

The negative determinism of Pussin's thinking is allied moreover with a more positive intention. For the employment of women who have gone through the experience of madness as support staff also signals the will to surround the patients with a truly comprehensive environment where the "paths of gentleness" do not depend solely on the imperative orders of the "internal police chief" but proceed from a personal and spontaneous understanding of the patient's persistent humanity. Apart from the very small number of specialists trained to study this special category of patients, where could one find people capable of an instinctive grasp of the enduring subjective dimension in the alienated patient, except among those who have lived through the same rending contradiction between self-annihilation and self-preservation? This is an ongoing concern; it comes back fifteen years later in E. Georget's writings, where the formulation is all the more trenchant in its acute pessimism. Simultaneously stressing the need for "the doctor in an insane asylum to make a special effort to instruct the individuals who exercise influence over the patients," and the extreme difficulty of conquering the prejudices that lead the insane to be treated with harshness, Georget reached a disillusioned conclusion: "It is almost impossible to make servants understand that the insane enjoy most of their faculties, with the exception of those servants who themselves have suffered from madness." But despite these unambiguous words, he does not pass judgment on the solution Pinel advocated. He simply mentioned it as a practice still in sporadic use, though it lacked the systematic character that its initiator sought for it: "At La Salpêtrière and at Bicêtre, they sometimes use patients who have been cured, to care for the others."[47]

To judge from a certain number of contemporary accounts, the best-known of which is by Auguste Comte, Georget neither exaggerates the problem nor makes the picture bleaker than it was. We know that Comte spent some time in "the private establishment of the famous Esquirol," as he put it, on the occasion of the "cerebral crisis" he suffered in 1826, and that he did not have very good memories of his stay; he blamed the "absurd treatment" that was inflicted on him for exacerbating his illness, turning it into a "pronounced alienation" that was finally declared incurable. He could hardly be more explicit in his complaints: he incriminates not the doctors' principles but the "extreme negligence with which that essential aspect of healing is carried out in these institutions," namely, moral treatment. The failing of these establishments, whatever their directors may promise, is that "all the intellectual and affective part of the treatment is in fact abandoned by them to the arbitrary action of crude low-ranking agents whose behavior almost always aggravates the illness that they ought to be helping to cure."[48] The patient's painful comments do not contradict the doctor's, as we have seen. Both evaluations provide a sense of the considerable—and not at all surprising—obstacles that the alienists encountered in their efforts to spread, share, and impose their new and paradoxical perception of the insane person as a being at once removed from himself and present to himself, and as a result incapable of being treated either as an individual in possession of himself or as an ex-subject who has become impersonal and "deprived of all sensitivity" (as Georget puts it). How could we be astonished at how difficult it was, how difficult it had to be, to gain acceptance for such a scandalous indictment of the alternative that was most solidly grounded in appearance as well as in the culture? Either one is dealing with an individual who is in full possession of his faculties, who knows what he is doing, and who must consequently be treated as someone responsible for his own words and deeds, or else one is dealing with an individual out of his senses, with whom it is completely useless to attempt to reason.

It is not only within asylums and over the use of the nursing staff, moreover, that advocates of the special science had to do battle to win acceptance for their view of madness as a challenge to the principle of noncontradiction. The confrontation with judges may have been the most arduous of all. In any event, a great deal of trouble, words, and time went into the effort to get the courts to acknowledge that a given accused party who responds quite clearly to the court's questions, who distinctly remembers what he is accused of having done, and who displayed skill, premeditation, and mental agility moreover in committing the alleged act, who is perfectly aware of what is happening to him, is nevertheless radically alienated, and acted from start to finish under the sway of his alienation. The theoretical difficulty here is identical to the one that made it so hard to get "warders" or "servants" to understand that a given patient who indeed enjoyed "most" of his faculties and who insulted or struck his caretakers was nevertheless acting, despite all his presence of mind, as an insane person, and that it was absurd to respond as if his outburst could be attributed to some sort of wickedness—a tenacious absurdity that an Auguste Comte, twenty-five years after the reform of La Salpêtrière and in the most advanced establishment of his day, could still experience in all its brutality. Conversely, it was equally difficult to get people to understand that a given patient in a state of complete delirium nevertheless remains present, appearances notwithstanding, to what is happening to him, and must in no case be treated as a being walled off from the world and unaware of others; he must not be treated with the harshness that one reserves, Georget says, for "beings deprived of all sensitivity."

Thus the alienists had to reckon with an unmistakable lag in public opinion. They had to struggle against a solid system of attitudes and beliefs; they had to undertake the patient work of reforming attitudes and training their staff in order to anchor the imperative that is so far from self-evident in its dialectical instability: always treat the patient *simultaneously* as an insane person and as a normal subject. As Pinel says, their task was "to ally two objects that seem incompatible, the repression of an insane person by countering his senseless desires with forceful resistance, and the fortunate gift of winning his confidence by managing to convince him that one has acted with such severity only in his own interests, and to contribute more surely to healing."[49] One must not leave the patient to his own devices, which would entail continuing to suppose at some level that the individual is so caught up in his own intentions and actions that he cannot understand that anyone might oppose them. But one must not interfere concretely either, as if one were in the presence of some "purely automatic" behavior where the issue is simply to ward off ill effects. One must face up to patients (one must not just act as if they were acting normally, but one must not think them so mad that they cannot understand and justify their own opposition). One must face patients without violence, even if one is backed by a powerful apparatus; more precisely, one must face up to patients without entering into the cycle of reciprocity in which the violence of those charged with caring for the patient *responds* to the patients' own violence (one must continue to treat patients with the respect that one owes to people in possession of their faculties, but without putting oneself on the same plane as they, without treating them as if they were like us, as if they were not mad).

We need to recall, too, that these developments unfold in a world of which violence is an essential component, within a society already largely pacified but still incomparably more brutal than ours. They take shape in the heart of a society where the insane are almost by definition violent, those subject to confinement in any case. The insane asylum is to a large extent the source of a universe of "furious" beings, while at the same time it uses "crude low-ranking agents" who are quite prepared to take harsh measures (moreover, at the time of the Pinelean reform, in as celebrated an establishment as Willis's, in Greatford, the domestic servants were explicitly authorized to return the patients' blows in kind).

But it was probably less a problem to proscribe violence as such than to break with the logic of reciprocity that had governed the use of violence according to a division as rigid as it was definitive: either one is excluded from the realm of reciprocity, and one exits from the circle of beings worthy of consideration, or else one belongs to that realm, and it is then inconceivable not to treat others as they treat you. What people had to be made to understand on a daily basis was the existence of a category of human beings who constitutively violated the fundamental articulations of human interaction. They were neither outside the circle of exchange nor subject to the imperative of reciprocity; they were inscribed within the space of the rule, but at the same time exempt from its effects.

Here we may well be touching one of the deepest of all the social causes that gave rise to psychiatry, namely, the opening of the special, fundamentally dissymmetrical space of interlocution where the properly psychiatric object appeared. We suspect that the symbolic exchange had to reach a certain degree of dissolution in order to produce a place where one could encounter not a non-subject but a subject called into question in his being as subject. The explicit social bond among individuals had to be almost completely dismantled—the bond that radically separated the social from the nonsocial, the human from the inhuman, and that related beings who resembled each other absolutely in the cyclic encounters of identity. Around 1800, quite clearly, there could not have been much left of the primordial social understanding of the necessary relation among individuals (and groups), an understanding that from time immemorial had been increasingly breached and damaged by the development of inegalitarian (statist) societies. More of that understanding may have remained intact than one might suppose a priori, however, especially on the level of the social institution of speech. At issue in particular is the way the conditions for discursive exchange—and thus the conditions for delimiting the field in which meaning circulates in such a way as to exclude the insane, to relegate them to a space outside of meaning—were understood. In any event, enough of the earlier understanding remained operative to make inconceivable the prospects of either attempting to discuss anything with a flagrantly delirious individual or trying any approach with an apparently accessible insane person other than reasoning, preaching, or even "directly ordering him to change." On the neighboring plane of attitudes and everyday relations, it was equally inconceivable that one could treat someone who was "out of her mind" as a full-fledged subject, and that one could fail to respond to an act of verbal or physical aggression committed by someone who seemed to know what she was doing. If these vestiges of the primitive symbolic constraint had not been ultimately overturned, if the indeterminate nature of encounters between individuals had not finally been disclosed, the strange intersubjective space where distance and listening, refusal and acceptance, identification and otherness meet could not possibly have come to light.

Even today, that space remains the stage on which the alienated face of any subject can be invoked and addressed. So we should not be surprised by the tremendous, almost insurmountable difficulties that the most determined reformers acknowledged encountering in their efforts simply to "humanize" the establishments devoted to the insane. The term *humanize* has become derisory; it elicits condescending smiles if not outright suspicion. As if it were difficult to be "human"! If it had only been a matter of decreeing, within the asylum, that good feelings would reign and that one would love one's neighbor, there would indeed have been nothing simpler—and nothing more problematic at the same time. However, what was actually at stake was something else entirely. The issue was how to respond in practice to the challenge represented by a phenomenon that until then had resisted the accepted understanding of the way individuals relate to one another. The way to be "human," that is, the way to respect the insane without being complicitous with their insanity, was not culturally or historically self-evident—not because of well-thought-out, doctrinal opposition, and not because of ill will, inherent insensitivity, or crass ignorance, but, much more profoundly and much more solidly, because of the unconscious weight of the past, because of the power of acquired reflexes and the invincible spontaneity of ancient, deeply sedimented attitudes. These reflexes and attitudes were by no means reserved for the "crude low-ranking agents" recruited inexpensively to look after the insane; it seems quite likely that they were more or less equally rooted in all levels of society.

This is the adverse context in which we have to resituate the autarkic, insular, "colonial" temptation that gripped the alienists when, once past the first enthusiasm for the possibilities of moral treatment, they had to establish an institutional system that conformed in its daily operations with the general principles defining the new approach to madness. In the face of an environment that was not hostile but closed, in the face of a certain pragmatic failure of understanding that was found even inside the hospital walls, how could they have avoided being literally absorbed by the mirage of isolation, the mirage of a small world in which they might succeed more or less in creating the conditions of an existence respectful of insanity, given the definitive understanding that on the side of social tolerance there was essentially nothing to hope for? In its caricatural extremism, the recourse to cured patients for staffing the wards is in this regard particularly eloquent: except for unusual individuals like Pussin, born reformers enlightened by reflection on their own experience, it was impossible to assume that any of the ordinary individuals who might turn up could be counted on to look after an insane person "humanely" under any and all circumstances. The use of cured patients was a desperate measure, and it was not practiced very long or very systematically. Instead, doctors resolved, in Georget's words, to "instruct the individuals in a position of influence over the patients."

The bleak skepticism of the starting point still remains pertinent, however. It is as if absolute priority had suddenly been given to the constitution of a milieu that would be thoroughly permeated by the special relational requirements of madness, a milieu in which one knows how to situate oneself in relation to insane speech and behavior, and in which, as a result, the patient can remain a "man" even while he is also an "other," neither rejected nor ignored by an imperative demand to behave the way everyone else does. And it is in this direction, we believe, that it is appropriate to seek the powerful roots of the inherently and essentially segregative character that the asylum as an institution tended to acquire.

The insane asylum was segregative not simply in the empirical sense that it was an instrument for setting aside a specific population, but also in the sense that it was a signifying mechanism, a device for conferring and renewing its inhabitants' tacit status as radically other, as unredeemable outsiders. It is essential to see that the principle of separation does not act, under the circumstances, and in terms of its most crucial results, as a negative principle of exclusion with respect to ordinary human beings, but rather as a positive principle of affirmation of a distinctive nature. The asylum accepts individuals who can be said to be rejected by society by virtue of their state. But that does not suffice to confer a segregative function on it. The asylum is much more profoundly segregative in that it tends in the end to set itself up as an active demonstration that individuals who are excluded from society because of madness can live in a meaningful way only within a specific, parallel universe, indeed that in their very being they belong to a different order. This must be directly connected with the primary project of forging an adapted environment within which the patient can draw on the subjective, social, communicative power he still has: the project of instituting, in other words, something like the authentic insane person's place, establishing a genuine society of insane people, in the sense in which Itard imagines a society of the deaf—that is, a space in which human beings who would be condemned to "moral isolation" if they were left to themselves in their communities of origin manage to gain recognition for the opening toward others they have maintained.

However, such a project is not neutral. It almost necessarily induces a certain displacement of ideas about the nature of madness, causing them to shift imperceptibly from the register of rupture and vital parenthesis to the register of a sui generis state, of personal constitution. No less logically, such a project secretes a certain notion of the goals of confinement that tends to relegate therapeutic motivations to the second rank. After all, why be overly concerned about sending back into an uncomprehending society people who at least benefit from the shelter of tolerance, behind the asylum walls? It is true that the shift toward an implicit policy of essentializing insanity and keeping the insane confined to asylums was actually brought about in the name of therapeutic imperatives alone; it is not as though institutional necessities had overwhelmed the medical outlook. On the contrary, the translation occurred under cover of therapeutic objectives, and quite precisely under cover of the establishment of the asylum as an instrument of cure.

This brings us back to the fundamental shift in moral treatment, which we noted in Pinel: the shift from a focus on the individual to a focus on the collective. The segregative instrument with which we are familiar, along with the powerful though concealed model of the asylum as a place to live, the asylum as a society, were produced when the special requirements that allowed genuine communication with the insane were extended to the entire institution. Officially, of course, there was never any question of setting the therapeutic dimension aside or relegating it to second place; it was not as if anyone made a deliberate choice to direct efforts toward improving the everyway welfare of insane patients instead of curing them. For the alienists certainly sought, on the contrary, to multiply the available therapeutic forces. The fact remains that the choice made was translated into a withdrawal of the confidence that had initially been placed in the immediate offensive resources of the "conversation of sane people." The institution became a mysterious medium from which beneficial effects were to be expected, but one whose influence was not subject to direct control. Most importantly, the doctor's primary task became in fact—independently of the happy therapeutic effects that were supposed to come about more or less on their own—that of organizing, governing, animating the irremediably separate world of the insane, as if the patients were expected (this perspective was not acknowledged, but it was obscurely influential) to stay there forever. Patients did leave the asylum, of course, and in large numbers. But the tacit shift in the institution's purpose had a lasting impact on the social image of madness, and the promptness with which the public forgot that asylums offered a cure was eloquent testimony to this shift. (Moreover, the image of seclusion—the one destined to last—showed up very early, around 1825.[50])

However, we still have to reckon with a supplementary factor that must have contributed a good deal, later on, to reinforcing the initial segregative option, namely, the rise of a radically pessimistic view of madness as expressive of a disorder atavistic in origin and inexorably destined to progress. This context led to a decisive disjunction between therapeutic perspectives and institutional imperatives. What else could be done with the irremediably disgraced beings for whose reintegration into society there was little hope, except to try to arrange a retreat that would be insurmountable in all respects, by creating a sort of microsociety of degenerates in the margins of a society that has no use for them? It is significant, from this standpoint, that the chief advocates of the new doctrinal orientation (we are thinking for example of Morel, Magnan, and, somewhat later, Sérieux) were also among the most ardent contemporary advocates of measures intended to "humanize" the asylums (for example, on the occasion of the well-known quarrel over the use of restraining devices).

More generally still, the reforming impulse that made itself felt starting roughly in the 1850s (for example, in the asylum-colony projects we have mentioned) probably cannot be separated, historically, from the accreditation of the idea that madness is durable, that it is rooted in the original constitution of the personality. Such views confuse madness with the destiny of the afflicted individual to such an extent that there is no conceivable practical solution except to enact in society the separation that is inherent in madness—not only by removing the individual from society, but also by giving full value to his social foreignness, by conferring on this state the effectiveness of an existence that is other, alongside, elsewhere.

The insistent appeal from without, the persistent mirage of a world ideally folded back on its own difference, led to the vast confinement warehouses with which we are familiar. These institutions were of course officially devoted exclusively to treating the insane, and thus they experienced considerable patient turnover. Still, insane asylums were so permeated by the hidden ambition of offering a properly social alternative, and thus so entrenched in the definitive, so oriented toward the long run, that they quite rightly came to be known as "factories for producing incurables." For it is not just that by leaving the insane at least morally on their own, the asylum would fulfill all the conditions that allowed its patients to plunge inexorably deeper into illness and to be transformed into incurables. In addition, according to the model that obscurely determined its organization, it would produce, both symbolically and concretely, individuals destined to remain unchanged, individuals assigned once and for all to their place and their destiny as insane, and not expected ever to return to their ordinary milieu, thus, in the end, becoming socially irrecuperable. Such individuals were often undeniably "adapted" to their special environment, on the one hand—indeed, many of them lived a quite "normal" existence except for their madness, in the framework of one of those activities of maintenance or subsistence secreted by an institution that intended to exist on its own. Those individuals were gently and imperceptibly destroyed, on the other hand, by their very adaptation to a way of life whose hidden deficiencies, even more than the visible ones, ended up blunting and finally breaking the deep mainsprings that guarantee the ultimate autonomy of individuals even while maintaining them in solidarity with their fellows.

For externality is a decoy, and with it the perspective of establishing a separate world in the margins of society, one that is nevertheless somehow on the order of a society. The space that is set apart from ordinary society can never be quite filled with the impalpable substance in which the living principle of the social resides. Whatever happens, that space remains marked by an irremediable lack, struck by an invisible, but central, absence that is impossible to fill; it is a sort of stunted space that is at most capable of an empty and mechanical operation, lethally haunted by what the mother-society has that it imperceptibly lacks. Not that people did not succeed, in the best of cases, in creating the conditions for an existence that was, to be sure, narrowly confined, limited, and routine, but relatively full and complete. And—we cannot emphasize this too strongly—such an existence was apt to be satisfying in many respects for a large number of its inhabitants, who settled in and never moved again. But what no one ever succeeded in doing was effacing the trace and the effects of the break with the outside world. They could think of all the substitutes that restore some sort of equivalence with the forms of ordinary life; they could anticipate all the ingredients that enter into the composition of social banality; they could organize a parallel universe in miniature right down to the smallest detail. Still, the fundamental separation from the collective space continued to count through absence, continued to work as an indiscernible and at the same time insurmountable lacuna, continued silently to undermine the plenitude of appearances. As if the institution, in closing itself off, had removed itself from the subtle element that ensured the spontaneous, unconscious cohesion of the social, the element that constituted something like its material soul—an element that can be neither manipulated nor fabricated nor imitated. What was instituted remained a semblance of an actual living environment; it was an artificial and in the long run necessarily destructive framework. The annihilating effects of that other, abstract existence were well-known, widely observed and reported. Even in the gentlest, most "humane" version, even in the most participative and richest asylum, it seems, the individual infallibly disengages in the end; he pulls away, becomes finally incapable of mentally moving outside the fixed reference points of his confinement, becomes incapable of reinscribing himself within the living indeterminacy of the common world.

Outside and Inside: The Work of the Institution

The institution thus succeeded in demonstrating its inhabitants' quite real capacity to adapt to the banality of a collective work life. At the same time, however, it turned out to be something like a mechanism for inducing loss of adaptation, a system that tended to paralyze or abolish the individual's capacity for integration. It revealed the possibilities of a system of socialization, and in the same movement it proved to be an instrument for desocialization, as ungovernable as it was effective. The contradiction clearly did not appear all at once; it developed over time. For it to become perceptible, the interminable, patient work of reconceptualizing insanity concretely on the basis of the patient's openness to others and to the world, with the asylum as the support structure, had to reach a certain degree of completion. The old images of madness as essential insensibility, confinement within the closed circle of one's own subjectivity, reduction of the individual to an exclusive concern with himself, were not entirely incompatible, once relativized, with the practical observation that exchange with the insane patient is possible. There are ways to enter into dialogue, but madness nevertheless remains a fundamental rift that isolates the patient within himself. As long as elements of those old images remained operative, it is not surprising that there was little concern about the pernicious effects of confinement within the asylum. The gap between the project and the results achieved can only appear at the end of a slow process of accumulation and accreditation, when the socializing operation has gone far enough to bring to light within the insane patient not only the active power to conceive of himself as existing among fellow human beings and in relation to the law of things, but also, and even more importantly, an inviolable kernel of autonomy, along with an inherent, indefectible mooring to others, an originary, constitutive, ineffaceable bond with the nearest human beings. That autonomy and that bond cannot be attacked without serious consequences.

The crucial influence of such a disclosure on the interpretation of the phenomenon of madness in general is not hard to discern. The early alienists tended to locate the origin of madness in the family. According to Esquirol, for example, "the moral cause of alienation often exists at the heart of the family."[51] Alienists saw this as a critical reason for resorting to strict isolation, since madness was almost always accompanied, in their view, by a reversal of moral affections, and still more profoundly by a sort of radical canceling out of the sense of other people that could only be exacerbated by the presence of close relatives.[52] All therapeutic treatment of insanity was based on the principle that the rupture inscribed in the malady itself had to be consummated; thus isolation made it possible to envisage the necessary reconstruction of the personality starting from scratch. That reconstruction in turn was supposed to enable the insane person to re-enter the ordinary circle of his relationships.[53]

In contrast, one can measure the scope of the reversal brought about by challenges to the notion that madness "isolates everything" and cuts off the individual absolutely, and to the associated postulate that strict seclusion is innocuous. It may indeed be the case that the source of madness should be sought in the family. But the personal bonds that were woven in its framework are not of the sort that can be dissolved, no matter how troubled they are. It is absurd on every level to think and act as if ties with others could ever be abolished, as if insane individuals could be completely cut off from the people closest to them. It is particularly dangerous to fail to recognize the need such people have, despite the feelings they manifest on occasion, to continue to situate themselves in relation to their relatives and friends, to maintain an opening toward them; and it will be unfailingly harmful in the long run to deprive them, by isolating them, of their usual communication with the people on whom their derangement is indeed crystallized ("it seems as though their moral delirium is preferentially fixed on the people they cherish most"), but who remain nonetheless the indispensible pivots of their continued existence as subjects. The practical recognition of the need to keep patients in steady contact with their original milieux, the need to avoid brutally severing their emotional ties, necessarily accompanies at least a tacit theoretical recognition that the individuals are primordially inscribed within the space of others; the self depends inherently and ineluctably on others.

This recognition, as we see it, creates the conditions for a renewed reading of the nature of, and also of the role played by, the mysterious bonds that irrevocably engage the affections of a subject. It is necessarily accompanied, too, by a complete change in therapeutic strategy: there is no longer any question of radically reconstructing a personality on the basis of its complete reduction to itself, once the fiction that a moral fissure separates the insane individual from others has been revealed as such. Once the illusion has been rejected, it becomes indispensable to respond simultaneously to a double requirement. On the one hand, practitioners must doubtless continue to take into account the familial causality of the illness and its dimension as an affective break; on the other hand, they must neither reify that subjective isolation nor take it literally. On the contrary, they must not fail to keep in mind that the break is never fully realized, that any distance, rejection, or indifference they may encounter needs to be interpreted in relation to and within the ties that the subject maintains in every case with the primitive objects of his "respect, gratitude, love, friendship."

A whole new field of investigation opens up here. At this point, we must close our sketch of a sketch, with no ambition but to suggest that ideas do not fall from the sky, nor do they spring up naked, pure, and perfect from the abyss. At a certain moment, practitioners reached the point of giving theoretical priority to the idea that personalities are not only shaped by but rooted in the universe of early relations with others. At the same moment, they became preoccupied on the practical level with the danger incurred in removing individuals from the intimate bonds that unite them with their usual milieux, declaring them cut off from those bonds, treating them as though they existed only on their own, constitutively independent and unconnected with anyone at all. It is not just a matter of chance that those two moments coincide. The internal movement that leads the institution toward self-questioning also encourages a new awareness that there is no such thing as solitary and self-sufficient subjectivity, that the self comes into being and structures itself only in relation to the other, that in the end an order of concrete ties to specific persons remains, irreducibly, the living armature of the inner world of human beings. This limited but precise testimony to experience, countering the classically abstract conception of individuality, is impossible to dismiss.

The institution's failure to reconstitute artificially a specific and authentic sociability leads it to focus, at least indirectly, on the fact that certain interpersonal bonds are so integrally a part of the individual's ineradicable core than they cannot be broken. This indirect focus constitutes the final phase in the process reintegrating alienated subjectivity within the sphere of common subjectivity. The process began when the representation of madness as a radical sequestering of the self was shattered, when practitioners discovered that the insane person's "moral isolation" was not as absolute as it had seemed to be, and that it was possible to enter into an intimate relationship with insane patients, who remain present to themselves and open to contact with others in spite of everything, even when they suffer from the most extreme forms of derangement.

Still, as we have seen, no matter how decisive this initial breakthrough may have been, in terms of the further developments it authorized, it did not suddenly transform the insane person into a subject who could be presumed intact in all respects, over and beyond the illness that afflicts and dominates him. The patient did cease—and this is a major, crucial change—to be viewed as inaccessible to all human contact, and especially to communicative contact. The circle of the insane person's self-enclosure is thus broken at a key point, and definitively relativized; however, it remains no less closed in other respects. Even though patients may engage in intelligible commerce with their doctors, from time to time, there is still a long way to go between that observation and the conviction that they can take others spontaneously into account on a daily basis, or can adapt their behavior to objective requirements. Thus the second phase in the dissolution of insane patients' primordial otherness is what might be called the recomposition of their abstract sociability. It has to be demonstrated not only that they are not closed off from all communication, not only that they are open to authentic exchange, since they remain subjects in their madness, but also that they are not so isolated that they cannot live among others, that they cannot insert themselves in a collective operation, that they cannot fully appreciate or even grasp the meaning of a common effort. Leuret's work has offered us a glimpse of this phase.

What remains, then, is the last circle of the patient's withdrawal, the affective circle, so powerfully labeled by Esquirol, which is alleged to cut the insane off entirely from those closest to them. From a strategic standpoint this form of isolation is critical, since it legitimates a rigorous separation of the patients from their original milieu. The institution's failure to constitute itself autarkically as an alternative society eventually calls that legitimation into question, for it brings to light the confined patients' ongoing need for the outside world. This final phase of the process (final at least in relation to the logic of the asylum system) might be called the phase of restitution, in which the insane regain their concrete subjective inscription.[54] However profoundly subverted the patient's feelings may prove to be, one must not imagine an absolute interruption of her affective commitments to others. At the same time, she remains profoundly attached, irreducibly anchored, to the original milieu from which her illness has removed her. Not for an instant does she cease to belong to it and to find in it her primordial space of reference. Consequently, nothing is more absurd and more harmful than the "extreme restrictions" put in the way of "communications on the part of the insane with persons on the outside," according to Pinel's canonical formula;[55] on the contrary, it is essential, even when confinement proves necessary, to strive to preserve the patient's openness to those ties through which she maintains her true inscription in the human world, under any and all conditions.

The history of the asylum can be represented as a long struggle on the part of the institution against itself. The most substantial challenges to the asylum arise from the very unfolding of its project. Under the circumstances, unless we resolutely close our minds to an understanding of the object and its development, we cannot be satisfied with facile images of the system as it is defined from the outside. These images portray a system assigned once and for all to a precise function, entirely adequate to its own ends, rigorously mastered by its agents and leaders—and thus deprived of all internal dynamism other than the inevitable erosion produced by time; the system was capable of changing only under the pressure of global society or owing to the evolution of ideas. What we have here is not mastery but an illusion of mastery: the asylum was caught in the grip of a project destined to utter failure, caught in a blind confrontation with the impossible. The history of the asylum is first of all the history of an untenable ambition, of a lure taking shape, of a mirage that dissipates almost imperceptibly in the slow and clouded return of reality.

What forces the institution to evolve first and foremost from within is the pitiless experimentation, the unavoidable testing of the ultimate inconsistency of the aim that drives and constitutes it. There is no mechanism capable of taking hold of souls and transforming them; there is no space separate from society where a self-sufficient social islet can be created. Those two closely related observations are the principal reasons for the bankruptcy of the asylum system. Within a few decades, the observations had become incontrovertible (though perhaps not insurmountable—that is another story). The singular "instrument for curing" known as the asylum was in fact instituted in the form of an autarkic colony essentially under the sign of that dual illusion of power and externality. Its twin goals—forging an institution with intimate and direct power over personalities, and establishing a self-contained, self-sufficient miniature world, the special society of insane people—constituted a double impossibility that had to be recognized in the long run from within. Its inevitable outcome entailed moral abandonment in place of the mobilization of minds, and deprivation through separation, leaving patients without the means to function in full correspondence with a collective order conceived specifically for them.

Still, this internal critique born of experience gradually took on irrefutable strength only in relation to the impetus of another dynamic factor. After all, one can always come to terms, more or less, with a gap—even a flagrant one—between aims and results. Except that here an aggravating element comes into play, a sort of supplementary stamp that helped the visible gap between the ideal of the institution and its wretched reality grow wider still. The mounting pressure of that element made confinement increasingly problematic in its very principle. What is at issue here is the very effective transformation of the insane person's status that came about silently and surely, in the asylum, in the name of and under cover of the otherwise aberrant institutional objectives. The communitarian opening of an originally cellular space, the socialization of everyday gestures, the collectivization of activity: all these were crucial changes, undertaken in the vain hope either of increasing the institution's hold over its inhabitants or of reinforcing its insular specificity. Nevertheless, their actual effect—as opposed to the anticipated ones—was the production of a new and different image of the insane person, a radical broadening of the field of possibilities in which he could be allowed to move, in which he could develop in complete humanity what was at the outset merely a vestige of reason. Although such a shift in perspective was never an acknowledged goal, since the illusions created by its explicit objectives masked the real character of the results produced, the machinery of the asylum reached the point of recasting the insane patient as a human being generally well enough endowed with presence to things and with spontaneous sociability for his strict isolation to come into question. The confinement system itself largely created the conditions that cast doubt on the soundness of the principle of confinement, to the extent that its internal development led it to dismantle the solipsistic representations of madness that had constituted the most solid bases for its legitimacy.

The crisis of the institution arose, we might say, from the conjunction of two series of mutually reinforcing factors: on the one hand, its failure to meet the objectives it set for itself, and, on the other hand, its involuntary success as an instrument not for curing but for radically reshaping society's perception of the insane. In contrast with the potentialities and requirements gradually revealed in insane patients as they went about their daily lives among other human beings, the dismal failure of the attempt to re-create artificially and in a self-contained environment the positivity of an authentic social milieu took on, over and beyond the crushing weight of the evidence, a definitive, insurmountable dimension of unacceptability. Conversely, acknowledging the impossibility of setting human beings apart from society in general without cutting them off from their intimate source of life brought clearly to light the extent to which sociability has to be characterized essentially as a primary, ineradicable inscription in a specific place of the human establishment. It brought to light the extent to which human subjects—even insane human subjects—depend on being moored originally to others, where they acquire a set of primordial attachments that cannot be broken or ignored with impunity. The historical condemnation of the asylum system was signed and sealed from within the mechanism itself, and much earlier than is usually supposed, at the point where those two movements converged. The asylum endured, it perpetuated itself, it wore itself out in attempts at self-renewal—but after the fashion of a tree that is dying at the core, a tree whose apparently intact vigor as seen from the outside hides the lengthy and inexorable process through which its vitality is being sapped.

ABSTRACT III

Crisis, Agony, and Repetition

The massive failure of the nineteenth-century insane asylum—a failure caused by the contradictory attempts both to isolate and to socialize the insane—led to a gradual disintegration of the institution, despite various attempts to revive it in the first half of the twentieth century. For the dream of total visual control over the insane, more recent psychiatry substituted the attempt to master the mentally ill by listening to their speech. Ultimately, however, this new method of control turned out to be as hopelessly utopian as the earlier approach.

ABSTRACT IV

Esquirol at La Salpêtrière

The appointment of Esquirol at La Salpêtrière as "supervisor of the insane" in 1811 signals the ascendancy of institutional treatment of the insane over individualized "moral treatment." Throughout his career, Esquirol vigorously defended the large hospitals in which a sizable population of patients could be rationally divided into categories appropriate to their behavior, then properly supervised and effectively mastered. Since Esquirol's method required the creation of a faceless mass of patients subjected to the will of the supervisor, his idea of a large hospital had a class dimension: in the small, expensive asylums reserved for the upper classes, the assimilation of individuals into groups could not be achieved as easily as in the large hospitals that served the needs of the poor.

PART TWO

The Passions as a Sketch of a General Theory of Mental Alienation

ABSTRACT V

Esquirol in 1805

Esquirol published his doctoral dissertation *Des Passions* at age 33. A continuation and systematization of Pinel's theses on mental illness, *Des Passions* is more directly oriented toward psychiatric practice than the writings of Pinel.

ABSTRACT VI

The Clinical Resolution

Des Passions rests on the assumption that an adequate clinical treatment can cure mental illness. While arguing in favor of a detailed analysis of all symptoms of mental alienation, Esquirol is never a mere empiricist; by postulating that the root of mental illness is located in the passions, he achieves a theoretical breakthrough in the understanding of madness.

ABSTRACT VII

Between the Will to Madness and Brain Lesions

According to Esquirol, madness does not affect the intellectual faculties alone; it is a total phenomenon that touches upon all aspects of human personality. Yet madness does not completely abolish the self; it allows the mentally ill to preserve part of their personality and presence to the world. For Esquirol, madness is neither simply a brain lesion nor a failure of the intellect, but a divisive force that affects the entire human being by turning the sick half against the healthy one.

ABSTRACT VIII

What the Passions Make It Possible to Think (Beginning)

Esquirol insists that madness cannot be understood without reference to the human body, yet the presence of madness in the body does not take the form of visible brain lesions. Pinel had already polemicized against the idea that madness is caused by incurable organic lesions. Mania, for instance, was in Pinel's view "a purely nervous state" that does not involve lesions and could be cured by an appropriate diet and moral treatment. Esquirol agrees with Pinel: madness affects the nervous system without destroying it physically.

Both Pinel and Esquirol subscribed to the theory that passions are governed by the epigaster. Although this idea had no factual basis and later had to be abandoned, it allowed the two alienists to root madness in the body, while detaching it from the brain. They were thus able to argue that alienation does not necessarily affect all the intellectual faculties of the patient, and they actively sought a cure for madness.

CHAPTER V

What the Passions Make It Possible to Think

A New Sense of Self

INTRODUCING THE PASSIONS into discussions of insanity offers a threefold conceptual benefit. First, it confers consistency on the idea that, in a general way, what is "altered, perverted, or annihilated" in alienation at a given moment nevertheless remains potentially intact. Second, it lends support to the idea that there is a certain distance between the patient and her illness, even though the illness affects her presence to herself and her power to separate herself from herself. The distance is grounded in anatomy and physiology, but it is experienced and sublimated as "psychological" distance. The ultimate image of the insane patient as someone whose moral faculties alone are disturbed, while her intellectual faculties remain perfectly intact, has to be understood strictly in terms of the extension of the disjunction that occurs between the site of thought and the site of madness (the passions); it may be seen as the clinical projection and the full development of that disjunction. The decentering of the place where alienation was believed to originate provided a practical and metaphoric means, as it were, for thinking that, even when the intellectual faculties are completely subverted, the subject retains a virtual exteriority to whatever is assailing her, invading her and disorganizing her from within, that even beneath the most manifest and most general derangement the thinking, conscious being retains at least a quasi-presence to self. The insane person is both specifically afflicted in her ability to relate to herself and shut off in an impregnable proximity to herself. A third crucial possibility is opened up, finally, by the recourse to a way of conceiving of sites in the body inherited from an earlier era: the possibility of intuitively pinpointing the idea that human alienation involves a person's status as subject, the possibility of providing a sturdy—if awkward and unsophisticated—form of expression for that idea.

The intellectual faculties as such are not in question: their disruption comes from elsewhere, from farther away. Nor are specific material lesions to be incriminated: if the animal economy is affected, it is in its general equilibrium and in its very principle of operation; it is impossible to relate its disorganization to the local affliction of one organ or another (except in the case of sympathetic alienation). The highly singular human dimension with which madness is involved is in itself a background. This dimension lies "beneath" thought; while it necessarily passes through thought, it cannot be confused with thought. At the same time, lying "beneath" the self, it is immersed in the depths of the body and espouses it fully; while it cannot be separated from the body's overall economy of thought, it cannot be confused with the objective body and the defined assemblage of the organs. In each of us there is someone who is always lagging behind the self, inexhaustibly reserved in relation to the self, at once an immutably distant spectator and someone inseparably soldered to the self, someone irresistibly involved with the body: in each of us, there is thus someone susceptible to becoming foreign to our self, while remaining present to the estrangement that besets that self. The aberrant focalization of madness around a so-called epigastric center made it possible to see the enigmatic face of that "someone" for the first time.

The place of the passions is a place from which all the physical and moral dimensions of a human being can be simultaneously mobilized, seized, and overturned, without the slightest harm being done to the integrity of the brain or any other organ. It is thus a place of maximum, inextricable individual unity, a place of immediate reciprocity between what belongs to the body and what belongs to the mind, a place where no modification in one register, however minimal, ever takes place without repercussions and instantaneous translation in the other register. But at the same time, it is a place that is in a sense external both to thought and to the regular physiological play of the organs; by that very token it can ensure their absolute convergence. It implicates them equally, it subjugates them indissociably, in a frenetic agitation of the body and a general effervescence of the mind; nevertheless, even under extreme conditions, it does so in the diffuse presence of the individual who is exploding in this fashion. Here again, the example of alienation, in its minimal form and thus in its pure state, brings the picture into sharpest focus. What is actually harmed in the insane patient who is "determined, dragged along, by a depraved will that leads him in spite of himself to act badly, even though he measures the harm he is doing and is conscious of it?" In a sense solely one small part of himself: his "moral faculties." But at the same time, and in a different sense, this limited topographical zone belonging to his personal set of functions and faculties is *all* of him; at least it is the patient as *himself*, the patient in his essence and his intimate structure as a subject. His intellectual faculties may not be affected at all in the way they operate, but he is still not able to use them freely, since he uses them irresistibly in the service of actions that he otherwise condemns.

While the operational efficacity of the insane patient's thought is not in question, what is in question, in contrast, is his relation to his thought as an instrument. Thus even if his moral faculties alone are disturbed, he surely does not experience his disorder as the disturbance of a single, defined, circumscribed part of himself, as would be the case in an ordinary illness. The dimension in which he is afflicted is very precisely the dimension through which he experiences himself as an indivisible unit, or, to take a negative tack, it is the dimension through which he experiences himself as incapable of differentiating himself from himself, of distancing himself with respect to himself, of considering himself as another.

The place of alienation in us is this vital source of subjectivity where no further retreat is possible in relation to the self, where there is only an unspeakable adhesion to the self, only a perception of the self in the mode of an indissoluble *identity*. This is why alienation has to be described as a radical or total state: it bears on the place in the subject where he coincides absolutely with himself and where it is therefore out of the question that he could observe himself in the process of operating a division between the troubled part of himself and the whole. He is alienated precisely in that he lacks mastery of the distance from his difficulty that would allow him to circumscribe, isolate, and reject it. He is alienated precisely in that his derangement operates in an ungraspable, uncontrollable proximity to himself.

However, the situation has a second aspect that needs to be taken into account. Even though it cannot be assigned to a broad or narrow but determinable zone of the subject, even though it cannot be separated from the subject considered as *One* and as *All*, alienation does not amount, either, to annihilation, to obliteration or destruction of the subject. Although it consists fundamentally in a vacillation of presence to the self and an uncontrollable evolution of the self, alienation most particularly and essentially does not signify the beginning of an absence to the self. Quite the contrary: the patient's condition is properly termed alienation only to the extent that someone persists for whom the condition of becoming-foreign-to-oneself exists and has meaning, someone who witnesses and experiences his own absence. This is also why all alienation must be characterized as partial, in a sense: by its very nature, alienation does not abolish the subject's virtual and indefinite transcendence with respect to herself; she always remains in some way *for* herself, even when her capacity to make distinctions is disturbed. The insane subject is compelled to entertain thoughts and carry out actions that she is unable to suppress, but she is not absolutely unaware that she is losing control of herself. Thus she always remains capable of staying at a certain distance from the place where her internal distance—the distance that confers on her the power to reflect and the ability to choose—is abolished.

Correlatively, then, and by way of the imputation of madness—as Pinel and Esquirol understood madness—to the passions, a new notion of the *sense of self* in general, or rather a new way of determining the content of that notion, is beginning to emerge. The tacit recognition of madness as the alienation of the subject could only have been carried out at the same time with a complete transformation of the way of conceptualizing the subject's apprehension by herself, the logical matrix, one might say, in which the idea of the self is produced.[1] It is as if a double articulation had been obscurely established. On the one hand, the experience of the self is the experience of the impossibility of detaching oneself from oneself—I am *myself* inasmuch as I experience myself in a primordial adhesion and indistinction; the self is that from which I cannot pull myself away or cut myself off; it is that with which, invincibly, I coincide. On the other hand, the experience of the self is a transcendence that is always renascent and inextinguishable with respect to the self. The self may have an infinite power of un-differentiation, yet one can never realize oneself in the form of an absolute detachment from the self, so that one might take oneself to be another; this brings us back to the ego as an inherent confusion of self with self. Alienation constitutes both a renewed questioning and an exemplification of this double articulation: in one respect, alienation is in a way an extension of the ego as incoercible adhesion to the self; but at the same time, alienation is the re-creation in a different place of the inexhaustible power of distance from the self.

We must emphasize once again that this double articulation could only be glimpsed, could only begin to be conceived and receive a semblance of intellectual form, owing to the decentering of madness with respect to the head and the concomitant recourse to an ancient, imaginary topography of the affective phenomena. Within the sphere of thought, it would certainly have been impossible to promote this new figure of the subjective phenomenon under its dual aspect of limitation of reflective power and simultaneous recognition of its inexhaustible and inextinguishable character. Instead, we have no trouble discerning how the fantastic focalization of the passions on the epigastrium on the one hand made it possible to make perceptible and credible the theoretically reflected intimate distance that is maintained in the most impenetrable madness, and on the other hand gave body to the representation of an immediate and opaque bodily adhesion to the self, an intimate dependence on a tangle of forces in which body and mind are inextricably mixed, an immersion in the material depths of one's own individuality.[2] Passions are the central truth of a two-faced being, a creature endowed with an invincible force of presence to and difference from himself, but essentially limited in his ability to turn back toward himself, prey to and locked in struggle with an obscure, unmasterable proximity with himself.

Beyond the Moral Idea of Man

What is astonishing in the story, if we step back and get a little distance from it now, is the phenomenon of condensation owing to which the definitive break with a moral interpretation of the intimate duality inherent in madness came about through the very notion that concentrated in itself the moral conception of madness. For in one sense, clearly, nothing is more false than Esquirol's statement that "few authors have studied the relations between mental illness and the passions" (*Des Passions,* p. 20). At the same time nothing is more significant: the denial is so massive and absurd that it becomes revealing. Esquirol was not—could not have been—unaware of the abundant literature that contradicted his affirmation in advance in the most flagrant possible way; yet his sense that he is locating something entirely new in the word *passion* is so strong that he is willing to proffer a manifest counter-truth. As it happened, he was right. The fact remains that there is something strange in this false terminological continuity, in this fixation on a word that is used only to signify the exact opposite of its classic meaning.

There is no more widespread, long-standing idea than that madness grows out of passion. Pride turns heads and arouses fantasies of seeing oneself as king, prince, or god. Giving in to the dictates of desire, yielding to passion's vehement appeal, preferring finally—indeed, resolutely determining—to satisfy them even when this means failing to accept the limits of one's own condition, failing to acknowledge the truth of the world and all the obstacles that stand in the way of appetites: generally speaking, these behaviors were understood as pathways to madness. The idea was further developed and systematized in Pinel's and Esquirol's day: there is a sinful will to madness which is a bias in favor of the passions, a deliberate choice of renouncing the self in favor of an illusion that leads to radical nonreflection and the unbridled, disorderly opacity of impulse. The idea is a powerful one: the resultant division that is thought to prevail in the insane individual between pure unreasoning decision and pure abolition of presence of mind makes it possible to integrate the contradictory data of experience; one can impute the remnants of reason that are sometimes discernible in maniacs to their inherent bad will while still continuing to regard them as beings currently absent from themselves. This way of thinking about insanity correlates with a paradoxical resurgence of the moral vision of disorders of the soul, which was aroused in turn by Pinel's "discovery" of the presence to themselves ordinarily maintained by the insane, such that one of the essential conduits for that discovery was the centering of madness around the passions.

Given the hesitant path Pinel followed before he finally decided to introduce the notion of passions explicitly and without reservations, we can readily imagine that he himself was well aware of the danger involved in using a notion with such a weighty legacy and such tenacious connotations. In a sense, the idea is there at the outset, in the "Mémoire sur la manie périodique ou intermittente." It lies at the heart of the model for a typical attack of mania that Pinel constructs in that text. He sees such an attack "as the effect of a reaction favorable to cure"; however, he carefully and very significantly avoids using the word *passion* itself in this strategic passage. "A lively affection, or, in more general terms, any stimulant at all, acts powerfully on the center of the epigastric forces and produces a profound disturbance there."[3] "*Any stimulant at all*" rather than "a lively affection," "the epigastric *forces*": Pinel prefers to invoke physical factors, and as little "psychological" influence as possible. Along with the statement's abstract medical emphasis, its reluctance to name openly an object that it so manifestly invokes indicates clearly enough the fear of uttering one word too many, a word that would reintroduce references and images that were to have been abandoned once and for all.

Now, in the *Nosographie*, which appeared the following year, the awkwardness seems to have disappeared. "It is easy to conclude," Pinel says straightforwardly this time, "that delirium without fever, far from stemming from defects in the organization of the brain, almost always depends on some strong, vehement passion, owing as much to the nature of the object of that passion as to the very lively sensibility of the one who is experiencing it. Now an inner feeling causes the effect of these disturbances to be related to the epigastric region."[4] But in the *Nosographie* the object is not mental illness as such; thus the expression becomes much freer. For this foray remains more or less isolated, and whether it is in relation to moral treatment, the classification of insane patients into distinct species, or anatomical research on the brain, Pinel's initial caution continues to prevail throughout, even when his topics seem to lend themselves exceptionally well to its transgression. Pinel deals with "moral affections" and "deep emotions"; he essentially avoids the passions altogether. He speaks of mania as a "purely nervous state," in the conclusion of a paper in which he dismisses the hypothesis of a defect in skull conformation in the insane; even in this context, which seems particularly suited to the term, he has nothing to say about the passions.

There is just one exception, and it is a noteworthy one, since it clears up both the reasons for Pinel's insistent reserve and the way he finally overcame it. In his "Research and Observations on the Moral Treatment of the

Insane," he evokes the theme of the passions twice, laterally, as it were. The first evocation, in the text, is critical; the second, which appears in a note, like a regret, is programmatic. While Pinel may have some reservations about the notion of passion, his avowal here is unambiguous. It comes up in connection with the use made of it by Pinel's mentor in analytic thinking, Condillac, and before him by an entire philosophic tradition. Pinel implicitly reproaches Condillac for failing to distinguish himself sufficiently from that tradition. When, in connection with an exemplary case, he criticizes "the principles of Locke and Condillac" regarding the insane, Pinel uses the occasion to throw a dart in the latter's direction on a more general level. "Condillac," he concedes, "has displayed equally his sagacity and profundity in the application of the principle of analytical inquiry to the development of certain mental emotions, such as inquietude, desire, the passions . . . But, connected with the history of the affections, there are important facts which it is the exclusive province of medical philosophy to unravel and to expose."[5] In plain language, where the passions are concerned, something other than analysis is needed, for analysis does not allow the practitioner to reach "real knowledge of the facts," and thus it reintroduces prepositivist views, in refined form. And in this connection, Pinel points out in a footnote that he intends to fill that gap. The gap takes on a strategic character for him, as he makes clear. "The medical history of the passions will necessarily be included among the preliminary notions in the treatise on mania that I plan to write later on; for how can the most frequent form of alienation be conceived, the form that comes from an extreme exaltation of the passions, if one does not first consider very carefully their moral and physical effects?"[6] When he notes that a path in the right direction has been opened "by an English author who vividly felt this truth," Pinel is referring to Crichton, "whom I have already cited," he says, without specifying that he had cited his book, *An Inquiry into the Nature and Origin of Mental Derangement*, in the context of stinging, ironic criticism.[7] Crichton's return to favor was destined to last: Pinel seems to have found the solution to his initial difficulties in Crichton's work.

In the introduction to his *Treatise on Insanity* (which appears to have been written after the work itself), when Pinel comes to the point of formally positing, developing, and defending the idea that the passions constitute "the most ordinary cause of disturbance of our moral faculties,"[8] his arguments are directly and closely connected to his summary and praise of Crichton's book. To be sure, traces of his earlier reservations remain. He describes the book as "more devoted to a preliminary knowledge of mental illness than suited to going deeply into the history and the treatment of that illness," but at the same time he recognizes it as "profound and full of new results from observations, according to the principles of modern physiology."[9] It is no exaggeration to say that Pinel found "the medical history of the passions," for which he felt an embarrassing need, ready at hand for the borrowing, in Crichton. Moreover, one sentence in the introduction sheds clear light both on the real cause for his earlier hesitations and on the specific point on which Crichton's work providentially unblocked him: "Crichton seems to have risen to a broad point of view that the moralist and the metaphysician cannot attain: it is the consideration of the human passions viewed as simply phenomena of the animal economy, *without any idea of morality or immorality*, and in their simple relations with the constitutive principles of our being."[10]

This crucial clarification is the only one that really allows us to understand the role and the somewhat singular destiny of Crichton's *Inquiry into the Nature and Origin of Mental Derangement* at the time. If we try to examine it closely from today's vantage point, we find it difficult to appreciate the acclaim it received in Paris as an event that assured it of an impact on the French scene that was highly unusual for a foreign book. It does not particularly stand out among the other texts of the period, and, if we take it on its own merits, the question remains, "Why this book rather than some other one?"—as the judgment of posterity seems by and large to have established. But in fact the book was greeted at the time as "one of those estimable productions that leave their mark on an era both among the literary splendors of a Nation and in the general history of the progress of the human mind."[11] It received favorable reviews everywhere and became an obligatory reference for a time. Its author was even briefly associated with Pinel and some of the others working to reform the treatment of the insane.[12]

However, if we look more closely, we notice that this short-lived infatuation with Crichton stems wholly and directly from Pinel. Crichton's book was first reviewed by one of Pinel's disciples, Moreau de la Sarthe, in the *Recueil périodique de littérature médicale étrangère*; the review was reprinted unchanged the following year in the *Décade philosophique.*[13] Now, in the same volume of the *Recueil*, we find Pinel's own annotated translation of a fragment of Crichton's book, under the title "Recherche méthodique sur la nature et les causes physiques du délire."[14] Moreover, given that Crichton is virtually the only author who finds favor in Pinel's eyes and toward whom he acknowledges a debt in the *Treatise on Insanity*, it is not too surprising that the educated public, not especially well informed on the topic, would espouse such an authoritative appreciation. Thus Pinel is at the origin of this ephemeral but remarkable movement of opinion.

It is easy enough to account for Pinel's enthusiasm, unlike that of most of his contemporaries. For Pinel, Crichton's work came on the scene providentially to resolve a thorny difficulty and take away a major obstacle that had been central to his preoccupations for some time. The problem was how to treat mental illness in terms of the passions, without falling into a moralizing rut or risking confusion with the old discourse according to which the person who cannot resist the urging of her passions ends up going mad. There is a clear and eloquent gap between Pinel's interests and those of his contemporaries, moreover: for example, Moreau de la Sarthe, whose attention was probably drawn to the book by Pinel, leaves Part Three of Crichton's work, the part dealing specifically with the passions, virtually unmentioned in his review,[15] whereas that is the part Pinel focuses on. He explicitly uses the substance of Part Three in the introduction to his *Treatise*, and this material finally allows him to adopt without reservation a hypothesis that was up to that point both necessary and virtually inadmissible, owing to "the consideration of the human passions viewed simply as phenomena of the animal economy, without any idea of morality or immorality." Mental illness must be related to the passions, but on the imperative condition of understanding the passions within a general science of the sources and laws of human behavior, freed from any moral perspective.

Pinel's prolonged reluctance to set out openly along a path that he had nevertheless recognized at the outset as the only possible one, and the circumstances that allowed him to get around the obstacle after all, attest in their modest but effective way that the advent of psychiatry cannot be separated from a profound revolution in the idea of man and very specifically in the idea of man's power over himself, that is, his moral strength. As the adversaries of the notion of monomania will protest to the alienists, some twenty years later, one is inviting immorality by admitting that an individual who, to use Esquirol's terms, "measures the harm he is doing and is conscious of it" is nevertheless irresistibly led in spite of himself to do harm and is thus irresponsible; if he is conscious, he necessarily has the power to prevent himself from acting and thus has responsibility. The proposition is not lacking in truth: to acknowledge that presence to oneself does not procure power over the self *ipso facto* is, in fact, to destroy the bases of the moral conception of the human being as it has traditionally been understood.

Now, this idea, unquestionably, is the basis of the imputation of madness to the passions, independently of any judgment of morality or immorality.[16] If traditional thinking had it that going mad by abandoning oneself to the urgings of one's passions was immorality, the reason was that the individual was credited with full power over his passions; he was thought to possess the ability to stand outside himself to such a degree that he ultimately had to have been in a position to opt knowingly for resistance or renunciation. Conversely, the idea that the fact of going mad owing to the intimate subversion of the passions has absolutely nothing to do with morality implies a totally transformed representation of the human being. According to this new representation, the individual theoretically lacks the radical distance with respect to herself that would enable her to determine whether she was for or against her inclinations, and that in turn would allow her in effect to choose madness. This view of the individual puts her at the other extreme; she is so wrapped up in herself, so immersed in "the obscure sources of her behavior,"[17] so rigidly committed and fixed in her determinations that she can do nothing about them, even when she benefits from full consciousness. On the other hand, still according to this new representation, one can reconcile the identification of a pronounced state of mental alienation with the recognition of a continued presence of the insane person to herself—for conscious distance in no way implies the power to determine one's own insanity, any more than injury to the subjective power signifies the abolition of the self as difference with respect to the self.

The double rejection on which psychiatry was based—neither choice of madness nor abolition of the subject in madness—thus has to be situated within and at the heart of an overall mutation of the anthropological reference points by which the intelligibility of the subjective economy was discreetly and decisively disconnected from morality. This shift itself had to be re-placed in the line of successive breaks that led to the appearance, in modern Europe, of the idea that specific laws, which were absolutely independent of the rules of morality, made political and economic phenomena autonomous and intelligible domains entirely unrelated to moral precepts. The constitution of a subjective field as a specialized field of science has to be understood in a similar way, and doubtless situated within the same general movement of emancipation. This new field has its own coherence; it functions as a whole, blending thoughts and passions in an autonomous way, according to an internal determinism that remains to be elucidated; at least there is agreement at the outset that the field is neither good nor bad a priori, and that it is entirely independent of ethical imperatives.

It would not be absurd, moreover, to take the comparison even further. One could argue that the intellectual schema of domination had to be overcome before the idea of a specific intelligibility of the political could emerge. There are laws of power, laws inherent in its very essence, against which the will of the prince is powerless. These laws command his action whatever he may do, and he does better to recognize them than to challenge them out of ignorance. In a somewhat similar way, the schema of will in general had to be overturned to construct economics as a separate domain in and for itself: there are laws of production, laws governing the growth and distribution of wealth against which both the global ambition to impose norms from without and the determination of any individual agent, prince or subject, are powerless. In this respect, emancipation in the moral context is also emancipation in the political context; one simply needs to know the laws before one acts. Now, if we consider the question of how psychic reality is set up as a space of investigation in itself, defined, governed, and articulated from within according to its inherent forms, its internal checks and balances, the undertaking is basically similar: here too, in the last analysis, it is a matter of liberating oneself from the schema of the will, from the myth of personal sovereignty, as if the individual, owing to the power conferred upon him by an ability to stand consciously outside himself, could dispose of himself at will.

The inaugural act, under the circumstances, is once again, first of all, an act of limitation. The prince, even though he keeps himself outside and above society, is nevertheless not entirely free to act as he pleases. In just the same way, to the extent that power and society do not constitute two distinct entities but two poles of a single reality governed by specific relations, the individual, even though he does in fact have at his disposal a certain distance with respect to himself, is nonetheless immersed in an overall organization of his being that unfolds according to its own laws. In relation to that organization, what the individual knows and the very fact that he knows himself confer on him no discretionary power; he cannot purely and simply abstract himself from that organization.

Hence the simultaneously emblematic and strategic character of the problem of the consciousness of the insane. The consciousness attributed to the insane is first of all a means—unquestionably used in complete ignorance of its real scope, but this has no relevance to its effectiveness—for signifying the essential limitation of subjective power. Consciousness of the act one is accomplishing does not preclude the possibility that the act arises from an uncontrollable internal compulsion. In the second place, the consciousness attributed to the insane is a means for confronting the traditional vision of the self's sovereignty over itself. This came strikingly to the fore around 1825 during the great debate over monomania and especially the homicidal variety. An act of homicidal mania is a premeditated, planned, and calculated crime that the accused remembers, and in detail, but that may nevertheless have been committed under the sway of alienation and may have to be viewed as the action of an irresponsible person. The figure of the conscious but alienated criminal brought to the social scene for the first time the core of the psychiatric discovery and its latent anthropological corollary, namely, the drastic restriction of the individual's moral autonomy and conscious power. To judge by the virulence of the reactions, this figure was not easy to tolerate. But it amounted in fact to nothing more than an extension of the figure confined within the circle of practitioners of the healing art, the figure that Esquirol was led to uncover by the logic of the passions: the figure of the insane person in whom only the moral faculties are altered or perverted, and who, even though his intellectual faculties are intact and perfect, appears to be impelled by a depraved will to do harm in spite of himself, despite his full awareness and his ability to assess the harm he is doing.

CHAPTER VI

Reducing Insanity: The Mirror of Alterity

WE HAVE MOVED from viewing the subject as abolished to making the subject responsible for his or her alienation: this sums up the break in the implicit overall understanding of madness that its causal decentering induced. Thus the manifestations of madness could be reinscribed within the space of what makes human sense; its signs and forms could be recuperated and incorporated within the general sphere of the comprehensible. This is the other aspect of the reconquest allowed by the interpretive recourse to the passions, which are now viewed as *symptoms*. Indeed, as long as the intervention of obliterating causes is postulated (and these causes may be physical or moral, but they are presumed in all cases to cancel out "presence of mind"), the world of madness can be defined in terms of a cleavage, a separation from the common order of the inner world, a passage outside the borders of what characterizes the human, an exit from the regular forms of humanity. In short, the insane are viewed as having entered a realm whose logical pinnacle and revealing index par excellence can only be an extreme projection onto the other-than-self and the other-than-man: "rage or fury," according to Hobbes (though he did not originate the expression). Whereas as soon as practitioners begin to think that the subject in person, as it were, however subverted he may be in his organization and his capacities, still remains active and alive at the heart of the feelings, thoughts, and acts through which he escapes himself, the interpretive perspective shifts. Are the marks of the subject's loss of self-possession instances of pure disorder, simple indexes of an indefinitely convertible and rigorously repetitive absence, or are they still expressions—unmasterable expressions, to be sure, but not at all unintelligible in themselves, and not at all impossible for an observer to identify with an author—of the divided human being that the observer still senses as "himself" beneath whatever alienates him?

To the extent that practitioners begin to recognize the persistence of a personal center of gravity, an authentic *reduction of insanity* becomes conceivable in relation to and starting from that center. Not only is the subjective dimension uneffaced, not only does the insane person remain somewhere present to his own illness, but the very thing that leads him astray and imposes itself on him uncontrollably, far from being pure nonsanity, continues to take on regulated, recognizable, universal subjective forms throughout: we know these forms as the passions. "All types of alienation have their analogy and as it were their primitive type in the character of each passion."[1] Madness does not uproot the individual from the ground of common experience, does not cause him to shift into innumerable and always identical forms of otherness in the emptiness of his position outside of sanity: every one of its manifestations can be assigned to a known moral category, can be decoded in the light of the most ordinary lived experience, can be understood within the varieties of personal experience considered in its greatest generality. "In sad melancholy, the face is pale, its features concentrated, its expressions pained; the eyes are hollow, dejected, the gaze suspicious, the movements slow. One hears only dull moans, whimpers, signs mingled with monosyllables that escape aimlessly. . . . Who does not recognize in this the characteristics of sorrow and the state of the man whom setbacks, misfortunes, and the injustice of his fellow man are pursuing and weighing down?"[2] In other words, every instance of estrangement from the self still marks an indestructible and positive participation in humanity, and all such instances can be traced to the common pathways of personal identity.

We do not wish to make Esquirol seem to be saying something that it makes no sense for him even to contemplate. It is clear that he does not articulate what we have reached the point of thinking today, namely, that it is always the subject who expresses himself in the discourse and the acts that constrain him and impose themselves on him as heterogeneous and unbearable; that it is the subject, directly and in person, who is expressing himself, thinking himself and seeking himself through the very aspect of himself that has become unmasterable and impenetrable to him; and, consequently, that one can envisage an enterprise of disalienation that would work by elucidating, recovering, and restoring to the subject the sanity that the subject had lost. It is clear that Esquirol's position is situated well below the threshold of this latest advance in the reappropriation of madness and self-recognition within madness. But his position must certainly be viewed and understood in this perspective, and it is no accident that we find ourselves obliged to ward off some confusion here. For while Esquirol certainly did not produce the content of our own position, he did create, historically, its conditions of possibility.

Esquirol does not relate the content of madness to the singular expressive necessities of a human being fated to expose herself in her profound uniqueness, even (and especially) when her speech can only find an outlet at the price of its own effacement. He simply reports the varieties of alienation, taken *as a group*, from the established forms of subjective experience considered *in general* and in the abstract. No doubt going mad, in his eyes, always amounts to leaving oneself. But it entails leaving *oneself* without exiting from the self's domain of continuity, proximity, and belonging. To go mad is to separate oneself from oneself only to find oneself nonetheless, and to reroot oneself, as it were, a bit further along, through a type of behavior that is in its broad outlines circumscribable and identifiable by others as measured by the knowledge they have of themselves. Thus madness takes on an essential human intelligibility, in relation to a presupposition whose decisive intervention can be discerned between the lines: it amounts to positing the limits of subjective organization as inescapable. From the field of the human, finally, one cannot exit. Not that its structure is in theory beyond all reach. On the contrary; here is precisely the enigma. That structure is highly susceptible to radical vacillation, if not to radical breakdown; and yet even within the disorder that upsets, disarticulates, or eclipses it, a coherent and sensible figure is recomposed that resembles it and proves to depend on its laws. A mysterious persistence and influence of the human in us forbids us to forget ourselves entirely, and keeps us from passing into the absolute other. This enigmatic force obliges us to try to identify a universal root and an overall consistency—among the passions, for example—in what seems to be a disorder emerging without origin or direction from the absence of the subject.

Human beings never cross the frontiers of the human, even when they are personally absent from themselves. This general principle posits a priori the possibility of identification. First, individuals can be identified with themselves in their biographical continuity—somewhere within their alienation they remain what they were; somehow their alienation is connected with their previous reality.[3] But in addition, the content and forms of alienation express elements of a comprehensible humanity with which other human beings can identify. Esquirol does not make these assumptions consciously. But in his writing there is some requirement operating from the secret underside of discourse. Still timid, naive, and awkward, this requirement is nevertheless irreversible as well as irrepressibly destined to take hold more and more deeply. The flagrant inadequacy of its first formulation, under cover of a dubious theory of the passions, rapidly leads it to retreat in prudent silence. Powerless to acknowledge itself, it will nevertheless continue insistently to impose itself on the understanding of madness, inflecting it toward increasing recognition of the singular subject in the dimension of her thought that proves to escape her, and toward increasing recognition of the subject in general in what is revealed by the specific paths of her alienation. The human being resembles her madness. Insanity holds up a mirror to her, in which the face of its own causes can be discerned. Structurally, Esquirol's work seems to set up this perspective of reflection by way of the inverse thesis: that madness resembles humans, that the passions and alienation are at bottom one and the same thing.

That thesis is literally untenable, however; it will be vigorously and legitimately criticized for erasing the pathological break.

Over and beyond the pertinent criticisms, Esquirol's initial formulation must be resituated in its own time and understood in its precise function if the true import of his idea is to be restored. Apart from any question of its truth value, it provided the means for overturning the representation of madness as exteriority, for reintegrating insanity within the space of the human. Once it had played its role, it could disappear, or it could simply be judged on its own merits. The mechanism for recognizing the human dimension of insanity and the latent imperative of identification with the insane subject that it had allowed to emerge remained for their part irreversible acquisitions that structured the field of knowledge from that point on.

The premises of the new approach to mental alienation entail, at least virtually, a complete shift of anthropological perspective. Unquestionably, it will take a long time for that shift to be completed. The processes through which any historical transformation is propagated, assumed, and assimilated in all its aspects generally do take a long time. The fact remains that from the moment systematic resemblance between the insane and the rest of humanity was outlined by the early alienists, a dynamic was set in motion that would lead to an explicit and integral recuperation of psychopathological phenomena within the space of the human, and to the idea that the unknown dimensions of the subject have to be decoded entirely in the light of what madness exposes. Surely no one can believe that, abruptly turning our backs on a millennial blindness and proscription, we have been led by some sudden insight or miraculous illumination to discover with the help of the subversion of the subject the authentic visage of humanity. In reality, this acquisition can only be explained as a cumulative process, as much a completion as a radical break: the gradually increasing visibility and acceptance of a silent and obscure reincorporation whose enactment and logical condition of possibility we are grasping here—the dissolution of the conception according to which the insane are in some way essentially external to themselves and to humanity. The advent of psychiatry can be traced to this point of inflection where what had relegated the subject to a position outside himself now turns inward and integrates itself with the subject as the image of a limit where that subject can be revealed.

ABSTRACT IX

Approaches to Healing

How to Speak to the Insane

Esquirol's originality consists in his incorporation of the therapeutic dimension into the definition of madness. By speaking to the insane, he aimed at reaching the human subject who is present behind his delirium and can hear the alienist. Esquirol sought to provoke a reflexive turn within the mad person's self. He thus discovered the singular power of verbal interaction: the ability to get in touch with the healthy part of the insane patient and mobilize it against the influence of madness.

CHAPTER VII

The Society of Individuals and the Institution of Speech

The Dissolution of Reciprocity

IN THE GENESIS of moral treatment, we can see distinctly the conjunction and articulation of the two basic factors whose determining role in the origins of the psychiatric phenomenon in general we have spelled out above: a revolution in the representation of human beings, and a revolution in the practice and in the symbolics of the relationship of one human being with another. It is easy enough to understand how the presuppositions of moral treatment are related to what we have called the reversal of the moral conception of madness. That conception has implications for the individual's capacity to make choices concerning himself and the way such a capacity may be affected in mental illness. On the one hand, one must not leave the patient shut off in his compelling delirium, either to focus on what remains of him in the objective sphere (his body), or to play along with the delirium in an attempt to undermine it. On the other hand, no ultimate distance is preserved behind and beyond the patient's complete self-enclosure that would allow one to call forth in him a pure and free decision to renounce his madness. There is always a vestige of difference and presence to self and to others that can be mobilized—not beyond madness and despite all appearances, but *within* madness itself, inside delirium, immediately visible and perceptible. And if one is therefore justified in placing therapeutic hope in the conscious power that subsists in the insane patient, this does not take the form of a radical choice on the patient's part to pull himself away from the captivity of illusion; it takes the form of a gradual, blind, spontaneous, and virtually automatic process of reconquest and recovery of self, a process that is neither truly conscious of itself nor truly intentional.

Moral treatment is rooted in something like a canceling out of the classic division between the view that madness entails a complete absence from oneself and the view that it entails full consciousness and an intact ability to make decisions about oneself (according to the latter view, such consciousness is both present at the origin of madness, allowing it to develop, and held in reserve as the ultimate and inextinguishable remedy for madness); the two terms are reciprocally integrated and correlatively relativized. In the creation of moral treatment, the terms *consciousness* and *madness*—terms that are at once mutually exclusive and mutually interdependent—were reunited, but at the price of a drastic reduction in conscious power, whose acknowledged coexistence with the most pronounced alienation signifies that the patient has neither the capacity to choose it nor the freedom to shed it.

That is true for the insane patient herself, considered in isolation. But the practitioner's *relationship* with the patient is another matter, which has to be looked at in a second stage. The theoretical coherence of this "diplopic" conception according to which madness is viewed in terms of the patient's loss of reflexive omnipotence has an exact parallel in a different register, the *practical* register of the rules that institute and govern the realm of symbolic exchange. Either one is mad, or else one is the conscious master of oneself. This alternative masks another, or is closely embedded in another, whose concrete influence we have already had occasion to assess: either one is operating within a situation of reciprocity, and treated as such (the insane person's aggressive inclinations will be met with blows), or else one is rigorously excluded from reciprocity, which means being "deprived of all sensibility," as Georget put it. Confronting the insane patient locked inside her own delirium, the practitioner should not waste his time seeking an impossible dialogue—or if talking with the patient is of paramount importance, there is no alternative but to "enter into her delirium," to fall into line with her chimerical beliefs, to restablish artificially a common code of discourse by agreeing to set up her insane condition as the norm; in short, the only way to reconstitute a space of possible reciprocity is on a footing of madness. As for the responsible subject presumed to be concealing herself behind the currently absent insane person, it is appropriate to address her, on the contrary, in the language of reason and morality, and to exhort her to get a grip on herself once and for all.

Passing over madness in the latter case as if it did not exist, the doctor appeals to the patient, who is presumed to be governed in some respect by the same norm as himself. The insane person is to be addressed in the language of his madness, yet as if he were not mad. There is no middle ground between these two possibilities. The constraint is the same in each case: one has to situate oneself without the slightest ambivalence within a frame of reference (whether "natural" or "constructed," reasonable or unreasonable) that allows the interlocutors to occupy positions that are ideally equal, symmetrical, and reversible. Neither says anything that the other could not have said; neither utters anything that the other cannot hear from his own place, as if he had formulated it himself. It is impossible to envisage a relation of confrontation not simply between opposing opinions but also, much more profoundly, incommensurate ways of thinking, heterogeneous systems of coordinates. Either there is no relation at all, or there is a relation established by force under the guise of identity. Either one seeks to continue to speak to the insane person only as to another self (obstinately addressing him with the discourse of reason alone and leaving insanity aside), or else one agrees to forget oneself by putting oneself on the other's ground and making the language of insanity one's own. At the same time that one finds oneself governed by a specific conception of madness and by the intellectual logic that splits madness and bounces it inexorably back and forth between two antagonistic poles, one typically finds oneself in the grip of a logic that has justifiably been called concrete—a logic that is no less rigid in its applications: the logic of reciprocity that founds and organizes symbolic exchange. This is the logic of the primordial articulation through which, from their very inception, as far as we can tell, societies have understood, reflected, and defined both the mode in which their members are present to one another, and the position of human beings in general with respect to one another.

It may seem surprising that we are attributing such survival power to an institutional principle that, while it may have prevailed exclusively for thousands of years in human history, at the heart of the egalitarian universe of primitive societies, has been considered essentially out of date since the advent of the state, of the principle of hierarchy, and of the nonreciprocal relation par excellence, the relation between commandment and obedience. And it may seem more astonishing still that we equate the time-honored principle with the recently created categories of the rationalist philosophy of the subject. It is obviously impossible to deal with each of these questions in the requisite detail. Still, a few clarifying remarks are in order. The birth of the state unmistakably signifies the end of the world of exchange, a world that positions itself against the state precisely by means of exchange.[1] This claim calls for one crucial reservation, however. The invention of domination and the appearance of a separate agency of power, while they virtually abolish the face-to-face relation required by reciprocity (for which they tend inherently to substitute at all social levels an irreversible relation of superior to inferior), are not translated immediately as such; they do not deploy their full potential at the outset.

The birth of the state does not imply the instantaneous realization of the possibilities intrinsically invested in the principle of the state. The penetration of society, its appropriation by the state, that is, the implementation of the aim of power that is structurally inscribed in the state organ, in fact requires thousands of years. But at the start, the state has a remarkable feature that many people have noted, including—with singular acuity—Marx. In its original despotic form, this feature appears as a sort of supplementary agency. It superimposes itself on the social mechanism, transforming it of course in order to adjust to it, but finally allowing it by and large to continue to organize itself according to its own norms.

Indeed, under the state, and independently of the hierarchical relation whose dissolving novelty it introduced, a social world subsists for a very long time, one that is perhaps not outside the state but that is at least quite perceptibly autonomous with respect to the state. Underneath its superficial upheavals it is deeply and obstinately in harmony with the values and structures of pre-state societies, and especially the well-structured societies where reciprocity was the rule. Moreover, even properly political relations between masters and subjects turn out to be defined (and distorted) under the circumstances in terms of reciprocal obligation. The relation of dominance will be expressed (and masked), for example, in an exchange between a despot who magically guarantees the fertility of the land and commoners who owe him obedience and tribute in return. But closer to our own day, in the context of European feudalism, we still find an analogous exchange between the guarantee of protection and the assent to subordination. Such compromises attest as much to the influence of a symbolic framework as to the need to disguise the realities of subjection. Even to express the opposite of the requirement of reciprocity, namely, the hierarchical imposition of inequality, there is still no language other than that of face-to-face confrontation under the imperative sign of identity and reversibility.

This observation invites reflection on the extraordinary solidity of the primordial form conferred upon the interhuman bond and its rootedness in the social body. Even though domination as such, descending from above, is inherently opposed to that primordial form, domination did not really suffice to destroy it, for the traditional philosophy of domination proved to a certain extent compatible with the implicit philosophy of exchange and thus sometimes allowed the latter to govern or to shape—below it, alongside it, in concert with it—entire realms of human relations (a given sector of the circulation of goods, for example, or kinship ties). Sometimes, much more modestly, the philosophy of domination allowed the philosophy of exchange to infiltrate or nourish marginal practices, residual attitudes that were not very spectacular but that were strongly rooted, like those we discover at the heart of the speech relation (which is perhaps the ultimate bastion of the traditional constraints).

According to the philosophy of domination, the foundation of social life is located at the top of society, on the side of power and the forces of reunion and coercion. The cohesiveness of the social body is ontologically primary; the individual is intrinsically included in the collectivity, and subordinated to it. Because it attributes absolute priority to society as a whole, traditional political thought remains consonant at bottom with the philosophy of exchange with which it nevertheless breaks in practice. For the philosophy of exchange also postulates fundamentally that relations precede the terms (individuals or groups) that enter into relations, that the form of any possible encounter among social segments or atoms is socially determined in advance, that the logical content and even the very existence of relations are primary as compared with what the concrete agents who find themselves in a given relation may do with it, may invest in it of their own personal will. It is probably in terms of the same anteriority recognized in the social realm that exchange and domination, despite their historic antagonism, could nevertheless be to some extent reconciled.

The decisive break, which definitively dissolved the last bases available to the principle of reciprocity in collective organization, and which deprived that principle of any social justification whatsoever, came about only quite recently. It coincided precisely with the shift in the social foundation, during the individualist revolution of the eighteenth century, that radically transformed both the image of political domination and its prospects, both the symbolic forms of the cohesiveness of the collective field and the elementary bases for relations among social agents. The source of this shift lay in a twofold process. On the one hand, the state affirmed its sovereignty, manifesting the specificity of a power incommensurate with any other form of authority or hierarchy. It claimed total administrative competence, and it thus acquired the aspect of an absolute reference in society; it became a source to which any member of society could relate directly, regardless of his concrete participation in a community, a family, or a corporation. The Tocquevillean state was a creator of equality; the state was a mirror of the new, detached, autonomous beings that existed by and for themselves, namely, individuals. On the other hand, the economy came to the fore: by economy we mean the complete separation, exemplified in the marketplace, of a sector of human activity that until then had been incorporated, "embedded," in the others. Correlatively, a direct mode of human relations is replaced by a type of relation increasingly mediated by things, one that presupposes mutual indifference, atomistic independence, and the absence of any personal commitment among partners (for partners are simply juxtaposed momentarily by the accident of an anonymous transaction and the "just price" fixed by a mechanical agency of regulation).[2]

These immense innovations were given a coherent and complete form by the democratic revolution, which brought the social foundation, as it were, back down from above to below. Henceforth, the social atom, the individual, has primacy; the cohesion of the social body is derivative, a product; sovereignty is delegated; power is an expression arising from within society itself. We have already shown how the legitimate installation of a system in which power proceeds in this way from the explicitly formulated collectivity will actually lead to an extraordinary expansion of the potential power of the state organ, even though that organ is now limited in principle to tasks of execution alone. Since power is nothing but what society wants for itself, there is no longer anything in society that can be said to escape power a priori. Everything in society stems from the collectivity's own enterprise of definition and organization, an enterprise of which power has become the instrument. Democratic power legitimately aspires to total control over the society in which it has originated, by virtue of the very fact that it originated from that society. Democratic power is no longer checked by autonomous modes of socialization, by traditional forms of collective cohesion, or by inherited types of communitarian organization independent of that power, anterior to it and subsisting on their own. For democratic power, there is no longer anyone below but individuals, independent units of citizenship; there are never indissociable, multipersonal entities expressing themselves as bodies, according to the principle that the whole takes precedence over the parts. Whereas above, the state finds itself credited at least implicitly with a monopoly of the collective dimension, since it is charged with translating the overall project that has arisen from the dispersal of individual agents into all spheres of social life, its task is to impose that project methodically and uniformly.

Thus, in the historical framework we have sketched out here, the democratic revolution has to be seen as the moment of something like a second birth of the state, the moment when, for the first time since it originated, the state finds itself actually permeating society through and through. It effectively dissolves in society the vestiges of the structures that carry the active affirmation of the precedence of the social bond over the individual human being, and it makes hierarchical dissymmetry and the political viewpoint prevail throughout society. The moment is one of accomplishment, of completion, in a sense—a moment of perfect co-penetration, of virtual fusion, between society and the state.

But the crucial feature that must be emphasized here is the correlation between this generalization of the statist principle and the individualist disaggregation of the social fabric. The full deployment of the potentialities in the very existence of a detached agency of domination necessarily implies the official liquidation of every vestige of the old modes of socialization at the heart of collective organization. Those old modes failed to take detached and autonomous individuals into account; conversely, they understood social agents only in terms of their already-established membership in the collectivity. They made it impossible for social agents to conceive of themselves apart from others, apart from relations with others. The necessity of those others is known in advance and is all the harder to ignore in that its form is strictly predetermined: this is in fact the profound and vital legacy of the early societies, of those tens of thousands of years of human history marked by an explicit, immediate, horizontal, collective cohesion, before the break that introduced, along with the state, five or six thousand years ago, the diametrically opposed postulate that society holds together only through the operation of the organ placed above and outside it, and human relations are only possible owing to the mediation and guarantees of a third party. Again, such postulates were never articulated as the official discourse of the state, but they were structurally contained in it as latent perspectives of its action.

For a long time, the state conceived of itself and presented itself within this primitive model of organic social solidarity, a model it was destined to subvert. And for a long time, too, it encountered a powerful obstacle to its own expansion in what survived of the original requirement that social agents posit themselves immediately for one another, inseparably from one another, with no need for a third party to bring them together—indeed while explicitly excluding, owing to the very order presiding over their encounter, any intervention by a third party.

This led us to speak earlier of the way exchange operates against the state. In fact, in the case of exchange, the aim of self-sufficiency and independence, which is inscribed in the very mechanism that governs relations of exchange, is exposed in a pure and virtually perfect form. All the factors that determine relations among individuals and groups are internal to the relation of exchange; all are wholly contained between the partners whom the relation brings into radical confrontation: this is one way to summarize the spirit of the threefold obligation to give, to receive, and to give in return. No prior social bond exists: an agreed-upon reciprocity creates that bond ex nihilo (concretely, within a given society, reciprocity repeatedly recreates the social bond, but always as if from scratch). In the modalities of the relation instituted in this way, nothing is owed to any external imperative. The rule of reciprocity does not come from the outside; it is immanent to the relation itself, whose conditions of possibility it limits itself to registering and expressing in action, namely, the fact that the partners are on the same level and in symmetrical positions (hence the potential reversibility of their behavior). Finally, the social bond in general entails nothing more than what exchange produces: exchange by itself is the social bond in its complete and perfected form. This accounts for the fissional, multiplicatory character of the societies it articulates, for their cohesion never presupposes the totalization of a whole; on the contrary, segments of society cohere by virtue of their mutual recognition, thus by way of their reciprocal autonomization according to a dynamics of schism and opposition that does not prevent the social bond from being rediscovered intact every time. Quite to the contrary, the social bond is continually recreating the conditions that allowed it to arise.

The advent of the state can be represented precisely as the introduction of the viewpoint of the One, the attribution to a separate agency of the task of producing the cohesion of the collective field, for only a constraining, global operation conducted from without can keep together elements that in themselves are destined to lead to asocial disaggregation. The social bond does not depend on us alone. It comes from elsewhere. In the last analysis, what brings us together is by nature external to the level on which we find ourselves: this would be one way to express the implicit philosophy of the state. It is a philosophy of the transcendent third party, at the opposite pole from the dual philosophy conveyed by exchange. Nevertheless, as long as a "holistic" mode of society continues to prevail, to borrow Louis Dumont's terminology, as long as such a mode guarantees the preeminence of interpersonal and communitarian solidarities over individual will, the affirmation of the state is necessarily destined to come up against sectors of society that subsist independently of the state. These sectors view themselves as having their own traditional consistency prior and external to the state, and in their organization they prolong the internal, immanent, autonomous principle of socialization for which the institution of exchange has historically provided the paradigmatic embodiment.

The state is not really perfected, is not fully in conformity with its own essence, until the day when, having become a pure and simple emanation of society, explicitly produced as such, it actually ceases to be brought up short by similar, regulated, independent forms of co-membership from before its time, forms with which one can come to terms from the outside, but that cannot be mastered from within. Only then does the state appear in its full specificity, and in visible separation, as the exclusive agency of the institution of the social, an agency established in terms of a rigorous disjunction between the viewpoint of the whole, from which collective unity and identity are produced, and the private viewpoint of individuals, in which each is egoistically authorized and invited to persevere. For the confiscation of the role of agent of the global cohesiveness of society by the political agency is also translated, in turn, by an emancipation. By the same token, anyone at all is free to assume fully his or her condition as a separate, private individual within the general framework that is constituted and defined by an Other, from the distinct place of power. Private individuals are free, in particular, to determine contractually among themselves the nature of their mutual relations, with the understanding that such relations maintained at the pleasure of individuals do not constitute in themselves the truth of the social bond, but that they presuppose its underlying existence, and that the fundamental conditions for the coexistence of individuals are instituted from elsewhere, from an encompassing viewpoint (the individuals concerned may then arrange these conditions as they see fit). This redoubtable equation makes subjective liberty dependent upon the omnipotence of power.

This is why the individualist-democratic revolution marks the moment when the bond of reciprocity disappeared, or rather when the last forms of support from which it could benefit in society were liquidated. As long as state control is fully developed, as long as the dimension of a primary, self-sufficient, collective cohesion exists outside the state, on the level of concrete human communities, there is room in the weft of the social fabric for remnants of the timeless imperatives of exchange to survive—obscurely, of course, but persistently and vitally. These imperatives constitute an original and maximal form of the way to posit simultaneously the immediacy of the articulation that holds people together and its regulated anteriority with respect to the existence of separate individuals. Within these archaic modes of socialization, even if they are residual, an instinctive faithfulness to the primitive logical requirement of symmetry and reversibility is invited quite naturally, as it were, to come into play: they supply it with a solid base, they continue to endow it with meaning, even when it is no longer recognized among the explicit norms. The systems of attitudes and the codes that individuals respect in their relationships remain potential conveyors, owing to the diffuse spirit that animates them, of a symbolic order that was its radical expression. Thus from time to time, in certain problematic cases or suitable situations, the ancient reflex comes to the fore as a recourse and as a rule.

This is precisely and typically what happens in the case that concerns us. When one is dealing with an insane person, the externality that he embodies, in contrast to the commonly accepted categories, represents a manifest challenge; it unfailingly awakens the buried but still available model of reciprocity. On the one hand, one does not know what to do with an individual who has gone over to the inconceivable outside of reason; on the other hand, the only thing about that individual that is certain is his retreat to the solitude of illusion and his break with the realm of communicable, shareable truth. Situating him in relation to exchange, under these conditions, is first of all a way of identifying him, assigning him a precise position, understanding him in terms of a defined status. If he is explicitly excluded from the space of reciprocal recognition, he at least acquires a clear place in the order of human beings, instead of the unbearable indeterminacy of nameless difference. But situating him in relation to exchange is also a way of reaffirming, in the face of transgression, the intangibility of the framework that conditions the existence of a relation among beings and thus the possibility of a human world. It is impossible to free oneself from this constraint, which means that we exist for others, ostensibly taking into account their presence and their reality. However absent he may seem, the insane person has to continue to depend on that presence and that reality at some level; he has to be forced to feel their imperious necessity. For the philanthropic concession belatedly inspired by the Enlightenment still consists in the spirit of the unavoidable obligation to rejoin the insane person on his own ground and to accept his insanity as a common frame of reference. To the extent that the insane person works against this in a blatant and radical way, he provokes, in contrast, the full-fledged mobilization of attitudes that we might have thought completely forgotten and that are indeed now scarcely discernible in ordinary social and personal relations. But in so doing, the mad person reveals to what extent—in a domain that is both hypersensitive and rather special, to be sure—the fundamental principle that has concretely codifed our obligation to exist for one another and the operation of our mutual recognition since societies began remains influential and imperative even though intangible.

The reign of the principle of reciprocity has come to an end virtually everywhere in society: the expansion of the market sphere, the development of political sovereignty and of the model of an at once rational and separate authority, the affirmation of the autonomous power to choose on the part of individuals, all these factors shape entire sectors of collective life that by nature escape its hold. But in dealings with the insane, in this last reserved space where the only thing at stake is the pure possibility of a relation among persons or shared membership in a collectivity, without regard to the content of that relation or that membership but considering their foundation alone, the primordial structure that establishes the position and the duties of each subject surfaces again when it is needed, intact and unsurpassable. For despite the ever-increasing space taken up by realms of activity organized according to norms fundamentally foreign to reciprocity in the broad sense (whether what is at stake is the law of value, the impersonality of the bureaucratic organization, or the unpredictable freedom of feelings as the basis of the family), the general spirit of society, by virtue of the persistent and embodied prevalence of the values of trans-individual cohesiveness, remains congruent in spite of everything with the underlying spirit of exchange. Not only does it not contradict that spirit, but it provides a vehicle for it, reserving a base for it from which it can intervene as circumstances require.

The break actually comes about only with the explicit advent of the society of individuals in the political order. But at that point it is decisive, complete, and irreversible. For not only has the domain of activities expanded in which the model of reciprocity is no longer operative this time, but the very foundations of the social ensemble and the principles presiding over human relations suddenly become globally and formally antinomic in relation to what had been from time immemorial the embodied spirit of exchange. With the recognition in law and in fact of the social atom as the basic element of society and the only source of power by delegation, the one thing in fact excluded is the a priori determination of the form individual relations should take, and the obligation for individuals to mold themselves according to a logic that is always defined in advance once and for all. Nothing is posited as anterior to the will of beings who are independent of one another from the outset: it is up to them to invent the tenor and elaborate the modalities of their relations, to negotiate them and establish their terms, within an open space whose cohesiveness a specialized agency—the state—now takes on the task of maintaining. In this indeterminate universe of the contract in which the bond between individuals results from their agreement and has no consistency other than the properly social bond that holds them all together, there is no longer any room at all for any rule or constraint that would by nature recall the anteriority of the collective order over the will of its agents, an anteriority that human societies had always affirmed up to this point.

The Uncertain Other

The event is unprecedented. For the first time in human history, the confrontation between individuals finds itself emancipated from any prior framework that is presumed to include and inform it. Individuals will henceforth meet under the sign of the *alea*, characterized by an absence of norms and by uncertainty as to whether coexistence is possible; in addition, a bundle of profoundly personal possibilities opens up every time. A separate study would be required to follow and analyze the series of crucial mutations that came about, at the crossroads between the eighteenth and nineteenth centuries, when this dissolution of the preregulated bond between humans took place, along with the liberation of a "wild" space of interpersonal relations. At the time no one understood or expressed what was at stake better than Hegel: he described the new era in which consciousnesses struggle to the death to be recognized. The struggle resulted ineluctably from the fading away of the traditional reference points that guaranteed the co-presence of the self and the other, that fixed the positions of each in advance and held them to reciprocal identification in a way that was completely independent of their private desires. With the loss of the certainty that the other is there and knows you are also there—a certainty inscribed in the very structure of the social bond—the ordeal of coexistence inevitably became a dramatic confrontation between two subjectivities that are at once mutually dependent on each other and mutually independent. Each is equally obliged to impose itself on the other in order to win recognition and to be confirmed in its being by the other, and each can refuse to take the other's existence into account.

Why not bring the philosopher's discourse back from the eternal heaven of Ideas down to earth where it was conceived, and confer on it primary value as an acknowledgment of a truly unprecedented situation? In our view, this is the best way to approach texts such as the one in which Sade urges his fellow citizens to exert more effort to become authentically republican: one must read it as another acknowledgment, or at least as a historic indicator, of the unleashing of mutual desire that derives from the reduction of human beings to the absolute solitude of their appetites. From this point on, indeed, how could commerce among human beings be anything else, at bottom, but a disorderly confrontation of requirements that are incommensurable a priori? Miraculous exceptions aside, this confrontation is the very one represented at virtually the same time by the image of romantic passion: a meeting of two creatures made precisely for each other, an encounter that is all the more ineffable for being unpredictable, all the more irresistible in that it might not have taken place—a mobilizing encounter that fully engages subjectivity, to the extent that it brings together and calls into question persons who are totally independent of each other at the outset, individuals who lack the community of belonging that had presided earlier in a more or less necessary way over interpersonal contact between individuals, and correlatively, to the extent that it takes place on a purely private level (and no longer within a framework that is presumed to define the conditions of encounters between the sexes in a general way, thus limiting perceptibly the intimate personal meaning of the encounter).

The disappearance of the imperative forms of reciprocal recognition applies, then, to the domain of private person-to-person relations. But in the anonymous field of social relations, the consequences of this disappearance may have been still more spectacular in scope—particularly where the political bond is concerned, and the relation of commandment and obedience that constitutes its core. For so long as that relation continues to be included within an organically coherent universe where superiors and inferiors exist in the first place together and for one another before they are hierarchically distinguished, so long as their relationship consequently continues to follow the paths of a relation of mutual recognition in which explicit submission responds to ostensible domination, the power of the former over the latter turns out to be strictly limited. Today, we are inclined to condemn as retrospectively humiliating the older, ritual aspects of obedience that direct the inferior to indicate in some visible way that he consents to its power and thus to his position. In view of more recent developments, it still behooves us to assess what such an obligation to assume one's own subjection explicitly preserves, and what it prevents; to assert that one is obeying of one's own accord, through a formal will to submit, is simultaneously to affirm one's own irreducible autonomy as an agent. Because I acknowledge this, that power has me at its disposal. The more I manifest my humble consent, the more I claim ownership of myself, in a way, as actor, as internal master of my own behavior, whereas modern power, freed from the constraints of a face-to-face confrontation in which signs of domination are exchanged for marks of allegiance, power that lacks apparent glory but that is in a way effectively transcendent, power that lacks any visible inherent difference but that is functionally detached from the level of its bestowers, becomes for its part, on the contrary, intrinsically manipulative. It becomes "power over bodies," and, as such, it is undeniably capable of taking full control over human beings, aiming to penetrate them in order to reconfigure their acts and behavior from within. It becomes power that seeks to produce and program agents rather than to impose submission on its subjects, because it is no longer impeded by the principle of the self-sufficiency of human beings, a principle that would guarantee their self-containment and their inviolable inner individuality, both of which the old ostentatious forms of subjection implied and kept constantly in view.

There is at least one other sensitive sector in which the transformation of the social conditions of interpersonal relations had, it seems to us, direct and considerable repercussions, namely, medicine. Medicine's status as a science is in fact rigorously conditioned by the human relationships in which it is applied and developed. Thus one would have to ask to what extent prescientific, preclinical medicine might have encountered, in the type of relation with the patient dictated by a society still based on solidarity, the most rigid and most insurmountable of its epistemological obstacles; and to what extent, to begin with, the mode of explanation and the style of practice that characterized medicine in general might be governed by the primordial requirement that one recognize the other both within his own, absolutely distinct reality, and as someone on the same level as oneself, in a position essentially symmetrical with respect to oneself. There is a constraining respect here, too, for a sort of inviolability of the other (the patient), an obligation to preserve something like his intimate ownership of himself, so that what the doctor has to be familiar with is the illness *in itself*, and not directly the patient with whom the illness is integrated. And the doctor has to do this in such a way that he encounters and diagnoses the symptom in an intermediate and finally neutral, "objective" space between him and his patient, given that he is always supposed to address the patient as if the latter were personally disconnected from his illness.

What one would quite probably end up bringing to light as the ultimate structure governing the operations of knowledge mobilized by classical medicine would be the historically and logically defined structure of the bond linking human beings to one another. Conversely, it is clear that the institution of pragmatic medicine went rigorously hand in glove with the establishment of a doctor-patient relation marked by radical dissymmetry and the absence of any dimension of reciprocity. What came into being with clinical medicine is exactly what traditional medicine disallowed. The clinician could now view the patient, an individual totality in which illness was lodged, as an object of knowledge. He could assert the right to investigate the patient thoroughly and to make decisions about the patient's person, by virtue of a rigorous cleavage between himself, the subject in possession of knowledge, and the other, who was reduced to pure objectivity under the clinician's gaze. The clinician's aim was simultaneously to appropriate the other (to gain an exhaustive grasp of the other in her most intimate materiality) and to expropriate the other (one knows the other in the other's place). Such a project would have been absolutely inconceivable in a universe where the values and norms of mutual recognition still prevailed. Thus it surely does not suffice to invoke the irresistible progress of rationality alone, considered independently of its point of application, in order to explain the appearance and the success of modern medicine. Here, on the contrary, everything leads us to believe that the concrete framework of medical practice first had to be overturned before the project of a strictly pragmatic investigation of the diseased body could emerge and triumph. In the realm of disease, the scientific spirit was no doubt able to prevail less through the logic of its internal development than owing to an extrinsic event that opened the way: the final dissolution of the symbolic order that had continued until then to determine relations among human beings.

Self-Possession and Interpretation

It is from this same change in the essence of the social bond, from this same unprecedented mutation in the way individuals situated themselves with respect to others and the way they assumed their coexistence, that moral treatment finally emerged. What made it conceivable, in the last analysis, was the abolition of the system of constraints in terms of which every space of interpersonal communication had been instituted up to that point. From this point of view moral treatment can be viewed less as a specific technique than as a perfect indicator, an exemplary—because limited—illustration of the new conditions of the speech relation in general that resulted from the advent of a society of individuals. The very existence of moral treatment signifies—in the dual sense of indicating and symbolizing—that the way for human beings to address each other and to understand each other has been radically transformed, right down to its ultimate underpinnings. And it signifies in particular that human beings are no longer bound by the type of reciprocal obligations that prevailed when verbal exchange still embodied an assertion of mutual membership in a collectivity, and was organized accordingly.

Among other things, the traditional understanding of the speech relation entailed a strict principle of separation between the interlocutors' positions, a separation that correlates with the determination of those positions as symmetrical and equivalent. There is the other, there is myself; in practice, recognizing this distinction amounts to positing simultaneously that it is impossible to occupy both positions at once (impossible to put myself, from my own place, in the place of the other), and that there is no need for a third party to hold the first two together. It is for the one to speak, then, and for the other to listen; it is understood that the roles are made to be reversed, but also that each participant must strictly confine himself to his own role, so that what the one utters is by definition presumed to be identical to what the other understands. I necessarily hear in the discourse of the other just what he put there, given that nothing allows me to put myself mentally in his place; nothing allows me to reconstitute from within either what he really meant to say or what his statement really means without his knowing it. What he said is what there was to say, from his point of view, without my having to add, single out, or detect some personal truth that escaped him. I can only accept and register a message whose content may be in itself problematic for me, from within, but whose meaning for the person who uttered it is judged to be, on the contrary, totally lacking in mystery. Interpreting the other's discourse, claiming to know in his place something he himself is unaware of, something that is exposed in his utterances, is not only unimaginable in a symbolic mechanism of this sort, it is structurally excluded. Communication is defined as the circulation, within a neutral intermediate space, of terms that are intrinsically "objective" in relation to the one who uses or receives them.

Here we find something similar to what we observed in connection with the commandment-obedience relation, that is, a tacit postulation of internal distance as the basis for autonomy on the part of the agent. As we have observed, no matter how thoroughly obedience is integrated into a system of recognition, it is not the same thing as automatic conformity with a preestablished norm or program. Obedience must be, and must show itself to be, free and conscious consent to a higher imperative, through which the individual affirms that he is in fact internally the master of his subjection. We find the same mastery and presumed self-possession in the partners in a speech exchange: the speaker is considered to be at sufficient distance from his own statement so that, on the one hand, he can know precisely what he puts into it, and, on the other hand, he can infuse it with an objectivity that detaches it from him. Thus the other has only to receive the statement with the same detachment. This may have to mean translating it for himself, struggling to assimilate it for himself, but it does not mean deciphering his interlocutor's private, hidden truth. The other may have knowingly concealed some intentions that have to be detected, but he is never understood to have involuntarily acknowledged some inner truth. Thus the relation of each partner to his own discourse is not open to question. No one has to come between the subject and his expression from the outside, since the subject has full mastery of his own expression, on the one hand, and since his expression engages him absolutely as the element in which he posits himself in person, as the means he uses to give himself knowingly to himself and to his interlocutor, on the other hand. There is no obscurity to dissipate; there is an imprescriptible right to be oneself, to possess oneself within the circle of the self, to be respected.

Here we touch the foundations of a traditional culture of speech of which we can find memories and traces close at hand. Each interlocutor has the duty to speak only knowingly, to weigh and measure his words, to behave as a man of his word, as a man who knows he is bound by what he says to the extent that in his speech his reflexive autonomy and his power to affirm himself are invested. And each has the reciprocal obligation to interpret a statement addressed to him the way the other offers it. One may certainly challenge, oppose, or reject the other's statement; one may not challenge the other's ownership of the meaning of his discourse or contest the other's full awareness of what he is proffering. One may certainly debate the truth of the other's statement; one may not cast doubt on its identity or seek to grasp in it, usurping the other's place, what his words reveal of him, independently of their objective pertinence; for example, to take an extreme case, one has no right to try to detect what the error in the other's words reveals about the truth of his being.

In such a framework, it is easy to see how the sketchiest view of this approach, which we customarily call interpretation (the decoding of the subject's singular implications in his discourse), is not only virtually inconceivable but could only be received as an intolerable attempt to transgress impregnable borders that shelter each individual from the inquisition of others. What has come to constitute the basic truism of contemporary psychological knowledge simply had no place in societies in which human relations remained determined by the original imperative of mutual recognition that was always already in place. It was not self-interested blindness that kept people from recognizing what has become self-evident for us on an elementary level; it was the instituted order governing the exchange of speech that ruled out the perspective that has become our own. Nor was it a heroic effort at elucidation that finally made the new conception possible; in reality, the change came about owing to the overturning of the old social structures and the concomitant dissolution of the principle of personal property that was inherent, somewhat paradoxically, in the collective organization that refuses to see the interlocutor as a detached individual. Here is a paradox indeed, one of the most perceptible paradoxes of modernity: the society that was based on the primacy of the collective dimension assured its members of a kind of inviolable independence and inner self-sufficiency, whereas, conversely, the society that constitutes separate individuality as its primordial element simultaneously institutes a law that places the subject at the mercy of, or at the disposal of, others, positing him as knowable, penetrable, and manipulable from without, while at the same time situating him as its own foundation and source.

These observations lead us to believe that the Cartesian philosophy of consciousness, far from corresponding only in a univocal way to the moment of the affirmation of the individual subject, proceeds in reality from the temporary and unstable conjunction of two contradictory historical inspirations, one rooted in the old symbolic order, the other linked to the modern process of individualist disaggregation of the social realm. It is undeniable that the conception of a reasonable being fully in control of herself and responsible for herself owing to her reflective distance from herself served as a virulent ferment of dissolution within an old world that viewed interpersonal bonds as anterior to personal will; the new conception has been a dynamic element in the general thrust toward a new universe in which individuals are viewed from the outset as mutually independent. Yet it is still important to see clearly that this vision of radical subjective autonomy based on reflective power gets its real grounding and a framework for its implementation from the system of interpersonal positions defined by the requirement of reciprocal recognition. At the deepest level, this vision presupposes the controlled distance between oneself and the other that is established by the symbolic mechanism; it presupposes the separation of places that that mechanism determines, the individual self-possession it postulates, and the inner sanctum it erects and defends. What the new vision makes explicit is nothing more and nothing less than the existence of the field delimited by the mutual imperatives and interdictions that have traditionally presided over the relation of communication. The new vision may be said to express, in terms of intrinsic articulations of the subjective space, dimensions that had previously been induced or defined from the outside in terms of relational rules. In particular, it makes explicit the dimension of individual self-sufficiency that is implicitly attributed to each of the partners in a speech exchange: each has to accept the other as constituting a world or bearing a principle of completeness in herself alone, as needing no one else in order to possess or know herself.

The operation is obviously not innocent. To transfer to the interior of the subject, as essential properties, what resulted from a projection of the modalities of her relation with others is to work directly to de-insert her, to constitute her as a detached individual, to position the subject as a primal cause that determines her own makeup. Even if at bottom it simply takes on the forms specified by the relation of recognition, the concept of consciousness necessarily tends at the same time to subvert and undermine the foundations of that relation. Moreover, the mere fact that such a concept could have emerged, the fact that the symbolic content invested in interpersonal relations can now be made explicit, suffices to attest that something crucial has changed in the overall social organization, something has already thoroughly altered the tenor of interpersonal relationships.

Legitimation of the human universe through tradition presupposes the intangible identity of culture in time, and thus in a way it sets aside the question of what is exchanged (for exchange is bound to involve the regular return of the same things) in favor of the very fact of exchange. It privileges the ritual existence of human relations over what those relations imply or what constitutes them; thus it leaves such relations to their intrinsically self-sufficient and mute repetition. In this way, when the fixed truth of the past is replaced by the fluid legitimacy of a reason that is continually in search of itself, the accent immediately shifts to the content of what circulates from one human being to another and the power that allows each person to find and sustain that content. In short, the individual status of these source-beings who are beings of reason becomes decisively problematic, even if what is involved for them is not the invention but the elucidation and identification of an order of truths that is, finally, eternal. Consequently, as soon as the organization that assures the subject of his full autonomy is defined from the inside, the process that will lead to the atomization of individuals who were originally presumed to be mutually independent is inexorably engaged, through the equal power to accede to truth that characterizes human beings.

Still, it would be a mistake to view this conception of integrally self-possessed consciousness as the philosophy par excellence of a triumphant individualism. This conception of consciousness certainly contributed to the advent of individualism; we may take that much for granted. But it draws its substance to a much greater extent from the old forms of social cohesion that individualism needed to liquidate definitively in order to impose itself; it constitutes the ultimate and transitory expression of those forms. With the disappearance of the last vestiges of the primitive rule that required human beings to recognize one another before they could test themselves in their individual singularity, the foundations for that way of looking at consciousness are gone. In the socially, externally detached individual, we encounter a being fundamentally limited in his capacity to distance himself from himself in order to know himself and to choose himself. He is destined thus to be known by the other; he is inherently exposed to the other's investigations. True, it takes official philosophy more than a century to notice the change (if indeed it has really noticed it yet): this is but one more aspect of the more or less complete academic degeneration in which official French philosophy has foundered after the fertile moment of German idealism, and one that has rigorously cut it off from the real movement of thought, whether society, history, or the psyche is in question (but there is no need to worry: recycled from conservation to "subversion," official philosophy perseveres).

Thus we have an overview of a process without academic credentials, a process in which, from Pinel to Freud, practitioners confronted the enigma of pathological forms of subjective experience. As this process unfolded, a stammering, hesitant, and conceptually insecure reflection slowly caused the representation of human beings to shift, as never before in history. It did so by gradually bringing into focus the new image of the power of the subject that had been obscurely introduced by the social revolution. It is essential to observe that psychopathological reflection has been the place where the anthropology of the democratic societies has been elucidated and developed. And it is no less important to assess that reflection: the philosophy of the individual reduced to himself is in no way a triumphant philosophy of self-possession. On the contrary, it entails the painful discovery of a subject who is no longer master of herself, just as she is no longer free in relation to the other. The victory of practical individualism has as its theoretical counterstroke the entry into a crisis of consciousness. Let us not be too sure that the discovery of the unconscious will come as a shock to the bourgeoisie. With the unconscious, the truth of the world in which it came into being has finally been found (and, significantly, it prefers not to know itself as such).

This crisis in the foundations of anthropology, which was coincident with the advent of the society of individuals, makes us somewhat skeptical about the possibility of reducing the process by which the modern approach to psychological phenomena has been constituted to a linear genealogy of confessional techniques. For confession can also be a way of positing oneself as master of one's own behavior: not only do I take responsibility for my behavior, but I dominate it sufficiently to be able to recount it in detail. This may be a way of liberating myself from the other. Her hold on me comes through what is inadmissible, what she knows about me that I dare not recognize. If I assume explicit responsibility for what I have done, I take away her power over me. She loses her advantage when I affirm my own impermeability to the knowledge to which she may have access. In religious and judicial traditions, confession manifestly functions in terms of this explicit recognition of self in one's own behavior; it entails a purifying obligation to reappropriate integrally for myself the guilty knowledge that can never really escape me. Everything changes when confession becomes, on the contrary, the obligatory way to grasp through the mediation of the other something in me that necessarily escapes me.

Traditional confession, even under compulsion or torture, is a sign of the subject's power (if the confession has to be dragged out, the reason is that the subject has the essential power to withhold it); psychiatric confession, in contrast, becomes a sign of the subject's consent to his own disappropriation (we moderns only really confess without our knowledge). Formerly an instrument of symbolic autonomy (I am guilty, to be sure, but I have full knowledge and complete retrospective awareness of what I have done), confession becomes an act of acceptance of my irremediable dependency on the other's constitutive gaze, directed not at my person but at my inner truth. However, the deceptive surface continuity conceals a radical divergence between two representations of the human being and his inner power over himself, a divergence stemming from the historical antagonism between two social logics. By itself, confession, as the forced exhibition of the subject's secrets to the gaze of another, can be reconciled with absolutely antinomic visions of what justifies or necessitates it: it can mean that the secrecy is meant to be overcome, or, conversely, that it possesses and binds us, that it alienates us from the person who is able to decode it. Thus it seems to us to supply only an artificial guiding thread if one wants to get back to the root of the structure of dispossession and dependency that has governed the relation of every individual to himself, virtually since the revolution that reconstructed the social realm on the basis of its individual atoms.

On Inequality as the Principle of Communication

These developments may look like digressions, but they are intended to situate as completely and precisely as possible the stake of an emerging practice that breaks with the order of reciprocity in a discourse like that of moral treatment. First of all, we see why philosophical rupture and practical innovation are necessarily bound up together in this context. Despite the undeniable heterogeneity of their development, the domain of attitudes and the domain of ideas, the (recent) representation of the subject and the (time-honored) way subjects relate to one another, stem in fact from one and the same situation. It is particularly important to grasp the way in which the cultural signification—in the strong sense of the term—of a circumscribed event like the invention of a certain speech mechanism, adapted to a limited number of cases and situations, goes far beyond its import as a concrete solution. What is involved, in fact, is only the perfecting of a system of attitudes and positions that can reveal in the insane person a fully competent interlocutor, while taking it upon oneself to modify the articulation that ordinarily governs the relations between speaking subjects. But beyond this punctual response to a very particular sort of problem, this is how a culture understands and organizes the coexistence of its members as beings connected by language. At stake, ultimately, are the instituted modalities of human exchange par excellence, and in particular the modality that would seem to be the least institutable, the most personal: that of meaning.

With the advent of moral treatment, the bond that people can establish among themselves symbolically enters a new phase, a new world of possibilities discovered at the heart of their relation, a new and singular power of one over another that takes shape in the element of personal communication. An unprecedented, subtle, penetrating violence slips into the cogs of interpersonal exchange. The relationship based on reciprocity certainly was not exempt from violence, as the example of the insane person would suffice to show. With someone who eludes self-evidence and shared definitions, the violence of exclusion allows no more discussion and indeed no more common membership in a collectivity than would be possible with a brute beast. Or there is the violence of imposition: the insane individual must be maintained within the common code (with which in fact he is not unfamiliar but which he simply rejects); thus he must be made to understand by force if all else fails. The advent of moral treatment corresponds to an attempt to overcome or escape this dialectic of rejection and constraint. Both pandering and preaching are disallowed; the therapist's aim is to assume the existence of the unreasoning gap. In other words the therapist must not act as if the gap did not exist, must not try to address the sane being concealed behind the insane one, but he must also avoid positing the gap as insurmountable, and he must not try to reduce it artificially by catering to the chimeras in which the alienated patient is isolating himself. However, the overt violence of denial (whether it belongs to the insane person or his madness) is conjured away only by means of the introduction of another, insidious form of violence, this time suppressed, but equally implacable in its way—precisely the form that the whole traditional system of reciprocity in verbal exchange managed in practice, if not by intention, to rule out: the violence of intervention within another's private sphere, the violence of interfering in the other's relation to his own discourse.

The definition of places and roles as symmetrical and reversible had a first and decisive consequence on the level of values, as we have emphasized: it entailed the demarcation of a strictly reserved personal domain, or, more precisely still, the complete subtraction of the space of the relation between oneself and the gaze or the grasp of an outsider. The elementary and capital rule of getting along with others consisted in remaining in one's place and in one's role and refraining from involvement in anything that might arise from inside another and from his intangible right not so much *over* himself as simply *to* himself. Let us note that attitudes of negation directed either at the insane person or at his madness, however harsh they may be, do not violate that rule. Even those who reject this person respect the general rule of conduct that applies to human beings as a whole. Speaking to the insane person as if he were sane in order to urge him to stop being insane is to attribute to him a mastery of his state that does not depend on the person who gives him orders or puts him on notice: it is to continue to recognize in him a sort of inner monopoly over decision making in which no one else has any right to interfere. The same thing is true when one deems the insane person so shut off in his insanity that it is useless even to address him: for this is still to posit that what stems from his engagement in his own thought is radically inaccessible to an outsider's grasp. It is his business; no one has the right to interfere.

The precepts of moral treatment constitute the exact opposite of this postulate of intimate autonomy. There is no more equality in principle, no more identity of level, no more reversibility of positions, to guarantee the existence in each party of a zone removed from the intervention of the other, but just the opposite: a relation based on the other's right to enter into oneself and to act in relation to what is happening within oneself. That woman is mad, thus she is under compulsion in her thoughts and actions. It is up to me to know this, to take it into account, and to behave accordingly. I know that she is not master of her conceptions or impulses: I have to accept her and accept those conceptions and impulses as best I can. But I also know that she is not completely caught up in the convictions to which she is subjected, and that I have to keep myself from going too far in her direction; I have to maintain an attitude of reserve that is firm but not directly confrontational. Under these conditions, such an attitude offers me a way to enter at least into harmony and perhaps into communication with the invisible reserve toward herself that allows the insane woman to continue to be counted among reflective beings. Thus instead of simply assuming the role that should be mine, from my own vantage point and taking only myself into account, I construct my position in terms of what I know of the other's inner state and its contradictions. While she remains blocked in immediacy, destined as she is to persist in her aberrant adhesion to herself, I myself acquire a position of the second degree by integrating what is given in her situation with what originally defined my own, as if I were maintaining myself in two places at once. I know myself through my desires, and I know her through her capabilities, whereas she knows only herself. I am not obliged to take anything from the insane person at face value. Her insane discourse is both accepted and neutralized in advance, to the extent that, instead of understanding it as anyone else would from her own place, I grasp it, in a sense, at its source. My listening to her utterance is subordinated to a preexisting idea of the conditions of enunciation. Subjectively, the insane patient does not dispose freely, not even covertly, of her own utterance (even if for the most part she remains instrumentally its master): it is thus completely useless to reject what she says in the name of reason and all the more useless to argue with her, to use persuasion or exhortation to try to bring her to recant her "errors."

Clearly, the new conception of madness emphasizes the dimension of irresponsibility. Giving up the presupposition of a will to madness meant recognizing the insane individual as all the more powerfully entrenched and implicated in her deviance, which she by no means chose but which imposed itself on her as if of its own accord, according to some mysterious necessity on the part of the stranger within the self. Still—and this is the key point—the insane person is not really a dupe of the uncontrollable conviction that dispossesses her. I must therefore respect the utterance produced under compulsion, out of concern for the person making it, who is not unaware that she is making it, who, even though acting under compulsion and absent from herself in what she says, means something in what escapes her this way, which somehow beneath its strangeness nevertheless resembles her. At the same time, I must also respect the person who is constrained by his own discourse and convictions and who experiences his own situation as painful. If I were to abdicate complacently in the face of the derangement that has the upper hand with him, or if I were to go along with it, I would be misunderstanding and ridiculing him; I would be acting as if there were not, within him, a human being suffering frightfully from his all-absorbing empty certitudes. To communicate with the insane person on such a basis means, in short, to posit that I know in his place, and moreover that I know better than he, the conflictual and ambiguous nature of the relation that implicates him in madness and separates him from it. The conquest of understanding and tolerance is accomplished here at the price of an exorbitant intrusion, a double operation of burglary and kidnapping making it possible to accede to the other's principle of speech and to substitute myself for him so as to appreciate the secret wellsprings, the actual determinations, and the true scope of that principle. If an authentic exchange is reestablished, if the individual who is prey to internal and external alterity is restored to the status of legitimate interlocutor, it is by virtue of the right his partner claims unilaterally to replace him in his faltering subjective function, the right to take charge of, and not just to take into account, what the other, for his part, no longer dominates: his relation of identity and difference with respect to himself, his place of adhesion and retreat with respect to his own discourse.

For moral treatment to be possible, changes had to occur within the social world so that, when two human beings meet, one of them should take upon himself the initiative of completely redefining the bases and conditions of their relation by positing himself not only as master of his own role but also as arbiter of the other's inner conflict. Without any question, this is one of the most enduringly inconceivable events in history, for the symbolic inequality and dissymmetry that it presupposes and advocates are at the opposite pole from the mutual recognition in terms of which human coexistence had been organized from the beginning. The type of power it mobilizes, the power of one human being over another, exceeds the bounds within which the collective order had never ceased until then to contain every aim and every enterprise with regard to fellow beings—not through its intensity, its reliability, or its barbarousness, but solely through its point of application, situated in a place where there was in principle no point of access: in the place where the other gives himself to himself and disposes of himself. This power, otherwise benevolent, disinterested, and intelligent, conveys a specific, unexampled violence that is perhaps mutely experienced at the moment of its appearance as more redoutable than that of the old mechanisms of coercion, for these at least stopped at the borders of a subject who was internally the owner of himself, if only to break him down or annihilate him. The violence of this comprehensive power is no longer inherently an obligation but an expropriation. It is the violence of a presence that envelops and surpasses you, that signifies to you in advance your impotence and your dispossession: whatever you may say, someone else is there who knows that behind what you say there is subjectively something other than what you are spontaneously led to utter—someone whom you can only recognize as justified in a systematic suspicion of your own power of meaning, dimly conscious as you are of the constraints that burden it.

However, beyond the sublimated but intense violence inherent in such a relationship, we need to look closely at the singular danger it entails, the dangerously personal aspect it is led to take on. For it is based not on a general rule posited in advance—a rule that is the same for everyone and that initially determines all relations among individuals as structurally equivalent, no matter how privileged their content may be—but on the initiatory act of one of the participants, who exceeds the limits of his ordinary role as a private individual to put himself once again, on his own initiative, in the place of the other. From this unilateral inaugural gesture, from this decision to make oneself count for two, a unique situation necessarily results. It involves a wild, radical confrontation of subjectivities, apart from any form that would intrinsically guarantee the separation of the respective domains of each interlocutor. There is no longer any principle that can call a virtual halt, that can require a distinction between what comes from the one and what depends on the other. Thus there is no longer anything but an aleatory and absolutely original conjunction of two pure individual singularities.

A relation understood in terms of reciprocity was a neutralized relation, in its narrowly personal aspects. Indeed, to the extent to which their content is always already defined, there are only universal relations, in a sense: the relation that I have with one person is one I could have with another; they are in potential communication, and they are equivalent. Here, summoned by the special stake created by the insane person's ambiguous adhesion to his madness, what one sees emerging instead is naked, indeterminate, untransmissible, all-encompassing contact between two human beings blending their particularities. And of course major risks are involved on both sides, both in the uncontrollable display of the most secret places of the self to an outside gaze, and in the power to penetrate in the other's place that which, in him, eludes his own grasp.

CHAPTER VIII

The Conquest of Dissymmetry

Talking Sense, Talking Nonsense

IN PRACTICE, it was exceedingly difficult for therapists to free themselves from the old attitudes and assume fully the new possibilities at the heart of the bond of communication, with all their uncertainties and dangers. One written account in particular offers exemplary testimony to the difficulties. Affecting in its honesty, the text is all the more enlightening in that its author was situated precisely at the crossroads between two periods. He could see clearly what strategy was required and what institutional arrangements were needed, but he was also invincibly held back, in spite of everything, by old reflexes and insurmountable inclinations; he was conscious, moreover, of his own hesitations and fluctuations. Our witness is one of the very few doctors who can be counted among the "pioneers" of the "philanthropic" reform that preceded the Pinelian break: Daquin de Chambéry was a typical representative of provincial enlightenment, but he also stands out as an exception. One of the few practitioners who participated in the network of the Royal Society of Medicine, he was considered progressive, because he was concretely and actively interested in the problem of madness—isolated, in a "remote countryside, as good as lost for the inhabitants of Paris," as he writes to Vicq d'Azyr,[1] and from where, indeed, his modest voice seems scarcely to have been heard. Writing in 1800, Pinel does not even mention Daquin's *Philosophie de la Folie*, which appeared in 1791, nor does he ever cite the second edition of 1804, although it is dedicated to him in dithyrambic terms.

To be sure, Daquin is not a striking innovator in essential matters. The image of madness that he continues to provide is even astonishingly archaic in certain respects. He characterizes the insane, for example, as "beings who most often do not even have an inkling of their own existence; most of them do not even think about the needs of daily subsistence or are totally incapable of procuring for themselves things of absolute necessity."[2] "Man," he adds, is "degraded in the finest and noblest part of himself . . . often incapable of receiving the slightest impression from speech, lacking fear of the elements, braving threats, insensitive to the cruelties that are too often practiced on him, and often, too, failing to give the slightest sign of pain at the blows inflicted on him or the punishment to which he is subjected, finally not even having, it appears, any idea of his own existence."[3] Or, in a remark that is rather disconcerting on the part of someone who dedicates his book "*to humanity*" and whose vocation is to console and comfort its most unfortunate members: "Their fate [is] much less to be pitied perhaps than one thinks, because lacking the true, correct feeling of what they do, they consequently become incapable of reflecting on their state and of appreciating the full extent of the misfortune into which they have fallen."[4]

And yet Daquin's definition of madness—which takes up a full page and requires meticulous decoding—adds some modern elements to a vision that is otherwise deeply traditional. The blend is illustrated, for example, by sentences like the following: "Madness, although it admits the exercise of all the operations of the soul, is exactly the opposite of reason."[5] But Daquin's classification, which includes the raving maniac, the calm maniac, the extravagant maniac, the lunatic, and the imbecile, remains squarely entrenched in semi-popular, semi-utilitarian categories (the harmless maniac versus the one who needs to be kept in a straitjacket). Still, despite the archaic aspects of his theory, Daquin's perception of the practical problem posed by the administration of "moral care" (he does not use the term "moral treatment") is undeniably of remarkable acuity, anticipating Pinel or Esquirol. It is safe to say that by 1792 Daquin had clearly established the fundamental elements of the question, in terms that would not be surpassed in any important respect. Once it has been acknowledged that the surest and most reasonable method for healing depends on "the diet, the exercise, the freedom" granted to insane people and requires "much gentleness in what one says to them and in the way one treats them," one still has to determine just how patients should be addressed, since their madness means that it is not possible to come to an understanding with them as one could with anyone else—assuming it is possible to reach an understanding at all (let us recall that Daquin claims that the insane are incapable of "receiving the slightest impression through speech").

"To cure madmen, would it be appropriate to encourage the object of their madness: or should one take the opposite tack?"[6] Practice provides abundant evidence: to irritate patients, to contest their ideas, is to run the risk of "augmenting their delirium, of overheating their imagination," often even "to an unbelievable point of exaltation." The brain produces "an overload of ideas that crisscross in a thousand ways, stifling one another, as it were, through the resulting confusion; and then only time and patience can calm the extraordinary movement that one has so imprudently caused."[7] However, Daquin continues: "I would not agree, either, that one should encourage up to a certain point the principal subject that is thought to have made a man mad; I do not think that one ought to go too far in supporting his ideas, because it would amount to seeking to perpetuate his state. He would go headlong in that direction, . . . and his imagination would continually revolve around a circle from which he would never exit, owing to the disposition his brain has acquired for producing and reproducing the same ideas endlessly." Thus we do not find ourselves facing an alternative but a contradiction. "There is thus a middle term to grasp, for the curing of madmen, between countering the object of their madness and encouraging it. I admit in good faith that this is the difficult point. Practitioners have given it little thought or have absolutely neglected it. As for me, I look at it as one of the principal aids for treating this illness."[8]

On the level of principles, Pinel and Esquirol say nothing more, nor do they say it better. We would even argue that they lack the luminous candor that allows Daquin to produce his vivid, convincing description of the patient torn between antagonistic demands. Let us be careful not to jump to the conclusion, however, that, from the very beginning of the Revolution, in the obscure liberator of the small number of insane patients that the hospice of Chambéry could hold, all the elements are already in place, and that the Parisian episode following the Revolution only constitutes a repetition, in a much vaster and much better lighted theatre, of an emancipation scene that had already been wholly written and enacted. For if we read Daquin's work attentively, we see that his difficulty in "grasping a middle term between opposing and encouraging the object of madness" is for him not only quite real, but also, it seems, virtually insurmountable. He can be clear and decisive when he is articulating a general rule, but when he is reporting his own actual behavior, or even, on an already more developed level, when he is confiding the concrete intentions that guided him, we can see that he is torn between incompatible attitudes, tugged in one direction or the other by uncontrollable forces. He does not succeed in finding a position of equilibrium from which he could prevent himself both from going along with the insane person and from opposing him squarely, while satisfying at the same time, in a certain way, the two imperatives of acceptance and refusal. He was able to see the point at which unreconcilable elements might be reconciled; he was unable to reach that point himself.

No sooner has he identified the core of the difficulty than he contradicts himself in a nonetheless admirable formula: "In these circumstances, the doctor must draw resources from his moral faculties, ply his character to that of the insane patient, and, as it were, become the patient himself."[9] But instead of going on, he heads off in the other direction: "It will no doubt be found paradoxical if I say that one must almost continually talk sense to madmen, even if they do not understand it, even though they do not pay attention and continue to talk nonsense: by dint of constancy and perseverance in this approach, one sometimes succeeds in bringing them back. It is true that that does not always happen; but I have observed more than one success with this way of proceeding."[10] Here, to be sure, something like an intermediate position emerges. One allows the insane person to talk nonsense; one abstains from contradicting him; one settles for maintaining the viewpoint of sanity in his presence, pleasantly and unobtrusively but also inflexibly, in the unavowed but transparent hope that unbeknownst to him he may end up being infused with it and will *come back* ("one sometimes succeeds in bringing them back," Daquin says significantly). There is no longer anything in the aim that would resemble an exhortation seeking to address, behind the patient's insanity, the invisible freedom of a subject capable of mobilizing himself against that insanity. The sharp corners of the approach have been carefully smoothed: instead of appealing directly to reason, one implies confidence in reason; instead of challenging the patient head on, one acts laterally; instead of seeking to elicit a decisive transformation, one hopes for a slow infiltration.

The fact remains that in order systematically to avoid the harsh forms of refutation or argument and scolding that are the rule, this way of situating oneself with respect to the insane person reintroduces the essential articulation of those forms and is rooted in the same set of presuppositions. It proceeds fundamentally from the same central interdiction: not to meddle with anything involving the insane person's private relation to his madness. "He continues to talk nonsense"; as for me, I persist in talking sense—but in no way do I authorize myself to intervene in his nonsense in order to try to get the attention of the subject who, in the middle of the delirium that absorbs him, nevertheless distinguishes himself from it. Daquin is quite conscious that one must not let the insane person "go too far in his own direction."

Thus it is clear that Daquin is not unaware of the intimate gap that can be brought into play, the remnant of an inherent reserve that keeps the insane patient from total adherence "to the idea that drove him mad." But what remains virtually inconceivable to Daquin is the attitude that leads one to try to disconnect the person who believes violently in that idea from the person who does not entirely believe in it, in order to communicate directly and personally with the subject who is aware, in certain respects, of his insanity and sensitive to the sane presence of his interlocutor. For Daquin, one can only try to make oneself heard indirectly and imperceptibly; it goes without saying that the patient will not hear the practitioner or pay the slightest attention to him. This is so because in every instance the movement of return can come from the insane person alone, because the cure for insanity stems exclusively from an internal process over which the practitioner may have some external influence but in which nothing allows him to involve himself directly.

The very same thing happens when the therapist urges the insane patient to return to reason. As therapist, I represent his situation and its unacceptable aspects to him; I remind him of his obligations; in so doing, I recognize, moreover, that I am addressing a human being who is at present removed from all contact, who is inaccessible in person; but I also understand that, once these encouraging or threatening words have been spoken, it is up to the hypothetic moral subject who has been summoned up to make a decision, to choose himself, by an act that is both hidden and sovereign, an act in which no one from the outside can intervene. Urgings and scoldings stop at the point where the subject's full power to make decisions for himself begins, a power whose exercise and progression I certainly attempt to influence by all possible means, but to which in the last analysis I must yield completely. It is against this hard, opaque, unbreakable kernel of the inner shell, a relation to a self structurally defined as impenetrable, that Daquin stumbles. For him, in contradiction, moreover, with everything he knows, this ultimate retreat of the subject is in fact inviolable, since the subject remains if not unthinkable, then at least unassumable in practice, for the prospect of playing consciously with the gap contradictorily unites the insane person with his madness.

Thus we find our author shifting unsurprisingly, even with a certain logical necessity, into the opposing but equivalent approach (equivalent in that it actually expresses the same possibility): he advocates talking nonsense with someone who is prey to nonsense. And indeed, having stressed the crucial necessity of grasping "a middle term between challenging and reinforcing the object of madness" and having proceeded to recommend "almost ceaselessly talking sense," Daquin returns to this passage thirteen years later, when he is preparing the second edition of his book. He extends it by adding an "observation" that in the most ordinary academic terms might legitimately be taken as an illustration and defense of his earlier statement. But this is not at all the case. "This observation," Daquin concludes at the end of his account, "is a striking example of the fact that insane patients can be brought back by speaking nonsense with them, and lending oneself to all their extravagant ideas."[11] He describes how he handled a woman about thirty years old who had fallen into maniacal delirium. She was "not at all dangerous"; he had advised that she be left at liberty within the institution.

> I saw her often, and although her alienation persisted, with less intensity, my presence calmed her each time. She remained in that state eight or nine months, drinking, eating, doing nothing but walking around and talking endlessly, without any coherence in her ideas or statements. I tried several

> times to approach her extravagant ideas and to talk nonsense with her; and I noticed, after some time, that this means had considerably diminished her alienation; but at the moment when I flattered myself with the hope of her cure, she suddenly became sad, sly, and silent; she would no longer get out of bed, and from that point on she refused to take any kind of solid or liquid nourishment, and even any drink whatsoever.[12]

Using skillful appeals and strategems, Daquin succeeded in getting her to accept food: "When she had thus managed by stages to eat more or less normally, and when she had recovered some of her strength, I made her get out of bed to walk about the rooms. Although she was still alienated, but to a much lesser degree than she had been before this last period, I continued to associate myself with her disconnected ideas, as I had done in the beginning, and by this means I succeeded in getting her to do everything I wanted."[13] But this time, success is complete: the work she agreed to undertake, the social habits, "the diversity of her occupations and the accompanying fatigue dissipated her disparate ideas little by little and imperceptibly restored her reason."[14] However, Daquin acknowledged that "this method is not a general prescription," and that he did not always answer "for its success in similar cases." "But it is quite certain," he went on, "that if I had taken the opposite tack here, if I had contradicted her statements and had not acquiesced in her ideas, I would not have succeeded: this is a delicate issue on which it is appropriate to proceed with special caution."[15]

Here an observation is pitted against a general precept, and the observation is presented cautiously as a special case: if we were to believe *La Philosophie de la Folie*, we could conclude that the patient effort to make the insane person listen to reason wins out by a long shot in the author's mind over sharing the insane person's nonsense. Another document exists, however, that makes it necessary to nuance our assessment and that reestablishes a sort of equilibrium between these divergent temptations of practice: an "outline of the journal kept since January 1, 1790 on insane patients visited at every phase of the moon, in order to observe whether that planet has influence on them." Daquin sent this document to the Minister of Internal Affairs on 20 Prairial, An IX (June 9, 1801), apparently in response to a request on the latter's part.[16]

To begin with, let us note the philanthropic leitmotiv, which will later serve as the basis for mythical narratives of "liberation": "I go into their cells alone: I treat them and speak to them with the greatest gentleness, and I even take pains to carry tobacco to give to those who like it and I keep fruit in my pockets, because I believe I have observed that most [patients] are eager for it. I use no means of repression, because I have noticed that there are very few cases in which such means are necessary; on the contrary, they almost always exacerbate their [the patients'] state." But what interests us in particular are detailed suggestions for approaching patients and starting conversations with them.

> During my visit, I converse with them; my questions deal at first with their general state of health, and with anything that might have happened to them between visits; it is rare that I end my visit without managing to take their pulse, and even conducting other investigations. Sometimes, they answer me appropriately throughout the entire conversation; most often, they talk nonsense; in those cases I talk nonsense with them, because I have noticed that that approach wins them over, puts their mind at ease and calms them.[17]

The feeling one gets from such statements is quite the opposite from what the book suggests: one may well conclude that the prevailing approach entails entering into the views of the insane, on the understanding that they are so thoroughly shut off within themselves that the only way they can exist (the only way they can be "won over") is for the practitioner to submit himself to the extravagant norms of a patient's world. What is novel is the sane practitioner's concern with pleasing the unfortunate people entrusted to his care, his desire to avoid leaving them in a state of complete moral abandonment, even if that means yielding to their insanity. But the bases on which this major concession is granted remain rigorously the ones that, in less friendly times, justified the exclusion of the insane person from all human conmmerce, for the patient's chimerical retreat into himself makes it impossible ever to find a legitimate common language.

This does not mean that, on the theoretical level, Daquin necessarily remains mired in presuppositions or convictions of that order. Reading him, one is even tempted to believe that to some degree he has essentially been freed from them. Thus, as we have seen, he is not unaware that to a certain extent one can prevent the insane person from plunging too deeply into his madness and thus that one may conceivably rely on a certain potential for restraint on the patient's part with respect to the ideas that possess him. The power of attraction that brings Daquin invincibly back into the orbit of inherited conceptions, whatever may detach him from it in other respects, must be sought, it seems to us, in the direction of the dense kernel of interpersonal practices and their logic. What brings Daquin up short are probably not so much specific representations of madness as the embodied principles of a time-honored tradition that govern the positions of all interlocutors toward one another and define their respective obligations. Daquin may unconsciously feel impelled to conform to the old rule of reciprocal abstention, a rule inherent in the imperative of mutual recognition: everyone is in his place and in full possession of himself; no one has to be concerned with anything involving the other's free relationship to his own speech. I am naturally free to reject it wholesale along, with the individual who proffers it, if it does not respond to the conditions that make a common space of reference and comprehension possible; I am also free to choose my position in relation to the other's singular position or to his disorder (this is something that the sinews of philanthropy suggest to Daquin); but in no case am I free to call into question what goes on between the other and his troubled discourse. I am not to speculate about what binds him to his discourse, what compels him to speak and at the same time allows him to understand at some level and to acknowledge that I do not adhere to his discourse. I can take it or leave it; I must not interrogate it.

The real, irreducible, insuperable difficulty on which Daquin runs aground is the problem of instituting a working relation with the insane in which the dominant factor is not the patient's literal discourse but the practitioner's knowledge of the fundamentally contradictory relation the patient maintains with that discourse. In this working relation it is thus no longer a matter of talking nonsense with the patient as if that is all he can accept; it is a matter of carving out a path for oneself at the heart of the patient's insanity to reach the person who inhabits and is constrained by it and who thus can be presumed to exist somewhere apart from it. Nor is it a matter of insidiously making him listen to reason, as if, beyond the ungraspable absent being, beyond the insane person, there were simultaneously another hidden self who could secretly continue to judge clear-sightedly. For it is within insanity itself that the trapped subject dwells. This subject is certainly not moved by arguments; still, owing to the skillful reserve of his interlocutor, he is restored to himself and is separated to some extent from his delirium. Daquin conceived of moral treatment; he did not actually institute it. Unfaithful to himself by his own admission, remarkable for his integrity, he may never actually have practiced it at all.

Rules and Reality

When we consider how manifestly impossible it was for Daquin to follow the principles he had set up for himself, it is easier to understand why writers like Pinel or Esquirol would insist that, with regard to the theory of moral treatment, "general maxims" are of little interest. However correct they may be, such maxims have nothing to say about the real difficulty, namely, how to interact concretely with insane patients, how to situate oneself with respect to them. Pinel speaks of sterile truths: "These precepts are only of partial utility, as long as the nosology of the disease is not established upon clear and extensive views of its causes, symptoms, and varieties. The influence of seasons and climates, the peculiarities of temper, character and capacity of the individual, together with the precise nature of the hallucination, are circumstances which must never be omitted in the study and treatment of mental derangement."[18]

Esquirol proves even more skeptical. As he says in substance in *Des Passions*, practitioners are now only at the stage of developing a groping inventory of special cases. "One day, perhaps, by multiplying the facts, by spelling out the cases in which moral treatment succeeds, we will be able to establish the principles of a moral therapeutics. But what intelligence, what habit, what sagacity, what tact must one not have to apply these principles and support them by all possible means?" (p. 78) The statement is rather curiously contradictory, moreover, for it begins by indicating that the principles in question are unknown, then goes on to suggest how difficult it is to put them into practice. We might call it expressively contradictory—for Esquirol surely does not mean that he is proceeding blindly, that he is completely ignorant of the principles that he ought to be rigorously following. Of course he knows something about them, but not enough to master their use; each particular application poses the problem anew in its entirety. After watching Daquin retreat before the obstacle of practice and give in on all points, we are scarcely astonished to find that his more fortunate successors locate the major difficulty posed by moral treatment not so much in its relation to doctrinal formulations as in the balancing point that Daquin succeeded in identifying but that remained permanently inaccessible to him. Each practitioner has to keep resituating that point in each case, in the here and now.

Normally, at the level of the relation as experienced by the practitioners involved, the principal and most solid resistance should be concentrated in fixed, inherited attitudes, in unconsciously adopted forms, in acquired reflexes. For each of the individuals who experienced the rupture of moral treatment had to face a challenge not only to his ideas, but also to a material culture he had received as his birthright, a culture that was virtually inaccessible to immediate reflective mastery. Embodied before it was desired, this culture was thus endowed with an autonomous, personal force of return and repetition that outlasted even the disappearance of its social substratum. The new relational mechanism based on a methodical, deliberate inversion of the norms of reciprocity could have been established only at the price of meticulous self-examination and struggle against the instinct that under all circumstances governs the modalities of one's own presence to others. Each individual had to rework and remodel this sector of the organization of her world, bit by bit, responding to the problem that is at once the most elementary, most insurmountable, and most perilous that the human subject implies: the fact of existing with others, and, what is more, of existing through others and for others. In this process, it was doubtless only a matter of grasping and translating the consequences of the immense social transformation that was restoring individuals to themselves and urging them to renegotiate and reorder the rules and forms of their common membership in a collectivity, starting from scratch. The fact remains that that mutation, whatever external forces may have called for it and carried it along, was achieved through the inner lives of human beings, where it conflicted with an already-constituted *ethos*, a crucial one under the circumstances, for it involved the reference points of personal identity, the perceived articulation of self to other. Daquin's declared, avowed abdication in the face of the objectives he set himself is proof enough that one does not easily leave such things behind.

Deep-rooted models of behavior and the subtle influence of the past are not all that is at issue here. For anyone who measures up to the task, a new confrontation is at stake, one that opens up a redoubtable perspective on the future. Before such a confrontation there is a temptation to hesitate or even retreat, for the historical stake of the operation is nothing less than the beginning of an all-out war of a new type: a war of subjects, without real victories or victims, in which love is a weapon as well as hate, a war no less present in the desire for good than in the will to evil, a war without respite or remedy. For what disappears along with the ultimate vestiges of the bond of reciprocity, as these had been embedded in speech exchanges, is what remained of the original symbolic procedure for pacifying the intersubjective relation within the strategically decisive order of meaning, a remainder that had continued to procure for people, in one of the major articulations of their universe, the essential dual assurance of self-possession and the presence of the other. That assurance itself was split into two: on the one hand, it is impossible for me to think that the other might not be there, thus I have an implied obligation to come to terms with the evidence of her existence; on the other hand, I am certain that the other recognizes me, that she knows and acknowledges my presence.

The new paradigm brings emancipation from the confining framework in which the positions of the interlocutors are fixed in advance in terms of symmetry and reversibility, and it entails the possibility, in the emptiness of the forms thus created, of situating oneself with respect to others in whatever way one pleases. For anyone who undertakes to use it, this new paradigm implies a harsh projection into a universe henceforth devoid of guarantees, in which nothing is taken for granted between myself and the other, beginning with the mutual acceptance of our coexistence (for the one can always be one too many, and nothing requires us a priori to ratify this presence that is in principle excessive), but in which anything is possible. For example, I can assure myself of the other from the inside, I can dispossess him of mastery over his own words, I can envelop him in a net of knowledge that allows me to hear him better than he hears himself and even allows me to discern in his place which elements of his discourse properly belong to him and which ones escape him. From Daquin to Esquirol, from the articulation of the attitudes required to converse effectively with those who are alienated precisely in their power to think and speak, to the systematic adoption of those attitudes in practice, an arduous and hesitant experimentation was required, an experimentation with the resources of the historically unprecedented science of substituting oneself for others. Practitioners had to learn to dominate the expropriating power that dislodged the insane patient from his own discourse, for his own good, and turned over his subjective engagement in it to the doctor's discretion.

It is worth noting that in 1805, fourteen years after Daquin's inaugural statement, for Esquirol to speak of moral treatment still amounted in part merely to circumscribing a domain and reporting examples; the time for theory was still deferred to an indeterminate future. Clearly, the problem remained intact, even if practical solutions were being found on particular occasions. The difficulty does not lie in applying rules, in bringing solidly established ideas down from on high into reality. The difficulty lies in transgressing norms in oneself to which one continues to adhere with all the fibers of one's being; it lies in using the newly acquired liberty with respect to the other, in handling the power of penetration of the other's world that has been suddenly conferred.

One cannot stress enough the concrete aspect of the approach and the specificity of the strategies required by each case. Still, between Daquin on the one hand and Pinel and Esquirol on the other, another element came into play that must have greatly facilitated things, if only by furnishing the indispensable auxiliary force without which the passage to a systematic practice could not have come about: namely, the transformation of the idea of madness in general. Daquin visibly lacks any way to represent for himself an anchor point at the heart of the insane person's universe. He notes that his presence suffices to calm certain of the patients entrusted to his care, and that he manages to win their confidence; in short, he remarks on the *effects* of an appropriate attitude, but he fails to question or even, apparently, to glimpse the *cause* that produces those effects in the patient. Daquin wonders about the approach he should adopt only from the outside, from his own vantage point; he counts only on himself, expecting nothing from his interlocutor. Pinel and Esquirol, for their part, seek to reach someone on whom they can exert pressure from inside the illness, in the person of the alienated patient himself. They start from the notion of a possible point of support within the person they are addressing. They know they can count on their patient's inner resources; the approach that will allow them to tap into and mobilize those resources remains to be found in each case, but the existence of the resources is not in doubt. This attitude is obviously crucially different from Daquin's uncertainty.

There is something to be grasped in the subjective interval left open by alienation. It tells us nothing, to be sure, about how to gain access to it, and nothing, either, about how to surmount the difficulties inherent in trying to do so. But it at least provides a focal point by which one can be continually guided and in relation to which one can adjust a way of behaving that is on its own almost impossible to define. This is why without the theoretical perspective opened up by Pinel's *Treatise on Insanity*, without the conception of an externality or a relative ex-centricity on the part of the subject, resistance to adopting, in practice, the rules of dissymmetry, irreversibility, and substitution that have to preside over the therapeutic relation might have remained simply impossible to overcome. These principles might have remained noteworthy conceptual approaches, infinitely renewed but definitively impossible to put into practice.

What prevents Daquin from crossing the threshold is also, then, the image of madness that he does not manage to surpass. While that image cannot be called absolutely traditional, it does not really integrate into a coherent representation the openings and intuitions that Daquin's practical aim nevertheless presupposes; consequently, it does not offer him the support he would need in order to entertain the principle of the alienated subject's essential accessibility. Pinel and Esquirol—and this is particularly clear in Esquirol's observations, as we have seen—give us the sense that they are exclusively guided by the way they understand their goal: to awaken and seize the patient's attention, to win over the reasonable human being hidden within the patient prey to insanity. By the same token, obsessed as they are with the precise end of their efforts, they no longer even see the problem of what method to use to reach their goal. Here, quite probably, it is their case-specific blindness, their intellectual confinement within the limits of the particular patient's situation, that in fact allowed them to dispense with developing a formal conception of the ways and means to deliver moral treatment; they were able to get around (or liquidate), by neglecting them, the substantial obstacles that made it harder to realize the idea than to formulate it. Conversely, it is just as likely that Daquin proved sensitive above all to the question of rules and the method to follow with respect to the insane patient to the precise extent that he remained blind to the possibility of gaining control of the patient from within, and thus to the extent that there was virtually no chance he could put the arrangements he conceived of (and conceived of all the more easily because he was unaware of the key that conditioned their application) into practice.

Madness as Suffering

In connection with the contrast between the "philanthropic" perspective and the work of the "theoreticians," the opposition has to be nuanced. According to the traditional image, madness radically severed individuals from external truth and from the world of their fellow humans. The break with that image has an immediate and important "philanthropic" consequence that makes it a humanitarian event as much as an intellectual one. Daquin dedicates his book "to humanity." He calls for a "gentle, vigilant, and studied pity," asking his readers to lend "a docile ear to the cries of these unfortunates." His own sensitivity spurred him into action: "What a crushing misfortune! and how can one be a man and not be interested in the deprivation of what gives him that superiority of rank in the universe? I would even dare suggest that anyone who sees a madman without being touched by his state, or who responds only with amusement, is a *moral monster*. It is that state that made me deeply sad."[19] Later, referring to the unfortunates who have been entrusted to his care for seventeen years, he writes:

> If I have lacked talent, I have not lacked goodwill or perseverance in being useful to them. I have always entered into their wretched quarters without fear, most often entirely alone and without a second thought, although since they are almost always ill-tempered, insidious, and endowed with surprising strength, they could threaten my life; but as my mind was always preoccupied with the hope I had of reducing their troubles, I did not even imagine that in their fits they might have the intention of turning their rage or their despair against me. I can even assert most truthfully that not one of them ever even turned on me, even though it is well known that madmen often turn against those who visit them or who are employed in their service.[20]

But let us look closely before we project onto this eloquent humanitarianism, on the basis of an overhasty labeling, what we moderns instinctively understand as compassion for others' distress. Is this really what is involved in the enlightened love of good or the candid sympathy for misfortune that Daquin professes?

At the very least there is a significant ambiguity here. When Daquin declares that "anyone who sees a madman without being touched by his state . . . is a *moral monster*," he is sympathizing with the objective situation, as it were, of the being who has lost his reason, with the lowering of the human species in general toward the condition of "brute beasts" that that state represents; he is not reacting to the intimate, personal situation experienced by the insane person himself. When Daquin evokes the desire to alleviate the sufferings of his wards, a desire that makes him oblivious to danger, he is speaking, to be sure, as a man moved by his own desire to do good, but not as a man impelled by empathy for the suffering of another or by identification with a state of dreadful pain. On the contrary, he stresses how little one can share with beings who are "almost always ill-tempered, insidious, and endowed with surprising strength," and thus eminently susceptible to threatening one's life. And it is all very well for him to remark that in the end they have never done him any harm; he does not go so far as to credit them with gratitude for his good care: one must do what one can toward improving one of the saddest fates imaginable, but one must not expect the parties concerned to be aware of it. From here we move directly to an unvarnished statement whose tenor we find rather surprising, coming from a "sensitive man": "Their fate [is] much less to be pitied perhaps than one thinks, because lacking the true, correct feeling of what they do, they consequently become incapable of reflecting on their state and of appreciating the full extent of the misfortune into which they have fallen."[21] What moves us in the condition of the insane person is something she herself can neither feel nor contemplate. Madness appears terrible to those who look at it from the outside, not to those who experience it. Is the insane person mistreated? She is in fact "insensitive to the cruelties that are too often practiced on [her], and [she] often fails to give the slightest sign of pain at the blows [she] receives or the punishment to which [she] is subjected."[22] It is appropriate to treat patients with consideration and gentleness, but not directly so as to spare them suffering that they are no longer capable of enduring; one ought to do so in the first place out of respect for human dignity in general, which is forgotten in someone who gives way to absurd brutality, and in the second place because bad treatment aggravates a state that is otherwise open to improvement.

In a similar way, finally, while Daquin condemns anyone who sees insane people only as subjects for amusement, he acknowledges as natural "the curiosity, despite the fear they inspire, [that] often impels us to visit these isolated men, abandoned by all of nature, men from whom others flee, who have to be locked up in cells like wild beasts" and whom others look at "like animals kept in a zoo."[23] How, after all, could the fact of being turned over to public scrutiny in this way affect someone who seemingly does not even have "any idea of his own existence." But in 1816 an enlightened thinker like Pinel's friend and colleague Moreau de la Sarthe, who had a direct interest in the developments of "mental medicine," says the very same thing: "Such an extraordinary change, this moral isolation, this sort of civic death: this is undoubtedly what strikes us the most, what moves us the most in the various situations of the insane, what makes the spectacle of madness less laughable than pathetic. It is true that one does not sympathize with the insane in the same way as with other patients; one even tells oneself that many of the mentally ill do not suffer, that some have very lively pleasures; and yet secret terror and involuntary commiseration surprise us as we walk through an insane asylum."[24] Moreover, Pinel himself suggests in connection with the Bicêtre patient who thought he was Louix XIX—Pinel, whose observation we have analyzed as an illustration of the premises with which he had to break—that "very lively pleasures," indeed, procured for the insane person by his certainty of greatness, constituted a virtually invincible obstacle to a cure.

The philanthropic movement, as expressed at its best by witnesses like Daquin, was widespread in the last two decades of the eighteenth century and it extended fairly far into the nineteenth century. It developed as a reaction to what madness signifies—"moral isolation" or "a sort of civic death," and not at all as a way of sharing what the madman experiences, even in a diffuse and remote fashion. "One does not sympathize with the insane in the same way as with other patients." Humanitarian concerns lead to proscribing mistreatment. But these concerns in themselves do not entail any questioning of the roots of mistreatment, of the reasons that led people to treat casual violence toward the insane lightly—the violence, for example, that Daquin deplores in his "nurse," who is "in truth honest, not at all a bad sort, but of a harsh nature, viewing the unfortunate patients perhaps as a burden on society, [and] incapable of supporting my views, despite all the counsel of gentleness I kept giving him."[25] But after pronouncing his (vain) prohibition of cruelty, he writes that the insane person is "insensitive to the cruelties that are too often practiced on him," thus legitimizing, a posteriori, all the justifications customarily provided for harsh treatment. A fashionable eighteenth-century physician, for example, could support a particularly energetic treatment of convulsive madness—beatings, in the case in point—as follows: "One must not be frightened of this way of curing; it appears cruel, but it is not; the patient has no feeling; as soon as feeling returns, the treatment is stopped."[26] Daquin has turned his back on the time-honored belief in the sovereign efficacy of blows; he strongly condemns their use in the name of the values of a kinder society; but he continues to rely on the representation of the insane person as a being shut off from the outside and absent to everything but his own dreams. And yet not so very much earlier, in a world more accustomed to violence, that same representation justified administering vigorous "remedies" when the opportunity arose, without any notion that one was being cruel, since the patient was devoid of feeling. There is no more "barbarity" in practice, but the major principle behind barbarity is perpetuated in thought and discourse.

This is why the Pinelian break represents an immense step from the specific viewpoint of philanthropy: with and through the discovery of what remains of reason in maniacs, it creates an opening for awareness of their suffering. Here the progress of sensibility passes through thought.

The desire to treat insane people well is one thing; the understanding of their inner state is another—as is, a fortiori, the possibility of conceiving of that state as inherently painful. So long as one sees the insane patient as a being completely absorbed in chimeras arising from his desire, one does not feel his suffering; one is rather tempted, on the contrary, to attribute to him intense satisfactions that he is suspected of having preferred to everything else, even in the face of his own degradation—except for cases where madness has a physical origin, where the body suffers. It is only when we perceive the insane person's own enduring presence to his malady, the difference that disconnects him from his own strangeness to himself, that we come to intuit the rift that traverses him and the moral pain that overwhelms him.

Even so, it took a long time to formulate this observation directly. Not until Esquirol's 1816 article on madness was it declared in a straightforward manner. Esquirol concedes that he has sometimes seen his wards in a seemingly happy state, but he hastens to emphasize that this is exceptional. "This happy state found in some insane people," he writes, "has caused many mistaken judgments about the patients. On the basis of a few who have been seen in that condition, people have concluded that insane people were all happy, that they did not suffer at all, whereas generally speaking they suffer both physically and morally."[27] He writes this, moreover, in a context where the figures of impenetrable autarky that have always constituted for example the basis for the thinking of people like Daquin, as we have seen, are methodically destroyed or dissolved. "Insane people become remarkably pusillanimous," Esquirol asserts; "they let themselves be easily intimidated; they are fearful, wary, suspicious."[28] Are they insensitive to "the elements," as Daquin says? Do they retreat even from meeting their needs at the subsistence level, under the exalting influence of vital forces? "These examples are very rare," Esquirol assures us. "Almost all insane patients gravitate toward the fireplace when they have an opportunity, almost all eat a good deal and very often. . . . These patients are not as impervious to environmental influences as some have maintained."[29] In reality, they are constantly prey to discomfort: "They are nowhere at ease; they want to be anywhere but where they are."[30] Even one's immediate physical perception of the insane is profoundly altered: "All insane people have convulsive facial features; their physiognomy bears the mark of pain."[31]

In 1805 this contrarian representation of the old images of complacency or indifference in confinement in itself had not yet been fully developed. However, we can see it beginning to break through, for example, via the quite new place allotted to the fears that sometimes assail the insane. It emerged in the way Esquirol approached a problem like that of insomnia, which regularly disturbed his patients, and which was one of the first points he wanted to clear up "as soon as he [was] freed from treating the insane"—a preoccupation that was already highly significant in its own right. "People generally attribute night screaming to delirium, but this is mistaken. How many errors remain to be corrected regarding these patients! I am convinced that the causes of their insomnia are few in number: reducible to pressing needs, frightening dreams, and sometimes to maniacal ideas." It is not simply that a disordered activity of the mind, indifferent in any event to time and place, is carried on even in the middle of the night. The patients' inner torments prevent them from sleeping, and to a certain extent these can be alleviated. "A burning heat devours them: a bath or oxicrat lotion applied to the head will often suffice to restore calm, if not to bring about sleep. We have less success in calming those who act cheerful and sing in the night: ordinarily they sing only to divert themselves from their insomnia, or to dull their suffering."[32] Behind the apparent gaiety, there is an anxious tedium or discomfort from which the insane patient is trying to flee. The reversal of the interpretation, the concern for getting back to the subjective roots of a behavior that is after all typically "insane," are of a particularly exemplary clarity here. Indeed, screaming and singing were traditionally taken as signs par excellence of the absence of the patient, whose retreat into himself is spectacularly manifest in these discordant displays, untouched by any preoccupation with external circumstances.

Esquirol for his part started from completely opposite principles of inquiry. He supposed that there was a reason for the insane person's behavior; he wondered to what the patient was reacting. And to the extent that he tacitly recognized the reflexive dimension at the heart of the insane person's experience, a dimension that allowed the patient to work through his experience, for example, in an attempt to conjure it away, that Esquirol was led to discern the suffering that that dimension entails. A world of immediate adhesion, complete and opaque to itself, can be either a world of satisfaction or else one of the perfect neutrality that is procured by the sleep of coincidence. The idea of madness as suffering could only emerge after this representation of blind confinement within the circle of delirium was dismantled; the perception of the insane person's maintained presence to himself had to come to the fore, and with it a sense of the inner division and struggle with which he has to contend. Only after one has understood the conflictual situation of the patient can one intuit the depths of his ordeal.

Let us avoid any retrospective illusions about the real motivations of the philanthropic movement that preceded the psychiatric reform per se. If this movement advocated a more humane treatment of the insane, it was not at all out of sensitivity to their inner pain: it was out of respect for their unfortunate loss of reason, out of a desire to honor human beings even in the extreme case where they no longer know they are human. The advent of another conception of madness, one in which a subjective function is at once questioned and recognized as indestructible, brought philanthropy closer to the insane person's suffering. And in the process the way that practitioners approached insane people was completely altered in other respects. For Daquin, the appropriate behavior had to be inspired by the physician's lofty sense of his responsibilities, by his "philosophy," in a word. For Esquirol, the physician's conduct must also be guided by the predictable manner in which it will be understood and received by the patient. Thus not only are harshness, blows, and all forms of mistreatment to be forbidden, even when the insane must be addressed with "an inflexible firmness," but in addition

> one must treat them with strict justice, and avoid giving them any occasion for legitimate complaint: they are naturally discontent enough, without giving them reason to be so. . . . One must resort to [repression] immediately after a fault has been committed: without this attention, they rebel against the presumed injustice, believing that they are the playthings of some individual's whim, either an enemy, or an envious person, or a barbarian. One must take care to make the patient feel that if he is prevented from doing something, it is because he is in the wrong; he must be fully convinced that he alone has made it necessary to take recourse to these means; thus, as soon as he yields, the repression must end. (*Des Passions*, p. 57)

We are apt to find this infantilizing pathos quite irritating today. But we need to read it in its own context, for despite the limitations there are elements of significant novelty. For Esquirol, philanthropy no longer implied that one must act toward the insane person as one would act toward anyone else, but rather that, whatever conduct one adopted toward the patient, one had to consider his feelings and reactions. The boundaries that Esquirol assigned to the patient's capacity for understanding appear ridiculously narrow today, but that is another matter. What is important is that Esquirol overturns the approach to the question by integrating—however little and however inadequately—a new parameter, in taking into account the insane person's presence to the treatment being proffered and his own interpretation of that treatment, in recognizing the patient as someone in whose place one can project oneself and whose behavior one can predict.

The word *philanthropy* has one meaning for someone who advocates gentleness even while declaring that the insane person is "insensitive to the cruelties practiced upon him," and quite another meaning for someone who does not deem it useless, for example, to investigate personally the effects of the shower treatment so freely recommended by most authors.

We learn this from Pinel, in support of the critics whom he invokes in opposition to the thoughtless use of a technique capable of provoking "a singular state of suffering in the head."

> Doctor Esquirol has subjected himself to experiments related to the use of showers, the curious details and results of which he will no doubt eventually publish himself. The reservoir of liquid was elevated ten feet over his head; the water was ten degrees colder than the atmospheric temperature; the column of water was four lines in diameter and fell directly on his head; it seemed to him at every moment that a column of ice was breaking against that part. The pain was very acute when the water fell on the fronto-parietal suture; it was more bearable when it fell upon the occipital. His head remained as if numb more than an hour after the shower.[33]

Between someone who wants to benefit the insane person, even if the patient himself cannot be aware of this, and someone who wants to know how this patient may experience the treatments administered to him, without doubting moreover that the patient feels the same thing, there is the distance between two different eras of madness, though not separated by very many years. In the interval, the insane person has been brought back into the order of sensible beings whose lived experience can be recomposed at least in part on the basis of one's own—human beings with whom exchange and even some measure of identification are possible.[34]

Thus we must not be too quick to credit a humanitarian tendency with transforming the conditions of confinement, in contrast to a theoretical undertaking that only provided a retrospective translation for the new perception that had already passed into practice and that governed the theory. For to do so would be to misrepresent in a fundamental way both the limits of the enterprise inspired by philanthropy alone and the crucially important effects of the advent of a different idea of madness. The attention that "the most unfortunate of men," beings "whose state is so afflicting, but perhaps even more interesting than it is afflicting,"[35] begin to attract toward the end of the eighteenth century, and the widely manifested desire to improve their lot, surely attest to an important shift in the representations of madness—particularly in the evaluation of its global anthropological signification. However, they do not entail any break at all with the central images of "moral isolation," personal self-enclosure, or absence to the world and to oneself that constitute the solid core of the traditional conceptions. The Pinelian break, as a radical shift in thinking about madness, not only overturned the immediate human understanding of madness by revealing it as suffering, but also created the conditions of a historical dynamic destined to keep on transforming the principles governing medical practice, by basing the latter no longer simply on the practitioner's ethical requirements but also on his capacity to put himself in his patient's place. This latter becomes a virtually infinite requirement; we can already detect its extraordinary expansion between Pinel's writings and Esquirol's. It has subsequently undergone many avatars and eclipses, but it has never ceased to have profound if sometimes obscure effects on the relation between doctors and these patients of a decidedly special type, since they are without a determinable status. The new requirement introduces a fantastic factor of instability that arouses constant criticism and brings forth new imperatives; even today we have surely not yet exhausted its powers of displacement.

Deliberate Interaction

To return from treatment in general to the question of moral therapeutics in particular, one more point is worth spelling out, in connection with the telling gap that separates the approaches, however close they may be in many other respects, of a Daquin and an Esquirol: the gap between their respective representations not of the techniques or mechanisms of therapeutics, but of the process through which they act. While Daquin advocates the use of moral assistance, by far the surest and most reasonable method for curing, he insists just as strongly that the grasp of a "middle term" between challenging and reinforcing the object of madness constitutes "the principal recourse against that illness"; he emphasizes the changes gradually induced by these "paths of gentleness" in patients' behavior, and he remains remarkably incapable of envisaging even for a moment the inner movement through which calm is reestablished along with confidence, the movement through which the practitioner's words act on the patient and slowly bring him back to himself. Here again, it is the vivid figure of the patient's perfect, blind adhesion to his insanity that stumps Daquin. How could one imagine any discordance between self and self within a being "who does not even have, to all appearances, any idea of his own existence"? From this point on, the only thing Daquin can describe is an overall development perceived from without.

In contrast, Pinel's discretion on the subject is more idiosyncratic. We cannot help noticing that in his *Treatise* he passes very quickly over the way the idea that has "vigorously struck him" works in the insane patient, once someone has succeeded in reaching him "by entering into his madness, as it were." For the way Daquin and Pinel situate the problem is quite different. In Pinel, the issue is no longer what attitude to adopt toward delirious notions, but rather how to conceive of the effects that are produced within the insane patient and perhaps even, in a way, at the very heart of his delirium. The overwhelming, determining step for Pinel is the possibility of penetrating into the insane person's universe, the possibility of addressing someone in the grip of the most pronounced insanity (thus someone who does not mistake himself for his own insane certainties). Pinel takes these possibilities for granted. Along the same lines, he implies that he believes skilled therapeutic intervention can produce a certain gap between the insane person and his insane convictions—not by reasoning, but indirectly, by way of the very flaw that delirious convictions entail: by arousing an echo within the patient and by mobilizing the invisible reserve toward these chimeras that he has been maintaining against all odds, the practitioner can make the patient himself perceive a sudden distance from the knot of certainties that just an instant before had been as irrefragable as they were irrepressible.

Pinel offers the picturesque case of a watchmaker confined in Bicêtre who is convinced that he has been guillotined and that he has gotten the wrong head put back on by mistake. One of his companions brings him up short with a well-aimed response during a skillfully directed conversation about "the famous miracle of Saint Denis," who carried his head in his hands as he walked along and kissed it repeatedly.

> Our mechanician strongly maintained the possibility of the fact, and sought to confirm it by an application of it to his own case. The other set up a loud laugh, and replied with a tone of the keenest ridicule: "Madman as thou art, how could Saint Denis kiss his own head? Was it with his heels?" This equally unexpected and unanswerable retort, [*sic*] forcibly struck the maniac. He retired confused amidst the peals of laughter, which were provoked at his expense, and never afterwards mentioned the exchange of his head.[36]

The example is noteworthy first of all because of the archaic nature of the model it adopts. Characteristically, it borrows its canvas and its form from the old therapeutics of realization or resolution. This brings out all the better, by contrast, the novelty that so struck Pinel's contemporaries: the disjunctive impact of the incident on the insane patient himself. In a specific context, someone succeeds in traversing insanity, as it were, and getting the patient's attention, thus awakening in him a suspended but by no means extinguished reflection that suddenly separates him from the blind imagining that had held him in its grasp. The achievement depends neither on a complicity with madness intended to bring it to its terminal point where it would evaporate on its own nor on arguments designed to win over a sane being hidden behind the lunatic's aberrant thinking. It is not logical argument that persuades, here; it is surprise—logical in nature, in this particular case—that leaves the individual speechless, shaken, and restored to the ground of perceptible evidence. Recourse to indirection has allowed someone to touch an obscure part of the patient that has remained out of phase with his delirious faith; it has helped dismantle his adherence to his delusions, an adherence that was not nearly as massive and as irremediable as might have been supposed.

Of course Pinel's example is naive, rustic, and elementary; it is easy to find fault. Still, under its crude cloak, it signifies a major discovery, one that was found fascinating in its own time, and for good reason. Pinel's example marks the advent of a fundamental possibility: the power to manipulate an internal difference that has not been absolutely eliminated in the insane person, appearances notwithstanding. At the same time, if the principle of grasping from within is clearly posited in this way, if the general notion of therapeutic action passing through the insane person's inner self and appealing to the hidden resources of that self (however halting or inadequate the language charged with expressing these moves may seem to us today), Pinel says nothing at all about the inner paths along which his watchmaker, for example, finds himself relieved of his tenacious illusions about having the wrong head. He offers nothing to designate the work that goes on in the place of the delirious conviction; he does not attempt to name what is happening inside the insane patient. It is as if he has encountered something there that remains unrepresentable. He observes that the watchmaker "never afterwards mentioned the exchange of his head," and that his reason rapidly reasserted itself.

Not until Esquirol do we find more or less direct and precise statements on this topic. He offers nothing systematized, no well-formed conceptions, just a series of hasty but explicit statements that point to an essential indication about how the therapeutic process works. These convergent statements are scattered throughout his writings. We can summarize their principal terms briefly: "Make the insane patient turn back within himself, begin to make him glimpse the possibility that he may be ill," make him "reflect on his current situation, on the reason he is staying in a strange house, on his state." However undeveloped it remains, in Esquirol we find the beginning of a definite, coherent conception of the distancing effects induced by adequate institutional arrangements and an appropriate attitude.

We can compare Esquirol's position with an example reported by Pinel: the contrast brings out with special clarity the difficulty, if not the impossibility, Pinel experiences in simply envisaging and naming this reflective dimension whose cooperation he nevertheless tacitly presupposes. Under the heading "The Advantages of Restraint upon the Imagination of Maniacs Illustrated," Pinel relates the case of "a young religious enthusiast" who had become maniacal owing to the suppression of the Catholic religion in France during the Revolution and who was led by a "misanthropy not to be equalled" and the idea of the torments of the afterlife, finally, to give up eating entirely, so that "on the fourth day after that unfortunate resolution was formed, a state of langour succeeded, which excited considerable apprehensions for his life. Kind remonstrances and pressing invitations proved equally ineffectual." Under these conditions Pinel asks:

> How was such a perverse train of ideas to be stemmed or counteracted? The excitement of terror presented itself as the only resourse [sic]. For this purpose, Citizen Pussin appeared one night at the door of his chamber, and, with fire darting from his eyes, and thunder in his voice, commanded a group of domestics, who were armed with strong and loudly clanking chains, to do their duty. But the ceremony was artfully suspended; —the soup was placed before the maniac, and strict orders were left him to eat it in the course of the night, on pains of the severest punishment. He was left to his own reflections. The night was spent (as he afterward informed me) in a state of the most distressing hesitation, whether to incur the present punishment, or the distant but still more dreadful torments of the world to come. After an internal struggle of many hours, the idea of the present evil gained the ascendancy, and he determined to take the soup. From that time he submitted, without difficulty, to a restorative system of regimen. His sleep and strength gradually returned; his reason recovered its empire; and, after the manner above related, he escaped certain death. It was during his convalescence, that he mentioned to me the perplexities and agitations which he endured during the night of the experiment.[37]

Pinel found that avowal intrinsincally interesting and must have returned to it frequently with his patient. It confirms the possibility of producing "agitations," "perplexities," and "internal struggle" in an insane person. Pinel refrains from formally attributing his "maniac's" return to reason to his passage through these states; however, this is what his narrative indirectly suggests. The logic of the approach is self-evident: it is impossible to get anything at all by the ordinary routes of persuasion; yet one is not dealing with an individual inaccessible to any grasp, "incapable of receiving the slightest impression through speech," and "braving threats," as Daquin would have put it; that said, it is pointless to confront him on the terrain of his delirious resolution, useless to seek to vanquish head-on by intimidation what one could not get around by requesting or begging; nor is it necessary to resort to some form of direct constraint that would subdue the patient physically. But once this whole set of possibilities has been eliminated, there still remains one way out, one possibility, the only good one, that of using a "disturbance of the imagination" to provoke an inner struggle, an internal debate, a conflictual gap between the insane person and his insane will, one that ends up dislodging him sufficiently from the invincible persistence in which he had been mired so that a gradual return of reason can be traced.

It is important, however, to see precisely where—between what and what—Pinel situates this salutary conflict. The limits that bring it to a halt are all in place. Pinel locates it between the young man's conviction that he must adopt "the abstinences and mortifications of the ancient anchorites" and the strongly felt idea of the threatened "present punishment" (pp. 62–63), between his own idea and the idea introduced from the outside, and not at all between the elements of his delirious faith and a confusedly accurate appreciation of reality, as Esquirol suggests in connection with patients who, expecting to undergo wretched treatments or else experience complete abandonment in the strange house to which they are taken, and encountering "care, attention, and consideration" instead, develop a diffuse doubt as to the validity of their fears. "This contrast of feelings between the presumed abandonment and the compassionate care provided by unknown people provokes an internal struggle from which reason emerges victorious": this time the struggle is between chimerical constraints and a delirious feeling of universal hostility on the one hand, and the realistic perception that those fears and feelings are essentially unfounded, on the other hand.

While Pinel does discern clearly that he has to operate via the patient's persistent capacity for inner struggle, that he has to count on the strength of the patient's own opposition "to the course of his sinister ideas," he remains characteristically incapable of conceptualizing the nature of that force and of localizing its point of application. He makes practical use of it, but he is blind to it intellectually. He completely misses the real tenor of what Esquirol recognizes as the patient's capacity to "reflect on his own state"—the capacity to bring in on his own some elements of reality that counterbalance his mad certainties, the capacity to find himself outside of his own delirium, to detach himself progressively, owing to that power of presences, from the beliefs in which he had become a stranger to himself. Thus, as the example we have just seen makes obvious, Pinel is unable to make any claims at all about the reasons for the effectiveness of moral treatment. At one extreme, he stresses "the painful state of fluctuation" in which the patient remains; at the other extreme, he registers the return to reason that follows the victory of the imperative of reality over the obligations imposed by delirium; but between the two there is no link that he can express or conceive of, even though everything he says indicates indirectly that such a link exists. For what remains inaccessible to Pinel is the idea of an inner struggle that not only pits insane convictions against the assessment of a genuine risk but that also entails a questioning, through the realistic perception thus triggered, of the adherence that binds the insane person to his delirium.

Speaking of the same sort of struggle, Esquirol says that it "makes the insane patient turn back within himself and glimpse the possibility that he may be ill." He says virtually nothing else about it, to be sure, at least on the level of reasoned explanation of the phenomenon. Still, he says enough to justify our observation that the idea behind moral treatment, laboriously sought ever since Daquin gave it its first authentic expression in the form of a problem to be solved, has now been explicitly articulated. What Esquirol's formulas tell us is that, for those of its promoters who actually managed to put it into practice (which was not the case with Daquin), moral treatment, already a practice virtually assured of its principal directions, was becoming aware of its own presuppositions and conscious of the reasons for its own effectiveness (which was not the case with Pinel). Esquirol's scattered remarks suffice to attest that he was aware of the foundations of an empirical theory limited to the sole element of the doctor/patient relation and the subjective principle in terms of which it operates. There is a way of relating to the insane person, of taking the absence of reflection that dominates him into account but refusing to confine him to it. Intrinsically and structurally, this approach results in sending him back into himself and reintroducing the reflective difference where it had been suspended or covered over. With Esquirol, this crucial point reaches the state of explicit conception; with it, in a sense, the first conquest of the notion of moral treatment is achieved.

The Inverse of Eloquence

"The moral treatment M. Pinel uses to cure minds that have strayed is, appropriately, precisely the opposite of the devices the art of eloquence uses to overwhelm the imagination and persuade people." Destutt de Tracy makes this claim in his *Elemens d'Idéologie*, in a note on Pinel's *Treatise* (a work that "cannot be too highly recommended" to readers).[38] Destutt de Tracy thus not only shows his acute sensitivity to the crux of the Pinelian invention, to the mysterious new sort of power revealed by verbal exchanges with the insane, but in offering a negative definition of that power as the inverse of the ordinary powers of discourse he also introduces a conceptual perspective that is destined to survive. Even today, there seems to be no better way to understand the mode of action inherent in the analytic apparatus except as the exact opposite of what happens in a situation of suggestion. It is as though we can comprehend the ability to produce a certain type of effects in the mind of another person only if we relate it to the thoroughgoing reversal of a different ability, the ability to influence by hypnotic suggestion. The latter is an immediately intelligible ability, since it stems from the received model of eloquence, albeit taken to its extreme limit; it remains within the traditional order of forcing another to espouse one's own ideas.

In the first place, the goals of the art of eloquence and the goals of moral treatment have something in common. Unlike neutral relations that involve only an exchange of information, eloquence and moral treatment both use speech to mobilize or alter the person(s) addressed. One might even say that in many ways they are the same thing, for in each case what is at stake is winning over one's interlocutor (winning him back to reason in general, winning him over to one's own reasons pure and simple).

In reality, the conjunction is formal and factitious; it masks an essential opposition. The orator seeks to compel his listeners to espouse his own ideas without reservations or second thoughts. The practitioner of moral treatment seeks, on the contrary, to rid his listener of the belief that alienates the latter from himself; the therapist attempts to introduce difference between the subject and a thought that is so close to him that he confuses himself with it and no longer dominates it. This goal can only be achieved by introducing difference within the discursive relation, by playing on the necessary, insurmountable gap between viewpoints, by making the other (the insane person) aware of the incompatibility between the places from which each of the interlocutors is speaking. As a therapist, I do not follow the patient onto his territory, nor do I try to bring him over to mine; I do not enter into his views, nor do I act as if he could share my own. This happens naturally within a space where exchange and communication have been fundamentally posited as possible: the incompatibility in question here is not the heterogeneity of two self-contained and mutually exclusive universes, but the hiatus between two human beings united by an initial identification, or rather two human beings one of whom has taken it upon himself, in a decision highly charged with consequences, to recognize that he and the other belong to the same collectivity, despite the derangement that isolates the latter.

We have thus already shifted from the opposition between the orator's goals and the therapist's to the profound procedural inversion discerned by Destutt de Tracy. The art of eloquence works through identification. It is not simply a subtle science of the wellsprings of conviction; the art of eloquence presupposes the gift of putting oneself in one's listeners' place, for this is the only authentic source for the turns of phrase and images that may correspond to the listeners' most secret expectations and that may literally reveal the listeners to themselves. Skillfully handled, the art of eloquence leads listeners to recognize themselves in the discourse they hear. Despite its superficial transgression of the forms of reciprocity (since it unfolds on the basis of a dissymmetry between speaker and listeners, eliminating the dimension of response), oratory stems in reality from the rule-governed universe of exchange. It fits completely into that universe and operates by relying on its major articulations.

The superficial dissymmetry between speaker and listener notwithstanding, eloquence produces perfect equivalence; the listener responds, in effect, by thinking, "That is exactly what I think; I could have said the same thing myself." If there is such a thing as an art of eloquence, it is in relation to this ultimate equality that allows me to find myself entirely within the discourse of the other, to shift over to his positions, to appropriate his argument for myself to such an extent that I may not even remember that the argument came from elsewhere. Thus eloquence allows me to experience the place from which the other speaks to me as fundamentally analogous to the place I occupy myself, as so symmetrical to my own that an obvious reversibility suffices to move me over to it. Although the interlocutors do not explicitly enact their mutual recognition, they are nevertheless engaged in a tacit relation of recognition. I recognize myself first of all in the speech of the other, and consequently I recognize what the other recognizes as belonging to me, since he is capable of making statements that could have been my own, statements that in any event I can experience in every respect through my own free inner movement.

For this is the other aspect of the orator's art that integrates it with the system of norms and values traditionally linked to the order of reciprocity. Eloquence involves the exercise if not of a power then at least of influence, or will; if it does not involve actually imposing one's thought, it at least involves conveying one's thought into the other's mind, solely on the basis of an appeal to an act of appropriation that emanates exclusively from the other. The art of eloquence consists precisely in creating a feeling of freedom in the listener, in using artifice to make the listener lose his awareness of outside pressures and believe that his assent is entirely personal and spontaneous. Ideally, the person being convinced has to feel that he himself is integrally the author and master of the position to which he is being led—he has to think from the place of the other, but to think himself there wholly.

The same observation applies to the relation of therapeutic suggestion; Freud clearly finds it interesting that the ideas induced in the hypnotized subject are later experienced by him as his own. And indeed, hypnotic suggestion remains affiliated with eloquence precisely because it relies on the same possibility of putting oneself in the other's place (to the point of failing to recognize what one owes the other), the possibility of occupying the other's place as if it were the same as one's own. Hypnotic suggestion and eloquence pursue the same objectives by different means; suggestion simply takes the goal of eloquence to its extreme limit. It does away with the rules of eloquence, replacing an ostensible respect for the listener's capacity to consent with an overt seizure of control by the speaker. Structurally, however, it poses no challenge to the organization of the intersubjective world that the relation of persuasion presupposes. Suggestion incorporates the two major terms of that relation: internal agreement with oneself and identification with the other. It pushes the listener's identification with the speaker to the extreme: the illusion that a skilled orator can create (making his listener forget that he is being swept away, confirming his sense that, on the contrary, he has always had those very thoughts on his own) is simply carried to its apogee when a hypnotized patient forgets that a suggestion has been made and is convinced of his own self-possession even as he blindly executes orders communicated by someone else.

It is not by chance that the matter attracts Freud's attention: for this is exactly the point of "the inversion of the orator's devices," the inversion from which the analytic mechanism stems, just as the principle of moral treatment did earlier. In place of the logic of masking and forgetting that leads me to believe that what the other has suggested to me is my own idea, the reversal might be described as the deliberate organization of an impossibility: I cannot fail to recognize the gap between what properly belongs to me and what comes to me from the other. Instead of manipulating illusions relating to the virtual identity of positions or to the reversibility of viewpoints, the practitioner resorts to the methodical use of an impossibility: the interlocutors' postures and roles cannot coincide. A science of disjunction has replaced an art of conjunction. With the new approach, it is a matter of preventing my interlocutor from being able even for a moment to believe that he is in the place I occupy. The technique of relationship is designed to make him feel that I am positioning myself with respect to him in a place that he can in no way experience as equivalent to his own, so that he is more or less confusedly obliged to tell himself, while listening to me, that he would not have said of his own accord what I am saying to him, and, similarly, when he speaks, he is compelled to think that I will not find in his utterances what he is convinced he is putting into them, but that from my position I will necessarily hear something different. In a word, he finds himself confronted with a potential gap unverifiable but unavoidable, between what he thinks he meant to say and what there is to be heard in his statement.

From a strategy of identification based on the possibility of exchanging positions on a basis of equality with the other that tends to confirm self-mastery (I know what I think, and I know why I think it, since I think the way the other does, and through him), we have moved to a tactic of difference, relinquishment, or evasion that disappoints the interlocutor's expectation of identity, for he finds it impossible to guarantee the other's agreement and reaction in advance, and this disturbs the basis of his own faith in himself. Thus in what I think and in what I say there is something of myself, according to this view, something of the reasons I have for speaking or thinking as I do, or in my manner of doing so, that escapes me. This elusive element provides my interlocutor with a justification for approaching it and for treating me differently from the way my discourse would seem to require at first glance.

It should be clearly understood here that we are talking about a difference or a gap—thus, in a sense, about the contrary of an opposition or a rejection. These latter in their own way restore to each interlocutor the feeling of complete and legitimate self-possession; structurally, they reproduce the symmetry and equivalence of the interlocutors' positions. The difference or gap we are talking about is not a rejection of the interlocutor's utterance as such, and yet, at bottom, it is nevertheless a refusal: the listener's refusal to hear the utterance as it is offered, as if the conditions of enunciation posed no problem, as if the interlocutor's statement incontestably condensed what he truly and univocally wanted to say. Properly speaking, as a listener I have no objection to what you say; I do not deny your right to express yourself as you do. I think and observe only that I cannot receive your discourse in the place where you are proffering it, on the level where you are locating it, as if you and it were one. We have shifted away from a situation stemming from the classical logic of speech exchange in which two systems of conviction and argument would clash; we have moved toward a situation similar to the one created by the orator's monopoly, in which there is only one discourse. The problem is that there are two ways of hearing that discourse: that of the person who utters it and posits it as his own, and that of the person who receives it but evades the symmetrical obligation to recognize it as the univocal expression of his interlocutor. The question of the validity of the other's discourse has been neutralized throughout; thus the very fact of uttering such a discourse is called into question for the individual who is speaking. The speaker confronts a listener who squarely refuses to attribute the statements he is hearing to the other, and who also refuses to consider himself implicated by those statements (for every utterance made by the other spontaneously implicates us: we hear it first of all as capable of being our own). Thus the speaker is led to wonder: Why do I say that, actually? And what if it were not absolutely I who am speaking and thinking in this discourse, which is nevertheless undeniably mine?

This way of conceiving of discourse entails a complete inversion with respect to the devices of eloquence. The sign of action is inverted, first of all: instead of speaking and anticipating that speaking will have some efficacity, in moral treatment one allows the patient to speak, and what is defined as efficacious is the fact of listening. (Listening includes everything that may count as a response to the patient; unlike the situation we find in ordinary interpersonal communication, such a response does not take the form of speech—it is literally inscribed in the patient's speech and has meaning only in those terms). Listening is efficacious because the speaking subject, however tightly bound he is to the self-evidence of his own discourse, remains sensitive in spite of everything to the constraint that governs his behavior. Thus in the presence of someone whose attitude signifies clearly that he is challenging the identity of the other's discourse, that he pre-supposes a certain gap in the patient's capacity to recognize himself entirely in what he affirms, the patient is in some sense automatically referred back to the internal discord at work within himself, back to his presence to himself and to the distance it implies in the face of the absence to himself revealed by his own forced speech. This is how he recovers "the awareness that he is ill," as Esquirol says naively but with intuitive accuracy. Doubtless nothing is carved in stone, at this point, but at least a process is set in motion that allows the alienating belief to be abandoned and the self to take hold of itself again, to return to self-possession and relinquish the thought that had been imposing itself radically and illusorily as its own. The forces required by this "internal struggle" (of which Esquirol also speaks) are mobilized by the intimate work of self on self; these are the only forces capable of ever ridding the subject of his madness, or of any other form of self-dispossession that comes about through the compulsion to find oneself in a discourse that in reality precedes and possesses you.

For the crucial feature through which, here again, moral treatment proves to be the inverse of the oratorical operation lies in the fundamentally indirect, mediate, and thus unverifiable mode of action that it presupposes. What happens takes place in the other, belongs to the other; I can induce it, but there is little more I can do. I credit the other with a receptivity to the listening attitude I adopt toward him; I postulate that somewhere in the other there is a gap in which I situate myself, and that he will somehow perceive the existence of that gap; moreover, I verify from the visible changes that manifest themselves in him that this is indeed the case. Beyond that, I also know that it is virtually impossible to address myself directly to the "healthy part" on which I rely. I can awaken it, conciliate it, and communicate harmoniously with it. Beyond that, I have no hope of getting hold of it and influencing it: there is no alternative to letting it operate on its own. In this respect moral treatment has nothing to do with an art of persuasion that irresistibly wins over minds by means of a tightly woven dialectic. On the contrary, the art of moral treatment is the art of creating for oneself an interlocutor whose inner meanderings escape one by nature from the outset, and who cannot be influenced through direct pressure.

There is an inverse of the bond of speech and more broadly of the relation of one human being to another as governed in all cases by an exchange of meaning. This other relation conceals a secret power, a principle for acting on individual human beings; such is the discovery that dawns with the advent of moral treatment. I may order, persuade, suggest; in one way or another I may obtain the agreement of my peers by shoving down their throats, as everyday language puts it quite colorfully, what I believe or desire myself. While the techniques involved and the pressure brought to bear may vary considerably, the path nevertheless always remains the same, and it has appeared to be the only path that permits not just a neutral exchange of information between interlocutors but influence or control by one interlocutor over another. As it happens, the insane person defeats this entire set of devices. Where his insanity is concerned, he is virtually inaccessible to argument, and still less to injunction; his unsharable convictions are actually reinforced by attempts to dislodge them that rely on the ordinary mechanisms of the power of speech. Thus the early practitioners of moral treatment faced an imperious obligation to innovate; and thus, through halting, groping efforts they brought a different power to light, one that was not complementary but contrary to the generally recognized powers of speech. They did not gain access to this new power in the interstices of the existing powers, or alongside them, but through a reversal of the principles presiding over the application of all known powers. The power they discovered is based on an exact inversion of the reciprocal recognition of identity that ordinarily governs the relation of speech exchange.

I know myself; he knows himself. I am fully self-sufficient when it is a question of what I am, what I think, and what I want; as a result, I can put myself absolutely in my interlocutor's place, on the necessary assumption that he is endowed in exactly the same way with full self-possession. When I reason this way, I am positing that human beings are radically independent of one another and completely self-sufficient, that they are rigorously equal, and that the positions they occupy are perfectly reversible. This double articulation that structures the field of discourse by attributing mastery to each interlocutor and positing the interchangeability of all is integrally subverted by the establishment of authentic communication with the insane person—that is, communication that respects the inherent contradiction in his position. On the one hand, the insane individual is specifically affected in his self-possession and his reflective capacity. On the other hand (and here is a discovery that underlies psychiatry), he is nevertheless in some sense present to the disorder that abolishes him as subject, and he keeps a certain reflective distance, at least virtually, from the nonreflection that dominates him. As a result, in order to take into account the element of human subjectivity that is maintained in the insane person, I am obliged to proceed by challenging the identity of his discourse and the ownership of his thought; I have to take it for granted, on the other hand, that he is capable of hearing my challenge in the first place; and then I have to assume that if I believe he can hear me and make my reasonable discourse his own I am closing my eyes to the reality of the constraint that makes him identify himself wholly with his delirium and espouse it blindly and uncontrollably. This problem seems to be virtually insoluble. However, it encompasses its own solution, which is the new-found power we have been describing. The power may well be the strongest force ever discovered for transforming human beings; at all events, it is the only force capable of calling back into question the alienation of human subjects from meaning, a relation of which madness constitutes only the extreme image.

If I have the contrary of a power to act on the other, I have the power to make him act on himself, but through my intermediary, and without needing to ask him anything; thus I have the power to make something happen in him, something that is both entirely of his own doing and wholly independent of his will. It is not the power to impose myself on him; on the contrary, it is the power to restore him to himself by allowing him to see the irremediable alterity of my own position, the place of the interlocutor. It is the power to make the subject's relation to himself problematic, the power to disconnect him from his own self-evidence, to awaken him to what binds him to his own exorbitant discourse, to make him aware of the idea on which he thinks his self-possession depends. It is the power to rid him of the illusory recognition of self in discourse uttered by another, discourse that is nourished and valorized by the ordinary mechanisms of interlocution. For a very long time, the institution of speech held that form of self-recognition to be beyond question, especially in the extreme form it took in the case of insane people. According to the traditional view, the insane individual was locked in the grip of a conviction so completely his own that he could not posit himself as a self with respect to it, nor could he conceive that others do not share it—the grip of his conviction was held to be absolute and unbreakable. But the traditional view was challenged by two intersecting sequences of events: the universe of reciprocity began to collapse, and a small number of practitioners dealing with madness began to grasp the intimate gap that kept the insane person from being totally imprisoned in his delirium. Where those two sequences converged, they made it possible to question the individual's relation to himself as that relation was exposed through his discourse, and they uncovered the particular need to question the insane individual's investment in his own delirium. The development of moral treatment allowed a power of an entirely new type to emerge: over the course of a century, starting from this narrow point of application, the development of this new power finally made it necessary to reexamine the whole idea of subjective organization.

This power, like the orator's, is thus exclusively bound up with speech, but, unlike the orator's, it does not emphasize the content of speech. Instead, it involves the inverse art of making manifest the listener's position with respect to what the speaker is saying, and of bringing out the difference between the interlocutors' positions. For the effectiveness of the mechanism depends entirely on this evanescent articulation. The only power at work here is that stemming from the relational structure instituted as soon as one person challenges the identity of another's discourse. In the case in point, this relational structure is instituted as soon as a practitioner stops behaving as if the insane patient were hopelessly closed off inside his madness and overtly presupposes a certain internal division in the patient.

The specificity of this structure lies in its radical irreversibility. The delirious patient is irremediably absent to the point of view of his interlocutor, physical proximity notwithstanding; the patient is made to feel from the outset that he will never have access to the place from which he is heard. An initial effect is thus achieved and the insane patient can be reawakened to the sense of an interlocutor's presence. I could behave differently: I could register his delirium or challenge it; I could yield to insanity and go along with the patient who has lost his reason, or I could do my utmost to make him listen to reason. But in either case I would be failing to acknowledge the duality that traverses him, and I would be reinforcing his isolation and his absence from the world of others. If he, on the other hand, is confronted by someone who shows himself to be sensitive to the contradictory truth of his condition, the patient can once more take into account internally, though perhaps only obscurely, the existence of another human being. He can begin to incorporate into his own world the dimension of shared participation in a collectivity; he can begin to integrate the fact that his own experience can be deciphered by others, can be shared with someone outside himself.

But while the other, the interlocutor, is reintroduced in this way into a place where he had actually never ceased to have a place, at the same moment this other is also recognized as ungraspable, as occupying a different place from any of the actual or virtual places that the patient himself may occupy. Thus the other is received under the auspices of a suspicion that is inherently impossible to overcome. The presence of the other is unimpeachable, but it takes the form of an inaccessible externality, an irreducible alterity. There is a place beyond myself, a place of which I cannot be unaware, from which the rift in which I live, appearances notwithstanding, is perceptible, a place from which the ultimate and painful ambiguity of my relation to myself is readable. But this place is by nature inaccessible to my grasp. As soon as something makes me credit an interlocutor with the capacity to discern the intimate contradiction that permeates me (and although I am no doubt already aware of this contradiction, I still have to discover that in a sense the other is more aware of it than I am, since he has been able to see it despite everything that I myself believe to the contrary), I am condemned to the ordeal of endless, unsurpassable self-dispossession. No matter what I do to the inner division that pits the blind mindlessness that dominates me against the reflective part of me that is aware of what is happening, the division moves and resurfaces out of reach; it is inexhaustible and therefore unmasterable. No matter where I go, no matter how I situate myself with respect to myself, the other remains in a position to call back into question what I think I hold from within; and in terms of that outside of which he continually reminds me he refers me to my own alterity. Here again, where I thought I was sure of myself, I nevertheless find conflict, constraint, separation, and alienation. A sharing with oneself that displaces itself indefinitely, a difference from the virtual viewpoint of the other, a gap constantly reborn and structurally impossible to fill—such is the strange system of interactions that emerges when one seeks to mobilize to therapeutic ends what remains of reflective presence in a human being prey to estrangement and absence from himself.

The crucial maneuver that sets the mechanism in motion depends entirely on the point of application that the therapist establishes for himself in his patient, a point of application presupposing, as we have seen, a characteristic break with the traditional order of speech: the patient's relation to himself. For in so doing the therapist reveals an abyss. Breaking with the principle that holds the personal sphere to be inaccessible, he breaks correlatively with the principle that the positions of participants in a discursive interaction are interchangeable, and he installs himself in a place that his interlocutor can experience only as inherently inaccessible. By the same token, as therapist I potentially open up the field of a boundless enterprise: I initiate the patient's return toward himself, his interminable referral to himself as he experiences the impossibility of identifying himself with the point of view from which I am relating to him and considering him. Practitioners at the beginning of the nineteenth century offered a practical response to madness. Their work demonstrated that, contrary to prevailing beliefs, access to the alienated subject, even access to his alienation itself, was possible—indirect access, to be sure, but access nonetheless, beyond question.

This access, discovered from without, constitutes the true mainspring of the work done from within, the work required to enable the patient to rid himself of his alienation. The inventors of moral treatment instituted an unprecedented articulation between self and other at the heart of the communicative interaction in which the identity of each is called into question, in which each interlocutor's presence to self must be endlessly rediscovered in a struggle against being carried away by meaning and against recognizing oneself mistakenly in the discourse of the other, factors that work ceaselessly in favor of self-dispossession. None of this is expressed, of course, or even envisaged for a moment by our advocates of moral treatment; they are absorbed in a narrowly circumscribed task and they are also, for reasons made clear by history, more preoccupied with trying to establish what their own approach should be than with trying to determine the exact nature of the process their work triggers in their patients. Nevertheless, the new-found power we have just characterized is what is fundamentally at stake in the therapists' efforts to free themselves from the tyrannical requirements of reciprocal recognition, which precluded any authentic entry into relation with the patient, and their practical struggle to find the right point of equilibrium from which to win over the insane person and make themselves heard by him without making concessions to madness.

When therapists succeeded in taking up a position in the in-between area evoked by Daquin, a position that neither contests nor panders to the patient's insanity, what they actually established was a relational mechanism corresponding to the subjective division that affects the insane patient. This mechanism is potentially capable, moreover, of calling into question the self-mastery and self-possession of any subject, insofar as these qualities are presumed to manifest themselves in particular through expression. When, following Esquirol's example, practitioners reached the point of glimpsing the mechanism that refers the individual back to himself and that institutes an inner distance between the subject and the thoughts that alienate him, they succeeded concretely in locating and fixing in place the principle and horizon of all action undertaken on the human subject from then on. These practitioners took the subject's nonreflective dimension into account and claimed to overcome it, even though they drew no general conclusions from their work and even though their field of application remained within narrow limits.

Between Daquin and Esquirol, then, we can trace nothing less than the emergence, the invention, and the constitution of a practical restructuring of the order of the positions that one individual can occupy in relation to another. As the resulting structure is developed and made more explicit, it is destined wholly to transform the representation of humanity. Moreover, this process of transformation is by no means complete. While at the concrete level the analytic mechanism has been devoted to the decisive deployment and the orderly exploitation of the dimensions of dissymmetry and irreversibility that had been painfully introduced into the approach to psychopathological phenomena a century earlier, while the goals and forms of the subjective process that mechanism authorizes have been the object of relatively elaborate developments, at the same time one can only be struck by the virtually complete absence of theoretical work on the properly structural effects of this process, effects that stem from the specific articulation of a certain way of speaking and a certain way of listening. The fact remains that the intrinsic influences of the logic of the system of free association and floating attention have to this day not been the object of any elucidation that stands up to scrutiny. The occasional pertinent insights submerged in pseudo-oracular Lacanian tall tales involving the so-called "signifier" clearly do not take the place of such an elucidation.

The absence of elucidation is a sign that we have not finished exploring and mastering the potentialities arising from the ruins of the order that has presided over human relations from time immemorial: in particular, the possibilities unleashed by efforts to find an approach appropriate to the subjective duality observed in madness. In many respects, in the now-familiar way of situating oneself in alterity or in absence with respect to the other in order to send her back to the division that separates her from herself, we are still at the point of using a principle of interaction whose real modalities escape us. With the collapse of the symbolic framework of reciprocity, we have witnessed the institution of a new space of interlocution, the practical discovery of an effective intersubjective operation that is bound up with the impossibility I experience, as subject, of taking refuge in a secure identity while putting myself—in order to hear myself—in the place of another, whose entire skill is devoted to eluding me. But we have also witnessed the start of a crisis of reflexivity, an irreversible questioning of the power to look at oneself as if one were another. This crisis and this questioning are as much presupposed by the new idea of madness as they are induced by the dissolution of the bases provided for them by the articulation of human beings according to the imperative of mutual recognition. Thus we find already in place, in the first decade of the nineteenth century, not only the underlying basis for the immense upheaval that thinking about human beings would undergo on the basis of madness, but also the concrete foundations for the enterprise of transformation and deciphering through which would be revealed, in the inverse of power over others, the fact that there is a correlated inverse, and a radical one, of the power of a subject over itself.

CHAPTER IX

Openings and Aporia of Moral Treatment

"They All Reason, More or Less"

ESQUIROL'S TEXT is remarkable precisely because it sets forth the first determining point of inflection of the not-very-linear historical process by which the newly acquired power over the other was explored and gradually elucidated. *Des Passions* constitutes a goal reached by indirection. In that text the notion of a reflective foundation on which moral treatment is betting—a notion that Pinel for his part fails to grasp and situate, as we have seen, even though he constantly presupposes it—achieves a more or less consciously assured expression for the first time. Furthermore, Esquirol does much more than simply spell out what remained implicit in Pinel: while he, too, deals with conceptualizations in a cursory and fleeting manner, he nevertheless draws a particularly decisive inference, as we shall see, from the new idea. In this way Esquirol definitively surpasses Pinel; he completes and provides a solid basis for the transformation of the image of madness that his predecessor inaugurated. But this development (which takes to the extreme limit the idea that there is always a way to appeal to the presence to himself that the insane patient has retained) has a counterpart in the other direction, namely, the discovery that there is an inherent limit to the therapeutic possibilities offered by the reflective return toward the self.

If one is seeking to cure the insane patient, there is little one can count on but the new grasp that brings the patient back to himself and pulls him away from his incoercible impulsive plunge into nonreflection. And yet this grasp does not suffice. The lucid distance with respect to his disorder that has been conquered can coexist, in the patient, with an invincible persistence of the same disorder. Something else is needed, something that Esquirol provisionally seeks, out of desperation, by reactivating the ancient doctrine of crises. However, he quickly localizes it instead in the instrument that is also capable par excellence of "making the insane patient reflect upon his state," capable of totally reshaping him, of recomposing his personality ex nihilo: the asylum. Thus the same movement that brings the insane patient back among the beings who have steady reasoning power also condemns him to immersion in the anonymity of the asylum mechanism.

The theoretical elucidation of approaches to practice thus has a rebound effect. For Pinel, this dimension of the reflective gap retained the status of an underlying but unformulatable intuition. By making it explicit, Esquirol finds in it the means to do away with the limits that his mentor assigned to moral treatment. On several occasions, Pinel emphasized that a particular form of alienation compelled him to free himself from the framework of "analysis" as established by Locke and Condillac; Pinel himself saw this form as emblematic of the novelty of his approach, and indeed, owing to its nature as a compromise formation, it symbolizes the historical ambiguity of his work reasonably well. He is referring to the well-known *"mania that consists exclusively in damage to the will,"* or mania without delirium. Pinel includes a whole chapter under this heading (in the English translation, "The Functions of the Will Exclusively Diseased") in the section of his *Treatise* devoted to moral treatment, precisely in order to mark the limits of which the therapeutic enterprise needs to be aware.

For an extended period of time, at Bicêtre, Pinel had in his care

> a maniac whose symptoms appear totally inexplicable upon the principles of Locke and Condillac. His insanity was periodical. His paroxysms generally returned after an interval of several months. The first symptom was a sensation of great heat in the umbilical region, which was felt to ascend progressively to the chest, neck, and face. To this succeeded a flushed countenance, wildness of the eyes, and great distension of the veins and arteries of the head. No sooner was the brain itself invaded, than the patient was suddenly seized by an irresistible propensity to commit acts of barbarity and bloodshed. Thus actuated, he felt, as he afterwards informed me, a contest terrible to his conscience arise within him, between this dread propensity which it was not in his power to subdue, and the profound horror which the blackest crime of murder inspired. The memory, the imagination, and the judgement of this unfortunate man were perfectly sound. He declared to me, very solemnly, during his confinement, that the murderous impulse, however unaccountable it might appear, was in no degree obedient to his will.[1]

Pinel offers this description in order to establish something self-evident: "It is easy to see, that paroxysms of this nature *admit not of the application of moral remedies.* The indication must, therefore, consist in their prevention by evacuants . . . or suppression by antispasmodics."[2] Nowhere is the speculative difficulty that has already invincibly stumped Pinel more obvious than in this description: the problem is how to incorporate explicitly the reflective dimension at the very heart of madness, how to conceive in a direct and sure way the intertwining of the subjective presence maintained by the patient and the radical challenge to it in his alienation. Here the tension is at its peak: tension on the one hand between the felt necessity to conceptualize the conflictual coexistence of a human being who remains entirely a being of reason—"the memory, the imagination, and the judgement . . . were perfectly sound"—and that same human being's absolutely unreasonable behavior, and tension on the other hand between that need to conceptualize and the nevertheless insurmountable impossibility of grasping the way those two aspects are intertwined and mutually present. On one side, there is undivided intellectual integrity; on the other, an "impulse" that is completely lacking in thought or meaning. An internal "contest" is being staged, to be sure, but between a subject who is purely external to the insanity of his acts, and a totally blind, rigorously senseless "fury."

The most traditional image of madness—a violence whose wild excessiveness is on a par with its wholesale absence of sense—thus turns out to be reintroduced even in the operation that destroys its foundations in other respects by recognizing in the insane person a clear presence to herself. It is as if Pinel can only introduce this conscious dimension (which, by and large, he does not succeed in integrating, and which he can only presuppose) explicitly if he posits it as unmitigated, except that he is appealing at the same time to the most archaic model of senseless automatism or nonreflection in action. For Pinel, either the patient's madness is tacitly recognized as mitigated (but then the reflective presence cannot really be designated within it), or else the patient is split between a straightforwardly identified conscious power and a subjective gap, but this time at the price of relegating madness to opaque impulsiveness and pure disorder.

At the center, the same crucial, irreducible, unthinkable element is pivotal: the idea that presence to self and estrangement from self may coexist, that they may be articulated in the same place, that one must in fact constantly hold them together. Thus one might say that it is when he succeeds in bringing the active core of his discovery to light, paradoxically, that Pinel turns out to be the most reactionary, putting the retrograde image of the "raging maniac" back into circulation, the image of an insane person who is enclosed (even if she is also somehow separated from it) within the blindness of a violence over which no one has any control. For after all, what weight can the ordinary rules of moral treatment have up against the juxtaposition of an intact understanding and an unbounded letting go? The insane patient's "dread propensity" (in a more literal translation, the "ferocious drive of a destructive instinct") marks the individual's complete absence to herself; it authorizes no hope whatsoever of awakening a remnant of return to the self. And, on the other side, the patient's undoubted "profound horror" for what she experiences as a "hideous crime" confers no power on her to restrain her propensity, her "wretched and irresistible inclination." The insane person is inaccessible in that she is raging; she is inwardly powerless even though in possession of her faculties.

It is on this point that the supplementary step Esquirol takes to clarify the active principle mobilized by moral treatment allows him to intervene in a way that at once dissolves the Pinelian categories and determines the representation of madness. Even in its embryonic state, Esquirol's conceptualization of the paths of the therapeutic process turns out to be a decisive instrument for generalization. To the extent that he himself is able to discern and name the latent power to "reflect on one's state" that the doctor's art must consist in recalling and bringing into play, to the extent that he ends up with a somewhat refined notion of the inextricable conjunction that brings together delirious adhesion and subjective reserve in the insane patient, he can only cast into doubt both the reality of the limit posited by Pinel and the existence of the pure embodiment of insanity that is presumed to justify that limit. For Esquirol, except in accidental circumstances that do not authorize us to come to conclusions about the essence of madness, there is no such thing as a blind explosion that absolutely escapes the one who yields to it. Even in the most virulent extremes, some personal presence always conveys the explosion and virtually offers an assured grasp of it to anyone who knows how to take hold. "Very often, what is called automatic determination, an irresistible impulse to do harm, is the effect of a well-thought-out and often quite methodically reasoned determination."[3]

It is because they have not taken into account this sense-governed activity, because they have not made a serious effort to "separate the principles from their determination" that people have up to this point failed to discover the way insanity is actually cured (ibid., p. 78). "They all reason, more or less; they appear delirious to us only owing to the difficulty we have in identifying the initial idea to which all their thoughts and reasoning, are attached. If it were easy to put oneself in harmony with that mother-idea, we would unquestionably cure a greater number of insane patients" (*Des Passions*, p. 79). If there is a limit to the effectiveness of moral treatment, it does not stem from the nature of impenetrable and unmasterable madness itself, but from our continuing inability to discover the secret roots of the insane person's behavior, to grasp its secret logic, to gain access to the hidden center of gravity (the *"mother-idea"*) that gives his universe its structure and meaning. But there is no such thing as complete absence to self in an impulsiveness that would be at once exempt from the will, imposed from the outside, and devoid of all meaning. Behind the apparently disordered manifestations of insanity, there is a human being who does not necessarily dominate them, to be sure, but who is present to them. They mean something to him; he often calculates them; he actively endows them with signification in every instance: "I could offer an infinite number of examples; they would prove that each alienated patient presents different determinations; that all are moved by an exaggerated passion, by initial ideas that we do not know: it is up to the person treating them to grasp the nuances of all these various disorders" (ibid., p. 80).

When it is a matter of making the point explicitly, things are not always self-evident for Esquirol. We find a telling confirmation of this in the same passage, in a short section where he attempts to account logically for something that observation reveals but that prejudice renders unthinkable; here he returns to a characteristically and significantly Pinelian approach. "Practitioners had not sought to know the patient's moral and intellectual situation: they had judged that his mental faculties were impaired, that they could never be exercised freely. In the greatest pain, are there not intervals of calm and even of pleasure? . . . If there are moments of respite in physical lesions, why would there not be times of remission in moral lesions?" (ibid., p. 79). The difficulty of conceiving of mental faculties simultaneously as afflicted and yet as potentially capable of some degree of free exercise is flagrant here. And what is remarkable about the palliative to which Esquirol appeals is that it is precisely the one that allowed Pinel to carry out the essential aspect of his break with the older view. Unable to pinpoint a site of interpenetration, one can appeal to the model of a necessary alternation between terms that are in some sense logically embedded each within the other. "Does not the vital force, in all circumstances of its activity, need a rest?"

As we have demonstrated in other contexts, Pinel was able to conceptualize the remnant of reason preserved in maniacs (a conceptualization on the basis of which he established his own system of classification) only by referring precisely to the intermittences of mania and by bringing obliquely into play the potentiality of a lucid interval within the crisis.[4] Confronting a problem of the same order, Esquirol uses the same schema: inside the "moral lesion" there has to be a principle of separation that preserves the place or the interval for the reasonable functioning to which the insane patient's reflective determinations attest. We can take this as one more sign, if one is needed, of the focal character of the intellectual obstacle constituted by the conception of the intimate duality that structures alienated subjectivity. Successively displaced, from Daquin through

Pinel to Esquirol, the obstacle was in part removed, but it continued to offer tenacious resistance.

Despite the lapse in Esquirol's thinking noted above, the fact remains that on the whole the point was firmly established for Esquirol as early as 1805. From the outset, he took it further than Pinel did, lending his own text the status of an event: "There are no unreflective determinations. The human being is not a machine: he feels and he determines himself," as he will say, still more clearly, some ten years later. It is true that

> in certain cases of mental alienation, someone who is in some sense withdrawn from the reign of the will no longer seems to be the master of his determinations. The insane are then dominated by their ideas and led to commit acts that they themselves disapprove of. Some, condemned to rest, silence, and inaction, cannot overcome the power that limits their activity; others walk, talk, dance, or write without being able to refrain from doing so; they have been seen to slip away from home with no motive except the need to walk or run for several days on end, scarcely stopping except for a bite of food: others give themselves over to acts of rage that they later regret.[5]

But appearances can be deceptive. "These irresistible directions, these automatic determinations, as the authors call them, seem to be independent of the will, and yet they stem from motives of which the alienated patient and those observing him are not very well aware."[6] Thus "a departmental tax collector, after undertaking a long and difficult accounting task, is afflicted with mania; the attack ends in melancholia complicated by dementia and paralysis. For several days he refuses to drink with his meals: the staff insists; he exclaims, *What, rogue, you want me to swallow my brother!*" What could be more extravagant, more devoid of any sort of foundation, more absurdly insane, at first glance, than such a remark? "Reflecting on this abrupt outburst," Esquirol continues, "I notice that the patient sees his own image in the bottle sitting on his table; I move the bottle, and from then on he drinks without difficulty."[7] There are always reasons, motives, logical threads. They are sometimes difficult to discern, but their intervention must be assumed to be a given in every instance. It is not because one does not understand that there is nothing to understand. In other words, there is always a singular, personal meaning ("each insane person presents different determinations") that the individual invests more or less obscurely in her own behavior, however alienated she may be. In however confused a fashion, she remains present, through this meaning, to the entirety of her own conduct—and consequently open to treatment. For the obligatory engagement of oneself in one's acts offers a point of access that the doctor can use; it even provokes the optimistic postulate that one could cure a patient's alienation almost without lifting a hand if one always succeeded in reaching its real roots ("if it were easy to put oneself in harmony with that mother-idea, we would unquestionably cure a greater number of insane patients").

Once he has conquered this initial idea, Esquirol continually returns to it, reaffirms it, and develops it in various respects. He uses it to dissolve definitively the old image of the insane person's fury, the emblem par excellence of the oblivion and external loss of self, the extreme case that is always discreetly required by someone like Pinel for the intelligibility of madness overall. Esquirol objects that fury is "just an accident, a symptom, the *anger* of delirium" from which no conclusion can be drawn as to the intimate essence of mental alienation. And he makes an observation that is infinitely more disqualifying for that familiar symbol of extreme insanity: "Like all the other determinations of madness, fury is never automatic, in the sense that raging maniacs never yield to their impulses without a motive. It is always to avoid or shunt aside some danger that they believe is threatening them, to resist real or imagined hindrances, or finally to take revenge on those whom they see as their enemies."[8] Esquirol takes up the same critique once more, this time explicitly, against the last operative avatar of the notion of fury that was constituted by the Pinelian category of mania without delirium—a category that *Des Passions* targets manifestly, though not explicitly —in his 1818 article "Mania." "It is still true that what has been called reasoning madness, mania without delirium, [and] maniacal fury, belong rather to monomania or to melancholia, and that the acts those insane individuals commit are always the result of delirium, however transitory one may suppose it to be."[9]

But the most noteworthy positive development to which Esquirol is led by this methodical refusal to acknowledge the existence of nonsense, unmotivated behavior, or raw disorder in the insane patient is doubtless the construction of the concept of hallucination. By looking beyond the external incoherence and the appearance of pure disorder for the logical connections between a thought and a behavior that are in the last analysis attached to a hidden source, by striving to "put himself in harmony" with the *mother-idea* in which delirium originates, Esquirol inevitably came to identify, outside of the orderly course of thought properly speaking, the primitive factor of rupture we know as hallucination. Moreover, if there is no intrinsic flaw in the order of reason in the mind, if we are not dealing with a disorganization of personal capacity as such, then madness must impose itself on the subject from the outset as an element at once external and in itself irrefutable. This seems to us to be the quasi-deductive reasoning that brought Esquirol from an inaugural postulation of meaning and subjective presence to the discovery of an original materialization of the content of alienation in the perceptual register. He saw the irreducible kernel of estrangement from the self as the unstoppable breach that has emerged in the reference points of the outside world.

We find strong indications of this in the first two texts in which the notion of hallucination appears explicitly. These texts also make it quite clear that Esquirol introduces this notion as a *cause*. First, the article "Delirium" in the *Dictionnaire des sciences médicales* (vol. 8, 1814):

> False sensations, without any perceptible alteration of the sense organs, and consequently dependent on an internal cause, presenting to the mind objects that do not really exist, *necessarily produce delirium*: such is the state of someone who believes he sees objects that are out of range of his senses, someone who persuades himself that his perceptions are the faithful image of external objects, because the sensations he is experiencing at the moment are as vivid, and seem to him as accurate, as those that the same objects aroused in him when he was not ill. . . . *Hallucinations* are the most frequent cause of delirium.[10]

In the same year Esquirol published a brief observation under the title "Suicidal Tendency Subsequent to a Hallucination of Hearing." He considered the term still unfamiliar enough at this point to warrant a note: "Hallucination: from the Latin *allucinatio*, 'error.'" "I have seen many nervous illnesses," he began, "many cases of delirium that depended on false perceptions of hearing. *The illusions of sensations are almost always the cause of delirium.*"[11] As a result, in our view, there is no room for doubt: what is being pinned down as Esquirol brings to light the phenomenon of hallucination is the quest for the mother-idea "to which all [the insane patient's] thoughts and reasoning are attached," a source idea whose synthesis between inside and outside, between the irrefragable aspect of what is perceived and the undeniable interiority of causation that is realized in hallucination provides a logically satisfying image.

We could look at the problem the other way around, moreover, and say that if Esquirol was the first to identify the hallucinatory phenomenon in its true originality, the reason was that the presuppositions governing his research could only alert him to the contradictory tension between the materiality of the manifestation and the ideality of its origin and tenor, between the positivity of its form and the subjectivity of its substance, between its perceptual certainty and the independence of its sense organs; he could then characterize this singular supplement of perception in its specificity, this perception so strangely lacking a world, in terms of that contradictory tension.

Esquirol returned later on to this source idea that continually and decisively inspired him, the idea that in the insane patient there is no act that does not refer to a constituted motive. He took it up again at the end of his scientific career, twenty years after his first formulation, but this time he limited its sphere of validity, or at least he recognized the existence of an order of phenomena that escapes such a rigorous determination. He accomplished this in the heat of the medico-judicial debate on responsibility, as it was crystallized around 1825 by the enigma of motiveless, cold-blooded murder. Putting his own authority behind theses that had already been publicly defended by his student Georget, and in the process retreating from the rigor of his initial postulate by conceding the existence of a noteworthy exception, Esquirol belatedly acknowledged a particular type of *homicidal monomania* "in which one can observe no intellectual or moral disorder."[12] Is this a pure and simple return of mania without delirium, "blind impulses," "irresistible drives," and other "unthinking determinations"? Only on the surface. For, in the first place, if these categories of absence to self do recur, they do so independently of the solid, traditional model of fury that, in Pinel's writings, overtly gave them coherence. There is no longer anything furious in homicidal monomania, no longer any uncontrollable effervescence or excess in the outburst. A murderer may make a sudden move, without provocation, and commit an atrocious act, but it is a precisely defined act. For, in the second place, if a flaw is revealed through which an image of the *senseless* appears (an image one might have thought abolished), the explanation is not that the fundamental constraint that had led Esquirol to posit that the insane person never acted without a motive definitively gives way before these surprisingly discordant behaviors. It is rather that, between the absence of a motive of which the subject is unaware and the presence of an avowed reason, we must introduce a category that is not so much intermediate as of a different order: the intervention of a motive of which the subject is unaware, but that can be, if not deciphered, then at least related to the fundamental elements of the subject's organization—with a system of instincts for example—through the objective determination of the act that escapes him.

Here is the beginning of another story in which, transformed but maintained, the imperative of referring every phenomenon and behavior indicative of alienation to a subjective foundation, however aberrant it may seem, will gradually unveil an unknown aspect of the human subject. We shift from a motive that is hard to discern from the outside, but positively present, however confusedly, in the mind of the alienated patient, to a motive that the observer can reconstruct in terms of the logic manifested in the act, but one that is radically removed from the consciousness of the individual who is acting. Such is the crucial bifurcation that is initiated with what we are tempted to call Esquirol's regressive renunciation, as he introduces the notion of homicidal monomania that he had earlier rejected in the name of the nonexistence of unthinking determinations. It actually provides him with a way of becoming receptive to something that could not have been accommodated within the initial framework on the basis of a conventional rejection of the senseless—for while the unmotivated may not exist, the unconscious does.

At the deepest level, it has to be understood that the dissolution of the traditional images of complete externality to self, a dissolution announced in *Des Passions*, ceases to be operative on the surface only because it has become definitively, structurally acquired. No one can see the impulse to commit murder "without interest, without motive, without derangement" as the equivalent of a paroxysmal forgetting of self manifest externally in the form of automatic violence; yet there is still a covert obligation, even if at the time it cannot be overtly assumed, to relate this act that has no immediately graspable motive to a personal root that in some respect makes it necessary from the standpoint of the psychic organization of the individual who commits it. To the extent that he can presuppose this limiting reading, Esquirol finally compromises on his primary requirement—to the extent that he views as irreversibly assured a process that he began to undertake along the two axes of passion and reflection, a process leading to the defeat of the view that the insane person is situated outside of meaning, unaware of herself, and fundamentally different from other human beings. Human beings continue to resemble one another even in madness, whose forms continue to resemble the human experience of passion. The alienated subject persists in his own behavior, which he keeps on endowing with order, connections, and meaning. The same work of deconstructing the alterity, the externality, and the heterogeneity of insanity goes on between these two poles. The individual who is prey to estrangement from himself does not abandon himself and does not pass into an undecipherable mechanistic void; alienation in general does not entail crossing the boundaries of the human. Just as the types of alienation remain within a space marked off by the known types of passion, the behavior of the insane person continues to inscribe itself wholly within the personal sphere of meaning. These are two moments, at two different levels, of the same process of integration.

From the outside, if we view them correctly, the manifestations of madness can be reduced to the various configurations that the violent affections of human beings can take on. The development of the idea of moral treatment, and in particular the attempt to combat the limit Pinel assigns it by guaranteeing it a foundation in universal law, leads Esquirol to add a second component to the initial reconquest of a principle of belonging and recognition. From the inside, for someone who can "put himself in harmony" with what is happening in the insane person, the statements he makes, like the acts he commits, have to be viewed within a logical framework of intentions and motivations whose original elements may escape us but whose underpinnings and influence, at least, can always be identified.

Thus by eliminating the vestiges of the archaic representation of madness that remained in Pinel's so-called mania without delirium (madness as self-abandonment and self-annihilation through blind impulse), Esquirol completes the Pinelian break and simultaneously spells out the thought that has inspired him from beginning to end: that the subject's alienation always entails a persistence of the subjective dimension, that powerlessness in the face of what has me in its grip does not prevent my active presence to what removes me from myself. Except that once this reinsertion of madness within the subjective circle has been successfully achieved, once this compulsory but conscious commitment of the *I* to delirium (to speak the way Esquirol began to speak in 1814[13]) has been explicitly recognized, the reflective dimension thus established, no longer revolutionary, becomes in turn an obstacle and a mask. That there is meaning for the subject is one thing; that she possesses meaning is another thing entirely. Granted, there are no "automatic" acts. But the commitment that binds the individual to what she does, no matter how powerfully determined and motivated, may very well still escape her, radically. Among all the forms of presence to self, in other words, might there not be one that passes specifically through the nonreflective dimension? A nonreflective dimension of a new type, most certainly. Not opaque randomness, not the raw disorder of the raging maniac, not the definitively fluent absence, in its materializations, of a being irremediably forgetful of herself, but a recoverable nonreflective dimension, open to elucidation, capable of being reintegrated into the field of reflection but rigorously cut off, indiscernible in its effective proximity and all the more disconnected in that it is immediately active.

This accounts for Esquirol's belated reversal, and his return to the problematics of the nonreflective dimension: these moves were called for not only by the circumstances but also by the internal movement of an exploration. Once the empty externality to self into which the insane person had previously been presumed to have fallen has been dismantled, once her subjective participation in the collectivity and conscious presence to the aberrations that permeate her have been established, what emerges very quickly is the existence of an internal heterogeneity. As long as one could place one's faith in images of a being who was absent to herself and who had become radically other both for herself and for other human beings, there was no reason to contemplate the possibility of an internal alterity that would have to be reconciled with the irreducible persistence of the subjective dimension; it made no sense. But as soon as one posits in principle that "in the middle of the most violent delirium," as in what seems to be the most incongruous isolated act, everything relates to the somehow reflective activity of an individual (as Esquirol says plainly, "the most complete disorder of the understanding can always be brought back to the *I*"[14]), the inevitable question arises: Might there be a flaw in this power of presence? In the mind of the insane individual, does everything really make immediate sense? Is everything truly attached to premises unknown to us but obvious to her? Does everything stem from motives of which she is aware (however delirious these motives may be in other respects)? These are the questions that confront Esquirol in the light of homicidal monomania and that force him to recognize the intimate heterogeneity at the heart of the reflective field that he had thought he would be able to reform. Apart from this, he can say nothing at all. He cannot even name that heterogeneity except by returning, in a regressive movement that is historically rather common in such matters, to the categories that he himself had banished earlier. And what emerges tentatively here will not be subject to extensive development anytime soon. The fact remains that in this completed trajectory of a thought, there is an irreversible problematic base, a yawning gap that will no longer close: between furious projection of oneself onto the outside and lucid proximity to oneself, between "automatic" nonreflection and reflective presence, there is room for an unnameable third term.

The Circle of the Passions

It is worth noting the hiatus to which his undertaking leads Esquirol (and of which he is aware) concerning the nature or rather the subjective place of madness. Esquirol is invincibly led to split that subjective place between the affective register on the one hand and the intellectual register on the other; he does not succeed in dominating the movement of exchange that takes him from the one to the other and that leads him to bring together the divergent points of view. Nothing attests better to this, indeed, than the split between the historical context of his thinking and the archaic nature of the notions on the basis of which (and largely because of that nature) the first psychiatric concepts were forged. Consequently, nothing better illuminates the necessary discontinuity of the subsequent history of psychiatry, which could only constitute a break in many respects with its founders' frames of reference. For if the backward character of the representations of the human economy on which Pinel and Esquirol relied served them well at first (in particular the imaginary physiology of an epigastric center), it quickly enclosed them in a network of inextricable difficulties: a perfect example is found in Esquirol's oscillations between the passions and the intellectual faculties. These are difficulties that only the elaboration of an entirely different anthropology could possibly resolve. Hence the inescapable subsequent displacement of the very bases for reflection: in order to continue, the development of the founding intuitions had to presuppose a pronounced break with the language in which they were formulated, and still more with the image of subjective organization on which they relied.

Esquirol starts with the passions. That is his only option. The eccentricity of the seat of madness in relation to the cerebral seat of the intellectual faculties offers for him, as for Pinel, the only way to represent the enigmatic survival of subjective power amid the shipwreck of reason. But since he, unlike Pinel, pushes the elucidation of this preserved personal presence quite far, through observing the effects of moral treatment, he is led directly to situate madness at the very heart of reflective power. This power is at once maintained (the insane patient continues to reason and to motivate her behavior) and affected in one of its essential properties (the insane patient, on the other hand, is not free at least in relation to a "mother-idea" that imposes itself absolutely on her). The idea persists in *Des Passions*, but Esquirol does not pursue it. He elaborates on it later, in correlation with a more extensive development of the critique of "automatic impulses" and "unthinking determinations" from which it stems directly. Thus he notes in the article "Délire" that the faculty of drawing away from or moving closer to "objects that are presented to the senses" is the one that seems specifically affected in the delirious individual; this accounts for the insane person's mastery of her relation to some of his representations. This idea is pinned down and refined in the article on madness as an attention disorder: "The insane patient no longer enjoys the faculty of fixing or directing his attention: this deprivation is the underlying cause of all his errors."[15] Thus madness is an intrinsic disorder of the power normally attached to the presence to oneself. That presence is not abolished, but somewhere the ability to deal appropriately with the things that present themselves to the mind (an ability that might have been thought indissociable from that presence) breaks down. Still, the ability does not entirely disappear. "The attention is so essentially damaged by one of these three modes in all insane persons, that if a pleasant sensation grips the attention of the maniac, if an unexpected impression distracts the attention of the monomaniac, if a violent commotion stirs the attention of the demented patient, the insane person becomes reasonable at once, and this return to reason lasts as long as he remains in control of directing and sustaining his attention."[16]

We have shifted from viewing the passions as the symptoms par excellence of alienation to viewing alienation as an intimate, special, "essential" disorganization of the faculties of understanding. The two views are not necessarily incompatible, moreover. For Esquirol, they are unrelated, but they coexist (in the same article on madness, he says again that "the causes that produce madness, the symptoms that characterize it imprint on mental alienation all the features of the passions"[17]). What is lacking, and for powerful reasons, is a unifying viewpoint from which the two aspects of the phenomenon can be held together, from which their mutual dependency can be investigated and the modalities of their interpenetration envisaged. The anatomical duality of their respective seats in the body is an insurmountable obstacle; the doctrine of the sympathetic actions of the epigastric center cannot reconcile the duality. To be sure, even in Esquirol's day, the disjunction is soon abandoned owing to progress in studies of the nervous system. Instincts and passions leave the viscera and return to proximity with the intellectual faculty in the brain, profoundly transforming the way the exchange and the connection between them is understood. The entire history of basic anthropology from this point on might be described as a history of the fusion between the two elements that are thus reunited anatomically, under the constant pressure of psychopathological data revealing their close association. All the same, if such is indeed the overall movement, it does not seem complete, nor is it destined to resolve all problems. To judge indeed by certain recent discussions, the problem of the intimate solidarity uniting "affect" and "representation," as we are inclined to say today, remains decidedly thorny. The clear difference that separates us from Esquirol is that we are convinced of the unity of the two orders of phenomena, whereas even though the logic of Esquirol's object led him to move from one aspect to another, he clearly did not see them as unified. But then again, even now we have not yet finished establishing this primordial junction whose existence we sense.

In *Des Passions*, Esquirol briefly hints that mental alienation is a specific disorder of reflective organization (later seen as an "attention disorder"), but he does not really develop the idea. Even so, he stumbles up against the division that his approach makes inevitable, and he has to acknowledge the other aspect that the passions, as "causes, symptoms, and curative means," simultaneously reveal and allow to escape. Thus he writes, of the difficulties and the extreme dangers of using repression as a "means of direction or treatment": "It is limited either to focusing the imagination, shocking it powerfully, or else to inspiring a feeling of fear that tames and subjugates the maniac, and allows him to give in to the impulses he is receiving. The effects of shocking the imagination must not enter into my work; they belong to the study of *the intellectual faculties considered as causes, symptoms, and means of curing mental alienation*; which must be the subject of another treatise" (*Des Passions*, p. 54). But how does "focusing" or "shocking" the imagination by a "powerful apparatus" differ from the other techniques that make "the insane person turn back within himself" or that lead him to "reflect on his state"—isolation, for example, which creates a sense of "the necessity of a dependency from which one cannot remove oneself"? What is happening here, quite simply, is that as he writes Esquirol is becoming aware of the drift of his undertaking, becoming conscious of the exact nature of the ways and means that he has constantly presupposed throughout his text, and he is making an awkward rhetorical attempt to put things right. Nothing is more artificial, indeed, than the programmatic symmetry he suddenly postulates between the register of the passions and that of the intellectual faculties. Not only is such symmetry belied by the overall economy of his argument, but apparently it will never be pursued or even mentioned again.

Like any other technique of moral treatment, "focusing the imagination" is a way of appealing to the insane person's ultimate capacity to take into account what is happening outside himself, his ability to hear and focus on what his interlocutor is saying. It is a way of playing on the therapist's power to reach the patient, despite all obstacles (including the patient's seeming absence), and of prompting the patient to come back to himself in the process. To be sure, this way of handling reflective difference presupposes that alienation consists somewhere, within the thinking sphere, in a certain "disorder" of the ability to relate to one's own thoughts. As Esquirol understands it, this is why all moral treatment entails an at least tacit understanding of madness as a disorder of the intellectual faculties. He puts that understanding to work later, but within the problematic sketched out in *Des Passions* and not in the form of a distinct and symmetrical second component corresponding to the first; here, he is obliged to recognize it briefly without being able to assume it or do anything but conjure it up in some confusion. It is a revealing way to acknowledge both that disjunction exists and that conjunction is the source of the problem.

The same exchange and reversal occur at the end of the text, but in the opposite direction. Esquirol begins by saying, as we have seen, that if moral treatment is possible the reason is that, contrary to the appearances that kept observers from looking more deeply, the insane actually do reason. They do not act without motives, and consequently one may be assured of gaining access to them through behavior in which they invest quite specific meanings and expectations. In other words, the effectiveness of moral treatment is based on the reflective power that alienation allows to subsist, and thus on the physician's power to play from within on the perceptible difference that continues to separate the patient from himself. Here there is a complete reversal of perspective. On the one hand, the therapeutic enterprise is rooted in what remains of the reasoning faculty in the insane individual; and then, abruptly, on the other hand, one can obviously not use reasoning to dispel alienation or to release the patient from it.

> If one looks at moral treatment as vain and illusory, the reason is that things have not been clear. Moral treatment is not limited to consoling patients, to building up their courage, to repressing their fury, to reasoning with them, to

> combatting the deviance of their imagination; we have never claimed to cure them by arguing with them, and such a claim would be belied by everyday experience: do the passions yield to reasoning? Are not alienation and all its various passions carried to the extreme? To treat them with dialectical formulas and syllogisms would be to be ill-informed about the progress of passions and the clinical history of mental alienation. All the opinions, advice, reasoning, and consolations offered are no doubt means of curing—we have seen many examples of this; but they work only by giving a moral shock, by placing the patient in a state opposed and contrary to his previous one before this means was adopted. (*Des Passions*, p. 82)

The active principle capable of "bringing back reason gone astray" does not lie within reflective difference, even when one has been fully able to mobilize and conquer that difference. "We do not cure by simple arguments; the patients may well hear them, and even understand them, but they lack the power of conviction, a power that is only acquired after a violent shock in melancolia, a type of alienation extremely difficult to cure" (p. 83). The extreme example of melancolia indicates that the insane patient may "be well aware of the disorder of his intellectual faculties," may follow arguments presented to him perfectly, may even try to believe what he is told, and still may not manage to exit from the circle of his cherished ideas; indeed, in the last analysis "he adheres [to them] all the more strongly the more one attempts to dissuade him." What is more, the insane patient himself may "feel the full ridiculousness of his delirium, know everything necessary to dissipate it, reason about his illness better than anyone," and as it were "apply moral treatment to himself" (*Des Passions*, p. 84) and still fail in his struggle against himself. "I know all that, but my idea is here, and I am not cured." He is lacking a specific trigger that in addition to separating him from his delirium and ridding him of it intellectually, would cut him off from it all at once or bring him out of it definitively—something that would dissipate, as Esquirol puts it aptly, the spell "that prevents him from conceptualizing what he understands" (ibid., p. 85). What is lacking is this supplementary impulse, this infinitesimal and critical force of rupture that would allow him to recover himself fully; instead, a mysterious and intangible separation prevents him from completely accepting what he nevertheless clearly manages to understand quite well, and this extreme degree of impotent lucidity adds the finishing touch to the argument that the missing element cannot arise from within the reflective sphere.

If there has to be a break in "the vicious chain of ideas" or a dissolution of their "desperate fixity," it can only come from the outside, not in the form of an increase in the acuity of the individual's sense of his own alienation, but in the form of a destabilizing irruption that upsets the equilibrium of the patient's relation to his own delirious conceptions. In other words only the intervention of a subversive power capable of completely overturning the order of thought, or of disturbing it locally but radically (even though that power itself is foreign to thought), can in the last analysis allow the subject to let go of the belief that invincibly keeps him from carrying out that operation himself—and where is that power to be found except in the passions?

Thus we have returned to the starting point, in a way; we have come back to the passions as the most logically plausible causes of mental alienation, since they can subvert the exercise of the intellectual faculties without abolishing them or threatening their essential integrity. The same reasoning brings them back in, in the final phase, as curative means that are in principle unsurpassable, for once the violent moment of their effervescence has passed, their anarchic force of destructuration without destruction leaves open every opportunity for reorganization. This gap proper to the passions, the gap between their current reign and their potential innocuousness, is what initially supplied the metaphoric support on the basis of which the reflective presence and the personal cohesion at the heart of madness could be conceived and discerned. This same gap returns at the end, where Esquirol is attempting to give credence to the idea that the obstacle discovered at the heart of the insane person's difference from himself might be overcome. Skillfully used, that difference might be expected to confer on him a certain power to get a grip on himself and free himself from his madness. "It is thus not in a series of arguments that the resources of the moral treatment of mental alienation can consist, but rather in the direction given to the patient's passions" (ibid., p. 85).

Crisis as a Way Out: An Asylum-Based Solution

At all events, what is at stake in this ultimate reversal is much more than the indefinite circularity to which Esquirol's premises and categories condemn him. What is at stake is bringing to light an authentic aporia: how to grasp a human subject who is insolubly split in two? The very features that establish the possibility and the effectiveness of moral treatment at the same time set its limit and make its outcome undecidable. Such an unsurpassable antinomy can be glimpsed behind the shift from the intellect to the passions; it is in part masked by this shift, to the extent that the shift is presented as a solution.

To appreciate the basic contradiction that is uncovered in the process and that the passions are called upon in the end precisely to surmount, we need only consider the fate of a single example. Esquirol uses it twice, in completely opposing contexts. In the first place, it illustrates the internal dynamics of the process of healing; in the second place, on the contrary, it points up the insurmountable obstacle to that process. The example stems from a patient's remark, which Esquirol saw as shedding particular light on the reflective relation of the insane patient to his disorder, the relation within which moral treatment operates. "'If I could believe, as you do, that I am mad, I would soon be cured,' one of them said to me," Esquirol reports the first time, "'but I cannot make myself believe it'" (ibid., p. 35). Esquirol recalls the incident to support his analysis of the chain reaction effects of isolation, from the shock provoked by the forced move to a strange place to the "moral contrast" aroused by treatments for which the patient is not prepared. "A healthy fear, the necessity of a dependency from which one cannot remove oneself, and hope will make him return to himself, will begin to let him glimpse the possibility that he is ill; and is not this result the surest guarantee of the patient's cure?"

The whole problem—and here is where the rupture of isolation comes into play in a decisive way—is how to provoke the initial movement of the patient's return to himself. From the moment this movement is triggered, a natural dynamic of awakening consciousness can only lead little by little to a total distancing from the state in which the individual had earlier been blindly trapped; correlatively, it must lead to the patient's complete recovery of his personality. As soon as the patient has been brought to the point of beginning "to glimpse the possibility that he is ill," the distance between the patient and his alienation then inevitably begins to widen on its own; the process can be expected to lead to complete separation and to the very clear feeling, the "conviction," as Esquirol says, on the patient's part that he has been in the grip of a pronounced estrangement from himself.

In Esquirol's example, his patient does not succeed in consenting to such an emancipation from his mad conviction; in this context, his statement illustrates an intermediate step in the process, as it were. Although he is still caught up in the net of his uncontrollable certainties, the insane patient is at the same time already lucid enough to see for himself what the next step toward cure ought to be; he is lucid enough to appreciate what separates him, no matter how narrow the gap, from giving up his delirious idea entirely. Whereas in a second stage, the insane person's same admirable lucidity about the infinitesimal step that would be required for him to be detached from his madness, about the tenousness of the screen that "prevents him from conceiving what he hears," becomes precisely the element that brings moral treatment to a halt. "'I hear very well what you are saying to me,' a young melancholic said to me; 'I have no trouble following your arguments; if I could understand you and if I could convince myself, I would no longer be mad, you would have cured me'" (*Des Passions*, p. 83). This is repeated to reinforce the passage cited above, where Esquirol shows that the patients may well "hear the arguments made to them, they may even understand them, [but] they lack strength of conviction"—that active supplement, more on the order of energy than logic, that the progressive awakening of their consciousness fails to procure for them as such.

As the patient, I may feel the full ridiculousness of my delirium; I may know what is required for it to be dissipated; I may be convinced that I am ill (to go back to Esquirol's first formulation), and I may be able to reason about my illness better than anyone else (to return to his second formulation [p. 84]); all of this, as we have seen, is by no means "the surest guarantee of cure." I may have acquired a certain distance from the idea that in other respects is controlling me, but I have not acquired the means to get rid of it. An enigmatic and irreducible gap subsists between my knowledge that the idea is totally groundless and the knowledge I would need in order to dissipate the idea effectively, the knowledge that would really abolish the mysterious subjective necessity that in spite of everything imposes the idea on me and subjects me to it.

Moral treatment thus reveals mental alienation as a specific disorder of the subject's relation to himself, of his presence to himself through his thinking (the malady Esquirol is attempting to name when he speaks of an "attention disorder"). Owing to its very nature, this disorder comprises the principle of an equally specific therapeutics that will involve the exploitation of that otherwise vacillating reflective power, and it will entail an effort to help the patient gradually reconquer conscious mastery of himself. In other words, given the nature of alienation, its treatment will quite naturally have to be carried out through an internal regrasping of the difference from onself that can always be assumed in the insane patient. In the last analysis, the therapeutic process that madness in a sense contains and the internal escape route toward which it beckons (the only true escape route on which one can rely) do not suffice to guarantee that madness will end.

In principle, madness can be liquidated through the progressive reflective process through which the subject rediscovers his own distance from the aberrant certainties that had gripped him. But this same process includes a mysterious stopping point of such a nature that full lucidity turns out to be compatible, in extreme cases, with an indestructible delirious deceptive enticement. Esquirol initially argues that, in its virtual dynamics, the movement that detaches the patient from his delirious conviction and restores him to himself offers the possibility of full emancipation from the belief that is costing him his self-possession. Yet Esquirol finally has to concede that the concrete efficacy of the process, even if we assume it runs its full course, remains ultimately undecidable. Here is the enigma of the conscious process: the factor destined to dissolve the human's estrangement from itself may also, on occasion, conserve and as it were contain that estrangement.

But from the standpoint of history the crucial point is not so much the challenge posed by the contradiction in itself as its prophetic value. For the contradiction calls for reactions; it demands responses; and these reactions and responses will have portentous, if not definitive, consequences for the future. There is thus an uncertainty to be lifted, a manifestation to be discovered, an undecidable element to be exorcised. As we have seen, Esquirol's first response was elicited by the entire economy of his argument, and it allowed him to bring the argument to an apparently satisfactory conclusion: passions, "moral shocks," and disturbances of the soul violently disentangle the strangely solid bonds that keep the insane person attached to his ideas despite his awareness of their aberrant nature. But if we take a closer look, we can see that a second response is emerging at the same time in Esquirol's work, a more extreme and more global response, as if the first one were insufficient. This second response can be subsumed by the term *crisis*.

The passage from shock to crisis is a continuous one. There is no cure, Esquirol writes, except "by giving a moral shock, by placing the insane patient in a state opposed and contrary to the one in which he was before this recourse was taken. Do not crises, in acute illnesses, act just the same way in giving the organism a powerful shock? Does crisis not provoke a difficulty, a disorder, an upset from which the whole nature emerges triumphant? Crises are to morbid alterations of solid and fluid what moral shocks are to the illnesses of intellectual and moral man" (p. 82). Thus what is first just an analogy (although an analogy highly charged with implications) is taken up later, as if the identity of the two orders of phenomena were now legitimately established: "Melancholia, like the illnesses that progress without violence and without character, the ones that tend to become chronic, are hard to cure, or to cure completely, unless a *physical or moral crisis* dissipates the thick cloud that obscures the intelligence, breaks the vicious chain of ideas, interrupts the habit of their harmful association, destroys their desperate fixity, or dissipates the charm that prevented the insane patient from conceiving what he heard" (*Des Passions*, p. 85). Esquirol's first important project after the publication of *Des Passions* (along with the beginning of his inquiry into establishments for the insane) consisted in a demonstration of the general validity of the point he had glimpsed in 1805: the doctrine of crises is "at all points" applicable to "the whole order of mental illnesses [*vésanies*]," and in particular to mania. He presented this thesis at length in his *Essai sur les terminaisons critiques de la manie*, which he read at the Société de l'Ecole de médecine on April 26, 1810, and published belatedly only in 1814.[18]

Esquirol's later use of his thesis unambiguously explains the need for such a restriction of the object of study. Perhaps Esquirol is dealing after all only with mania, even if he specifies that the task would have been "much easier" for any other type of illness stemming from "the whole order of mental illnesses," and that precisely the difficulty of the case, and thus its exemplary value, claimed his attention.[19] In fact, what is under discussion is "mania," understood in the sense it has in Pinel's *Treatise on Insanity*. The text in question was included basically unchanged in *Mental Maladies*; in 1838 it becomes "critical terminations *of insanity*." Where in 1810 Esquirol wrote, "I propose to demonstrate that this doctrine [of crises] is, in all respects, applicable to mania," in the definitive version he corrects himself: "in all respects, applicable to *mental diseases*."[20] The term *mania* from the first version is simply eliminated in the same way throughout and replaced according to circumstances by *insanity*, *mental disease*, or *mental alienation*. Thus the key statement summarizing the text's contribution, "Mania *terminates by resolution*,"[21] becomes, in 1838, "Mental alienation *terminates by resolution*."[22]

If crisis emerges in this way at the heart of Esquirol's thinking about mental illness in the immediate wake of *Des Passions*, the reason is that something in the earlier work calls for resolution: the intimate contradiction, in the insane person, between lucid distance from his insanity and powerlessness to break away from it. This contradiction reveals that moral treatment may still find itself in an impasse. Thus we cannot expect a guaranteed outcome, an ultimate deliverance, in the natural continuity of the reflective return that restores the individual to himself. Only an explosive contradiction, an internal revolution, an overturning of the patient's entire being can guarantee personal freedom with any certainty, can bring about an irreversible detachment from the dark shadows of madness, reducing to a sudden shambles the pernicious compromise worked out between the subject and his disorder and requiring a complete reconstruction of the individual's subjective organization. Direct movement from delirium to conscious emancipation of the sort described in *Des Passions* is not impossible. But as Esquirol goes on to say in 1810, "I have constantly observed that the cure for this illness is only palliative or temporary when it is not judged by crises."[23] Nor does moral treatment lose all interest from this viewpoint. On the contrary, more than ever, it allows the doctor to guide the patient toward a favorable outcome. Moral treatment spurs the patient to reflect on his condition and thus sets up in him the conditions for a bitter internal struggle, with the understanding that only the critical paroxysm, which abolishes the conflict by bringing it to its full development, will ultimately terminate or resolve it.

It is not hard to see why the "moral shock," the "shaking up" that is provoked by judicious direction of the passions appeared insufficient from the outset to Esquirol and obliged him to seek a more radical solution at once. The effects of the passions remain punctual and local. No doubt a moral disruption at an opportune moment may be able to detach the insane patient from the idea to which he has been adhering with hopeless obstinacy. But such a disruption stops short of questioning or putting at stake the overall personal economy in which the delirious conception has its place. This is why it remains superficial, "palliative or temporary" in its effectiveness; it lacks the subversive impact needed to accomplish a total restructuring, to reduce contradictions on the level of the individual's entire physical and moral being—an impact that has to come from the explosion of the contradictions themselves—and as a result it lacks the biographical rupture for which the "crisis" logically offers, in contrast, a metaphoric or imaginary model.[24] Esquirol takes what the neo-Hippocratism of the day—which was professed moreover by his mentor, Pinel, and generally shared by the Salpêtrière school[25]—can offer him. The recourse to the notion of crisis and the doctrine it implies is not what really matters. What is important is why such recourse was taken at a given time and in a given context; what matters is the problem for which the recourse to crisis would be the solution.

For as we return to the original difficulty, to the aporia of moral treatment that is discovered like a yawning gap at the end of *Des Passions*, and as we reconstitute the chronology of Esquirol's attempts to surmount it or surpass it, we observe that alongside the doctrinal response constituted by the introduction of the crisis model, there was another response, a practical one (though no less marked by the imaginary) that had more serious consequences, because it ended up taking concrete form on a broad scale, and because it endured. Esquirol may have developed the idea of critical termination in a solid and systematic way in 1810, but he did not move to La Salpêtrière to carry out the work with which we are familiar until the following year. Might it not be that something more than crisis was required? Might the indetermination at the heart of the process through which the madman is apt to exit from his madness call for a manifestation of a different order, a manifestation now materialized in an institutional system simultaneously capable of managing the undecidable aspect of the cure and of responding to it effectively?

The asylum was invented in its definitive form around this time, through the extension of moral treatment to the institution as a whole and the correlative definition of the institution itself as an "instrument for curing." To a certain extent, the asylum can undoubtedly be viewed as one of the developments that resulted from the radical uncertainty about the possibility of overcoming alienation, as that uncertainty was being revealed in the immediate, personal practice of moral treatment. It can thus be seen as one attempt among others to meet and overcome the therapeutic challenge posed in that context. However, this does not suffice to explain the form it actually took. The asylum's form becomes intelligible only if one considers other aspects of the encounter between the problem raised and the social imaginary inherent in the new perspectives of power and history. Historical circumstances alone precipitated the emergence of the asylum as a mechanism with a thoroughgoing therapeutic aim; one aspect of those circumstances has now come under the spotlight. An obstacle assigns an insuperable limit to what the doctor can do with his patient in the context of their direct relation. How can that obstacle simultaneously be acknowledged and overcome? Such is the underlying question that, in addition to pushing him toward a long and methodical study of the application of the crisis model to mental alienation, determined the major thrust of Esquirol's career, as represented by his assumption of the directorship at La Salpêtrière, and involved him, in the framework of a large hospital, in the search for an impersonal system of action to exercise a hold over the mind of the insane patient that would be at once indirect and constant—in short, the search for an institutional mechanism that would transform personalities.

On the one hand, we have the violent resolution of internal struggle through crisis, which allows Esquirol to maintain and reaffirm the essential idea of a specific dynamism of madness that brings it to a favorable outcome. On the other hand, we have a reckoning with the uncertainty about the outcome that this same internal struggle entails (unless a crisis comes along) when one has succeeded in arousing it. This reckoning leads to the assumption that it is useless to push any further in the direction of a reflective gap which, by itself, does not produce detachment from delirium; thus it leads the doctor to give up hope of having any individual impact on the patient. At the same time, there is the possibility of surmounting these obstacles through the use of an overall mechanism that allows the doctor to have complete control over patients without having to deal with them head on.

In one respect, this mechanism generalizes the effect of moral treatment: it diffuses the doctor's presence to its fullest extent without requiring that the doctor actually be in a particular place in person, properly speaking; thus the mechanism constantly refers insane patients back to themselves. But in another respect, this same mechanism simultaneously overcomes the limit of moral treatment and eradicates the aporia of that approach, owing to the silent, invisible but unstoppable operation of total restructuring of subjective individuality that it authorizes. What the explosion of a crisis produces naturally and violently is achieved slowly and imperceptibly, but implacably, by the insane patient's incorporation and dissolution within the anonymous collective body of the asylum. On the one hand, there is a spontaneous break; on the other hand, there is the work of the healing art and the passage of time. Thus the initial history of moral treatment closes around a double imaginary solution to the fundamental problem it was able to raise. But the problem, now covered over, remains henceforth ineradicable, and the illusion in which it was buried has been traversed and dismantled by the work of another history. Insoluble and fecund, the problem will come up again, in another light.

EPILOGUE

Social Divide, Division of the Subject, Mad Rupture

WE HAVE CHANGED. We have become individuals, primary, free, and self-sufficient social atoms. The constitutive paradox of the anthropology of democratic societies is that human beings are for the first time recognized as possessing original and inalienable rights that antedate the collective phenomenon. We are masters of ourselves before the law, externally independent in terms of the community to which we belong; and we are also, and correlatively, the first beings to discover that we are subjugated from within, internally dependent, dispossessed of ourselves by something that comes from nowhere but ourselves. The social emancipation of the individual has as its consequence or fundamental counterpart the revelation of psychic subjection. Ever more in possession of herself from the viewpoint of others, the modern individual is simultaneously a subject who encounters and experiences herself in her own intimate sphere as determined by an aspect of herself that turns out to be inherently inaccessible to her own power. The history of individualization—for the individual continues to come into being, to separate herself, to enclose herself in her own privacy, to affirm herself in her own self-sufficiency—is moreover, and necessarily, a history of personal dispossession or subjective destitution.

We have examined only a minuscule moment in this vast movement, preferring for the time being to take a depth sounding and a stratigraphic pulse rather than offer an overview of the long haul. The moment we have chosen is a privileged one, too, and—to shift our frame of reference from time to space—it is a precisely determined *point*: the point at which what is latent in history is projected into the field of the anthropologically efficacious, the point at which an obscurely renewed vision of the human subject is applied to the specifically human phenomenon of madness. And it is also, by the same token, the Archimedes point owing to which the world of the soul can be raised and shifted. For it is here, for reasons that we have sought to elucidate in part, and for other reasons too that remain to be explored, that the anthropological reversal embedded virtually in the political revolution succeeded right away in becoming operative. The undermining of the powers traditionally attached to consciousness was concretized and condensed in an inaugural figure as a transformation of the idea of becoming-other-to-oneself. Displacement and redistribution from activity to passivity within the subject, simultaneous recognition of an indefectible presence even at the heart of the most pronounced estrangement from self: this is how the rupture with the order of internal mastery, corresponding to the dissolution of the bonds of external dependence that had retained the individual, was initially achieved, in the contradictory representation of a being never sufficiently distanced from herself to alienate herself in a deliberate way, but also never really incapable of absenting herself from herself.

For over a century, a university-based philosophy entirely disconnected from the real historical movement managed to remain ignorant of that event, as of everything else; from the lofty heights of its speculative monopoly, it could continue to recite the antiphon of pure reason, of clear conscience and the moral imperative, thus creating the illusory impression of an immobile and as it were obligatory perpetuation of the classical system of the subject, centered on voluntary force and the free disposition of the self. At the same time, the infinitesimal fissure that opened up around 1800 at the boundaries of human experience continued to widen, disaggregating the monolith behind its immovable surface. The will to evil as embodied in crime, the transgression of the natural laws of desire as exemplified for example by sexual deviation, the known and yet uncontrollable and inexhaustible varieties of the intimate compulsion to believe and to act, the constraining weight of the past in each individual and the invincible logic of personal development, the powerlessness of human beings to bear the spectacle of their mortal limits: there are so many areas in which the presence-absence to self that was originally discovered in mental alienation has been extended, bringing about a complete reconfiguration of the subjective space.

One day it will be necessary to retrace the way in which this doubled figure of difference was silently disseminated, starting with the delirious paroxysm in which it was first imposed and moving on to various forms of rupture with general norms, continually enlarging the domain of the pathological at the expense of the realm of ethical judgment, and ending up with no discernible boundaries between its own domain and what is presumed to be the domain of the normal. But what one will infallibly find at the source of the subject's decentering, is the moment when the fundamental ambiguity of the proximity of man to himself became perceptible experience. Hegel, the last true philosopher, was clear about this in his own way. Without being able to discern the many-faceted and decisive future, to be sure, nor to guess its overall implications at the time, he was at least able—and this alone suffices to differentiate him from his pallid successors—to grasp the extraordinary intrinsic interest of the paradoxical division the alienists revealed in their patients.[1] This was the last encounter between the great tradition of conceptual invention and the genuine process of illumination at work in history. Beyond, there is the landscape of ruins where we still camp out—old words empty of substance, representations floating without language, notions that are at once inevitable and inaccessibly inadequate to the object that they express; a proliferation of useless discourse and an arid silence of felt experience.

But this point of departure near which we have narrowly positioned ourselves is also a point of arrival. It presupposes a lengthy, weighty genealogy, and it blends the results of several histories. It would take another book to sort out the multiple fibers through which the crucial change in the vision of the human being, which has been our principal focus here, is linked to the past, and to situate its meaning within a global transformation spread over centuries. In order for the question of the subject of madness to emerge—the question of madness as a specific disorder of the subjective function and the question of the insane individual as preserving some element of his power as subject—the dimension of the subject as such still had to arrive on the scene. In other words, the founding operation of modern thought still had to be carried out, in a process that extended from Montaigne to Descartes: it consisted in removing the human faculties from the various stages in the ontological hierarchy where they had been dispersed and gathering them together in the single foyer of an agent of knowing who would be henceforth opposed to the world.

The process is itself inseparable from the gestation of Western individualism, which we apprehend under a name without precedent in history, that of *subject*, this being only the internal aspect of what we grasp from the outside under the no less original aspect of the *individual.* Replaced in this way within the social movement in which it appeared, the classical vision of the human being as a reflective being stands as an intermediary formation, at once radically novel owing to the separation and autonomization of the agent of knowing and yet faithful to the ancient symbolic order stemming from the inclusive preeminence of the social over its particular terms.

It would still be necessary to follow the development of this work—the process through which the subjective core presumed to subtend the activity of knowing is discovered—from within, from the Humean moment that marks, with the end of intellectual intuition, the abolition of the last link that maintained humans in immediate and receptive communication with ultimate levels of being, to the Fichtean affirmation of the *I* as the living principle of science. Quite remarkably, moreover, this construction of a subjective core—which turned out to be at once and inseparably a subject of science and an ethical subject—coincides chronologically with the practical triumph of the individual, with his revolutionary entrance into politics as sovereign, but it also coincides with the crisis, in the sphere of psychopathological phenomena, of the conscious power of self over self. In this connection, we would have to look toward what was developed during the eighteenth century around the psychological *I* and its uncertainties or eclipses in order to discern the background of the challenge to the frameworks of self-possession that was posed by the treatment of insanity. How was it possible to move from the subject of reason to that for which we do not yet have a true concept, but only a strong intuitive apprehension, the subject of madness, which both presupposes the philosophers' indivisible *I* and radically challenges it?

Exclusion, Inclusion

Similarly, what we have described as the initial undermining of the insane person's alterity would not have been conceivable without the metamorphoses that embodiments of the Other in general had undergone during the preceding centuries of Western history. These transformations did not materially alter the exclusion of the insane or the perception of the excluded as irremediably different; nevertheless, they made it possible to question both the exclusion and the perception, and even to get around them. The turning point of the 1800s marks the beginning of a third age of madness, an era in which insanity was integrated into human organization as a limit case. This could not have come about without the henceforth famous era of exclusion. Breaking with the time-honored inclusion of insanity among the explicit dimensions of culture, separating the insane from ordinary mortals, the era of exclusion actually permitted each individual to emerge and be recognized in the gap that was in this way shifted toward uncontrollable estrangement. For if it is correct to say that the societies that existed before classical reason and the politics of confinement traditionally reserved a place for madness, each recognizing it in its own way, if it is correct to say, in short, that ancient societies knew how to cope with insanity, we still need to understand the content and the implications of that apparent familiarity or proximity.

In a religious universe, madness has its place, first of all, as an eminent manifestation of the ontological difference between two reigns. Given the abyss that separates human intelligence and divine wisdom, what is instinctively good sense for us is always rightfully suspect as madness in God's eyes; conversely, what seems mad to us may well appear reasonable to God. Thus human beings are necessarily destined to behave like insane people in relation to a supreme and inaccessible wisdom, owing to the limits of their earthly condition. What is more, a "good" madness is possible: the deliberate madness that resolutely turns its back on the stunted maxims of human reason and assumes the impenetrability of ultimate truths is a pathway to the profundity of God. Between those two poles, ineluctable madness and elective madness, the dark shadows of insanity take on the thickness of a constitutive dimension of the human world. They do not by any means exhaust the special problems raised by "natural" madness, but they situate those problems against a background that tends to reduce them to the level of particular cases, especially given that, within the same speculative economy, the submersion of the faculties of the soul by an obscurity emerging from the body is an easily foreseeable special case that attests in its own way to the imperfections of the human condition.

To this we must add, in the second place, the insertion of madness within the collective fabric, an insertion directly linked to the archaic logic of society with which it is the distinguishing characteristic of the modern state to have broken for the first time. What we are describing can be characterized as the explicit reproduction of order starting from disorder, the ritually manifested reinstitution of culture against nature, of the inside against an outside that is by the same token integrated in a way within that for which it serves as a foil. The division between inside and outside is not a de facto division but a formally instituted one; it comes into being, as it were, within the human species, and the insane person, cast out onto the side of nature, primordial savagery, or even straightforward animality, nevertheless remains a figure for humanity at its extreme limit. The insane person is at once a materialization of the other with respect to humanity and an indispensable embodiment within humanity itself of the externality against which humanity has explicitly to be reconquered and constituted. At all events, within such a framework, and apart from any individual experience of madness, we find madness in the form of periodic subversion and ritual reversal, regulated inversion of customs and roles, formally enacted mockery of all things; in short, here again madness takes the form of an internal alterity compared to which the established order is to be restored while its deliberate character is marked. This latter is a wholly social "madness," in no way to be confused with madness as a disorder of the body or with any individual instance of insanity; however, both types of madness have a cultural status that make their recurrence in the collective landscape more or less predictable.

Finally, there is a third, closely related point to consider: all this takes place in a society in which man is fundamentally an other for man. In this society the hierarchy of functions is rooted in the difference between the "races"; the bond of subordination implies an inherent distinction between master and serf; political division is projected, as it has been since the birth of states, as a separation of beings into species. But above and beyond political divisions, all of social life finds itself informed by the representation of a bond between human beings based on an intimate estrangement, in such a way that all true inherent difference finds itself translated in that bond and reflected as alterity of status.

The most striking case in point is obviously that of women, the object of the most ancient inegalitarian division we know, even antedating the one that precipitated all the others through the birth of the state and the introduction of domination within human space. This ancient division can be attributed to "nature" in the social and symbolic sense of the term: the body is invested not only with procreative power but also with a natural force that is external to the human order properly speaking but without which any reproduction of culture would be impossible. Here is an exemplary case of an outside against which a society posits itself in order to institute itself and which then passes inside the society, an outside that until quite recently was universally understood as having to validate itself by excluding women from the most authentically cultural of collective activities; it called for a watertight division between masculine and feminine roles, a clear confinement of each sex within its unlikeness to the other.

But in a world wholly articulated in terms of the postulate according to which essential divisions exist among human beings, more broadly speaking any sort of feature that marks inherent singularity becomes the source of a social gap. In the ancient societies of Europe, the fate of unfortunates of all sorts—people who are inherently set apart because of infirmities that keep them from communicating or belonging, the blind, the deaf, the mentally retarded, the insane, but also those simply marked by nature as deformed or misshapen, for example dwarfs or physically handicapped people—could be understood only in terms of the culture of alterity in which that fate is rooted and integrated. Unlikeness as principle of the social relation: here is the key to the status, so ambiguous to our eyes, of these excluded-included individuals. They are excluded to the extent that they are assigned to and literally confined within the difference that afflicts them. The manifest gap becomes an ontological disjunction: just as master and slave, lord and serf, have nothing in common in the sense that the one finds nothing resembling himself in the other, a person in possession of his faculties has nothing in common with one who is "out of his senses," a person who has "lost his mind."

Having exited from common reason, the insane person is perceived under the sign of essential or species-based externality. This externality is aptly translated by a key cultural feature: the insane person becomes the stuff of spectacle. No one could possibly recognize any aspect of himself in the deranged creature: thus he is very interesting to look at, and still more amusing to arouse and goad—but no more and no less than any other carnival monster or street attraction. There is no surer indication of attitudes toward madness than the instinctive popular tendency to set it up as a curiosity. It was to remove the insane from public mockery that Father Joffré and Saint Jean de Dieu established the confinement of the insane in fifteenth-century Spain. However, the phenomenon of public mockery was simply transferred inside the institution's sheltering walls. Bedlam was closed to visits by the curious in 1770; Bicêtre and La Salpêtrière remained open until after the French Revolution, and it was well into the nineteenth century before the public was prevented from gaping at asylum inmates in the farflung French provinces.

This shift away from making a spectacle of insanity is one of the most reliable indications we have of the content and impact of the psychiatric revolution. Psychiatry is invested, on the contrary, with an assumption of identity that is inscribed in the general process of equality. But at the same time, it is true that the status of alterity is intrasocial; it implies neither rejection of the other nor denial of his existence. Just as master and slave, or a fortiori husband and wife, live in proximity as complementary (because heterogeneous) elements of a social whole even though they view each other as absolutely dissimilar, the insane person is admitted as one type of creature that enters into the plan of the world, a specific and necessary fragment of the universal truth, no matter how much he is presumed to be set apart in his difference. This mode of social relation has a fundamental ambiguity that is hard for us to grasp in retrospect. It establishes solidarity on the basis of difference, indeed inherent difference; it links beings all the more inseparably in that it divides them; it makes them indispensable to one another to the extent that it makes them deem themselves incomparable to one another. We can thus speak quite justifiably of the socialization of the insane person in such a framework, or of her integration into the collective landscape, but only provided that we consider the fact that the socialization and the integration in question are anchored in a social arrangement that is at precisely the opposite pole from recognition of identity, in which our own reference points as believers in human equality and human likeness would make us approve such a socialization or integration. It is precisely to the extent that I find nothing at all of myself in an insane person, to the extent that I encounter her as perfectly other, that I accept her at the same time as an inevitable link in the great chain of being—while not letting that acceptance deprive me of the joyous cruelty authorized by difference that the good souls who preach to us today about the warmhearted virtues of traditional communities would do well to ponder.

The celebrated "Great Confinement" corresponds to the spectacular collapse of the coherent traditional organization in both of its aspects. It corresponds to the dissolution of the bonds that integrated madness into culture and kept the insane person at the heart of society, but it also marks the opening of a breach in the alterity that shut the insane person off within himself. Also destined to disappear, in the course of the vast religious overhauls produced by the Reformation and the Counter-Reformation, were the great themes of Christic Folly or the Madness of God, which had provided human insanity with metaphysical dignity. At the same time, under pressure from the authorities, festivals and other carnival rites of the insane, faded away, along with a whole system of popular culture that had been focused on the same need to signify, by clowning mockery or mad subversion, the regular rebirth of the established order within the collective cycle. The phenomenon had deep connections with the new role taken on by the decisive player of the era: the absolutist state. The mechanisms of symbolic institutions lost their ancient forms as a direct consequence of the affirmation of the political function; the agency of domination was irresistibly taking over and tending to take monopolistic control of the entire set of tasks connected with maintaining and ensuring collective cohesion.

There is no more need for communities to do any recurrent internal work on themselves, once an ostensible and unimpeachable locus of power stands out, a locus of power capable of imposing the preeminence of its own viewpoint everywhere, and thus capable of making constantly perceptible the conformity of the course of events to the decrees of a higher will. Here we can grasp the articulation of the two aspects of the transformation: on the one hand, the eradication of the vision of madness as a dimension of the human world—an eradication that in a single stroke strips madness bare and naturalizes it, or rather reduces it to its naturalness, to its contingent factuality; and, on the other hand, in close connection with the control newly won by political authority, the advent of brand new pragmatic forms of behavior—which can be subsumed under the generic term *exclusion*—with respect to insanity, insanity having been restored to its raw individual truth. Two factors have to be taken into account: the substitution of the viewpoint of equality for that of alterity, and the reshaping of the division between the social inside and outside.

When the state becomes sovereign, when it posits itself as a specifically political reference, at once unique and general for the social body as a whole, there is fundamentally no more room (we are speaking of the logic of the process that underlies a slow and complex unfolding) for the notion of an interhuman alterity like the one that prevailed in earlier societies. In the first place, and this is a key feature, there exists henceforth in society a place compared to which all human beings are potentially alike inasmuch as they are political subjects: hence the idea of equal rights that is contained implicitly in the very fact of sovereignty, and the inexorably leveling action of the central authority.

But it is not only the definition of the personal status of the "outside" of each individual taken separately in his relation to power that changes. The definition of the "inside" of direct relations among individuals also evolves. We now know that we are part of the same whole, which is moreover a homogeneous whole from the viewpoint of the agency that manages it. Between myself and any other member of the community to which I belong, there is necessarily *likeness.* It is impossible for me to look at anyone purely from the outside, to view her as absolutely separated, without common measure with myself—impossible thus to view her in the ways that, in older societies, used to go hand in hand with full recognition of the radically other in all its legitimacy. According to that earlier view, we were ontologically different, thus mutually indispensable. The egalitarian revolution conveyed by the modern state replaces that system of dissimilarity with one of reciprocal belonging, forcing beings to discover themselves substantially in one another instead of simply having to recognize and acknowledge one another's existence.

The new system has an inevitable corollary: in the presence of a true other—an insane person, for example—who exhibits a difference that is apparently as irreducible as it is intolerable, there is need for rejection, denial, even elimination; those are ways, after all, of achieving the general likeness of beings by severing from the whole any who might pose a problem for the collective identity. In earlier times, when one could apprehend others under the sign of perfect strangeness, there was no reason for exclusion. What gives rise to exclusion is not the fabrication of an other where one had previously found likeness; it is, on the contrary, the secret obligation to decode likeness where one had gotten along very well with unalloyed alterity. The vacillation of the symbolic framework that produced the obvious alterity of the insane person, and the perspective of the essential community of human beings that was imperceptibly imposed by the political mechanism, made problematic and unbearable the social presence of the mad creatures who had become other both for themselves and for their fellow human beings. With the advent of modern democracy, it became impossible to assume a proximity that was nevertheless obscurely acknowledged, threatening, and all the more incomprehensible in that the cultural forms that in a way necessitated the insane person's existence had unraveled. There was no longer any fundamental reason for madness to exist: this is what severed it from the world and, very significantly, removed it from sight, even though in reality it continued for some time to be exposed inside hospital walls to the gaze of ordinary people avid for the spectacle. The lag is nevertheless telling. It was no longer absolutely certain, at least for the enlightened advocates of the policy of confinement, that one could contemplate the insane person's lunacy from the outside without feeling at all implicated oneself.

Thus the positive institutionalization of difference in the form of confinement signals the opening of a crucial breach in the system of natural difference. We must be clear about the meaning and the destiny of exclusion pronounced in this way: insanity confined, and simply by virtue of the fact that it is confined, is insanity destined to pose the problem of its de-confinement. The problem will take three full centuries to explode. But it was inscribed from the outset in the gesture that removed the insane person from the rest of civilization. Nevertheless, the insane inmate in a hospital or prison (and we must not exaggerate the proportions of the phenomenon: only a small proportion of the insane were locked up, while the rest circulated freely, as before, or were kept under watch at home) continued to be massively and univocally perceived as self-enclosed, if only in terms of a legacy that included images of animality and the notion of a being in the grip of invisible forces and thus situated *elsewhere* in the strongest sense of the term, a legacy that had a lasting influence over the prevailing representations of insanity. Without directly challenging that vision of an inaccessible monad, the advent of the subject of reason nevertheless introduced a destabilizing ferment at its core. Recycling and reshaping the elements of the religious idea of madness as either sinful or holy, depending on whether it attests to a person's feeling of the signal weakness of his intellect or whether it stems from his powerlessness to remain on the level of ultimate ends, the emergent postulation of a subjectivity consisting entirely of activity is reflected in a moral conception of madness according to which madness proceeds from a deliberate choice of illusion over the truth of the world as willed by God. As we have seen, this conception does not alter the representation of the insane person as radically shut off in a universe of dreams in which there is no way to reach him. What is more, it means insanity is condemnable; it associates one pole of madness with other forms of the will to evil and highlights its aspect of alterity. But at the same time it formally designates a living source of decision-making at the shadowy heart of absence to self; it posits the terms of a fundamental contradiction between the imputation of subjectivity to the insane individual and the abolition of subjectivity in that individual. What we know as psychiatry grew out of the resolution of this contradiction: it entails neither an escape from insanity nor an obliteration of the self in insanity, but, at one and the same time, the indissociable co-presence of the subject and the subject's other.

Meanwhile, along with the explicit invention of the individual, the eighteenth century produced "the sensitive man," the man of equality, the one who sees himself in his fellows and takes a philanthropic interest in the destiny of the wretched inmates locked up in asylums. But he takes just as much interest in the fate of animals. He opposes mistreatment and cruelty toward mute beasts, and he undertakes to bring other beings naturally excluded from human communication, blind and deaf people, out of their moral isolation; he also takes a passionate interest in the rehabilitation of female nature. These anthropological inclinations of the new "sensitive man" converge at a nodal moment that we have sought to grasp from within, in its maximal specificity. At the same time, the nodal moment is merely one among myriad moments in the immense process through which alterity is dissolved in all its forms, a process that constitutes the line of force of recent Western history.

Concerning the particular history of madness, this key moment marks a crucial reversal that we can characterize precisely, with respect to philanthropic sensibility, as the passage from external identification (I pity the insane person because I put myself in his place, but he cannot be aware that I pity him any more than he can be aware of his own condition) to internal identification (he is to be pitied because he is not without a wrenching awareness of his estrangement from himself). Along with the meanderings of the history of the insane asylum, we have followed the slow displacement of the possibilities opened up by that simple entry into the internal universe of the insane patient, up to the institutional explosion of the principle of confinement. But here again, the disintegration of the distance at which madness had been held, a disintegration that literally incorporated madness in us, is not socially separable from the movement that has simultaneously absorbed the difference that had been embodied from the outset by the proletariat. This latter movement reduced the daily violence of human relations to an extraordinary degree, subverted the timeless proscription weighing on women, awarded individual rights to youth and eventually even to children, made the savage a social and cultural being whose practices are equivalent to our own, and called into question the boundaries that separate us from animals.

What actually inspires the writing of history in terms of exclusion? What is the source of the social echo that it has known and that it continues to encounter, in a world subject over the last twenty years to a revolutionary acceleration of progress toward equality? Where does it get its mode of truth, if not directly from that movement and the values it conveys? It is our own rejection, *here and now*, of externality in human space that makes us so sensitive to its manifestations as a central phenomenon in the past; in this realm, the polemical effectiveness of historical knowledge is without parallel. The spotlight Foucault's *History of Madness* focused on the edict of 1657 declaring the creation of the Hôpital Général unquestionably played a telling role in the considerable transformation that the psychiatric apparatus and social attitudes toward abnormality in general have undergone since 1960. But this powerful inscription in a process that is still under way also tends to blind us to the complex trajectory the work of eradicating alterity has followed over the last several centuries. In particular, in terms of our present reference points, it tends to mislead us about the respective meanings of an actual visible severing and of an estrangement experienced as unproblematic.

We understand confinement quite well: it is the familiar social gesture that sanctions alterity in our world, against which we position ourselves directly. What has become completely unintelligible to us, on the other hand, is the order of a world in which a human subject is naturally an "other" human, in which daily contact among human beings is based on the feeling of belonging to different species. Hence the retrospective optical illusion and the diffuse myth of an age of acceptance of madness antedating the modern break with insanity. Yes, madness was tolerated; but we must also see that tolerance postulated such radical dissimilarity that the existence of the other went without saying and was situated at the opposite extreme from the imperative of recognition under which we operate today. The gesture of confinement has to be read against the background of the specifically Western historical break with the order of the Other that has dominated our societies since their beginnings. It then becomes clear that what instinctively appears to us as intolerable exclusion was the means for, and marks the beginning of, a process of inclusion.

The principle of the dissolution of confinement inscribed in the very act that institutes it can be brought to light from still another standpoint, related to the role of the state. As long as the work of reproducing the collective framework stems from a process that is at once ritually explicit and immanent to the life of communities, as we have seen, the outside against which society stands in relief and symbolically restores itself is in some sense necessarily internal to it. "Primitive" individuals (from whom we have a compelling need to distinguish ourselves) are nevertheless in their own way social beings. The inverse of sanity—the thing we must explicitly proscribe in order to give sanity its proper seat—is nevertheless part of the world of sane people. However, this dimension of internal externality turns out to be abolished when the state sets itself up as the monopolistic specialist charged with keeping society together, making it intelligible and preserving its conformity with the order of things. From this point on, the collectivity considered as a whole is logically subordinated to the state that provides for its global identity and its cohesion. As time goes on, there is no more need for contrarian figures in relation to which the specificity of the human order could be situated and marked. Hence the vast movement of deculturation whose influence on representations of madness we have stressed in passing. There is no more room inside the social space for figurations of the other or embodiments of the outside.

We could even show, indeed, that there is no more symbolic "outside," as the institution of the social becomes positive and ceases, with the loss of its explicit character, to fall back on its fundamental foil, *nature*. This is so, moreover, at a time when the conception of nature is undergoing a radical transformation from the viewing of nature as animated and inseparable from human participation, even though it represents the opposite of the human, to the viewing of nature as objective, brute, materially foreign. Similarly, the symbolic outside disappears from the social realm and becomes a physical outside: it becomes quite precisely what the practice of exclusion brings about. Whatever marks human difference has no place within a community whose existence has meaning only if it is homogeneous. Whatever the other is (and confinement is in its essence abstract and heteroclite), it must be transferred to the watertight margins of a universe that ought ideally, as a universe of generalized homogeneity, to be open to itself in all its parts. The shutting off of the excluded is on the same scale as the project of internal visibility, mutual exhibition, or transversal accessibility of the *public space*—that stems, with the modern state, from the submission of the whole to the law of homogeneity.

But the operation is intrinsically contradictory, from the viewpoint of the social logic from which it proceeds. We arrange an outside within a society for which there is fundamentally no possible or tolerable outside. Moreover, we confine: we do not expel, or banish, or send back to the borders. Instead of chasing away vagabonds, the poor, and the insane, as was the practice in the Middle Ages, given the assumption of a world always open to the outside, we take charge, on the tacit postulate that one way or another those others belong to the collectivity, even if the mode of their belonging requires us to institutionalize their non-belonging. We cannot abandon the individual who, as in the singular case of the insane person, embodies the transgression of the limits of the human species; we cannot leave her to her self-sufficiency as an other. Her existence concerns authority and demands authority, even apart from any element of danger or distress that might require protection or consolation. Here indeed is what distinguishes the modern spirit of confinement from the spirit underlying the measures of charity or repression to which the medieval world resorted. For, in the Middle Ages, insane people—and others—were occasionally locked up, but one by one, depending on the circumstances or the urgency; the gesture did not imply any special relationship of status between public power and the human beings who might need to be brought together or contained but who were presumed to entail their own principle of existence. The fundamental presupposition that subtends the policy of confinement, on the contrary, is that anything having to do with the social outside (those outside the social bond, such as the homeless; the presumed counter-society of beggars; those excluded from participation in humanity owing to an impaired ability to communicate, such as the blind and the deaf; those absent to their fellows owing to madness) is the direct and immediate responsibility of the agency charged with producing and maintaining the identity of the social body. The first movement of that agency, quite logically, is to impose homogeneity by repressing and cordoning off all discordant singularities, separating them from society properly speaking. Except that, owing to its very acknowledgment that those human beings outside the norm pose a problem, owing to the very fact that it looks after them, the political agency implicitly—and not only implicitly—recognizes their membership in the community of beings that it is responsible for governing. By excluding them, it integrates and incorporates them.

On the one hand, it cuts them off so that there will be no more manifestation of the gap, no more being-outside, within society. On the other hand, in so doing, it obviously creates another universe within society, an abscess of difference against which the development, affirmation, and consolidation of its own ideals will lead it to turn later. In the long run, the logic of power that gave rise to institutions of confinement inevitably had to reverse itself and become the logic behind the abolition of these same institutions. The same state that instituted the system of exclusion had to reach the point—still in terms of the same social demand that led it to posit a separation—of calling back into question the initial division. The demand for sameness in society determined exclusion; the same identificatory aim at work within the social-human space today commands the end of exclusion. That demand needed exclusion in order to shape and assert itself; now it needs to put an end to exclusion in order to accomplish itself fully. A long period of time was required—the virtually geological time of the great historical mutations—for the tendency to be reversed. Indeed, the reversal has only begun to occur in the last few decades, and it is still very far from complete. The fact remains that it was present from the beginning, structurally contained in the act that regrouped, circumscribed, and symbolically exorcised the human incarnations of the other than human. We are heirs of confinement, whatever we may think, and whatever may be suggested to us by the flattering imagination of rupture. The same concern that secreted the dark enclosures where the figures of disinsertion and detachment were kept is the one pushing us now to require their destruction: there must be no place of the other, no sphere of the outside, no separate universe of difference within society.

Confinement does not come about, then, without a challenge to the margins thus created. The operation that institutes confinement deposits the seed of its own subversion in the process, within the world of confinement itself. The ostensible shunting aside is at the same time a tangible demonstration of an obligatory, unsurpassable integration from which no one is exempt. And the gesture amounts indirectly, in consequence, to conferring a social identity on the very beings whose social nonexistence is being sanctioned and materialized. Invisibly paralleling the process of rejection, a process of necessary insertion begins at the same time. The act that consciously institutes the universe of exclusion takes place only by introducing within itself, unknown to its advocates, a hidden obligation and power of social being. This new power will take time to crystallize, first of all, and then still more time to unfold in all its effectiveness, but it is destined from the outset to permeate and shape the institution from within, to the point of subverting its external boundaries.

The history of the asylum has allowed us to reconstitute one episode of this movement of challenge from within, an episode that is at once exemplary and limited. In it we move from the regrasping of the human bond with the insane individual to the imperative to bring that individual back and dissolve him within the ordinary social bond; in the process, we pass through the fiction of a countersociety adapted to the specific breakdown of the faculty of belonging that characterizes the insane. This movement is only a moment—a privileged one, to be sure, owing to its clarity as well at to its symbolic import—in the global process of dissolution and reabsorption of the figures and forms of the outside, a process that has been under way now for a little more than three centuries, with the emergence of modern politics and the continued work on society accomplished since then by the sovereign state in the course of its metamorphoses.

The Invisible, the Body, the Truth

There is one last special history to bring into our account over the long term: the history of the division of the subject. By this we mean the history of the culturally defined forms that have been successively adopted by the experience of a rift within humanity; what we know as the structural division of the subject represents only the last avatar of that rift. For a very long time these forms were understood independently of psychopathological phenomena. Later, they were gradually incorporated into madness, and finally wholly absorbed; mental alienation, becoming-other-for-oneself from within, was established as the indicator or key figure on the basis of which all the others could be understood. Madness was finally available to conceptualization, over and beyond the occasional alienation: the essential alterity of madness became the constitutive principle of subjectivity. The original, central factor from which we must begin here is the division of the world between the sacred and the secular, between visible reality and invisible forces, between the natural and the supernatural—along with the obligatory consequences of that division for the representation of human experience. The history of the division of the subject, during the time period that interests us, is nothing but the other side of the history of a reduction, precisely, in that division of the world.

The division can be followed along two axes: the axis of truth and the axis of the body. As long as ultimate meaning is thought to proceed from the invisible, as long as it is localized in a radical elsewhere, the encounter with truth has for human beings, one way or another, the character of objectivity. Truth exists independently of us. It manifests itself in an autonomous way in relation to us, whether in the form of revelation or in the form of display through perceptible signs. The extreme case, spectacular as well as demonstrative, of that objective power is the one in which truth speaks through the mouth of an individual who is absent as an individual, in which truth expresses itself through the subject and by supplanting the subject, manifesting its transcendent consistency in the articulation of its human embodiment and in the obliteration of the faculties of the one through whom it is uttered. There is nothing abnormal or unbalanced in that sort of oracular, visionary, or prophetic experience: it is the actualization that necessarily emerges in one place or another, when the cultural framework makes room for it, of the division of the world (understood for example here as the division between matter and spirit) in the form of a rift in the subject. The aforementioned division may take the opposite path, which also leads to the display of a rift in the subject: the subject may remain present to herself but may be made to witness the removal of her body; she may have to experience her body as prey to the invisible.

In a culture for which there is a fundamental cleavage between the natural and the supernatural (that is to say in the entire set of known cultures, with the unique—and relative—exception of our own), the strictly "phenomenological" observation of the coexistence in us of a visible part, the body, with a part that no one has ever seen and no one will ever see, called the soul, consciousness, or the self, necessarily takes on ontological significance. However one conceives of human individuals, they are a mixture straddling two orders of reality, which explains precisely why the disjunction of those two orders finds them a privileged terrain on which to declare itself. The religious refraction of the intimately experienced division is translated in all cases by the minimal postulation of an internal exteriority that disconnects the individual from her body and that is revealed in exemplary fashion when the body begins, in short, to live its own life, owing to the invisible element that has it in its sway. Convulsions are a case in point: through the ostensible escape of movement from personal control, convulsions bear witness to the all-powerful presence of the invisible and make the schism within the subject and her dual membership somehow tangible: she belongs to the realm of the visible, and her visible part suddenly exists and animates itself objectively, as it were, or in any event independently of the subject; thus the subject also belongs to the realm of the elsewhere. These phenomena, too, are perfectly "normal," socially predictable, within a certain framework, which necessarily and as it were anonymously calls for them, apart from any sort of personal psychic need, even though such needs naturally tend to be channeled in the same direction.

Here we should make it clear that we have in mind only the deep logic governing the production of experiences that cut us off from ourselves—always in the form, finally, of a participation of a part of ourselves in the invisible. In reality, things are of course less clear; they are often confused or tangled, overdetermined by the context, recycled in more or less hedged or delayed forms. We have simply been seeking to establish the cardinal points in relation to which the true nature of the modern anthropological revolution becomes intelligible. We can discern what it really involved: not at all the abolition of the dimension of an objective truth independent of the subject, manifesting itself under any and all circumstances, and in the subject's place if necessary, but on the contrary the integration, under the name of the unconscious, of the autonomous and invincible power of the truth to exhibit or express itself, through the subject and without the subject's knowledge, within human beings. What is more, the modern anthropological revolution made that integration the fundamental feature of human structure. It did not efface the alterity of the body, as a naive vulgate declares, but it simultaneously internalized, dematerialized, and radicalized that alterity. For if we can say that there was reappropriation and subjectivization of the body (of which the trajectory of the passions from the epigastrium to the brain, and their metamorphosis into affects or feelings, with the passage from material exteriority to the subtlety of inner emotion, provides a partial illustration), the end result was not at all a full and perfect presence of self to body as such, but, on the contrary, an ultimate unknowability of the body by the subject.

Nothing prevents us from identifying with this body that we are (and let us point out in passing the extraordinary change in the culture of the body that such an identification implies: we shift from viewing the body as permeated, independently of ourselves, by its belonging to the world and as traversed by its currents, to viewing the body as personal, controlled, and separated from things); however, this body with which we identify turns out simultaneously to entail, beyond the psychic face in which we recognize ourselves, another face that is at first unnameable and then, par excellence, unknowable. The difficulties of the notion of drive in psychoanalytic theory, for example, provide a telling illustration of this dilemma. A drive is a force that comes from the body; it nourishes and determines the psyche; but it remains ungraspable as such for the body; we can never come to grips with anything but its symptoms. Beyond the psychic sphere, which includes the body, an other of the body is revealed, this one radically inaccessible. What serves as support and driving force in the body is irremediably situated beyond what we are capable of grasping from within ourselves. A body concealed corresponds to the body espoused; this concealed body is at once absolutely impossible to separate and to objectivize (and in this sense it is absolutely internal) and absolutely impossible to apprehend or to possess, for the subject immersed in it. The truth has an irrepressible autonomy, the body an unfathomable strangeness: at the same time that they are vanishing from the order governing the world, the powers of the invisible have transferred themselves into us.

A history of this displacement ought to begin with an examination of Christianity's crucial impact on the experience of the invisible. The Christian vision of the relations between God and the world is entirely different from the previously identified forms of that relation as manifested in the visible dimension. This history would include an analysis of a pivotal episode that occurred at the dawn of the modern age, the "great witch hunt." We would first have to look at the strange division of the world staked out in that episode, the division between the works of God and the powers of evil; we would have to consider the type of secularization of the invisible implied by the persecutional phantasmagoria of a countersociety dedicated to the devil here on earth. In this episode we would encounter the familiar notion of possession once again, but imputed to a pact with the devil and attributed to personal will, to the guilty choice no longer to belong to oneself. Finally, we would find the constraint of truth spectacularly restored to human power through exorcism: with God's help, the other can be obliged to admit what he is. We would have to deal with all these elements, without of course omitting the emergent reading of these experiences of alterity in terms of madness (a reading that is in fact overestimated by the tradition; it is not particularly significant in its own right); here it would be a matter of showing that those experiences mark a dramatic reshaping of the relations between the visible and the invisible that announces the entrance of their cleavage into the intrahuman sphere, and its shifting from the objective realm to the subjective.

Let us skip over the convulsionary phenomena of the seventeenth and eighteenth centuries, and the striking gap they illustrate (in a world now almost exempt from the struggle between good and evil, and a collectivity significantly more inclined to suspect simulation than possession); let us move on to the crucial turning point constituted by the episode of "animal magnetism," also known as Mesmerism or, today, more commonly as hypnotism. This episode interests us to the extent that it is contemporaneous with the revolution in the idea of madness that has been our focal point. It is not coincidental that that episode was included from the outset by powerful minds in the chain of classically identified manifestations of the invisible. The two fundamental forms under which the division of the world is actualized in us are contained in it: both the convulsive removal of the body from the individual's control and, very soon, with somnambulism and "lucid sleep," the unmasterable expression of truth by the subject in his absence as subject. But the structural salvaging of these two components—and this is the decisive element—goes hand in hand with a complete transformation of their status, which can be summed up by two concepts: naturalization and domination. On the one hand, the division that is revealed here between the visible and the invisible is entirely internal to the human order. If it brings to light the existence of two principles in us, the principles in question are natural ones (however their ontological status may be interpreted). On the other hand, the division, once recognized, enters entirely into our power: we provoke its manifestations, direct them, and use them as we please.

Unquestionably, in this connection, the Mesmerian moment must be considered a crucial turning point in the history of the other interior: specifically, the moment at which the force of the outside comes back into the human orbit. It would be important, moreover, to examine carefully the correlation between this discovery of a duality of subjective experience with the imputation of madness to the subject during the same time period. On the one hand, then, there is the disjunction and the succession of a presence and an absence to self (an artificially provoked absence that creates, in the suspension of the reflective property, the conditions of an extrasubjective lucidity or veracity). On the other hand, there is the wrenching gap of an active presence to self preserved even at the core of the absence experienced.

Clearly, the two figures are not unrelated. On the contrary, the supplementary and final step taken at the end of the nineteenth century, thanks to the encounter between hypnotism and hysteria, might legitimately be described as having arisen in a profound sense from their co-penetration—the conjunction between the contradiction of alienated subjectivity and the duality of levels of psychic exercise produces the idea of a dissociation of the personality and reveals in a more general way the aptitude of the subjective function to split in two. At all events, it is no accident that the event had hysteria as its framework and pretext. Hysteria is the traditional accompaniment to all experiences of the outside, from the oracular faculty through witchcraft to the magnetic crisis, and it is in fact a natural pendant, necessarily evoked through counterreaction, to every sort of manifestation of the externality that is invisible in oneself, that is to say in the absence of self or in the powerlessness of self over self.

What turned out to be signified in hysteria was also an externality, woman's, but one operating within woman and cutting her off from herself. The externality of procreative power was symbolized by the functional independence of the womb, which was virtually a person within the female being; it lived its own hyperlife and occasionally manifested its autonomy—and at that point it recalled, either separately or together according to circumstances, precisely the autonomy of the living process that traversed the human species anonymously and supplied it with the natural framework from which it must cut itself off in order to institute itself in its cultural identity, the alterity that excluded women in part from culture, or the simple externality of the body.

As human beings, we are not riven by the invisible force of the supernatural alone; we can also be riven by the invisible force of nature that passes through us and infinitely surpasses us as individuals, the force that supports us and yet against which we affirm ourselves as something other than nature. Thus it is not by chance that the reduction of the invisible other through the internalization of subjective division was paralleled by, or, more accurately, carried out on the basis of, a reduction of the natural other as manifested in the division of the female body (we can discern the symbolic stake of the etiological displacement that shifts the seat of hysteria from the womb to the nervous system, then from a physical source to a psychic source).

The crisis of hysteria in the final decades of the nineteenth century, a crisis of the fundamental identity of the feminine function, supplied the stage on which the alterity of the body could be projected. We are familiar with the consequences: first, the subjectivization of the procreative faculty, which constituted the child as a product of desire and thus upset and continues to upset the traditional economy of reproduction, on both the physical and the psychic levels, within our societies; next, and correlatively, the transformation of the image of woman, specifically the removal of the original danger that caused her to be relegated to the social outside; finally, the broad elaboration, as a counterpart of the new possibility of espousing one's own body that is now available to the subject, of a no less unprecedented vision of sexuality as the force that radically separates subjects from themselves.

We must add that all this came about in the context of a global restructuring of the relations between humanity and living creatures in general. That restructuring led to the surreptitious emergence of a contradiction between the psychic individual—a belated offspring of the political individual, born of the internalization of the values of self-sufficiency that defined him socially, and convinced him that his end lay in himself—and the pitiless law of the species, destined to remind the psychic individual of his condition as an anonymous and by himself insubstantial link in a process that in the last analysis is the only thing that counts. Under the conditions thus created, owing to a complex interaction between social circumstances and learned representations, the primordial content of the unconscious managed to reveal itself at least in a confused way: the phantasmatic denial of the limits imposed on the subject by his materiality as a biological segment (he is born, he has a sexual identity, he must die). This denial detaches human beings from their membership in the collectivity of living creatures and makes them exist for themselves; on the basis of a hard kernel of unreasoning denial of reality, it institutes the field of a possible culture.

The tenor and form of the subject's internal rift thus prove to be in harmony with the movement that effaces the old externality in favor of intimate identification with the body and transfers the sense of separation to the inside. Similarly, we would have to trace the shift, also imposed by hysteria, from the subject who has the power to speak the truth about himself, in spite of himself and in a state of suspension from himself, to a subject who is structurally absent to his own truth.

We can see how the incorporation of personal alterity that is achieved this way provides the key to the inclusion of madness. Every sort of division of the subject henceforth finds itself not just naturalized but integrated into the register of the pathological. Natural absence no longer coexists with pathological alienation: subjective dissociation is the central fact of psychology. This dissociation has varied manifestations, moreover; conversely, every manifestation of a rift cutting human subjects off from themselves has to be understood as belonging to the realm of the pathological, a realm that thus turns out to be perceptibly enlarged (this is the moment when neuroses, in the contemporary sense of the term, come to the fore and proliferate). But at the same time, the decisive separation and opposition between a normal realm and a pathological realm become untenable: the pathological cleavage of the *I* constitutes only a particular expression of a division that is universal in scope, only a specific actualization of the self-estrangement that organizes the subject. Simultaneously, the entire book of human experience can now be decoded in terms of pathology, and the pronounced cleavage of self from self is simply transformed into an enlarged reflection of the essential alienation in which the human condition is rooted. Such was the means that finally allowed the long, subterranean task of recuperating madness, a task begun several centuries ago, to reach its end point: the regrasping, within human beings, of a division of self that had been attached from time immemorial to their relations with the invisible.

The Evolution of Insanity

A dissolution of social alterity and of the status of difference conferred from without on the insane; a reduction of invisible alterity and an internalization of the expressions of exteriority in human beings—how could such a general and large-scale process have failed to affect the very manifestations of the rift within the self we call insanity? And indeed, just as there is a history of the place set aside for the insane person by the collectivity, just as there is a history of the split between the visible and the invisible within the subjective sphere, there is a history of the forms of madness, of the modalities according to which it succeeded in becoming concrete and in signifying itself as a process of becoming-other-for-oneself. The experience of being taken over by invisible forces, whether they invest the body or replace the personality, undoubtedly also entails an experience of estrangement from oneself. Moreover, the homology of these phenomena has had a lasting impact on the way insanity is understood and approached, either because observers are intent on deciphering a prophetic meaning in the statements of a maniac, or because they respect the "visionary's" legitimate absence from the world and his supposed dealings with another world. But the distinguishing feature of madness, despite this contamination at its borders by the register of the instituted invisible, is that the caesura from the self is inscribed in the raw order of nature, in an intrahuman register; furthermore, instead of concerning the relationship between an individual taken in isolation and the powers of the beyond, madness essentially concerns the subject's relation with others, calling into question the very existence of others for him.

A disturbance of one's power over one's self, a removal of self from self, madness is at the same time and fundamentally an absence signified to others, a marked nonbelonging with respect to the rest of humanity. A disorder of presence to self, it has no meaning unless it is turned simultaneously toward others, unless it is addressed to the beings in whose company the insane person lives. And that is what largely determines the modes of its manifestations, inserting them into a history whose major parameter will be the way in which a society understands the common participation of its members. It is one thing to be insane in a society in which the communitarian bond is viewed as primary, as antedating the existence of any separate and unsurpassable individuality; it is something else to be insane in a society that acknowledges the existence of inherently autonomous and self-sufficient individuals. It is one thing to be prey to a delirious conviction—a conviction that I share with no one, though I am not absolutely unaware that I am alone in possessing it even while I am powerless to resist it—in a universe where existence for others is the rule; it is something else to succumb to such a conviction in a universe where each member enjoys a sort of autarky in his own singular beliefs. Hallucination—a perception that I alone experience, an irrefutable perception accompanied by a feeling of terrifying solitude—does not have the same personal import, does not even manifest itself to me in the same way, does not trigger the same reactions in a world where sharing with others whom I take to be indissociable from myself is a cardinal dimension of instituted experience, as it does in a world whose logic leads individuals to turn inward.

This is quite precisely the gap that separates us from Esquirol's insane patients, or Pinel's; their brutal paroxysms, their physical appearance, and their stories, apart from any retrospective nosographic subtlety, stem first of all from a social mode of production of the gap between self and self and between self and others that is different from the one with which we have become familiar. The unmistakable difference obliges us to measure the extent to which madness itself has changed; it is fundamentally a difference in the way the singular subject is inscribed within the collective framework. The earlier madness, one might say, is madness for others. Consequently, it situates itself quite naturally under the sign of rupture, whether in the form of an uncontrollable explosion (mania) or a savage withdrawal (melancolia), because it constitutes itself for the gaze that will be cast upon it, in relation to the presence of a fellow being inherently recognized as unsurpassable.

If this third-party point of view that structures the subject—the ability to look at oneself as an other among others, an ability that indissolubly links the reflective presence to self and the presence of the other—begins to vacillate from within, the consequent disorder, a disorder of self-disposition inseparable from a disorder of the assurance that one is experiencing life in the same way others do, in the same world as they, can be expressed socially only in relation to the preeminence of the interhuman bond. Psychologically I experience an eclipse of the power to situate myself at a distance from myself, and thus to establish my identity with others. In relation to what, from this point on, am I to externalize this intimately experienced absence, if not in relation to the social obligation to be for others, and, furthermore, to the impossibility posited in principle of not being for others that I continue to feel? What I then exhibit unambiguously to others is what prevents me internally from maintaining myself among them.

In such a framework, madness is destined to use the expressive pathways of direct and open contradiction with the signs and forms of collective belonging. Hence the paroxysmal violence that regularly accompanies it; the archives of that violence emphasize its excessiveness with repetitive complacency. Hence, in a more general way, the aggressivity of the symptoms that express a communicative intent even when the insane person appears calm. The ostensible severance from the communal order in fact represents only one aspect of the expressive logic of belonging at work here. My need to signify the gap, the externality, corresponds to a no less acute need to make others recognize, acknowledge, and share what is cutting me off from them. I neither hear nor believe the same thing as you do, and I cannot mark this vehemently enough; you must hear what I hear, you must follow me where the evidence obliges me to go. It is as imperative to bring out the difference as it is indispensable to act as if the difference did not exist.

The contradiction becomes, pathetically, a quest for an impossible identity—each of us is equally charged with symbolic aggression toward the other, whether you are relegated to a distance from an experience that I hold out to you as impenetrable, or tacitly ordered to give your assent to the unbearable. We are thus both equally invested with virtual violence or with components of rupture, all the more so in that the viewpoint of the insane person and the constraints that determine both the formation of his symptoms and his way of assuming his disorder cannot be separated from a system of collective attitudes founded on the same bases and constituting part and parcel of the behaviors to which he is committed. If he is obliged to situate his madness with respect to others, the others in question are no less led to situate themselves with respect to his madness. If it is essential for the insane person to display himself under the virulent sign of the other—indissociably, in relation to himself, in his body, in his language, in his affections, in the continuity of his existence, and in relation to the rest of his fellows—it is just as customary for the people around him to relegate anyone who violates the common norm to the fringes of humanity. If madness still nevertheless manifests itself in terms of a communicative aim, it is also socially incorporated in the element of communication; there is even an insatiable appetite for the dialogue of derision that it authorizes. What is more amusing than conversation with an insane person besotted with wild notions of which he tries to convince you or that he defends to the utmost? Moreover, the mechanism of production inevitably operates in other respects as a mechanism of selection: while it shapes the figures that madness is capable of producing, it also defines socially the type of phenomena that may be considered as arising from madness. The transformation of the system of expression of alienated subjectivity and the modification of the reference points allowing the identification of the reality of alienation will go hand in hand.

With the movement of individualization, we witness a progressive retreat of madness to a position within personal space. Once the obligatory bond with others—a bond that antedates oneself—has been dissolved, once the subjective monad has been restored to itself, as it gradually learns to exist for itself alone, in an insidious and irrepressible forgetting of the dimension of shared belonging, madness imperceptibly becomes less and less *madness for the other* and more and more a *disorder of identity*. This disorder will be translated especially, to go straight to what is most obvious, by a *historicization* of madness that corresponds to its increasingly pronounced insertion within the fabric of singular existence. Madness had been a decisive caesura, marking a clear absence to others; it now becomes a progressive development, closely associated with the trajectory of a life. No doubt it always leads to severance from ordinary people, but this severance comes at the end of a more or less lengthy evolution, one that may have been at work since the origins of the individual (perhaps it had even been initiated among our forebears). Under the circumstances, it can only express the progress of an intrinsically abnormal constitution; it can only end up producing a being who is other in herself, in her particularity, rather than a being who manifests an active and open break from others. This real movement is inseparable from the movement of ideas, and especially, in the nineteenth century, the century of the discovery of history, from the imperceptible and diffuse penetration of the categories of temporal development within the personal sphere.

The key that made it possible to reach the end point in this realm was the counterstroke of the Darwinian revolution, which consisted in projecting the immense duration of phylogenesis onto the shortcut of ontogenesis. Darwin represented the initial period of life that leads the individual from conception to adulthood as a repetition and recapitulation of the formation of the species, of the complete process of hominization. This representation paved the way for the conception of a radical institution of the human within us, however the repetition and recapitulation may have been understood subsequently (Freud, for example, understood it as a subjective institution). The perspective of a self-constituting personal history that was irresistibly brought out in this way obviously helped draw attention to the evolutionary temporality of the phenomena of alienation. But the history of representations of the disorder cannot be disconnected, under the circumstances, from the transformations of the very way in which the disorder was materialized—transformations linked to the invisible work of anthropological destructuring in which the earlier framework that required all people to conceive of themselves and situate themselves in terms of their co-belonging with others was dismantled. Commensurate with the dissolution of the reference points that rendered personal identity indissociable from the presence of others, and with the constitution of a purely subjective, purely internal identity that resulted from it, madness came to be manifested as the imperceptible progress of a wholly internal gap, an immanent estrangement, an isolation through indifference to what is not the self.

As long as madness can be understood and externalized only as madness for the other, it remains fundamentally impersonal. What is important in madness thus understood is the relation whose impossibility it expresses, the fact that there is rupture. The rupture itself matters much more than the content that causes it; the content as such is in a way of no interest at all. Conversely, what is important for madness understood as essentially confined within the circle of the self is its content: those aspects of the subject that are refracted in it, those elements that the subject as a singular being assigns to it, the relation of expression that connects him to it. We have seen how Esquirol established the resemblance of madness to the subject in general through the passions. The fundamental step remaining was the reading of madness as a projection of the particular individual, in direct connection, once again, with the display of madness as such. The same thing holds true for its manifestation as a deep disorder of the organization of the personality, stemming more from a dislocation of the internal structure or a dissociation of the elements of the psyche than from the external expression of a rupture within the self. In the extreme case, perhaps we are well on the way to witnessing the disappearance of the classical forms of strangeness to self and absence to others as a whole, with the continued progress of the fold back into subjective immanence. It makes less and less sense to escape from the self only to fall immediately under the gaze of the other. Thus it no longer makes sense to leave yourself in the guise of a body arrested in an immobility where that body ceases, owing to the dead objectivity it acquires, to belong to you, or in the guise of a convulsed, riven, paralyzed body that exposes your removal from yourself in every way.

But in the absence of catatonia or hysteria, there are the unspeakable pains of incarnation, there is an infinite discomfort in the intimacy of the body. The body will never again be absent, but it is henceforth richly endowed with the lived experience of disaggregation. In the same way, there are no longer very many of the spectacular neurotic schisms in which a virtually pure alienation of self from self was displayed, in the contrast between an intact consciousness and an irresistible impulse or an impregnable obsession. What tends to be effaced is precisely the dimension of objectivity (externality) of the symptom, whatever it may be, the dimension that once projected it—even though it was unique, even though it reflected the most cryptic part of human individuality, the part most inaccessible to the intelligence of others—onto a field of readability open in principle to others. At the root of these disturbances, we are beginning to see that there is not the slightest eternal necessity; rather, there is a determinism that is entirely historical, even though it has proved to be particularly resilient.

From this point on, even the cardinal forms of delirium or hallucination are affected by this shift. It is not that the ultimate essence of the phenomenon of madness has been perceptibly modified. At bottom, it is still a matter of putting into play the key element of the subjective institution that allows each individual to situate himself symbolically as one among others, as one resembling the others, witnessing the same things as the others, giving words an equivalent meaning, and experiencing nothing that cannot be comprehensible to others. Only madness ceases to manifest itself, as it has in a long tradition, as a perception independent of the self, alienated because irrecusable, at once empty of the presence of others and opposed to others. Madness ceases to signal visibly or positively a withdrawal in relation to the register of common experience. The identity intimately threatened by alterity, the powerlessness to lead one's life on a plane in which one has to compromise or connect with others: these are the emerging figures of an alienation that is entirely incorporated in the sphere of presence to self; signs of a world in which subjects no longer have to exit from themselves just as society no longer entails exteriority. This world entails a de facto severing of the self from others, but a severing that is no longer signified as such. Psychic space absorbs the symbolic outside. We do not know what shape the madness of the absolute individual will take. At least we are learning, from the rapid changes that affect our knowledge of madness, to anticipate the difference.

Notes

FOREWORD

1. The only book comparable to Foucault's work I know that can be said to have raised a similar set of issues by way of an independent inspiration is Klaus Dörner, *Madmen and the Bourgeoisie: A Social History of Insanity and Psychiatry*, trans. Joachim Neugroschel and Jean Steinberg (Oxford: Blackwell, 1981). The German original, *Bürger und Irre*, was published eight years after Foucault's book on madness, in 1969. For Gauchet's account of his and Swain's encounter with Foucault, see his introduction, "A la recherche d'une autre histoire de la folie," in Gladys Swain, *Dialogue avec l'insensé: Essais d'histoire de la psychiatrie. Précédé de: A la Recherche d'une autre histoire de la folie, par Marcel Gauchet* (Paris: Gallimard, 1994).

2. For some new information on these developments, see Dora B. Weiner, *The Citizen-Patient in Revolutionary and Imperial Paris* (Baltimore and London: Johns Hopkins University Press, 1993). This book contains an extensive and exemplary bibliography. Pinel's act of removing chains had been anticipated a few years earlier at Bicêtre by Jean-Baptiste Pussin, the lay practitioner and former inmate who was a pioneer in methods of human treatment. See ibid., 257, where a famous picture of the scene at the Salpêtrière, by Tony Robert-Fleury, is reproduced.

3. Michel Foucault, *Madness and Civilization: A History of Insanity in the Age of Reason*, trans. Richard Howard (New York: New American Library, 1967), 199. This English version was made from a truncated French edition. In the original version, *Folie et déraison: Histoire de la folie à l'âge classique* (Paris: Plon, 1961; rpt. Paris: Gallimard, 1972), the passage appears on p. 505.

4. Translated from the French by Oscar Burge, with a foreword by Charles Taylor (Princeton: Princeton University Press, 1997).

5. For recent but conflicting views and additional information on them, see Jan Goldstein, *Console and Classify: The French Psychiatric Profession in the Nineteenth Century* (New York, Cambridge University Press, 1987), and Dora B. Weiner, *The Citizen-Patient in Revolutionary and Imperial Paris*, which contains an extensive annotated bibliography.

6. For the first point of view, see the work of Klaus Dörner, *Madmen and the Bourgeoisie*, cited above; the second view is strongly present in Jan Goldstein, *Console and Classify*.

7. See Gladys Swain, *Dialogue avec l'insensé*, xlvii ff. The work of Foucault referred to appeared in English as *I, Pierre Rivière, having slaughtered my mother, my sister, and my brother: A Case of Parricide in the 19th Century*, ed. Michel Foucault, trans. Frank Jellinek (New York: Pantheon Books, 1975).

8. For Gauchet's discussion of this difference, see his essay "Tocqueville," in *New French Thought: Political Philosophy*, ed. Mark Lilla (Princeton: Princeton University Press, 1994), 91–113, esp. 101–2.

9. See, for instance, Carlo Ginzburg, "Clues: Roots of an Evidential Paradigm," in *Clues, Myths, and the Historical Method*, trans. John and Anne C. Tedeschi (Baltimore, Johns Hopkins, 1989), 96- 125.

10. See, for instance Ronnie Po-chia Hsia, *Social Discipline in the Reformation: Central Europe, 1550–1750* (London, Routledge, 1989).

11. For examples of how directly and self-consciously late-eigh teenth-century writers faced the dilemmas and problems of indi viduality, see Gerald N. Izenberg, *Impossible Individuality: Romanticism, Revolution, and the Origins of Modern Selfhood, 1787–1802)* (Princeton: Princeton University Press, 1992).

INTRODUCTION

1. The expression echoes the title of a work by Robert Owen, *The Revolution in the Mind and Practice of the Human Race* (London: E. Wilson, 1849); we return to this text below.

CHAPTER I
LA SALPÊTRIÈRE, OR THE DOUBLE BIRTH OF THE ASYLUM

1. This administration was not yet the Conseil général des Hospices; that body was not created until 27 Nivôse, Year IX (January 17, 1801). The administration in question was the Commission administrative des Hospices de Paris, created on 16 Vendémiaire, Year V (October 7, 1796). Concerning the circumstances of the creation of the Conseil général, see the dissertation of Florence-Ella Cassaigne (Ecole des Chartes, 1975, available at the Bibliothèque de l'Assistance publique in Paris).

2. Ibid., especially chapter V.

3. Cf. *Le Discours du Préfet du département de la Seine, en prononçant l'installation du Conseil général d'adminstration des Hospices civils de Paris*, 5 Ventôse, Year IX (Archives de l'Assistance publique, Imprimés a 2204[2]).

4. The minutes of the deliberations of 19 Germinal include the following statement: "I propose as a result that the Conseil should invite the Prefect to inform it about a *project that was presented to him several months ago*, having to do with the establishment of a hospice for the insane. . . ." (Minutes of the deliberations of the Conseil général d'administration des Hospices civils de Paris, Archives de l'Assistance Publique, Fosseyeux 136, vol. 1, 37, f° 46–47), whereas the report of the Conseil to the minister on 24 Germinal indicates that the Prefect "*had been working for six months on the project* of forming a hospice specially intended for curing [the insane]" (Minutes of the deliberations of the Conseil général des Hospices, vol. 1, 50, f° 71). This source will be cited henceforth as *Minutes du Conseil*, followed by volume, minute, and folio numbers.

5. *Minutes du Conseil*, vol. 1, 37, f° 47.

6. *Rapport fait au ministre de l'Intérieur par le Conseil général des hospices civils de Paris sur l'établissement d'un hospice destiné à la guérison des aliénés dans les cy-devant Couvents de la Madeleine de Trénelle et des filles de la Croix, Minutes du Conseil*, vol. 1, 50, f° 69.

7. The two buildings were located near the Pension Belhomme, where Pinel had begun his career as an alienist.

8. *Rapport sur la formation d'un hospice d'aliénés, Minutes du Conseil*, vol. 1, 50, f° 68.

9. *Rapport fait au ministre de l'Intérieur, Minutes du Conseil*, vol. 1, 50, f° 72.

10. Armand-Gaston Camus, *Rapport au Conseil général*, p. 80. We have found traces of a third attempt, made later still, at the end of 1802, when the conseil was resigned to renovating the Salpêtrière facility as satisfactorily as possible. This attempt is of a different order from the first two. In the first place, the purchase request now focuses on just one of the two houses in the Faubourg Saint-Antoine, "the former Traisnel convent." In addition, the aim is no longer to set up a treatment establishment, but rather to transfer to the new facility the incurable lunatics who are "crammed in at Bicêtre" in a way that is "an outrage to humanity. The conseil invites your Excellency to judge for itself the impossibility of leaving these unfortunate creatures where they are any longer." As for the actual treatment facilities, the conseil seems to consider the question closed at this point: "Charenton and La Salpêtrière will be adequate for the treatment of insane persons from all the departments" (letter, 9 Frimaire, Year XI, Archives Nationales, f° 15, 1863).

11. *Sur l'établissement d'un hospice consacré à la guérison de la Manie, Minutes du Conseil*, vol. 1, 37, 19 Germinal, Year IX, f° 46–47.

12. *Rapport fait au ministre de l'Intérieur . . . sur l'établissement d'un hospice destiné à la guérison des aliénés*, 24 Germinal, Year X, *Minutes du Conseil*, vol. 1, 50, f° 72.

13. *Sur l'établissement d'un hospice consacré à la guérison de la Manie*, 19 Germinal, Year IX, *Minutes du Conseil*, vol. 1, 37, f° 72.

14. The treatments administered at the Hôtel-Danieu clearly fall into the latter category. The report of 24 Germinal, Year IX, to the Minister of Internal Affairs not only deplores them because they are badly administered, but it criticizes them squarely for doing more harm than good, owing to their theoretical inadequacy: "The copious bloodlettings, the purges, the showers, the only means of treatment used by the twelve doctors who rotate in two-month shifts, weaken the patient to such an extent that passing insanity generally develops into imbecility and idiotism, which are deemed incurable" (*Minutes du Conseil*, vol. 1, 50, f° 69). Thus the misguided intervention of medicine creates an artificial and incurable problem where in the beginning there was only an inherently "passing" insanity.

15. The *Traité médico-philosophique sur l'aliénation mentale ou la Manie*, 2nd ed. (Paris: Brasson, 1809) is dated Year IX, which has traditionally been translated as 1801, since Year IX coincided for the most part with that year. In reality, however, the *Traité* appeared in the early months of Year IX, that is, in 1800, or perhaps even toward the very end of Year VIII. We have proof of this in the transcripts of the Class of Mathematical Science and Physics of the Institute, which register the receipt of Pinel's book on the occasion of the session of 16 Fructidor,

Year VIII (September 3, 1800), some twenty days before the beginning of Year IX. This does not absolutely determine the date the book actually went on sale in shops, but it does make it possible to situate the moment toward the very beginning of Year IX (September-October 1800)—to be precise, October 27, according to the *Journal typographique* (we would like to thank Thierry Gineste for his kindness in communicating this information).

16. These means were of two sorts. In terms of personnel, he was able to appoint Pussin; and in terms of sites, he was able to proceed with an elementary reorganization of the insane women's workhouse. Pinel had been attempting for a long time to get the warder whose talents he had admired at Bicêtre to follow him to La Salpêtrière. As early as 26 Vendémiaire, Year VII (October 17, 1798), he had written to the Minister of Internal Affairs, François de Neuchâteau, to describe his difficulties and his imperative need for enlightened assistance. "For the more than three years that I have been working at La Salpêtrière," he wrote, "it has been impossible for me to undertake the treatment of insanity or even to make any precise observations of that illness, because of the kind of disorganization that reigns in this part of the hospice. . . . Everything falls into confusion and disorder without a consistent method in the governance of this category of patient, and I must here pay a genuine tribute to Citizen Pussin, who combines a rare intelligence and several years of experience with the happy harmony of humane feelings and imperturbable firmness, all necessary qualities for managing the staff and gaining control over the minds of some of the patients. . . . Thus I ask," he concluded, "that Citizen Pussin be from now on charged with the internal Management of the madwomen of La Salpêtrière."

In the hope of being more convincing, Pinel made a point of having his letter countersigned by several well-known and imposing personalities such as Cabanis, Roussel, and Touret; each one added a word or two in support of Pinel's request, and the entire text was accompanied by a brief essay entitled "Observations faites par le citoyen Pussin sur les fous" (a document recently exhumed by Mme Dora Weiner [Archives Nationales, 27 AP (8), doc. 2], who published it in an article entitled "The Apprenticeship of Philippe Pinel: A New Document," *Clio Medica*, 13, 2 (1978: 125–33). But Pinel's efforts were futile. Not until 3 Thermidor, Year IX (July 22, 1801) did the Conseil des Hospices issue a decree to that effect, a highly ambiguous one moreover, since it decided that "Citizen Pussin, first warder of the insane at Bicêtre, will carry out the same functions simultaneously for the insane persons at La Salpêtrière (*Minutes du Conseil*, vol. 1, no. 174, f° 263. Unless he had a special gift for ubiquity, it is hard to see how Pussin could have risen to the dual task.

There follows a murky imbroglio at the end of which Pussin's appointment was definitively confirmed, and he was transferred to La Salpêtrière on 14 Frimaire, Year X (December 5, 1801) (ibid., vol. 1, no. 380, f° 621). Meanwhile, on 3 Brumaire, Year X (October 25, 1801), the conseil had issued a decree designed to eliminate the most noteworthy abuses prevailing in the workhouse. Furnishings to be supplied included "clothing, sheets, blankets, mattresses, straitjackets, in sufficient number," as well as "combs, brooms and buckets." "Madwomen and serving girls" were forbidden "to sell their food, . . . to raise and feed chickens, rabbits, dogs and other animals within the confines of the said workhouse . . ., to bring in people not associated with the service." The conseil decreed, finally, that "the sane persons who have reached retirement in the madwomen's workhouse will be distributed among other workhouses of the facility" (ibid., vol. 1, no. 324, f° 514–15). But at the session of 14 Frimaire, the very session in which Pussin's appointment is confirmed, the administrators are obliged to acknowledge that "these dispositions have simply not been carried out," in particular the most important ones, namely, "to remove from that workhouse 40 sane persons who for the most part are living at the expense of the madwomen" and to guarantee that "rations be provided in full measure" (ibid., vol. 1, no. 380, f° 621). All these details make it obvious that if the reform of the treatment of the insane did not follow the paths described by the legend, it nevertheless constituted, at its humbler level, a very laborious undertaking.

Beyond these elementary measures intended to end the most flagrant anomalies, the decisions of Germinal, Year X, seem to have dealt in the greatest detail with a restructuring of the sites themselves. A double separation made it possible to create a dedicated treatment space. A special building was created on one side for epileptics, who had been previously mixed in with the insane female patients, and the older female patients were "confined in a particular site" on the other side. Long since abandoned and forgotten, these elderly women had reached a state that no longer justified much hope for a cure. The workhouse for the women undergoing actual treatment "was enlarged by a two-acre lot planted in linden trees." It was eventually divided up into three major sections, the first for women who were "highly agitated or raving," the second for those who had "already undergone a quite favorable change," the third for those whose delirium had completely dissipated, and whose consolidation was to be fostered by hand work before they were returned to their families. We should note that dormitories were set up for these convalescents (instead of the cubicles that prevailed in the first two sections) as well as a "large sewing workshop" (according to Camus, *Rapport au Conseil général*, p. 83, and Pinel, "Recherches sur le traitement général des femmes aliénées," *Le Moniteur universel*, 281 [June 30, 1805]: 1158–59). Despite the constraints of the site and the mediocrity of the resources available, we cannot fail to recognize in this tableau a certain number of fundamental features of the asylum order, clearly established from the outset.

17. *Rapport fait au ministre de l'Intérieur . . . sur l'établissement d'un hospice destiné à la guérison des aliénés*, 24 Germinal, Year IX, *Minutes du Conseil*, vol. 1, 50, f° 69.

18. Esquirol *Des passions considérées comme causes, symptômes et moyens curatifs de l'aliénation mentale* (1805; rpt. Paris: Librairie des Deux Mondes, 1980), p. 6.

19. Pinel could still maintain in 1809, however, that after his six years of experience "there is a 0.93 probability that the treatment adopted at La Salpêtrière will meet with success if the insanity is recent and has not been treated elsewhere" (*Traité médico-philosophique*, p. 437). The arrival of patients cared for (badly) elsewhere, or held too long without treatment, had a negative effect on the results. Under ideal admission conditions "more than 9/10" of the insane were actually cured.

20. "Résultats de nouvelles observations faites sur les aliénés de la Salpêtrière en 1812, 1813 et 1814," *Journal des Sciences médicales* (1816): 82–83.

21. Ibid., p. 24.

22. Pinel himself indicates elsewhere, moreover, that an observation tending in that direction was his starting point: "I noticed first of all, in the Bicêtre hospice, that mania, when it was of recent origin, could be cured by the forces of nature alone, if one managed to set aside the harmful obstacles and direct the moral and physical regimen wisely, which was the initial object of my efforts" (*Traité médico-philosophique*, p. 8).

23. "Recherches sur le traitement général des femmes aliénées dans un grand hospice," *Le Moniteur universel* 281, 11 Missidor, Year XIII (June 30, 1805), p. 1158.

24. In saying this, we are leaving ourselves open to such an obvious objection that it would be unseemly not to point it out. Does not the idea of the institution as remedy have a much longer history, where insanity is concerned? In particular, had this idea not already been forcefully expressed by Tenon? Unquestionably. But let us take a closer look at what Tenon means by it. "What are hospital buildings, for patients other than the insane?" he asks. "Purely auxiliary means suited for providing a favorable regimen and for enhancing the action of the medicines. But hospitals for the insane are quite different: they themselves fulfill the function of remedy. The insane person, during his treatment, must not be thwarted; during the periods when he is under surveillance he must be able to leave his quarters, proceed along the gallery, go to the walkway, do some exercise that relaxes him in keeping with his nature" (*Mémoires sur les hôpitaux de Paris* [Paris, 1788], pp. 211–12). Tenon's thesis is clear: the hospital "fulfills the function of remedy" to the extent that, within the shelter of its walls, it allows the excessive energy or concentration afflicting the patient to manifest itself and thus to dissipate, as it were. This thesis is to have considerable historical impact; it will be taken up again by all the reformers and will actually constitute one of the underlying principles of the institutions newly devoted to curing insanity. But despite the deceptive continuity of expression, it has nothing to do with the idea of the asylum as an "instrument for curing" in Esquirol's sense. Let us be clear: as an *instrument*, the asylum is a means that is wholly docile in the hands of the doctor; it guarantees him moral control over individuals by virtue of the organization into which he incorporates them. Tenon's idea, in contrast, and despite its novel elements, is still based on a pre-Pinelian idea of madness. It still relies on the implicit supposition that the patient is someone who is cut off from others, someone to whom direct access is impossible; the best one can do is to let the patient's aberration dissipate on its own, without challenging or thwarting it. In contrast, the project of transforming the asylum into an instrument for curing, while it endorses and integrates the initial refusal to counter the manifestations of insanity, is based at the same time on the theoretical rupture implied by the advent of moral treatment (the insane patient does not present an unconquerable subjective isolation), and it entails the extension of moral treatment to the entire institution: it is possible to organize an establishment in such a way that it provides those in charge with simultaneous internal access to the souls of its insane inhabitants. The similarity between the verbal formulas and the continuity of practices must not obscure the break that occurred and the profound shift in goals. Even before the revolution, a vision of the hospital as a remedy for insanity began to emerge. But something absolutely un-

precedented arose sometime between 1800 and 1810, with the goal of establishing an internal order (actually a system for adjusting individuals to the institution, as we shall see) that was capable of controlling individuals both personally and collectively, capable of diffusing within its collective body—which miraculously reconciles intimacy and anonymity—the controlling impulses of the doctor.

25. We are of course alluding to an often-cited statement from the *Traité médico-philosophique*: "Directing a hospice for the insane is like running a small government" (p. 221).

CHAPTER II
THE POLITICS OF THE ASYLUM

1. Alexis de Tocqueville, *Democracy in America*, ed. J. P. Mayer and Max Lerner, trans. George Lawrence (New York: Harper & Row, 1966), vol. 2, part IV, chapter 6, pp. 666–67.

2. Michel Foucault, *Discipline and Punish. The Birth of the Prison*, trans. Alan Sheridan (New York: Vintage, 1979), with reference to *l'Ordonnance du 1er janvier 1766, pour régler l'exercice de l'Infanterie.*

3. "The object of the legislator being to determine the conduct of citizens, he must know all the mainsprings of will. He must study the simple and composite forces of all motivations; he must know how to regulate them, combine them, combat them, provoke them, or slow them down at will. These are the levers of the forces he uses to meet his needs." These lines are by Etienne Dumont, presenting and condensing the theses of Jeremy Bentham in the *Discours préliminaire* placed at the head of his edition of the *Traités de législation civile et pénale*, "a work excerpted from manuscripts by the English jurist" (Paris: Rey and Gravier, 1830), vol. 1, p. 22. This indispensable science of behavior has two parts, one devoted to the study of "the sensibility of man considered as a passive being" (Bentham calls this "mental pathology"), the other devoted to the study of "motivating forces" (or "spiritual dynamics"). "These two sources," still according to Dumont summarizing Bentham, "have a marked correspondence in medicine. One must first study the passive being, the physical state of man, and all the variations that that animal machine can undergo through the influence of internal and external causes. One must next discover the active principles, the forces that reside in the organization, in order not to thwart them, in order to slow down those that would be harmful and to excite those that are apt to bring about beneficial changes."

4. This passage and the preceding citations from Bentham are from Dumont's reading of the original edition of the *Panopticon*,

5. Fabre d'Eglantine, *Rapport sur le Calendrier républicain* (3 Brumaire, Year II [October 24, 1793]). The quotations are from Fabre d'Eglantine, *Oeuvres politiques* (Paris: 1914), pp. 173–203 (see especially pp. 174–78). Mirabeau had already had something to say about the need to combine with the "cold wisdom," the "justice," and "truth" of the new institutions "what man grasps with all his senses": "Man obeys his impressions more than his reasoning. It is not enough to show him truth: the crucial point is to get him excited about it. Serving man in the

objects of primary necessity counts for little, *if one does not also get hold of his imagination*" (*Sur les fêtes publiques, civiles et militaires*, in *Travail sur l'éducation publique trouvé dans les papiers de Mirabeau, fait et publié par Cabanis* [1791], Cabanis, *Oeuvres complètes* [Paris: Bassange 1823], vol. 2, p. 451 [emphasis added]. Bronislaw Baczko examines the revolutionary variations on this theme in B. Baczko, "Former l'homme nouveau, utopie et pédagogie pendant la Révolution française," *Libre* 8 (1980): 89–132. See also Baczko's remarkable *Lumières de l'Utopie* (Paris: Payot, 1978).

6. Robert Owen, *A New View of Society*, in *A New View of Society and Other Writings* (1913: rpt. London: Everyman's Library, 1927, pp. 44–45).

7. Robert Owen, "An Address to the Inhabitants of New Lanark," in ibid., p. 110.

8. Louis Peisse, *La Médecine et les médecins*, Paris, 1857, vol. 2, p. 4.

9. *The Revolution of the Mind and Practice of the Human Race* (1849). A. L. Morton, who selected and presented the texts, naturally includes the idea among Owen's "weird notions," along with his belief in phrenology and the religious language he uses to evoke the "New Jerusalem." As if the religious dimension of utopian socialism could be counted as an aberration. As if phrenology, because it had been a "pseudo-science," did not nevertheless mark a crucial turning point in anthropological conceptions. What is "weird" in the case in point lies in the area of the anachronic suburban rationalism that prevents a thought from being understood in the complexity of its context, where "error" conveys as much meaning as, or more than, the banal positive truth.

10. The idea has something of a history at the time of Owen's writing. It appeared at the end of the eighteenth century. It is found in Tenon: "The first remedy," he wrote in his *Mémoires sur les Hôpitaux de Paris*, "is to offer the madman a certain freedom, to make it possible for him to give himself over in moderation to the impulses of nature" (Introduction, p. xxv). The idea was taken up again by all the reformers, Daquin, for example, who recommended that mad patients be left "free . . . to walk about, to come and go as they please . . . in a vast, spacious and pleasant enclosure" (*Philosophie de la folie* [Paris, 1792], p. 52). But it was actually more or less during the years when Owen was writing that that "liberation" acquired its symbolic significance, retrospectively; it was crystallized in particular in the Pinelean myth of the abolition of chains.

11. The formula is Pinel's, from "Recherches sur le traitement général des femmes aliénées dans un grand hospice," *Le Moniteur universel*, 281 (June 30, 1805), p. 1158.

12. *L'Architecture considérée sous le rapport de l'art, des moeurs et de la législation* (Paris, 1804), p. 68.

13. *Traité médico-philosophique*, 2nd ed. (Paris: Brosson, 1809), p. 251.

14. Ibid, p. 194. In counterpoint, let us cite a remark by J. A. Miller in his study of Jeremy Bentham's panoptic machine: "Bentham repeatedly uses one particular expression: in juridical matters as in logical matters, one must always be able to situate oneself 'at first glance.'" And, elsewhere: there must remain "no dark spot." Bentham uses the same expressions in extolling the panoptic construction ("La Machine panoptique de Jeremy Bentham," *Ornicar?* 3 [1976]: 19).

15. *Traité médico-philosophique*, preface, p. iv.

16. Esquirol: "In a way, the doctor has to be the life force of a hospital for the insane. Everything must be set in motion through him; he directs all activity, for his role is to regulate all thoughts. He is the center of activity, and all issues concerning the inhabitants of the establishment must be referred to him" (*Des Maladies mentales* [Paris: Baillière, 1838], vol. 2, pp. 527–28).

17. And in fact at least one asylum was built on an island: in Scotland, "on one of the islands of the beautiful Lake Lomond, chosen so as to increase the patients' isolation, so that they could take walks and get exercise without inconveniencing or endangering the neighborhood; this asylum was entrusted to the care of Doctor Arnold" (according to an article by Black on institutions for the insane in England, published in 1805 in the *Bibliothèque britannique*, sciences and arts, no. 70, p. 69; cited in F. E. Fodéré, *Traité du délire* (Paris: Croullebois, 1817), vol. 1, p. 179).

18. E. Georget, *Dictionnaire de médecine* (Paris, 1824), *s.v.* "Folie."

19. Prospectus of the *Etablissement pour le traitement des aliénés des deux sexes fondés en juillet* 1822 à Vanves près Paris par MM. les docteurs Voisin et Falret.

20. Fodéré, *Traité du délire*, vol. 2, p. 215.

21. Ibid., p. 200. Esquirol says, for his part: "The first effect of isolation is, to produce new sensations, to change and break up the chain of ideas, from which the patient could not free himself" (J.E.D. Esquirol, *Mental Maladies: A Treatise on Insanity* (1845; New York: Hafner, 1965, vol. 1, p. 73).

22. Let us note in passing that the alienists' continual recourse to educational metaphors must clearly be related to the radical aim of reconstructing personalities. ("The insane are but grown up children, children too, who have received false notions and a wrong direction. So many points of resemblance do they bear to children and young persons, that it will not be surprising if one and the other should be governed on similar principles" [Esquirol, *Mental Maladies*, vol. 1, p. 73]). Critics regularly stress the prominence of this goal in order to bring out, generally with good reason, the paternalistic idiocy of the approach. But beyond these superficial effects, might we not need to be sensitive to the exorbitant aim implied by the analogy? Is it not urgent to reflect on the excessive and aberrant aspect of the underlying ambition to take human beings at the starting point, jettisoning the previously acquired "false notions and . . . wrong direction," in the tranquil, naive intention to rebuild them from the ground up, to begin them all over again, to re-form them totally?

23. Esquirol again: "Isolation is not less useful, in combating the disorder of the moral affections of the insane. The disturbance unexpectedly occurring in the nervous system, changes the nature of the sensations and often renders them painful. The natural relations with the external world are no longer the same. Externally, every thing seems to be thrown into confusion. The patient who believes not that the cause of these phenomena is within himself, is at variance with all that he sees or hears; a circumstance which excites his mind, and places him in opposition to others and himself" (*Mental Maladies*, vol. 1, p. 74).

24. Prospectus, *Etablissement pour le traitement des aliénés* (cf. n. 19 above); emphasis added. For an architectural study of these "quite special arrangements," see the works of Dieter Jetter: "Das ideale Irrenhaus im Spiegel historischer Baupläne," *Confinia Psychiatrica* 5 (1962): 1–29; "Die psychiatrischen Kran-

kenhaüser als Anstalten besonderer Art," *Confinia Psychiatrica* 9 (1966): 198–222; "Ursprung und Gestalt panoptischer Irrenhaüser in England und Schottland," *Suddhofs' Archiv*, 46, 1 (1962): 29–44; and *Geschichte des Hospitals*, especially vol. 1, *Zur Typologie des Irrenhaüser in Frankreich und Deutschland* (Wiesbaden: Steiner, 1971).

25. Georget, *Dictionnaire de médecine*, *s.v.*, "Folie."

26. Fodéré, *Traité du délire*, vol. 2, p. 200. It may be useful in this connection to mention the way the notion of isolation is used by certain hypnotists. Thus Puységur writes that "the first distinctive feature of somnambulism . . . is *isolation*, that is to say, a patient in this state has no communication or relations except with his hypnotist; he hears only him, and retains no relationship with external objects" (*Recherches, expériences et observations physiologiques sur l'homme dans l'état de somnambulisme . . . provoqué par l'acte magnétique* [Paris: Dentu, 1811] p. 43). Isolation is the condition of sovereign authority, but it is also, as the analogy suggests, the means for an exclusive relation entailing wholesale dependence and total influence.

27. The idea appears in Cabanis, at the end of his "views on public aid"; he himself explains that these views were inspired by his experience as a member of the commission on Paris hospitals in 1791, 1792, and 1793. "We have observed," he writes, "that a political constitution based on the nature of man and on the eternal rules of justice must in the long run almost completely eradicate the traces of poverty, and distribute without upheavals, in a more equal way, all the means of enjoyment." And he continues, in a fine spurt of political optimism: "I dare add that, through the effect of the wise institutions that constitute an authentic republic, dementia and all the disorders of the mind must also become rarer. Society no longer degrades man; it no longer binds his activity; it no longer stifles in him the passions of nature, so as to substitute artificial and miserable passions, suited only to corrupt reason and habits, to produce disorder and unhappiness. Revolting authorities and tyrannical prejudices cease to make war on man; the customs of ignorance, unreason and poverty no longer surround him with their contagion from the cradle on. Subject only to the suffering that is inseparable from his nature, he will ignore all the alterations of the mind that are directly produced by the disorders of a bad social state, and consequently, the damaging corollaries that its influence develops. Finally, the moment may come when madness will have no source other than a primitive disturbance of organization, or those singular accidents of human life that no wisdom can prevent" (*Oeuvres philosophiques* [Paris: Presses Universitaires de France, 1956], vol. 2, p. 59). Medical realism is there to forestall an overly absolute affirmation: to be sure, there will always be a few idiots suffering from a congenital deficiency, or vital shocks that lead to personal debilitation. A residue of "accidental" madness is inevitable. But it is the end of all "essential" madness that we are promised by an adequate organization of the human world.

28. "To bring order to the ideas of the insane, one must establish order around them. All their movements are regularized" (Archambault, *Rapport à M. le préfet de la Meurthe sur le service médical de l'asile d'aliénés de Maréville pendant l'année* 1842 [Nancy: Raybois, 1843], p. 16). Morel expresses a similar view of behavior in a medical report on the hospital of Maréville: "Agitation has gradually

faded in the element of general tranquillity" ("Des gâteux dans un asile d'aliénés," *Annales médico-psychologiques* 2 [1850], p. 100).

29. Esquirol, *Mental Maladies*, p. 76.

30. Scipion Pinel expresses a similar idea: "The distributions of the establishment are calculated to produce a continuous impression on the imagination of the patients, and this action is so general *that one observes its effects even on those who do not suspect it or who claim to be exempt from it*" (*Traité complet du régime sanitaire des aliénés* [Paris: Mauprives, 1836], p. 127; emphasis added).

31. Morel, "Des gâteux dans un asile d'aliénés," *Annales médico-psychologiques* 2 (1850): 100.

32. Bouchet, "Du travail appliqué aux aliénés," *Annales médico-psychologiques* 12 (1848): 307.

CHAPTER III
IMPOSSIBLE POWER

1. See especially the two volumes of *L'Expérience du mouvement ouvrier* (Paris: Union générale d'éditions, 1974), and more particularly the introduction, "La Question de l'histoire du mouvement ouvrier" (vol. 1), and "La Lutte des ouvriers contre l'organisation de l'entreprise capitaliste" (vol. 2). The second article appears in English as "On the Content of Socialism, III: The Workers' Struggle against the Organization of the Capitalist Enterprise," chapter 8 of Cornelius Castoriadis, *Political and Social Writings*, trans. and ed. David Ames Curtis, vol. 2, 1955–60: *From the Workers' Struggle Against Bureaucracy to Revolution in the Age of Modern Capitalism* (Minneapolis: University of Minnesota Press, 1988), pp. 155–92.

2. See especially Marandon de Montyel, "L'Hospitalisation de la folie et les nouveaux asiles ouverts pour aliénés," *Annales d'hygiène publique et de médecine légale*, 3rd series, 34 (1895): 411; "La Nouvelle hospitalisation des aliénés par la méthode de liberté," *Annales médico-psychologiques* 1 (1896): 60; and "Asiles d'aliénés à portes ouvertes," *Annales médico-psychologiques* 2 (1896): 390. Marandon de Montyel began to experiment with an open door policy at Ville-Evrard around 1888. The movement, which originated in Scotland, was already widespread at the time in England and Germany (the colony-asylum of Alt-Scherbitz in Saxony, a pilot project constantly cited as an example, was created in 1876). Despite their belatedness, Marandon's discussions still seem to us particularly trenchant, because they are not limited to presenting the open-door policy in the framework of an agricultural colony as a happy and humane solution to the problem of incurables and other retarded souls, as was the common practice, while the time-honored principles of disciplinary surveillance remained in force for patients "in treatment." For Marandon, it is a matter of putting the *entire* asylum system on a new footing; his condemnation of the traditional system as it was practiced is absolute and unequivocal. His articles are not at all innovative on the level of practical suggestions, but they have the singular import of signifying an *intellectual break.*

3. "La Nouvelle hospitalisation des aliénés par la méthode de liberté," p. 60.

CHAPTER IV
A SOCIALIZING MACHINE

1. The best historical panorama in this area remains Esquirol's article, "Maison d'aliénés," in the *Dictionnaire des sciences médicales*, vol. 30, Paris: Panckoucke, 1818; see especially pp. 48–61, reprinted in *Des maladies mentales* (Paris: Baillière, 1838).

2. In Strasbourg "they have thought of establishing, at the far ends of the rooms and along the sides, something like cages or wooden cupboards that can at the very most contain a man of medium height, raised half a foot above the floor with a slatted floor. These cages or cupboards are strewn with a little straw on which the insane patient lies, naked or half-naked; here he takes his meals and here he relieves himself; the liquid waste flows through the slats onto the floor of the room, which gives the miserable cubbyhole a permanent stink" (F. E. Fodéré, *Traité du délire* [Paris: Croullebois, 1817], vol. 1, p. 19). At the hospital in Martigues, "in the courtyard, they had built a hangar with very narrow boxes, where the wretches lay on the ground, obliged to pass their heads through a hole made under the door, like a cat door, the only place where they could benefit from air and light" (ibid., p. 94).

3. J.-L. Moreau de la Sarthe, "Médecine mentale," in *Encyclopédie méthodique*, *s.v.* "Médecine."

4. Mourre, *Observations sur les Insensés* (Toulon: Surre Fils, 1791), p. 9.

5. Berthier, *Excursions scientifiques dans les asiles d'aliénés*, 4th series (Paris: Savy, 1866), p. 51 (Evreux) and p. 45 (Pontorson).

6. Cited in Ferrus, *Des aliénés* (Paris: Huzard, 1834).

7. Report to the Minister of Internal Affairs of 24 Germinal, Year IX, *Minutes du C.G.H.*, vol. 6, no. 50, f° 71; emphasis added. Cabanis, in his *Rapport au département de Paris sur l'état des folles détenues à la Salpêtrière* of December 6, 1791, wrote the following, in the article entitled "Traitement à établir pour les fous": "A house of treatment for madness should combine several advantages that are lacking in the boxes at La Salpêtrière. It must be possible to place the patients alone, *each in his own cubicle*, and that cubicle must contain a clean bed" (reprinted in A. Tuetey, *L'Assistance publique à Paris pendant la Révolution* [Paris: Imprimerie Nationale, 1897], vol. 3, p. 491; emphasis added).

8. Camus, *Rapport au Conseil général des Hospices* (Paris, Imprimerie des hospices civils, Fructidor, Year IX [September 1803]), p. 81.

9. "Folie," in *Dictionnaire de médecine*, 1st ed.

10. "Recherches sur le traitement général des femmes aliénées dans un grand hospice," *Le Moniteur universel* 281, 11 Messidor, Year XIII (June 30, 1805): 1159. Pinel counts 59 convalescing insane women among 255 inhabitants overall.

11. Ibid.: 1159.

12. *Traité médico-philosophique sur l'aliénation mentale*, 2nd ed. (Paris: Brosson, 1809), p. 248.

13. Ibid.

14. Pastoret, *Rapport sur l'état des hôpitaux, des hospices et des secours à domicile à Paris* (Paris: Huzard, 1816), pp. 182–83. Moreover, traces remain of the pressure Pinel and Esquirol put on the administration to bring about these trans-

formations more quickly: at the meeting of the Conseil général des Hospices on January 5, 1820, reference is made to a letter from the two Salpêtrière doctors "in which they give an account of the good effects that have resulted from the elimination of low boxes and from placing the patients that formerly inhabited them in more healthful dormitories; they express the desire to see prompt completion of the building intended for the convalescent patients, owing to the considerations of the greatest interest that they have developed in their letter." Unfortunately, the letter itself has been lost (*Minutes du C.G.H.*, vol. 62, 28 724, f° 119).

15. Pastoret, *Rapport*, p. 179.

16. Parchappe, *Des Principes à suivre dans la fondation et la construction des asiles d'aliénés* (Paris: Masson, 1853), p. 216. Doing away with boxes became a ritual obligation, one of the first items on the agenda of every forward-looking alienist who arrived in a departmental facility after the promulgation of the law of 1838 and found it necessary to struggle against outdated practices and thinking. For example, when Morel arrived in Maréville in 1848, he discovered "wooden cells, separated by a corridor, and stone-vaulted boxes. Nothing was lacking from the standpoint of solidity: iron bars and thick oak doors, seated firmly on their hinges and equipped with formidable locks." Still, despite his repeated entreaties he did not find it easy to have them eliminated. They were not torn down until the following year when Renaudin was named head doctor. This represented just one significant episode among a dozen similar ones (according to Sémelaigne, *Les Pionniers de la psychiatrie française* [Paris: Baillière, 1930], vol. 1, p. 314).

17. Berthier was head doctor of the insane asylum of Bourg-en-Bresse. His *Excursions scientifiques* were published in four series: in 1862, 1864, 1865, and 1866 in Paris and Lyon (cf. n. 5, above).

18. We find a significant example at the Bon Sauveur in Caen, where dormitories are divided into wire cages, one for each bed, so each inmate can be locked up individually for the night. See Claude Quetel, *Les Cadres de la folie au XIX*[e] *siècle, le Bon Sauveur de Caen* (thesis, 3rd cycle, Paris-Sorbonne, 1976).

19. Pinel, *Traité médico-philosophique*, p. 236, note.

20. "Maison d'aliénés," p. 78.

21. Ibid., p. 79.

22. Ibid., p. 78.

23. *Des Maladies mentales* (Paris: Baillière, 1838), vol. 2, p. 526.

24. This passage and the preceding ones are cited from *Le Traitement moral de la folie* (Paris: Baillière, 1840), pp. 170–71.

25. *A Treatise on Insanity*, p. 216.

26. Ibid., pp. 216–17.

27. Ibid., pp. 194, 216.

28. Ibid., pp. 64–65.

29. Ibid., p. 193. Such remarks point to Pinel's ambivalence, to the historical ambiguity of his thinking. Thus he declares that it is possible to get the patients "in even their most furious state" to work; but in the same passage he also declares, "The return of convalescents to their primitive tastes, pursuits, and habits has always been by me considered as a happy omen of their final complete re-establishment" (p. 217). If the return to the dimension of work is a sure indication of the return to reason, this implies that madness at its height entails a withdrawal from

the possibility of well-regulated activity; it means that, for Pinel, madness remains in some form, even if no longer in its essence, *idleness.*

30. From this viewpoint, the reversal became complete when work stopped being just a useful distraction for convalescents and became, on the contrary, the privilege of calm chronic patients. Thus in 1860, the *Rapport sur le service des aliénés du département de la Seine* points out that if the number of working patients has been continually decreasing in recent years, the reason is that patients deemed to be calm, able-bodied incurables are being shipped out to the departments (p. 13). Clearly, one can remain insane for life, one can suffer from a progressively worsening disorder, and still be perfectly fit to work. The disjunction is much less "self-evident" than one might think; indeed, this understanding had to be acquired, and it represents a considerable step in historical terms.

31. *Le Traitement moral de la folie*, pp. 165–66.

32. If there is a single transformation that translates the fantastic growth of insane asylums during the nineteenth century (for France, at least a fiftyfold increase, with nearly a twentyfold leap between 1800 and 1840 alone), it is probably the expansion of the criteria for confinement. This was a direct effect of the theoretical break that took place in the early years of the century. As soon as the truth of madness was no longer situated in the radical alterity of the individual, one could begin to count as "real" madmen a whole series of patients who would not have been judged insane under the classical criteria (this is precisely the meaning of the debate between judges and doctors over monomaniacs). A statistical investigation of the evolution of the thresholds of confinement will shed decisive light on this question.

33. Leuret, *Le Traitement moral de la folie*, p. 168.

34. Unfortunately, few monographs go into sufficient depth to allow us to follow this process of generalized increase in patient population in any detail. We usually have to settle for impressionistic notations (several patients in a cell intended for one, beds in the corridors, and so on). Let us note that Claude Quetel's thesis, *Les Cadres de la folie au XIX*[e] *siècle, le Bon Sauveur de Caen* (3rd cycle, Paris-Sorbonne, 1976) constitutes a happy exception. Quetel took pains, for example, to assess the evolution of the ratio of support staff to patients: from 1 warder for every 4.5 patients in 1838, we move to a ratio of 1:9.6 in 1903. Thus we see a return, under the pressure of the influx of patients (from 120 in 1820 to 1,500 in 1900), to the conditions at La Salpêtrière at the turn of the century. "The governing bodies allow one nurse for every 10 patients," Esquirol indicates in 1818, judging that number "very ill-proportioned to the infinite and ever-growing needs of these patients" ("Maison d'aliénés," p. 80).

35. The failure of the asylum's most fundamental project—asserting collective control over human beings by means of an adequate mechanism—began to come to light much earlier than is generally supposed. It was openly expressed as early as the 1860s. Medical influence, such as is guaranteed in principle by the system of classification and discipline, is misleading, according, for example, to Mundy in 1862 (in a paper presented at the annual meeting of alienist doctors in England, in *Annales médico-psychologiques* 2, 4th series [1863]: 389). Marcé writes in 1862 that "the patients, under overcrowded conditions and *without intellectual or moral guidance*, become incurable, most of the time, for the simple reason that

they are not being treated" (*Traité pratique des Maladies mentales* [Paris: Baillière, 1862], p. 656). And in 1868, Griesinger writes: "The idea of mass treatment, with the discipline of the barracks, of insane patients still capable of leading a more human life, has had its day; it has no future" (cited by Sérieux, in his 1903 *Rapport* [Paris: Imprimerie Municipale], p. 26). It is impossible to understand the criticism that was developing at the same time on the outside and that has received more widespread attention without relating it to this internal criticism. The two cannot be dissociated.

36. *Le Traitement moral de la folie*, p. 178.

37. Ibid., pp. 181–82.

38. Ibid, p. 180. Archival material allows us to continue to follow the progress of Leuret's reforms, especially an interesting exchange of letters in which the Prefect of the Seine Department asks the Minister of Internal Affairs "to approve in principle of the addition of 44 persons to the personnel of the hospice for the insane." These additions were deemed necessary in order to extend the application of measures "that have produced good results" with a limited number of patients. As the Prefect explains, "many of the insane who up to now have been kept locked up can be released and restored to social habits through work and distractions" (August 28, 1841). He attaches to his letter a copy of the minutes of a session of the Conseil général des Hospices, which notes the successes achieved owing to "walks taken outdoors, distractions or means of working indoors, classes, meals in common in the dining hall, meetings and musical evenings," and he spells out the staffing needs that stem from this "new organization," from interns, a teacher and a pianist (for the singing classes) to a carter and "brigadiers responsible for taking the patients to work in the fields" (April 14, 1841; Arch. Nat., f° 15, 1968).

39. Parchappe summarizes quite aptly, in his way, the basic internal evolution of the asylum system. "A serious error," he writes in 1865, "has long presided over the perspectives of therapy and practice where the insane are concerned. It consists in believing that the isolation of patients, so often advised as the primordial condition of effective treatment, must be understood as if it were a matter of removing the patient from all human contact, from every act of social life. We have finally understood that if it is of primary importance, for curing madness, to remove the patient from the conditions of social life, from those in which he has contracted his illness and those in which he has subsequently enacted his delirium, it is no less important to restore calm and reason in his soul, and to prepare him to resume one day the role that belongs to him in collective life, to create for him, in an orderly way and under a regimen that is at once gentle and rigorous, conditions of existence preferable to those that he has been forced to leave behind, and yet analogous to those he will have to take up one day and which are necessarily part of the human destination" ("Aliénés, asiles," *Dictionnaire encyclopédique des sciences médicales*, vol. 3 [Paris: Asselin and Masson, 1865], p. 99). Everything is here, between the lines: the initial temptation of the cell (radical reduction of the individual to himself, removal from "all human contact, every act of social life"); the conversion to the opposite aim of resituating the individual among others, reimmersing him in the conditions of "collective life," conditions that are at once special and analogous to those prevailing outside; and the temptation, finally, by the same token, to set up the asylum as a small society set apart, equivalent to ordinary

society but "preferable" in its autarky because specifically conceived to meet the needs of the insane patient.

40. Esquirol, *Des Maladies mentales*, vol. 2, p. 426; emphasis added. In 1895 Marandon de Montyel writes: "I showed last year in the *Tribune médical* how the asylum could be set up so as to give such a complete illusion of a village that an outsider arriving on the public square, not knowing where he is, will come into the shoemaker's shop, or the tailor's, to place an order; he will ring at one of the houses to inquire about renting" ("L'hospitalisation de la folie," *Annales d'hygiène publique et de médecine légale* 34, 3rd series (1895): 432. This point remained central to arguments over asylum architecture. It was perhaps made most sharply during the debates over the cottage system in 1865–75.

41. Three series of factors are inextricably mixed, in fact, at the origin of the projects of "colonization": (1) early doubts about the possibility of gaining control of the asylum population as a body, and about the real benefits of disciplinary confinement; (2) the need to reduce the numbers of inhabitants in overcrowded asylums (as Foville says, "the colony has to take in the crowd of harmless chronic patients that constitutes the overflow population of the asylums"); (3) finally, right in line with the original utopia, the search for a system making it possible simultaneously (a) to succeed in keeping the patients busy, (b) to put in place an architecture reconstituting "village" conditions of ordinary life, and (c) to constitute, on that basis, a true small society of insane patients. Hence the ambivalence of the theme: sometimes the texts seem to be evoking warehouses, while at other points they celebrate the ideal form of the psychiatric institution. The ambiguity is perhaps not without significance. Might a certain strain of alienism not have been tempted to make permanent arrangements for the existence of the insane instead of treating them? We return to this point below. The most noteworthy and most telling text on this question, owing to the historical consciousness it displays and the feeling it expresses of an ongoing development in which change is brought about by the experience acquired over more than twenty years in the asylum, seems to us to be H. Belloc's *Les Asiles transformés en centres d'exploitation rurale, moyen d'exonérer en tout ou en partie les départements des dépenses qu'ils font pour leurs aliénés, en augmentant le bien-être de ces malades et en les rapprochant des conditions d'existence de l'homme en société* (Paris: Béchet Jeune, 1862). See also, in connection with the colony projects, the *Annales médico-psychologiques*, the responses to a work by Jessen in 1861, "Sur les colonies d'aliénés" (vol. 7, p. 619), by Mundy in 1863 (vol. 2, p. 387), the discussion of the problem in 1862 (vol. 8, pp. 650, 674, 683), the article by Auzouy in 1864, "Des fermes asiles ou de la colonisation des aliénés" (vol. 4, p. 407). Sérieux devotes a good deal of attention to the problem, focusing on the German example, in his *Rapport sur l'assistance aux aliénés en France, en Allemagne, en Italie et en Suisse* (Paris: Imprimerie Municpale, 1903).

42. See especially F. Berthier, *Sur l'opinion de feu le Docteur Itard relative aux facultés intellectuelles et aux qualités morales des sourds-muets* (Paris, 1852).

43. For a more detailed analysis, see Gladys Swain, "A propos de l'enfant sauvage de l'Aveyron," *L'Evolution psychiatrique* 4 (1976): 995–1011.

44. Itard, *Traité des maladies de l'oreille et de l'audition*, 2nd ed. (Paris: Libraire médicale de Méquignon-Marvis, 1842), vol. 2, p. 331.

45. Pinel, *Traité médico-philosophique* 2, p. 226. Pussin himself tells a very similar story in his *Observations sur les fous*, a document transmitted by Pinel to the Minister of Internal Affairs. When he was charged with overseeing "thirteen years before" (thus around 1785), he reports, "as one of my principles was never to allow the insane to be struck under any circumstances, and because I had formally declared my intentions in this respect, the serving boys sought to rebel against me, saying that they were not safe and objecting that if I was not spared myself, they were much more exposed; but despite their clamor I persisted in my resolutions, and in order to follow through on my plan I was obliged to fire almost all of them, one by one, when they disobeyed. Thus I had some difficulty meeting my goal, but I have finally reached the point where the serving boys never strike any patients, even when they are the victims of their fury. I am not unaware that those whose job it is to look after the insane are exposed to great dangers, but I am certain, too, that there is less peril in gentleness than in severity" (Arch. Nat., 27 AP [8] doc. 2; cf. Dora Weiner, "The Apprenticeship of Philippe Pinel," *Clio Medica* 13, 2 [1978]: 131–32).

46. Pinel, *Traité médico-philosophique*, p. 226.

47. Georget, "Folie," *Dictionnaire de médecine*, 1st ed.

48. "Examen du *Traité* de Broussais" (*De l'irritation et de la folie), Journal de Paris*, 1828, reprinted as an appendix in *Système de politique positive*, vol. IV, p. 227. On this episode, see Georges Dumas, *Psychologie de deux messies positivistes, Saint-Simon et Auguste Comte* (Paris: Alcan, 1905); Dumas's book is still the most complete discussion of the topic available.

49. Pinel, *Traité médico-philosophique*, p. 284.

50. There is a sign of this contrary image in a polemical brochure published in Montpellier in 1826, *Supplément au voyage en France de M. Leigh.* Its author tells us that clinics and other asylums had acquired the picturesque popular label "Pinelières." The brochure is especially interesting for us in that it turns arguments drawn from the break with the idea of complete madness against the alienists: the very arguments that the alienists were trying to impose at the same time before the courts on the occasion of the widely publicized trials of "homicidal maniacs" (Léger, Lecouffe, Papavoinen H. Cornier). One may be mad and still be conscious of what one is doing. But if one can thus be a mad person "without looking like one" (without satisfying the criteria of deviation and absence on which the classic diagnosis was based), then any alienist can declare that anyone at all is mad, the pseudonymous Leigh retorts. If madness escapes manifest, wholesale perception, then the mad can also be arbitrarily identified and sequestered. Thus the suspicion of arbitrariness surrounding the psychiatric enterprise arises out of what was actually the most innovative and "progressive" aspect of its view of mental alienation—and, not coincidentally, at the moment of its direct confrontation with the most retrograde notions on the topic, those that were particularly influential in the judicial structure. The fact is that in this complex context an authentic social unease is emerging. This is attested elsewhere by the Debelleyme circular in 1828, the first of the sort to make strict rules governing the admission of insane patients to clinics and hospitals (in Paris) and to place admissions under judicial control.

51. *Des Passions* (Paris: Librairie des Deux Mondes, 1980), p. 43.

52. Ibid., p. 29. Two excerpts from the article "Folie" in the *Dictionnaire des sciences médicales* are also pertinent here. "In an institution for the insane, social bonds are broken, friendships end, confidence is destroyed, habits are altered; people act without respect for social conventions, they obey out of fear, they do harm without hatred; each one has his own ideas, thoughts, and emotions, his own language; each one lives for himself; self-centeredness isolates everything" (vol. 16, p. 153). "The insane develop an aversion for people dear to them; they insult them, mistreat them, flee their company; this is a consequence of their defiance, their suspicions, their fears: mistrustful of everything, they fear everything. Some seem to constitute an exception to this general law, by conserving a sort of affection for their relatives and friends; but their tenderness, which is sometimes excessive, exists without confidence in the persons who before the illness had directed the patient's ideas and actions" (ibid.), p. 160.

53. "The return to the moral affections within their proper limits; the desire to see one's children again, and one's friends; the tears of sensitivity; the need to pour out one's heart, to find oneself surrounded by one's family, to resume one's habits, offer a sure sign of cure" (ibid.).

54. On the practical level, this phase corresponds to the rediscovery of *individual treatment*, as considered from a radically new standpoint, on the basis both of the patent failure of mass treatment and of the acknowledged impossibility of making do with an abstract approach to individuality. The first "moral treatment" was individual, but in an archaic sense; it tacitly reintroduced the idea that one could only address insane patients by accepting them in their inherent isolation. It seems more "modern" to us because of an illusion of perspective. The fluctuations of the asylum mechanism were necessary so that an absolutely unprecedented aspect of the individual phenomenon could appear in contrast, negatively: the individual is first of all an irreducible singularity that cannot be dissolved in any community or mass (some would call it a "subjectless process"); second, that singularity is made up of mysterious ties and attachments, concrete anchor points that are knotted together and offered in the course of a unique history. Here we have the "individual," by no means given in advance in his content, but *constructed and produced*, with whom treatment will deal henceforth. The need for individual therapeutics, instead of and in the place of the "block treatment" or "collective therapy" that were in current use in asylums is a central polemical theme in the reform literature of the 1890s and the 1900s (for an overview, see Sérieux's 1903 report; for details, see Marandon de Montyel, *Rapport au Préfet de la Seine*, in *Procès-verbaux de la commission de surveillance des asiles d'aliénés de la Seine* [Paris: 1892]).

55. Marandon de Montyel describes the practice of withdrawing the insane patient from the circle of his ordinary relations: "They were firmly convinced that it was necessary to place the patient in a milieu completely different from the one in which his mind had foundered and to shelter him from all emotions, even the gentlest and most legitimate ones. As a result, they judged family visits dangerous and disturbing, and such visits were forbidden; only after long months of absolute isolation was a very short one authorized. Even writing was deemed harmful. And the patient did not emerge from that profound withdrawal until the cure was com-

plete" ("La Nouvelle hospitalisation des aliénés par la méthode de liberté . . . ," *Annales médico-psychologiques* I [1896], p. 61).

CHAPTER V
WHAT THE PASSIONS MAKE IT POSSIBLE TO THINK

1. At the same time, moreover, in another register and probably without the slightest point of demonstrable contact, philosophers are pursuing the development of this same notion of selfhood, which Mauss for his part views as the end result of the process through which the person as "psychological being" has been brought into relief, a process that has gone hand in hand, in the modern West, with the tendency toward the political affirmation of the individual. "Kant posed, but did not settle, the question as to whether the 'self,' *das Ich* (ego), is a category," Mauss writes at the end of his essay on *the notion of person* ("A Category of the Human Mind: The Notion of Person, the Notion of 'Self,'" in *Sociology and Psychology: Essays*, trans. Ben Brewster [London: Routledge & Kegan Paul, 1979], p. 89). "The answer that every fact of consciousness is a fact of the self or 'ego' was finally given by [Johann Gottlieb] Fichte, thus founding all science and all action on the 'ego.' Kant had already made individual consciousness, the sacred character of the human person, the precondition of Practical Reason [1949, 1966]. It was Fichte who made it also the category of the 'ego,' the precondition of consciousness and science, of Pure Reason [1817]. Since that time the revolution in our mentalities has been achieved, we each have our own 'self' or ego, an echo of the Declarations of Rights which had preceded Kant and Fichte" (Mauss, "Category"). Let us simply note the parallel: while the two operations of thought are rigorously independent of each other, and while their respective stakes are absolutely different, they are surely not without historical and logical relation. How to characterize that relation is another matter; its elucidation would require us to go back to the highly obscure roots of the cardinal mutation of anthropological reference points that accompanied the advent of historical-individualist-democratic-industrial-bourgeois society, about which we still know so little. The social history of the *subject* considered as a specific production of the modern state-capitalist universe remains to be written in its entirety: what we are describing here are two moments or two aspects of it that are probably both complementary and contradictory.

2. Hence the purely accidental character of the programmatic evocation of a work on "the intellectual faculties as causes, symptoms, and means for curing mental alienation" (p. 54), which was to complement the work on the passions, but which in reality was never begun; nor, apparently, was it even alluded to later on. We shall come back to this perspective that was opened up for a moment and then abandoned, but which was fertile in meaning in its context. Hence too, perhaps, Esquirol's singular perseverance in epigastric localization, which will lead him, for example, to publish a series of observations on the displacement of the transverse colon in mental illness (*Journal de Médecine* 62 (1818): 341–58; 63 (1818): 176–84 and 289–91 [not included in *Des Maladies mentales*]), where he strives in fact to find a precise anatomical basis for the famous epigastric pain that

the insane were initially believed to feel. He wrote these observations at a time when his students were unanimously seeking the *cerebral* seat of alienation; as leader of a school, Esquirol follows, encourages, and supports his students' research. While he tolerates and understands the need for new orientations in harmony with the requirements of the times, he remains obstinately faithful for his own part to what he continues to understand as the enabling conditions of his own research.

3. *Mémoires de la Société Médicale d'Emulation* for Year V, 1st year (Paris: Richard, Caille, and Ravier, 1797) (Year VI), p. 114.

4. *Nosographie philosophique*, 1st ed. (Paris: Crapelet, 1797) (Year VI), vol. 2, p. 11.

5. "Recherches et observations sur le traitement moral des aliénés," *Mémoires de la Société médicale d'Emulation*, 2 (1797) (Year VI): 238 (*A Treatise on Insanity* [trans. D. D. Davis, Birmingham: Classics of Medicine Library, 1983] pp. 83–84).

6. Ibid., p. 238 (*Traité médico-philosophique sur l'aliénation mentale*, 2nd ed. [Paris: Brosson, 1809], p. 80; the note is not included in the English translation.)

7. "I cannot help admiring the courage of Dr. Crichton, who has lately published two volumes upon maniacal and melancholic affections, merely on the basis of some ingenious elucidations of the doctrines of modern physiology, which he extracted from a German journal, and which he accompanied by a description of the moral and physical effects of the human passions" ("Recherches et observations"; rept. in *A Treatise on Insanity*, p. 51.)

8. *Traité médico-philosophique sur l'aliénation mentale*, Introduction, p. xxii (not included in the English translation).

9. Ibid., p. xxi.

10. Ibid., p. xxii; emphasis added. Here Pinel is borrowing directly from Crichton, who says: "The passions have to be considered, in a medical point of view, as a part of our constitution, which is to be examinated [sic] with the eye of a natural historian, and the spirit and impartiality of a philosopher. It is no concern in this work whether passions be esteemed natural or unnatural, moral or immoral affections. They are mere phenomena, the natural causes of which are to be inquired into" (*An Inquiry into the Nature and Origin of Mental Derangement*, vol. 2, [London: Cadell and Davies, 1798], pp. 98–99).

11. By Moreau de la Sarthe, in *Recueil périodique de littérature médicale étrangère* (Paris, 1798) (Year VII), p. 143.

12. Itard, for example, represents Crichton—even though he is associated with Willis—as the father of "the sublime art created in England [moral treatment] and recently spread in France through the successes and the writings of Professor Pinel" (*Mémoire sur les premiers développements de Victor de l'Aveyron* [1901], reproduced in L. Malson, *Les Enfants sauvages* [Paris: Union générale d'éditions 10/18, 1964], p. 137). In his *Promenades poétiques dans les hospices et hôpitaux de Paris* (Paris: Trouvé, 1826), Alhoy, the administrator of the Conseil général, depicts Crichton as a reformer of the treatment of the insane on the same level as Pinel: "Greetings to you, Chricton [sic]! Greetings to you, Pinel! Generously opening up your paternal breasts to the insane, you have, in England and in France, by studying them better, relieved their suffering" (p. 309). "It is to these two men," he

insists in a note, "that the insane will forever owe a treatment more appropriate to the nature of their ills" (p. 324).

13. *La Décade philosophique* 35, 20 (1799) (Year VIII), 4th quarter, Fructidor: 457–64.

14. *Recueil périodique de littérature médicale étrangère* 1 (1798) (Year VII): 401–18 and 463–78. The translation of an excerpt is included in vol. 2 under the title "Du principe de l'irritabilité et de ses lois," pp. 342–50 and 357–66. The name of the translator is not given; it is reasonable to think that Pinel may have been continuing his work.

15. Cf. *La Décade philosophique*, p. 463. Moreau, however, is one of the most outspoken advocates of "moral medicine." He contributed a significant article called "Quelques observations sur différentes circonstances de maladies à la guérison desquelles les ressources pharmaceutiques n'ont point concouru" to *Mémoires de la Société Médicale d'Emulation* (vol. 2, 1798 [Year VII], pp. 178–215). Moreover, Pinel would explicitly borrow his classification of the passions in the second edition of his *Traité de l'aliénation mentale.* Moreau has a sentence that expresses particularly well the physiological orientation of the medicine of the passions he is promoting: "One must look not at the effect of the passions according to popular opinion, but at the passions themselves as various modifications of the nervous system" (p. 183). He declares that he had "often thought" in this spirit about "the formation of a pathometer" (p. 182).

16. The care that both Pinel and Esquirol take to exonerate the insane of the suspicion of constitutional immorality is worth emphasizing. According to Pinel, "This means clearly enough that people of both sexes endowed with an ardent imagination and deep sensitivity, those who are open to the strongest and most energetic passions, have a disposition closer to mania, unless a healthy, active, and energetic reason has taught them to counterbalance their impetuous enthusiasm—a sad reflection, but constantly true, and quite suited to arousing interest on behalf of the unfortunate insane. I must doubtless make some exceptions and recognize the existence in hospices of unhappy victims of debauchery, misconduct, and extreme moral perversity. But in general I can only offer striking testimony to the pure virtues and strict principles often manifested in the cure. Nowhere except in novels have I seen husbands more worthy of being cherished, more tender fathers or mothers, more passionate lovers, people more attached to their duties than most of the insane happily brought to the period of convalescence" (*Traité*, p. 14; see also p. 123). According to Esquirol, "Those on whose behalf I am advocating are the most interesting people in society, almost always victims of prejudice and ingratitude on the part of their fellows. They are family men, faithful wives, honest brokers, skilled artisans, warriors valued by their fatherland, distinguished scholars; they are ardent, proud, and sensitive souls" (*Des établissements consacrés aux aliénés en France* [Paris: Huzard, 1819], p. 4). "I have penetrated into the asylum of unhappiness *where virtue often whimpers*," Esquirol says in the preamble to the same text. But the influence of the traditionally received ideas remains such that Pinel concludes the second edition of his *Treatise* in the following terms: "One cannot deny medicine the advantage of contributing powerfully to the return of healthy morals by producing the history of the ills that result from forgetting it" (p. 492).

17. The expression is Crichton's. The entire formula is worth citing: in certain respects, he writes, man "may be said to contain within himself the secret springs of his own conduct" (*Inquiry*, vol. 2, p. 96).

CHAPTER VI
REDUCING INSANITY: THE MIRROR OF ALTERITY

1. *Des Passions considérées comme causes . . .* (rept. Paris, 1980), p. 21.
2. Ibid., pp. 25–26.
3. Cf. ibid., pp. 28–29: "Almost all the insane patients entrusted to my care had offered some irregularities in their functions, in their intellectual faculties, in their affections, long before falling ill, often starting in early childhood; irregularities that their parents had missed, but that I got them to remember, by questioning them about the state prior to the one for which I had been consulted."

CHAPTER VII
THE SOCIETY OF INDIVIDUALS AND THE INSTITUTION OF SPEECH

1. On this point, see the definitive analysis by Pierre Clastres, "Exchange and Power: Philosophy of Indian Chieftainship," in *Society against the State: Essays in Political Anthropology*, trans. Robert Hurley with Abe Stein (New York: Zone Books, 1987), pp. 27–47.
2. Two important books deal with this break: Karl Polanyi, *The Great Transformation* (New York, 1944); and Louis Dumont, *Homo Aequalis* vol. 1, *Genèse et épanouissement de l'idéologie économique* (Paris, 1978).

CHAPTER VIII
THE CONQUEST OF DISSYMMETRY

1. Letter of March 16, 1787, expressing thanks for a prize awarded by the Royal Society of Medicine. The letter has been removed, along with part of the author's dossier, from the archives of the Royal Society and added to other, later texts in the Archives of the Society of the School of Medicine, at the Academy of Medicine (box D). In this set there is also a cover letter for a "work that I have just finished on *madness*," dated 10 September 1791. On Daquin, see Claude Caron, *Joseph Daquin et les malades mentaux en Savoie à la fin du XVIII*[e] *siècle*, medical dissertation (Lyon, 1964).
2. *Philosophie de la Folie* (Paris, 1792), foreword, p. xv.
3. Ibid., p. 2.
4. Ibid., pp. 1–2.
5. Ibid., p. 8.
6. Ibid., pp. 49–50.
7. Ibid.
8. Ibid., pp. 51–52.

9. Ibid., p. 52.
10. Ibid.
11. *Philosophie de la Folie*, 2nd ed. (Chambéry, 1804 [Year 12]), p. 118.
12. Ibid., pp. 113–14.
13. Ibid., p. 117.
14. Ibid., p. 118.
15. Ibid., pp. 118–19.
16. This is suggested by the accompanying letter. The Minister forwarded the dossier to Thouret, Director of the School of Medicine; hence its presence in the archives of the Society of the School of Medicine (box D). "Citizen Minister," the letter says, "I am sending you herewith the meteorologico-medical observations of May and Floréal. In response to your request, I am attaching a summary of my journal on the insane, and a little brochure produced recently to encourage my fellow citizens to adopt the vaccine."
17. *Plan du journal sur les fous.* The substance of the summary is taken up again in a noticeably extended form in the second edition of the *Philosophie de la Folie*, pp. 208–14. On the point that interests us, however, the second version is both more incidental and more restrictive. "It was important to keep from countering their fantasies or challenging their ideas, in the days of greatest influence [let us recall that Daquin is speaking about the influence of the moon]; on the contrary, it was necessary to condescend on those occasions in some way to almost all of their wishes, and to talk nonsense with them: this was the only way to analyze their intellectual state rigorously and to bring calm to their minds" (p. 214). What is presented thus as an ordinary means in a first phase is reduced here to the proportions of a means adapted to critical circumstances.
18. Pinel, *A Treatise on Insanity*, p. 48.
19. *Philosophie de la Folie*, 2nd ed., foreword, p. xiii (the first edition has a similar passage).
20. Ibid., pp. xiv-xv.
21. Ibid., pp. 1–2.
22. Ibid., p. 2. Hence, for example, the opinion attributed by Fodéré to the "famous doctor Willis, who considered it a good sign, it has been said, when the patient showed fear; *for he was then beginning to pay attention to external objects*" (*Traité du délire* [Paris, 1817], vol. 1, p. 488; emphasis added). Blows (which Willis authorized the servants to repay in kind) and coercion were seen as a way of breaking through the subjective autarky; pain was used to reawaken the insane patient to the presence of things.
23. *Philosophie de la Folie*, 2nd ed., p. 3. (The first edition has a similar passage, p. 2). Daquin offers the example of a girl he saw during a visit "to the small houses in Paris, [a girl] whose madness consisted in claiming and actually believing that she was a man and not of her own sex; thus she was seen in her lodgings dressed as a man." He may well pass harsh judgment on those who make sport of madness; still, what holds his attention here are the picturesque and piquant details: "Her garb made a quite ridiculous contrast with her sex." He may be a philanthropist, but he uses dangerously energetic expressions to depict the state of rage into which contradiction plunges the "poor unfortunate girl": "Transformed

by a single word into a ferocious beast in whom only the human face remained to establish the difference" (ibid., pp. 65–66). Now, going to stare at insane people is known to have been a widespread practice. However, it has never been the object of a systematic study that would confer on it its true import as an index to mentalities. Two points in particular to which Daquin's text refers are worth looking at more closely, one involving its content and the other the date. Contemporary accounts appear to agree as to why people went to see "lunatics": they went to amuse themselves (Daquin did not proscribe this practice frivolously). Fodéré, born in 1764, recalls the insane people he saw outside of situations of confinement, "in [his] birthplace in the Savoie": they were "allowed to wander freely in the streets and in public places," when they were not dangerous, and they served "as the butt of jokes among children and the populace" (*Traité du Délire*, vol. 1, p. 167). The wandering lunatic followed by a crowd of children who make fun of her more or less cruelly with the complicity of adults: here is an old image that can be traced to the dawn of the twentieth century in countries that had not been overly "psychiatrized" (Greece, for example, as the works of D. Ploumbidis show). But we must not be misled: within the world of confinement, the situation and attitudes were not so very different. Thus in 1756, the doctors of the Hôtel-Dieu in Paris complain in a memorandum about the behavior of the servants who deal with "persons whose minds are alienated": "Every day the men and women assigned to serve in these wards are seen to behave as if they were not used to these sorts of illnesses: they cluster around the patients, focus on their madness, laugh at their extravagant behavior; on other occasions they amuse themselves by opposing them, contradicting them, making them angry" (quoted in Martin-Doisy, *Dictionnaire d'économie charitable* [Paris, 1855–64], vol. 1, p. 476). But Pinel himself still complains in the first edition of his *Treatise* that he has been unable to get the administration of Bicêtre to restrict "the visits of strangers and other curious people. . . . To see the unfortunate beings there confined, already too much the objects of pity, made the sport and the spectacle of the unfeeling and the mischievous, calls no less for redress than for sympathy. I recollect to have once seen a madman, who, towards the decline of a maniacal paroxysm, was excited to great fury and violence by provocations which he received at the window of his apartment from an unfeeling bystander, who treated him with contemptuous merriment" (*A Treatise on Insanity*, p. 213). It still remains to be determined just when these practices actually disappeared. In 1817 Fodéré asserts that "public visits take place in France in all the hospitals in Provence" (*Traité du Délire*, vol. 2, p. 254). This information is corroborated locally in a dissertation by Jacques Léonard: in Rennes, at the Petit Saint-Méen, visits by curiosity seekers are authorized until 1835 (*Les Médecins de l'Ouest au XIX*[e] *Siècle* [Lille, 1978], vol. 3, p. 1365). A systematic investigation of the question would undoubtedly produce some surprises.

24. "*Médecine mentale*," *Encyclopédie méthodique*, s.v. "Médecine," 1816, vol. 9, p. 141.

25. *Philosophie de la Folie*, 2nd ed., foreword, pp. vi-vii.

26. Joseph Raulin, *Traité des affections vaporeuses du sexe* (Paris, 1758), p. 242.

27. "*Folie*," *Dictionnaire des sciences médicales* (Paris, 1816), vol. 16, p. 159.

28. Ibid.

29. Ibid., p. 161. Pinel, for his part, acknowledges "the constancy and facility with which some maniacs support severe and long continued cold." But "there are many, on the other hand, who are severely affected by cold, even during their accessions. How common is it in the winter season to see the patients at lunatic hospitals crowd about the fire?" (*A Treatise on Insanity*, pp. 32–33).

30. *Dictionnaire des sciences médicales*, vol. 16, p. 159.

31. Ibid., p. 161.

32. *Des Passions considerées comme causes, symptômes et moyens curatifs de l'aliénation mentale* (1805; rept. Paris: Librairie des Deux Mondes, 1980), p. 68.

33. *Traité médico-philosophique sur l'aliénation mentale*, 2nd ed. (Paris, 1809), pp. 331–32n.

34. Let us note that Daquin began by explicitly stating the impossibility of such a state of affairs: "What a sad science, in which the individual who makes it his study is obliged to examine other individuals of the same nature as himself but who, however, not being himself, appear to occupy only an intermediary status between man and brute" (*Philosophie de la Folie*, p. 1). The individuals under study resemble the researcher but are nevertheless afflicted with an irreducible difference; they are all the more other in that they remain "of the same nature."

35. The expression is from Camus, *Rapport au Conseil général des Hospices* (Paris, 1803), p. 81.

36. *A Treatise on Insanity*, p. 72.

37. Ibid., pp. 61–63.

38. "Idéologie proprement dite," in *Elemens d'Idéologie* (Paris, 1826–27, p. 203 (the note appears in the second edition of *Elemens*, in 1804).

CHAPTER IX
OPENINGS AND APORIA OF MORAL TREATMENT

1. *A Treatise on Insanity*, pp. 84–85.

2. Ibid., p. 86; emphasis added.

3. *Des Passions considérées comme causes* . . . (rept. Paris, 1980), p. 79.

4. Cf. Gladys Swain, *Le Sujet de la folie* (Toulouse, 1978), especially §8, "la leçon des intermittences maniaques et l'engendrement de la classification" (the lesson of maniacal intermittences and the way the classification is generated).

5. "Folie," *Dictionnaire des sciences médicales* (Paris, 1816), vol. 16, p. 158.

6. Ibid., p. 157.

7. Ibid., p. 158.

8. Ibid. 1816, vol. 17, p. 155. The formula according to which fury is the anger of delirium comes from the article "Délire" in the same dictionary, 1814, vol. 8, p. 254. The information that is simply evoked here in the wake of *Des Passions* is the object of a systematic investigation by Gladys Swain, "D'une rupture dans l'abord de la folie," *Libre* 2 (1977), especially "De Pinel à Esquirol: La Découverte du sens," pp. 208–24.

9. "Manie," ibid., 1818, vol. 30, p. 454. And in the same dictionary, under the heading "Suicide": "Insane persons have been spoken of as wretches obeying a

blind fate: I think that I have learned better than anyone how to read the thoughts of these patients, and to prove that their determinations are motivated, but that they result from a false idea" (1821, vol. 53, p. 232). This is what Esquirol himself viewed as his own personal contribution.

10. Ibid., 1814, vol. 8, p. 251.

11. *Gazette de Santé* (November, 1814), pp. 242–43, 258–59.

12. Note added to the translation of Hoffbauer's *Médecine légale* (Paris, 1827), reprinted as *Mémoire sur la monomanie homicide* in *Des Maladies mentales* (Paris, 1838), vol. 2, p. 804.

13. "Délire," *Dictionnaire des sciences médicales.* Cf. Gladys Swain, "D'une rupture dans l'abord de la folie," *Libre* 2 (1977), especially pp. 221–24.

14. "Délire," *Dictionnaire des sciences médicales*, 1814, vol. 8, p. 253.

15. "Folie," ibid., 1816, vol. 16, p. 162.

16. Ibid., p. 163.

17. Ibid., p. 158.

18. Archives de la Société de l'Ecole de Médecine, Académie de Médecine, Mémoires EFG box (attached to a report by Pinel and Laënnec dated July 19, 1810) and *Journal général de médecine* 50 (May-June 1814): 3–85. The text seems to have remained incomplete as far as the initial project is concerned. The manuscript ends as follows: "After speaking of physical crises, I shall say a few words about moral crises," and the published article announces a continuation in forthcoming issues that never appeared. Apparently, then, this second part of the investigation into moral crises does not exist.

19. "Terminaisons critiques de la manie," p. 4.

20. *Mental Maladies*, p. 174.

21. *Journal général de médecine*, p. 12.

22. *Mental Maladies*, p. 175.

23. "Terminaisons critiques," p. 6.

24. Indeed, crises generally tend toward just such an outcome: the completed break between a before and an after, the "perfect cure" whose features Esquirol indicates so as to be able to judge accurately, he says, whether the critical episode is over or not: "The patient must not retain any painful memory of his illness; he must speak of it with indifference, see without repugnance the people who took care of him, and the places where he was treated. He is reasonably skeptical, and adopts forthrightly the recommendations given him for the preservation of his health" ("Terminaisons critiques," p. 13).

25. Pinel provided some examples of critical termination of alienation in his *Treatise*; Esquirol went on to generalize and systematize the theme. Moreover, the article written on crises for the *Dictionnaire des sciences médicales* (7 [1813]: 370–92) was prepared by Landré-Beauvais, Pinel's associate at La Salpêtrière and Esquirol's future colleague. He invokes the authority of his master and the numerous cases to which "the students who took [his] courses in clinical medicine at the La Salpêtrière hospice" can attest (p. 390). Finally, let us not forget the spectacular reactualization of the doctrine of crises carried out by Mesmer in a context that was not so very different. The eventual convergence of perspectives would be worth examining.

EPILOGUE
SOCIAL DIVIDE, DIVISION OF THE SUBJECT, MAD RUPTURE

1. See Gladys Swain, "De Kant à Hegel: Deux Époques de la folie," *Libre* (1977): 174–201.

List of Works Cited

Alhoy, Louis François Joseph. *Promenades poétiques dans les hospices et hôpitaux de Paris.* Paris: Trouvé, 1826.

Archambault, Théophile. *Rapport à M. le préfet de la Meurthe sur le service médical de l'asile d'aliénées de Maréville pendant l'année 1842.* Nancy: Raybois, 1843.

Auzouy, Théodore. "Des fermes asiles ou de la colonisation des aliénés." *Annales médico-psychologiques* 4 (1864): 407–25.

Baczko, Bronislaw. "Former l'homme nouveau, utopie et pédagogie pendant la Révolution française." *Libre* 8 (1980): 89–132.

———. *Lumières de l'Utopie.* Paris: Payot, 1978.

Belloc, Hippolyte. *Les asiles transformés en centres d'exploitation rurale, moyen d'exonérer en tout ou en partie les départements des dépenses qu'ils font pour leurs aliénés, en augmentant le bien-être de ces malades et en les rapprochant des conditions d'existence de l'homme en société.* Paris: Béchet jeune, 1862.

Berthier, Pierre. *Excursions scientifiques.* 4 series. Pardis and Lyon: Savy, 1862, 1864, 1865, 1866.

———. *Sur l'opinion de feu le Docteur Itard relative aux facultés intellectuelles et aux qualités morales des sourds-muets.* Paris: 1852.

Bouchet, Camille. "Du travail appliqué aux aliénés." *Annales médico-psychologiques* 12 (1848): 301–22.

Cabanis, Pierre Jean Georges. *Oeuvres complètes de Cabanis.* 5 vols. Paris: Bossange, 1823–25.

———. *Rapport au département de Paris sur l'état des folles détenues à la Salpêtrière.* December 6, 1791. Rept. in A. Tuetey, *L'Assistance publique à Paris pendant la Révolution*, vol. 3. Paris: Imprimerie nationale, 1897.

———. *Oeuvres philosophiques.* 2 vols. Paris: Presses Universitaires de France: 1956.

Camus, Armand-Gaston. *Rapport au Conseil général des Hospices.* Paris: Imprimerie des hospices civils. September, 1803 (Fructidor, Year XI).

Caron, Claude. *Joseph Daquin et les malades mentaux de Savoie à la fin du XVIIIe siècle.* Dissertation, Faculty of Medicine, Lyon, 1964.

Cassaigne, Florence-Ella. *Le Conseil général des hospices de Paris.* Dissertation, Ecole des Chartes, Paris, 1975.

Castoriadis, Cornelius. *L'Expérience du mouvement ouvrier.* Paris: Union générale d'éditions (coll. 10/18), 1974.

———. *Political and Social Writings.* Trans. and ed. David Ames Curtis. Vol. 2, 1955–60: *From the Workers' Struggle against Bureaucracy to Revolution in the Age of Modern Capitalism.* Minneapolis: University of Minnesota Press, 1988.

Clastres, Pierre. "Exchange and Power: Philosophy of Indian Chieftainship." In *Society against the State: Essays in Political Anthropology.* Trans. Robert Hurley with Abe Stein. New York: Zone Books, 1987, pp. 27–47.

Comte, Auguste. "Examen du Traité de Broussais (*De l'irritation et de la folie*). *Journal de Paris*, 1828. Translated into English as "Examination of Broussais' Treatise on Irritation," in his *System of Positive Polity*, London: Longmans, Green, and Co., 1875–77, vol. 4, pp. 645–53.

Crichton, Alexander. *An Inquiry into the Nature and Origin of Mental Derangement Comprehending a Concise System of the Physiology and Pathology of the Human Mind and History of the Passions and Their Effects.* 2 vols. London: T. Cadell, Jr., and W. Davies, 1798.

———. "Recherche méthodique sur la nature et les causes physiques du délire." Trans. Philippe Pinel. In *Recueil périodique de littérature médicale étrangère* 1 (1799 [Year VII]), pp. 401–18, 463–78.

Daquin, Joseph. *Philosophie de la Folie.* 1792. 2nd ed., Chambéry: Cléaz, 1804 (Year XII).

Destutt de Tracy, Antoine Louis Claude. *Elemens d'Idéologie.* Brussels: A. Wahlen, 1826–27.

Dörner, Klaus. *Madmen and the Bourgeoisie: A Social History of Insanity and Psychiatry.* Trans. Joachim Neugroschel and Jean Steinberg. Oxford: Blackwell, 1981.

Dumas, Georges. *Psychologie de deux messies positivistes, Saint-Simon et Auguste Comte.* Paris: Félix Alcan, 1905.

Dumont, Etienne. "Discours préliminaire." In Jeremy Bentham, *Traités de législation civile et pénale.* Paris: Rey and Gravier, 1830.

Dumont, Louis. *Homo Aequalis*, Vol. 1, *Genèse et épanouissement de l'idéologie économique.* Paris: Gallimard, 1978.

Esquirol, Jean Etienne Dominique. *Des Passions considérées comme causes, symptômes et moyens curatifs de l'aliénation mentale.* 1805. Rept. Paris: Librairie des Deux Mondes, 1980.

———. "Délire." *Dictionnaire des sciences médicales.* Vol. 8. Paris: Panckoucke, 1814.

———. "Essai sur les terminaisons critiques de la manie." *Journal général de médecine* 50 (May-June 1814): 3–85.

———. "Hallucination." *Gazette de Santé* (November, 1814): 242–43, 258–59.

———. "Folie." *Dictionnaire des sciences médicales.* Vol. 16. Paris: Panckoucke, 1816.

———. "Maison d'aliénés." *Dictionnaire des sciences médicales.* Vol. 30. Paris: Panckoucke, 1818.

———. "Manie." *Dictionnaire des sciences médicales.* Vol. 30. Paris: Panckoucke, 1818.

———. "Observations sur le déplacement du colon transverse dans l'aliénation mentale." *Journal de Médecine* 62 (1818): 341–58; 63 (1818): 176–84, 289–91.

———. *Des établissements consacrés aux aliénés en France.* Paris: Huzard, 1819.

———. "Suicide." *Dictionnaire des sciences médicales.* Vol. 53. Paris: Panckoucke, 1821.

———. Note added to translation of J. C. Hoffbauer, *Médecine légale.* Paris: J.-B. Baillière, 1827. Rept. as *Mémoire sur la monomanie homicide* in *Des Maladies mentales*, vol. 2.

———. *Des Maladies mentales.* Paris: J.-B. Baillière, 1838. Translated into English as *Mental Maladies: A Treatise on Insanity.* Facsimile edition of vol. 1 1845. Rpt. New York: Hafner, 1965.
Fabre d'Eglantine, Philippe François Nazaire. *Oeuvres politiques.* Paris: Charpentier et Fasquelle, 1914.
———. *Rapport fait à la Convention nationale: Dans la séance du 3 du second mois de la seconde année de la République française, au nom de la commission chargée de la confection du calendrier.* Paris: Imprimerie nationale, 1793.
Ferrus, Guillaume Marie André. *Des aliénés.* Paris: Huzard, 1834.
Fodéré, François Emmanuel. *Traité du délire.* 2 vols. Paris: Croullebois, 1817.
Foucault, Michel. *Madness and Civilization: A History of Insanity in the Age of Reason.* Trans. Richard Howard. New York: New America Library, 1967.
———. *Discipline and Punish. The Birth of the Prison.* Trans. Alan Sheridan. New York: Vintage Books, 1979.
Gauchet, Marcel. *The Disenchantment of the World.* Trans. Oscar Burge. Princeton: Princeton University Press, 1997.
———. "Tocqueville." In *New French Thought: Political Philosophy*, ed. Mark Lilla. Princeton: Princeton University Press, 1994, pp. 91–113.
Georget, E. *Dictionnaire de médecine.* Paris, 1824.
Goldstein, Jan. *Console and Classify: The French Psychiatric Profession in the Nineteenth Century.* New York: Cambridge University Press, 1987.
Itard, Jean Marc Gaspard. *Traité des maladies de l'oreille et de l'audition.* 2nd ed. Paris: Libraire médicale de Méquignon-Marvis, 1842.
———. *Mémoire sur les premiers développements de Victor de l'Aveyron.* 1901. Rept. in L. Malson, *Les Enfants sauvages*, Paris: Union générale d'éditions (coll. 10/18), 1964.
Jessen, Peter. "Sur les colonies d'aliénés." *Annales médico-psychologiques* 7 (1861): 619–21.
Jetter, Dieter. *Geschichte des Hospitals.* 6 vols. Wiesbaden: F. Steiner, 1971.
———. "Die psychiatrischen Krankenhaüser als Anstalten besonderer Art." *Confinia Pscyhiatrica* 9 (1966): 198–222.
———. "Das ideale Irrenhaus im Spiegel historischer Baupläne." *Confinia Psychiatrica* 5 (1962): 1–29.
———. "Ursprung und Gestalt panoptischer Irrenhaüser in England und Schottland." *Suddhofs' Archiv* 46, 1 (1962): 29–44.
Landré-Beauvais, Augustin-Jacob. "Crise." *Dictionnaire des sciences médicales.* Vol. 7. Paris: Panckouke, 1813.
Ledoux, Claude-Nicolas. *L'Architecture considérée sous le rapport de l'art, des moeurs et de la législation.* Paris: Chez l'auteur, 1804.
Léonard, Jacques. *Les Médecins de l'Ouest au XIXe Siècle.* Lille, Workshop for Thesis Reproduction, 1978.
Leuret, François. *Le Traitement moral de la folie.* Paris: J.-B. Baillière, 1840.
Marandon de Montyel, Evariste. *Rapport au Préfet de la Seine.* In his *Procès-verbaux de la commission de surveillance des asiles d'aliénés de la Seine.* Paris, 1892.
———. "L'Hospitalisation de la folie et les nouveaux asiles ouverts pour aliénés." *Annales d'hygiène publique et de médecine légale* (3rd series) 34 (1895): 411–34.

Marandon de Montyel, Evariste. "Asiles d'aliénés à portes ouvertes." *Annales médico-psychologiques* 2 (1896): 390–412.

———. "La Nouvelle Hospitalisation des aliénés par la méthode de liberté." *Annales médico-psychologiques* 1 (1896): 60–85.

———. "Asiles d'aliénés à portes ouvertes." *Annales médico-psychologiques* 2 (1897): 264–288; 2 (1898): 470–92.

Marcé, Louis Victor. *Traité pratique des Maladies mentales.* Paris: Baillière, 1862.

Martin-Doisy, Félix. *Dictionnaire d'économie charitable.* Vol. 1. Paris: J. P. Migne, 1855–64.

Mauss, Marcel. "A Category of the Human Mind: The Notion of Person, the Notion of 'Self.'" In *Sociology and Psychology: Essays.* Trans. Ben Brewster. London: Routledge and Kegan Paul, 1979, pp. 57–94.

Miller, J. A. "La Machine panoptique de Jeremy Bentham." *Ornicar* 3 (1976): 19.

Mirabeau, Honoré Gabriel Riqueti, Comte de. *Sur les fêtes publiques, civiles et militaires.* In *Travail sur l'éducation publique trouvé dans les papiers de Mirabeau, fait et publié par Cabanis.* In Cabanis, *Oeuvres complètes*, vol. 2.

Moreau de la Sarthe, Jacques Louis. "Médecine mentale." In *Encyclopédie méthodique.* Vol. 9, *Médecine.* Paris: Panckoucke, 1816.

———. *Recueil périodique de littérature médicale étrangère.* Vol. 1. Paris, 1798 (Year VII).

———. Review of Crichton, *An Inquiry into the Nature and Origin of Mental Derangement.* In *Recueil périodique de littérature médicale étrangère.* 1798. Rept. in *La Décade philosophique* 45 (1800 [Year VIII, 4th quarter, 20 Fructidor]): 457–64.

———. "Quelques observations sur différentes circonstances de maladies à la guérison desquelles les ressources pharmaceutiques n'ont point concouru." In *Mémoires de la Société médicale d'Emulation* 1 (1799 [Year VII]): 178–215.

Morel, Bénédict-Augustin. "Des gâteux dans un asile d'aliénés." *Annales médico-psychologiques* 2 (1850): 72–101.

Mourre. *Observations sur les Insensés.* Toulon: Imprimerie de Surre Fils, 1791.

Owen, Robert. *The Revolution in the Mind and Practice of the Human Race.* Ed. A. L. Morton. London: E. Wilson, 1849.

———. *A New View of Society and Other Writings* (1813). London: Everyman's Library, 1927.

Parchappe de Vinay, Jean Baptiste Maximien. *Des Principes à suivre dans la fondation et la construction des asiles d'aliénés.* Paris: Masson, 1853.

———. "Aliénés, asiles." In *Dictionnaire encyclopédique des sciences médicales.* Vol. 3. Paris: Asselin and Masson, 1865.

Pastoret, Claude Emmanuel Joseph Pierre, Marquis de. *Rapport sur l'état des hôpitaux, des hospices et des secours à domicile à Paris.* Paris: Huzard, 1816.

Peisse, Louis. *La Médecine et les médecins.* Paris: J. B. Baillière, 1857, vol. 2.

Pinel, Philippe. *Nosographie philosophique.* Vol. 2. Paris: Crapelet, 1797 (Year VI).

———. "Recherches et observations sur le traitement moral des aliénés." *Mémoires de la Société médicale d'Emulation* 2 (1797 Year VI). Rept. in *A Treatise on Insanity*, pp. 83–84.

———. *Mémoires de la Société médicale d'émulation pour l'An V.* 1st year. Paris: Richard, Caille and Ravier, 1798 (Year VI).

———. "Recherches sur le traitement général des femmes aliénées dans un grand hospice." *Le Moniteur universel* 281 (June 30, 1805 [11 Missidor, Year XIII]): 1158–60.

———. *Traité médico-philosophique sur l'aliénation mentale.* 2nd ed. Paris: J. A. Brosson, 1809.

———. "Résultats de nouvelles observations faites sur les aliénés de la Salpêtrière en 1812, 1813 et 1814." *Journal des Sciences médicales* 1 (1816): 82–94.

———. *A Treatise on Insanity.* Translated, with a historical commentary by D. D. Davis. Birmingham: Classics of Medicine Library, 1983.

Pinel, Scipion. *Traité complet du régime sanitaire des aliénés.* Paris: Mauprives, 1836.

Polanyi, Karl. *The Great Transformation.* New York: Farrar and Rinehart, 1944.

Prospectus, Etablissement pour le traitement des aliénés des deux sexes fondés en juillet 1822 à Vanves près Paris par MM. les docteurs Voisin et Falret.

Puységur, Armand Marie Jacques de Chastenet. *Recherches, expériences et observations physiologiques sur l'homme dans l'état de somnambulisme naturel, et dans le somnambulisme provoqué par l'acte magnétique.* Paris: J. G. Dentu, 1811.

Quetel, Claude. *Les Cadres de la folie au XIX*[e] *siècle, le Bon Sauveur de Caen.* Thesis, 3rd cycle. Paris-Sorbonne, 1976.

Rapport sur le service des aliénés du département de la Seine. Paris: Dupont, 1860.

Raulin, Joseph. *Traité des affections vaporeuses du sexe.* Paris: J.-T. Hérissant, 1758.

Sémelaigne, René. *Les Pionniers de la psychiatrie française.* Paris: J.-B. Baillière, 1930.

Sérieux, Paul. *Rapport sur l'assistance aux aliénés en France, en Allemagne, en Italie et en Suisse.* Paris: Imprimerie municipale, 1903.

Supplément au voyage en France de M. Leigh. Montpellier, 1826.

Swain, Gladys. "A propos de l'enfant sauvage de l'Aveyron." *L'Evolution psychiatrique* 4 (1976): 995–1011.

———. "De Kant à Hegel: Deux Époques de la folie. *Libre* 1 (1977): 174–201.

———. "D'une rupture dans l'abord de la folie." *Libre* 2 (1977): 195–229.

Dialogue avec l'insensé: Essais d'histoire de la psychiatrie. Précédé de: A la Recherche d'une autre histoire de la folie, par Marcel Gauchet. Paris: Gaillimard, 1994.

———. *Le Sujet de la folie.* 1978. New ed., Paris: Calmann-Lévy, 1997.

Tenon, Jacques René. *Mémoires sur les hôpitaux de Paris.* Paris: P.-D. Pierres, 1788.

Tocqueville, Alexis de. *Democracy in America.* Ed. J. P. Mayer and Max Lerner. Trans. George Lawrence. New York: Harper and Row, 1966.

Weiner, Dora. "The Apprenticeship of Philippe Pinel: A New Document." *Clio Medica* 13, 2 (1978): 125–33.

———. *The Citizen Patient in Revolutionary and Imperial Paris.* Baltimore and London: Johns Hopkins Press, 1993.

Index